Roger Payne

AMONG WHALES

SCRIBNER

New York   London   Toronto   Sydney   Tokyo   Singapore

CHARLES SCRIBNER'S SONS
Simon & Schuster Inc.
Rockefeller Center
1230 Avenue of the Americas
New York, NY 10020

Manufactured in the United States of America

1   3   5   7   9   10   8   6   4   2

Library of Congress Cataloging-in-Publication Data is available.

ISBN 0-684-80210-4

ACKNOWLEDGMENTS

This book had a gestation period of many years, during which I received help in myriad forms from a legion of friends. As I set out to acknowledge that help I know I am going to forget several people I should have mentioned. I only hope they will forgive me when they someday encounter an equal chaos in their own brains.

In the very earliest days, Jim Bird and Linda Guinee transcribed endless pages of all but illegible notes I had written on envelopes (and worse) and then indexed them so I could find relevant ones later. My gratitude to them for this is total. Pamela Dyson and Mia Grifalcone helped me with this process as well, and Ollie Brazier helped in hundreds of ways with the research on right whales. In much later days, Kendra Fanconi, Lisa Harrow, Nigel Piers Hooper, Sharon Hustler, Katy Kjellgren, Colette McClennan, Caroline Renton, and Carl Wilson spent long hours helping me correct the various edited versions of this manuscript.

My thanks go to Peter Evans and Ed Parsons for major help in researching specific points in the text, along with John Atkinson, Justin Cooke, Kendra Fanconi, Tom Ford, Chris Hallus, Kim Marshall, Carey Newson, and Vicky Rowntree.

For help with specific points and for discussions about points in the book, I thank: Peter Best, Richard Dawkins, Ron Christensen, Phil Clapham, Justin Cooke, Chris Clark, Theo Colborn, Eleanor Dorsey, Tom Ensign, René Eyerly, Joe Geraci, Jonathan Gordon, Bill Jordan, Scott Kraus, Jon Lien, Stormy Mayo, Ed Mitchell, Kate O'Connell, Holly Payne, John Payne, Katharine Payne, Laura Payne, and Sam Payne, Judy Perkins, Jorge Reynolds, Vicky Rowntree, Jon Seger, Karen Steuer, Steven Swartz, and Douglas Webb. Several of the above read full chapters. In all cases, their comments greatly improved the final manuscript.

Michael Williamson kindly shared with me his unpublished calculations of the volume of water engulfed by blue whales. Paul Winter and Chez Liley drew my attention to the Brian Swimme lecture from which I have quoted, and gave me copies of their notes on it, while Trever Bowen introduced me to the excerpt from Camus' diary which I have quoted. I am grateful to all three.

There are several people who, though they did not assist me directly on the text of this book, helped me with the rest of my life as to free my time for writing it. Chief among these are: Guy Anderson, Steve Aikenhead, John Atkinson, Karen Baker, Kirstin Findlay, Mia Grifalconi, Sarah Haney, Nigel Piers Hooper, Annie Johnston, James Ronald Keating, Iain Kerr, Jean LaPidas, Jerry and Ani Moss, Andrew Morse, George Perry, Chat Reynders, Vicky Rowntree, and Pritam Singh.

There are several organizations without whose help the research on which this book is largely based would never have been done. Chief among these is the Wildlife Conservation Society (formerly the New York Zoological Society), in particular its Director, William Conway. I am grateful for the help of many friends during my many happy years at that institution, particularly Frank Larkin, Howard Phipps, the late Nixon Griffis, and the late Landon Thorne. I also received support for work reported here from the World Wildlife Fund (with particular thanks to Tom Lovejoy, Russell Train, and Mike Sutton), and from the National Geographic Society (where my special thanks go to Mary Smith, as well as to the late Barry Bishop, Gil Grosvenor, Bill Graves, and Ed Snider, and Steve Stettes). Many other foundations and individuals have helped with funding for our expeditions to study whales as well as with the analysis of the resulting data. In some cases their help has been not only financial but personal as well. My thanks to all of them.

In Argentina our expeditions received invaluable assistance from many institutions and individuals. My deep thanks go to Amalia Lacroze de Fortabat and the Fundación Alfredo Fortabat; to the Museo Argentino de Ciències Naturales, especially José Maria Gallardo; Parques Nacionales, in particular Felipe LaRiviere and Arturo Tarak; and to the Government of Chubut's Direcciòn de Turismo (now the Organismo Provincial de Turismo), whose directors Antonio Torrejón and Juan Pepitone were especially helpful, as were Donato Gioiosa, Adalberto Sosa, and Jorge di Pascuali; I am especially grateful to Teresa Ortiz Basualdo, and the late Alberto and Augustina Pereyra-Iraola, the late Emilio Ferro and his family, Carlos Garcia, Juan Carlos Lopez, Diana de Lopez, Nestor Monocchio, Juan Olazabal, and Santiago Ortego, who helped my family and me in numberless ways—always with the greatest generosity and warmth. I am grateful as well to the Aeroclub de Trelew (and to their pilots, Hugo Callejas, Ruben Osinalde, and Pablo Pascual), to Centro Nacionál Patagónico, and to Guillermo and Patricia Harris, of Fundación Patagonia Natural.

Cormac McCarthy read nearly the entire text and made innumerable improvements to it. In the margins of my most sophomoric diatribes he wrote such comments as "Yawn, yawn," and "No Sale," thus sparing me much wider embarrassment later on (though whether enough, only time will tell). I also value deeply our many discussions about biological points in the text. In my experience there is no precedent for someone not a professional biologist being so well-read and so clearly informed about biology.

My deep thanks go to my long-suffering editor Wendy Batteau, all of whose suggested modifications were great improvements, including such non-trivial suggestions as "Why don't you put all that stuff on ocean acoustics in an Appendix? And why not just leave out the second appendix, plus that chapter on monsters; I don't think they belong here. [Pause, then brightly:] Perhaps in some other book." I cannot imagine so willingly accepting such basic suggestions from anyone else. She has about her a kind of genius in this regard. My thanks also to Bill Rosen, for his support as this book's first publisher and its last editor. My deepest thanks as well to an anonymous copy editor who made countless improvements to the text. I fear I tested the patience of everyone at Macmillan (now Simon and Schuster) to the nth degree. I can only hope that any success this book enjoys will make the past easier for them to forget. My deepest thanks also go to my agent, Amanda Urban, who kept us all speaking to each other.

My former wife, Katharine Payne, lived through the years from which most of this book came, and though we separated before I began writing it in earnest, I feel her presence and help in all aspects of its genesis. My gratitude for both is unwavering and eternal. Although I failed her on precisely the counts of unwavering and eternal, I have since learned to value these human qualities above any others. Nor is this just the breezy sentiment of the recently converted. It is the deepest feeling of the Captain who respects most that reef on which he lost his ship.

Both of my families endured this book. I am grateful they still speak to me, and hope it will become more frequent. The people whose lives were most punished by it are my wife, Lisa Harrow, and my youngest son, Timothy Harrow, both of whom bore it all with the best of will. Lisa was always there to help freely and willingly whenever I needed it. Thank you, my darlings. Yes, we can now have a more normal existence, and I won't be so late for dinner.

Long ago when I was in the deepest throes of book writing I wrote along the following lines to some old friends, Holly and Gon Leon, apologizing for not being free to abandon my book long enough to spend a weekend with them:

That moth which is my soul is making an annoying, dry sound as it flutters and flutters under its bell jar, where it has been so long trapped by this backbreaking book. When the book is finally done my soul will fly arrow-straight, boring at a thousand meters a second into some velvet vein of cool black night. Thus refreshed it will commence to make barrel rolls and freeform polygonic, polytechnic, Polynesian, pyrotechnic, wheelies and helices and madcap whorls, scrawling *VICTORY!* in four hundred languages all over the bat-black night, and rewiring all the constellations, connecting all the million-million dots to form all the fantasies ever fantasized. And with the air sizzling past its finally free-to-fly, free-to-breathe, free-to-envelop wings, it will spin and leap and fire dance out past the fringes of all its pent up dreams until it reaches the very edge of its universe, where it will stand with wings trembling and there . . . sing its goddamn heart out.

OK, moth, the time is finally come. Now! *Go* for it!

In token
of my admiration for his genius,
this book is inscribed
to
CORMAC McCARTHY

&

In token
of my admiration for her genius,
this book is inscribed
to
LISA HARROW

CONTENTS

PREFACE

This book is about a life spent among whales—sometimes with whales as companions, sometimes far from them and from the sea—but always with whales in mind. It is about how the lives of whales conjoin with ours and is written from the perspective of a scientist—but hopefully one who realizes the limits of his science.

Like any field biologist, I have spent far too much time desk bound, or in the lab analyzing data, or on the phone, or in some perpetual meeting, or fund-raising, or in some other wise pouring the sands of my life through a sieve of wide mesh. But there have also been wonderful moments when, having driven down the last track to some deserted beach, I have stepped into a waiting skiff and set forth into the world of whales—everything landish left miles behind. This book is about those times and about what I learned from them.

Because I wish to convey the lightness of being of these largest and most apparently ponderous of animals, this book is not intended to be a compendium of information on whales—there are many such books available. It is about the things I know about whales that intrigue me most and about what I think whales can teach humanity. For I believe that the principal gift that whales offer humanity is that they are the only animals that can impress us enough to persuade us to change our minds about the importance of the wild world.

Although I am a scientist, I believe that C. P. Snow was deeply wrong and that the gulf he perceived between the sciences and the humanities is just that, perceived, not real, a "Visual Cliff"—one of those clever perspective drawings beyond which kittens, and other ingénues, are afraid to go.

One of the features of spending a life as a scientist is that you only get to publish what you have proven to be true (or believe you have so proven). There's not much chance to put down deeply held suspicions. The suspicions get voiced, but mostly in informal discussions with fellow scientists. These usually take place around a dinner table, or over beers in some pub— a letting-down of our guards that the public seldom gets to see. Yet for many of us it is the most interesting part of our jobs. After all, it's often fascinating, even riveting, to hear someone's hunches about a subject they have spent much of their lifetimes pondering. As Ralph Waldo Emerson said, *"A friend is a person with whom I may be sincere. Before him I may think aloud."*

I have biologist friends who can lead you down the garden path and into their world of beliefs the way a great storyteller weaves a spell. Though sometimes it's years later, the final payoff comes when their theory is proved (or disproved). Hearing theories from friends which they have not yet proven against all possible assaults but which they have solid reason to expect to be true is like being on the inside of news before it breaks, or learning about some cover-up while the politicians are still denying its truth.

There is all but no room in the scientific literature for such speculation— which is exactly as it should be. However, I thought that in addition to hearing about things that are well demonstrated the reader might enjoy being in on some fairly outrageous speculation. If this annoys my colleagues, I can at least find solace in imagining the pleasure they will get as they tear the corpses of my arguments limb from limb, and snap and snarl over the bones. If it causes anyone to set out to disprove my favorite theories, then it will have served a useful function.

However, my main target is the general reader, as I try to explain some of the reasons that many of us are so deeply fascinated by whales, and why it is that we object to people killing them.

—Roger Payne, London

AMONG
WHALES

CHAPTER 1

Whales

The deep sea. When we think of it, it is usually the surface we picture; an area of sparkling sunlight and ceaseless motion, of dancing waves and teeming fish moving in shoals like showers of silver. We forget that this is only the very thinnest, uppermost layer, only 5 percent of the mass, and bears no relation to the deep bulk of the ocean, a place that is perpetually dark, cold, and still, stirred only by slowly drifting currents. By comparison with the surface film there is little life in the abyss. It is sparsely populated by a variety of outrageously baroque, inordinate fish adapted to live under the immense pressures of its major depths. Some of them live in little bands, and most have tiny lights sprinkled over their bodies with which they are presumed to light their way and keep in touch as they move in concert through the void, like slowly drifting clouds of stars or majestically wheeling galaxies.

One of the most intriguing creatures in the void is a small squid that glows so faintly its light can only be perceived with dark-adapted eyes. This animal lives at great depths and adjusts its dim glow to match the faint light falling upon it from the surface so far above. Were it not for its faint luminosity, the squid would be seen by prey below it as a silhouette against the surface. But when such prey looks up, the squid is invisible, the light it produces exactly matching the amount of light penetrating from the surface.

In the darkness of the abyss another manifestation of life permeates everything—the calls of distant whales. They carry over vast distances, the sounds traveling in long, majestically curving paths and completely filling the vast, vaulted spaces—at times echoing off the ceiling a mile or two overhead, or off the oozy floor as far beneath. To many human ears these sounds are very beautiful, even though whales and people have vastly different evolutionary histories and therefore might be expected to appreciate very different kinds of sounds.

Many people view the ocean as a flat and featureless plain. But this is an erroneous perception. In truth it is a place of great complexity and diversity, filled with excitement and hidden drama. The extraordinary things that occur within its vast spaces and corridors must in most part be deduced, for the sea is not a great communicator but the strong, silent type—a mute and patient (though sometimes wildly destructive) companion.

There are two major groupings of whales: the toothed whales, which have teeth (e.g., dolphins, porpoises, killer whales, sperm whales, beaked whales, etc.), and the baleen whales (which include the biggest whales), which contain baleen strainers instead of teeth in their jaws. (The term *cetacean* is used to indicate the entire group—toothed as well as baleen whales.)

The largest species of whales are called the "great whales"—a loose association usually considered to contain (in rough order of decreasing length of large individuals) the blue whale (30.5 meters long), fin (26.8 m), sei (21 m), bowhead (19.8 m), sperm (18 m), (right 17 m), humpback (16 m), gray (14.1 m), Bryde's (14 m), minke (10.7 m), and pygmy right whales (6.4 m), that is, all the baleen whales plus the sperm whale.[1] This is not a very logical list since it omits species like the bottle-nosed whale (9.8 m), which is larger than the pygmy right whale. However, by the standards of the terrestrial animals with which we are most familiar the great whales are, undeniably, "great" in size—the smallest of them weighs more than some adult elephants.

As a consequence of their great size, whales escape much turmoil. With increasing size comes increasing serenity. Large creatures find less and less that is significant enough to be annoying and therefore experience fewer extremes, less upheaval. Small things lead frantic lives. When a passing ant sets its foot in a drop of water, the amoebas in that drop experience raging tidal waves, while to the ant the footsteps of a mouse on the roof of its galleries must rattle all the cupboards and shake the pupae off the walls. Consider the effects of a thunderstorm on these same amoebas—a disruption of such violence as to be beyond not just human experience but human comprehension.

With size comes tranquility. For a whale a passing thunderstorm is but the footfall of an ant, and a full gale an annoying jiggling of its pleasant bed. If you were a whale, all but the grandest things would pass beneath your notice.

As the largest animal, including the biggest dinosaur, that has ever lived on earth you could afford to be gentle, to view life without fear, to play in the dark, to sleep soundly anywhere, whenever and however long you liked, and to greet the world in peace—even to view with bemused curiosity something as weird as a human scuba diver as it bubbles away, encased in all that bizarre gear. It is this sense of tranquility—of life without urgency, power without aggression—that has won my heart to whales.

Conducting scientific research on this most difficult of groups can be compared to viewing a whale through a keyhole. The bulk of the animal glides past from time to time while we try desperately to figure out what on earth it is. In spite of lots of sparks and smoke, we have so far accomplished little more than a small enlargement of this keyhole. Someday—perhaps in the next hundred years—we may have a picture-window-sized keyhole and will finally see what the whole whale looks like. But even then the enigma of the whale will still stand, undecoded, before us.

I have been studying whales continuously since 1967. One of the delights of that experience has been discovering that there is no way to get a whale to adopt a human time scale. This is no more possible than it would be for a human to adopt a weasel's speed of living. Whales are unhurriable. It's one of their most endearing traits. Nowhere is this more engagingly seen than in trying to figure out what a whale is doing when what you are watching is, say, play but you have not yet figured that out. The difficulty comes from the fact that one of the major clues to the function of a behavior pattern is the rhythm of its occurrence. Because we commonly associate play with quick motions, the key to being able to recognize play in whales is learning to think differently—in terms of long, slow rhythms, where things occur very lingeringly (it would be a comparable problem to learn to recognize play in snails, or sloths, or tortoises). To understand whales one must be deeply patient, must slow way down and be content to observe passively for a long time. Only at the end of, say, a day may one say to oneself, "Now let me see; what did I see? Well, I saw the whale do this . . . and then it did this . . . and then this . . . and then . . . For heaven's sake, it was *play* I was looking at." In order to observe whales, you must be willing to set your metronome on adagio. Then, to understand what you have seen, you must fast-forward through your observations by setting your metronome on allegro.

During the first ten years of my career in biology I was an experimentalist. I worked in neurophysiology and behavior and did experiments on how bats determine the direction from which a sound is coming, how owls locate their prey in total darkness by hearing it, and how moths determine the direction from which a bat is approaching (so they can make evasive maneuvers to avoid it). When I started studying whales—a group of species upon which it is all but impossible to experiment—I worried whether I would find the work stimulating enough or whether it would seem boring simply observing, without ever being able to manipulate anything—or do an experiment. I had enjoyed experimental work—at that time of my life I liked manipulating things, but I had very little idea of how to make good, passive field observations. But one does, eventually, grow up, and I soon appreciated the greater rewards of finding things out through passive observation. It's a lot like astronomy—another field in which you can never perform an experiment but must wait for nature to present you with something interesting to observe. I soon realized that the constraints posed by passive observation can be more challenging than those posed by experimental work. It is rather like the constraints of the sonnet form, which make composing poetry exquisitely challenging. Passive observation is a different kind of challenge than experimentation, but I believe it requires a subtler way of thinking, and that the result can be sonnets rather than ballads.

One reason whales maintain such a hold on our imaginations seems to be their omnipossibility—their unexpected and unpredictable appearances off all coasts, invariably arriving on their own schedules, showing up for reasons we do not understand. Sometimes whales even make their way up rivers. Humphrey the wrong-way humpback whale was the most famous of these river vagrants. Humphrey somehow got headed up the Sacramento River toward the city of Sacramento, the seat of the California government, and it took a small navy of boats to turn him around. (One wonders what it was that Humphrey so urgently wished to convey to the California Congress, and why he wasn't aware of how powerless they would almost certainly be to do anything whatever for him.)

In many areas of Africa finding elephants or lions in your backyard, though uncommon, is a perpetual possibility. If you live in Japan or America it is not. But regardless of where you live, if your house fronts on the ocean, you could conceivably see a whale at any moment. However, whales seem so exotic to most of us that no one expects they will see one, so most people never look. I have several times stood with my back to the sea in Hawaii with several groups of humpback whales in full view behind me within half a mile of shore and asked local people, "Do you ever see whales in these waters?" Almost invariably the answer goes something like, "Well, yes, occasionally. I saw a group about two weeks ago when we were out fishing. They came right up to the boat."

For three months, the region is loaded with humpback whales. You can see a blow anytime you look. But no one sees whales even though they are the largest of animals. People seem to think it isn't possible for whales to be there. Whales must present themselves so close they can no longer be overlooked before most people notice them.

In 1970, while working out the migratory destinations of humpback whales in the Caribbean, I visited fourteen islands in two weeks in order to interview native fishermen and captains of charter boats about seeing whales. Many of the native small-boat fishermen were afraid of whales, so they were on the lookout for them all the time and, consequently, saw them frequently. I encountered one charter boat operator who said to me, "Listen, my friend, you may think there are whales here but believe me there aren't. I take ten loads of tourists up and down this chain of islands each winter—all on two-week trips—and I never see whales. Trust me, if there were whales here we'd see them." The trips he was taking passed through the center of a concentration of humpback whales—enough of them to support a local whaling industry.

When I went to the next wharf and spoke with the local fishermen, one of them said, "Oh yes man, we see plenty whales. We see whales all the time." I eventually stopped asking charter boat captains. With a few notable exceptions it was a waste of time.

Though we distinguish between the Pacific Ocean, the Atlantic Ocean, the Indian Ocean, etc., there is really only one ocean, and it holds all the whales that exist—all, that is, except for the river and freshwater species. Whales can pass along your coast, or come into any harbor or bay that is deep enough to float them, no matter where you live . . . and sometimes they do. When it happens it always sends a message that speaks to you directly— one capable of setting up waves that propagate right into the core of your being.

The single most obvious characteristic of whales is their size; they are animals so large that figuratively speaking it's hard to get a grasp of just how large they are. In Argentina there is an old female right whale named Troff who has had many calves. One of her favorite haunts is beneath an observation hut we built on top of some cliffs near our research station. On windy days, Troff often hangs out there for hours without moving. Her mass and extraordinary strength are made manifest simply by her lying there, immovably, like a submerged reef, while waves break over her body. It is a noble spectacle—one I have watched for hours: the immutable whale over which the seas burst without effect. One does not tire of such a sight.

But right whales are dwarfed by blue whales. In the Miocene, there were ancestral whales as long or longer than modern whales but they didn't weigh as much as the largest blue whales. Blue whales are larger than the largest animals that have ever appeared on earth—bigger even than the biggest dinosaur yet discovered, the astonishingly immense *seismosaurus*—in fact between one and a half and four times its mass, depending on who is estimating the size of *seismosaurus*.

Since an entire blue whale is so unfathomably big, let us focus for a moment on just one of its organs—we'll consider the heart. In a large blue whale the heart weighs about four thousand pounds (that's two tons) and probably pumps about sixty gallons with each beat. Its valves would be about the size of a hub cap, and a child could crawl through the aorta, the largest blood vessel leaving the heart. So large are the arteries that even sixty feet aft of the heart, where the main artery has narrowed down to a diameter needed to support just the last few muscles attached to the last few vertebrae, this vessel is still about the size of the sewer pipes that carry waste water away from the average house—large enough, that is, to allow a good-sized trout to swim leisurely along it. So here is a new way of studying the anatomy of an animal, by dispatching children to transit its aorta, or fish to navigate its arteries and veins.

Were we able to listen to the heart of a blue whale beating (no one ever has, though Colombian cardiologist Jorge Reynolds recorded the gargantu-anly slow whooshing of a humpback whale's heart beating) we would find that even at a time when the whale was exerting itself to the maximum and its heart was beating wildly—the way yours or mine would feel after a footrace—it would be contracting only about 18–20 times a minute, or once every three seconds. Compare this with our 120 beats under similar circumstances, or the roughly 800–1,000 beats per minute achieved by a heart the size of a rice grain, a heart housed in the world's smallest mammal, a shrew.

A surgeon who went whaling back in the 1950s—long after the largest blue whales had been killed—noted that it took six strong men with flensing hooks to drag the heart of a blue whale across the deck of the factory ship, even though the deck was always so slippery with blood and fat that men frequently commented on what enormous loads they could pull across it.

Another measure of the extraordinary size of blue whales is their appetites. For example, during the first few weeks of its life a blue whale calf is believed to make a net gain in weight of 250 pounds each day, growing at a rate almost fast enough to be seen. The effect of monitoring such growth can be compared to gazing long and closely at the hour hand of a steeple clock, the gargantuan form of the baby swelling visibly, almost menacingly, before one's eyes. This incredible growth rate is based entirely on mother's milk. But due to natural inefficiencies, the mother probably produces milk at least three times the weight of the calf's gain—that is, about 750 pints a day of a milk that is richer in fats than cream (750 pints is ninety-four gallons—almost two fifty-gallon drums full of heavy cream). For adult whales, however, the statistics grow even more incredible: scientists have found one ton of food in the stomach of a blue whale. This is equivalent to the meat in eight thousand quarter-pound hamburgers. Imagine sitting down to a meal of not eight or eighty or even eight hundred hamburgers, but eight thousand. And don't forget that if you were a whale you'd be hungry a few hours later—and ready to eat another eight thousand.

The food that these giant animals eat is, of course, far smaller than hamburgers. It comprises millions of tiny animals that have to swim slowly enough for a whale to be able to catch them as it lunges forward, its huge mouth open like a barn door. The major diet of blue whales in the Antarctic Ocean—the area of their former major concentration—is krill, a minute form of crustacean.

I once saw a black-and-white snapshot taken by the whalers who caught the largest blue whale ever known. It was not taken on the flensing platform where the whole body would have shown, but in the water as it lay next to the catcher boat—an indistinct blob lying beside a nondescript catcher boat. As I leaned forward, straining my eyes trying to see more detail, I realized I was actually seeing less and less, just more grain, the image coming apart before my eyes the way the beauty of a whale is reduced to rubble when it is cut up to be boiled down for its oil.

That snapshot is the only known photograph of the largest-known individual of the most mammoth species of animal ever to live on earth—which means the largest animal for which we have any evidence anywhere in the universe. This female blue whale was killed in the Antarctic in February of 1928. The contemporary description of what turned out to be humanity's encounter with the largest animal ever known to have existed only gives the whale's sex, length, and the day and place she was killed. It also notes that her companions were especially large animals.

So there you have it, the sum total of all information passed along to us in the eye-witness account by one of the handful of people who saw the biggest animal that any human since the dawn of time has ever laid eyes on; in fact, the biggest of which our own species has ever been aware.

A few hours after this historic moment was immortalized on film, the whale had been stripped of its blubber coat and the carcass set adrift to make way for processing the next one. The narrator is careful to inform us that at the time they were only interested in the blubber, because they had found an area with so very many big whales that they were in a bit too much of a rush to be able to spare the time over such niceties as cooking the oil out of the roughly 140 tons of meat they must have discarded when they set the body of this whale adrift to make way for the next blubber coat from the next whale. Other than measuring its length, no one took any measurements from this largest of whales—they were in a terrible hurry, so we have no idea what the span of its tail was, or its girth, or how high a hill it made later as it lay on the deck of the flensing plan, or anything else. And no one saved the bones, either. If the whale weighed 160 tons, which seems to be a safe assumption for this very large female, the blubber probably weighed at least forty-five tons and would have brought about as much as the cost of a two- to three-bedroom house.

But suppose one of the whalers who killed her had had the vision to save one of her bones, perhaps the smallest finger bone (probably about fifteen inches long). What would that bone from the world's largest animal be worth?

Suppose they had saved two bones, or the whole skeleton. What would the skeleton of the world's largest animal be worth? I have a friend who mounts whale skeletons for museums and aquarium exhibits. He estimates that a complete skeleton of the world's largest blue whale could bring up to half a million dollars in today's market, with sales of images of it to all forms of media and entertainment being worth more.

Or let us ask the ultimate question: what if instead of *killing* the largest whale and her outsized mates the whalers had never gone whaling and we had done without all the margarine we got from whales, making it instead from vegetable oil as we do now? In that case others—tourists, say—might have the chance of seeing the largest examples of the largest animal that has ever been known to exist in the history of life on earth (in fact, in any part of the known visible universe). It is unclear what the opportunity to see huge whales in the Antarctic would be worth, but operators of tour boats to the Antarctic are well aware that the sighting of a whale is often the most memorable event of a trip. About fifty thousand tourists have visited Antarctica since the beginning of this rapidly increasing industry, paying between two thousand and eighteen thousand dollars apiece for the privilege (exclusive of airfare). The current receipts of the Antarctic tourist industry are between fifty and seventy-five million dollars a year—money which is made, of course, by a business that is currently conducted without any reasonable chance of seeing a blue whale, let alone a large example of one, even though the boats conducting this business pass through former centers of concentration of blue whales. Though I don't know what an accessible group of extra large blue whales would earn for the tourist industry in today's dollars, it would undoubtedly be more than those who killed the largest blue whale realized for the oil in her blubber—I imagine the figure might be between a hundred and a thousand times more.

Using an economic argument as if it were the soundest basis for judgment is, of course, at the root of the tragedy of our times. One could hardly find a clearer example of what such reasoning leads to than the present state of whales. Simply stated, putting economics first is the myopia of this the most shortsighted of all civilizations; it is the view for which our era will be remembered the longest, the addiction for which we will someday be judged more harshly than the most ignorant and prejudiced medieval society. They had an excuse: they simply didn't know any better, whereas we do know better—we have access to the data that proves our folly but because it says uncomplimentary things about what we have become accustomed to accept as "normal" we won't pay attention to it. The ultimate expression of our madness is that we revere as wise those who put economic considerations above all else and sneer at those who see the madness of such a system of values, labeling them as unrealistic. Meanwhile, we spend all of the capital of our children's inheritance to maintain ourselves in the myth that what we are doing is viable. I would offer that this is the most deeply flawed, most expensive belief ever adopted in the history of our species.

The real mistake modern whalers make is in assuming that what they are part of is a good and long-standing business. Whaling on the blue, fin, sei, Bryde's and minke whales wasn't possible in the Antarctic before the invention of the steam-powered catcher boat, the exploding harpoon, and the air compressor (the latter being essential since corpses of these whales must be inflated with air to make them float).

The modern whaler's greatest manifestation of greed and shortsightedness is his refusal to admit, even to himself, that what he is part of, in fact, is a wildly out-of-control hunt made possible solely because of the industrial age, and that it is not a matter of debate but a point of crystal clarity that no population of living things can ever withstand the full force of uncontrolled twentieth-century technology. What modern whalers were pioneering was perhaps the most reckless, most selfish, most greed-motivated hunt of all time—madder, I would suggest, than any that occurred in the previous history of our species. There is good evidence that our pleistocene ancestors wiped out several species, including the woolly mammoth, the woolly rhinoceros, the giant sloth, and so forth. But they didn't have the benefits of science, wildlife laws, government conservation departments, newspapers, magazines, radios, international conventions for the regulation of hunting and so on. They were simply ignorant. It is their refusal to show restraint when the evidence for the need to do so is so overwhelming that gives modern whalers their most indelibly black mark. It is what makes them, in my view, the undisputed champions of shortsightedness in the history of our species.

There is another way that may help us to understand how big a large blue whale is, and that is to think of it making the simple maneuver of going from its normal horizontal position (when it is breathing on an even keel at the surface) to a vertical position (when it is head downwards in the water with its tail just sinking beneath the waves). In order to make this simple maneuver without hitting her head on the bottom, our 110-foot whale would have to be, of course, in at least 110 feet of water. And when she did so she would have experienced a difference in pressure from the tip of her head to the tip of her tail of over three atmospheres.

What consequences this pressure differential has on the life of the whale has never been seriously examined. It may have no significant effect, since the increasing pressure from the tip of her lips to the tip of her tail is balanced by the increasing pressure of the water in which she is positioned.

But let us hold our whale in our imagination in this vertical posture for a moment while we wait twenty minutes for her to come back to the surface to breathe. We will spend our time trying to get a better idea of just what an enormous animal she is. Her tail is at the surface, but the tip of her is at a depth which only the most experienced divers can reach while holding their breath. But if you have donned your tank and dived down to examine this whale for the past twenty minutes (as she returns your gaze with her enigmatic eyes, the size of grapefruit), when she tilts upward to return to the surface, should you wish to follow her, you would have to be able to take steps to avoid getting the bends: you would have to return to the surface no faster than one foot per second (a fraction of her speed) and would have to stop at a depth of fifteen feet and decompress for fifteen minutes.

So how does she avoid this calamity when she returns without hesitation to the surface? This is a complex question. Part of the answer is that she is not breathing air under pressure the way you and I are. The only air she has available is what she took with her from the surface. This has caused some scientists to guess that in order to avoid the bends whales may sometimes empty their lungs just before diving deeply. But there is a disturbing aspect to that suggestion; many whales, including blue whales, vocalize while submerged. If their sounds are made with air as most scientists assume, they must have air.

Though the three-atmosphere pressure gradient on a large blue whale may not be of consequence underwater it may be of great consequence when the same whale breaches (leaps) into the air. If our female leapt straight up out of the water until her tail cleared the surface, the pressure differential on the column of blood lying in her main arteries would be, briefly, over three atmospheres. I have never seen a blue whale breach, but I have seen thousands of breaches by humpback and right whales, and when you are positioned correctly in relation to them to observe their angle of exit from the water, it is clear that they don't really leap vertically. Also, when their bodies do clear the water completely (which is very rare), they don't clear it during the initial upward rush but only as the whale is falling back into the sea—when its body is horizontal.

I suppose it is possible that a contributing cause of the failure of large whales to rise vertically into the air like a Poseidon missile is the need to avoid the shock on their systems of a two- or three-atmosphere surge of blood pressure. However, it seems clear enough that there is another very good reason not to leap so high. Water is relatively incompressible—not all that different from rock (you can push water aside, however, but this requires acceleration of a large mass of water at the moment of impact, which is not much different from hitting stone). This means that if you leapt high enough to bring part of your body to an altitude of a hundred feet, you would then have to drop back from that height. There are lots of tricks that a whale can and does use to avoid the shock of a belly flop landing, but every now and then things are bound to go wrong, and then any part of its body that is at the top of a fifty-foot arc (or higher) will hit very hard indeed. (If you picked up a whale with a crane and dropped it flatwise into the water from a height of between fifty and a hundred feet you would know that what you were doing would not be likely to do the animal much good.)

Even though it exits from the water belly downward, one of the tricks that a breaching whale uses to avoid belly flops is to roll about its long axis while in midair so as to land on its more rigid back. Near the end of a sequence of a dozen or more breaches, whales often seem to surge forward so that only half of their bodies leaves the water. These surges are done at a lower angle than the earlier breaches, so the whale is not dropping down onto the water directly and does not roll so as to land on its back as it exits. As it lands from a surge, a whale pushes the water as much forward as up. Nevertheless, it is the undersurface of the whale that takes whatever impact there is. When a right whale does this a bit too early in a sequence of breaches and at a time when the breaches are still quite high, the result is a gargantuan belly flop in which the head hits so hard that the mammoth lower lips are sprung outward and one wonders whether the lower jaw has not been dislocated. This looks as though it may hurt, because after such a belly flop a right whale doesn't breach again for a long time.

So here, finally, alive and swimming, is the animal we have been talking about—the giant of giants, the blue whale. When you are in the water and see a blue whale pass very close, it's a bit like standing on a train platform watching the train go by, hoping that the wind isn't going to suck you under its wheels. Of course, when you are underwater, it is the wash from the whale that worries you most, but it never seems to pose any real problem.

In an effort to fit the size of a whale into some frame of reference—to somehow steady its waxing/waning image in one's mind—it is useful to find an animal that is as small when compared to us as we are when compared to a whale. Squirrels fit this bill: they compare in size to us as we do to a gray whale—one of the smaller whale species. It may also help to compare two animals that relate to each other in size as we do to the whales. Ignoring their spindly legs, deer have about the same body mass as we do. So the next time you visit a deer park and see squirrels foraging for nuts and mast among the deer, what you are seeing is equivalent to a human diver searching for clams and shellfish among the whales.

A friend of mine was once harvesting scallops in Golfo San José in Argentina when a right whale swam directly above him, lingering to play in the bubbles from his diver's hookah. He said that the whale blotted out the sun and that what impressed him most was the size of its shadow on the bottom of the gulf.

In human lives straight lines figure prominently. When there is no natural boundary like a river or a coast, we often make the boundaries between our nations with straight lines. We set up states and towns the same way, as well as the borders not just of our properties but of the subdivisions within them, the fields, the gardens, the pastures, the woodlot, etc. We are now discovering that our ancient ancestors incised straight lines, "lay lines," in the earth. Our natural tendency is to plow and plant and harvest in straight lines. We had to be taught contour plowing, even though it should have been easier to plow that way, and before we embraced it fully our straight-line farming had cost us hundreds of millions of cubic yards of topsoil. We stretch our fences straight though this gives us fits in enclosing the rising and falling landforms that they cross. The lines in our architecture are for the most part straight, as are the lines in most furniture. We mount sculptures on square bases and we cut the edges of our books and magazines and newspapers straight and frame our paintings with straight lines.

We are glad when someone "straightens" up the room or "straightens" out some terrible confusion in our lives. We admonish our children and our politicians to "straighten up," and we speak of making progress by sticking to the straight and narrow and admire someone because they are straight with us. In many instances there is no reason why we could not get along just as well with curved rather than straight lines. Indeed we often do: we have curved as well as rectangular place mats. The same is true of carpets (but in both cases straight-edged ones sell much better). And we have circular buildings (rare) and circular barns (rarer), even though the Shakers built a circular dairy barn claimed by many to have been the most efficient dairy barn ever built (why wasn't it widely copied?). In a few cases circular wins out with us over straight. For example, we prefer circular to square plates, bowls, glasses, and cups. This may once have been appropriate, given the way glassblowing and pottery wheels work, but with modern techniques this is no longer an important consideration. One is forced to conclude that there is often no rhyme or reason for this aspect of ourselves; we seem simply to be truly in love with the straight. Although much of what we do follows curves or cycles, we are in general a most angular species.

So much of the lives of whales is cyclical, or annular or cycloidal. They live in cycles within cycles within cycles. The motion experienced by a whale being borne inside an ocean swell is circular. The bigger the swell, the bigger (and slower) the circle through which the whale's entire body is passively carried. As we shall see, the migratory routes of many whales (e.g., bow-heads, right whales, and humpback whales) seem to be curved paths more than simple oscillations back and forth along a straight line. When whales view the sky from underwater it is visible through a circular window above their heads, beneath whose center they are always inescapably located (the skylight above them like a kind of halo that won't dislodge—I refer here to a halo of light, not one of sainthood). When a whale in midocean lifts its head above the water to look around, the horizon is a circle (just a larger one) in whose center the whale is always exactly located. And no matter how far it swims in the open sea, a whale can never get out of the center of its circular horizon. (Of course, the acoustic horizon of a whale is the same.) There is for whales also, as for all life, the daily cycle of light and dark, the yearly cycle of warmer and cooler, and the lunar cycle that affects the tides and is super-imposed on an annual tidal cycle of springs and neaps.

When you add to this the endlessly recapitulating songs of humpbacks (about which I will have more to say in chapter 4), which keep cycling back over and over, and add to this the roll of the sea, and to that the whale's visits to the depths and returns to the surface, and to that the annual (and annular) migrations, and the lunar waxings and wanings . . . you see that much in the lives of whales is somehow a cycle that returns and completes itself. Indeed it is from the circular motion of a whale rolling at the surface to breathe that whales derive their very names. The word "whale" is believed by many to derive from the old English word for "wheel"—the idea being that when viewed from a boat or from shore, a whale breathing at the surface looked, to our unlearned ancestors, like a wheel revolving slowly in the sea.

I like the image of a whale as a giant wheel turning the sea. To me this finally makes sense, because it offers a concept commensurate with the grandeur, resplendence, and dignity of whales—not just a wonderful merger between symbol and reality but a fittingly gracious concession to the idea that maybe it is whales and not we who are the sovereign wheels and cogs of this planet—the inerasable manifestation of the *true* benefits of mind. If you think me overboard in this matter, realize that it is whales, not we, who would most impress a group of alien tourists visiting Earth from other worlds on a Cook's "Two-week Holiday Package Tour." After all, when you visit a deer park, it isn't the squirrels you remember.

Most baleen whales experience warm winters and cold summers—just the opposite of what most of us experience. They spend their summers feeding in high latitudes where the seas are rough and the water very cold, and their winters in much lower latitudes where the seas are calmer and the water warmer. They experience spring as a time of increasing cold as they swim into their cold, high-latitude summer feeding grounds, and autumn as a time of increasing warmth because they are moving into their warm, low-latitude winter breeding grounds. It is probably in late spring that whales experience the coldest water, as the water they are entering when moving poleward has not yet lost its winter chill. It is much the same with the many migratory bird species that winter in the tropics and nest as far north as the Arctic. Their summers include snow flurries, while their winters are balmy. It is probably only sedentary species like ourselves that dislike winter, simply because we stubbornly stay in one place and allow winter to wash over us while we stand, our teeth chattering, building a hatred of it. Our insistence on staying put is what gives us the concept that winter is a time of privation and cold and causes us to welcome spring with the deep relief born of want. Whales and songbirds don't let the seasons roll over them. Instead they follow the changing seasons to their new destinations.

Because most large whale species make long migrations between summer feeding grounds in high latitudes and winter assembly grounds in low latitudes, the energy necessary to push such large animals through several thousand miles of water is enormous. So why do they do it? Why do they make the effort? What's in it for them? And while we're at it, why are whales such enormous animals anyway? And why do they have such thick blubber coats?

And why do some species make sounds that carry (as we shall see) clear across oceans? I believe that all the answers to these questions have the same root—they all represent the baleen whales' responses to their principal prey—krill.[2] (There are several foods eaten by baleen whales, but for several species the principal prey is krill.)

Because the once-great herds of whales were particularly badly decimated in the Southern Hemisphere it is sometimes hard to realize that the Southern Hemisphere was the center of concentration of baleen whales. There are, of course, major herds of several baleen whale species in the Northern Hemisphere, but prior to whaling, the mother lode of baleen whales was always the Southern Hemisphere, where their principal feeding area was the Antarctic Ocean and their principal food (in some cases their exclusive food) krill—a ten-legged crustacean, which looks like a miniature shrimp. Most shrimp with which we humans are familiar grow in warmer water than the Antarctic, but it is in the Antarctic that krill thrive best. For much of their three-year lifetimes they are widely distributed here, but during their mating seasons they come together in large concentrations, and this is when the whales gather and eat their way through the mating swarms, devouring krill by the ton.

Everywhere that krill occurs in the Antarctic, it provides a major food source for a variety of predators—seals, all of the penguin species as well as several species of flying seabirds, and at least five species of baleen whales.

The size of large krill swarms can be astonishing. A team of Russian researchers found a single school of krill that they estimated to contain a hundred million tons. One hundred million tons is more than humanity's entire annual catch of fish from all the oceans of the world, which is to say that if the estimate was correct, that single giant school of krill had more tons of food in it than all the fish extracted from the sea by the entire human race fishing all the oceans of the world for a full year. And that was just one school of krill that year. Krill is a truly incredible food resource.

How strange that this kind of feast is served up in the Antarctic Ocean, which most of us tend to think of as a bleak and relatively lifeless place. That perception, however, is totally wrong. During Southern Hemisphere summers, the Antarctic Ocean supports more tons of living things per square mile—more biomass, as it is known—than any comparably sized body of water on earth. The reason for this is that the Antarctic Ocean is rich in nitrates and other essential chemicals that are largely missing from sunnier places like equatorial midocean waters.

In midocean there is no mechanism to return these essential minerals to the surface. When an animal or plant dies, it sinks to the bottom, taking the nitrogen and other essential elements bound up in the compounds of its body with it. Once a corpse has reached the bottom, the only way its nitrogen molecules can get back to the surface is for something to carry them there. In most places no mechanism to do this exists, and no nitrogen or minerals return to the surface to be available to plants for constructing new cells. The result is that midocean waters are nutrient depauperate—they are deserts compared to antarctic waters.

The main force that returns nitrogen to the surface is the upwelling of water. These upwellings occur where deep ocean currents strike island arcs or continents. When they rise to the surface, deep ocean waters bring with them the nitrogen and other essential substances that have been drifting along in bottom waters ever since their original sinking. Because the net circulation of ocean water is toward the poles, deep ocean water in the Southern Hemisphere flows toward the antarctic continent. Thus many of the nutrients from the entire ocean are imported into the Antarctic. When they reach the surface plant life explodes, and the animal life which depends on it develops to an unsurpassed degree. This plant life is, of course, the basic food for all animal life in the region. However, although krill can catch the larger species of single-celled plants, krill also consume zooplankton, which have fed on plants themselves.

As I have mentioned, it is when krill is concentrated in its huge mating swarms that whales gain their best access to it. At other times of the year, krill appears to be too spread out to be worth a whale's effort to collect it. The populations of other krill predators are limited by the availability of other species of prey during the months when krill isn't available to them; such predators must find other things to eat while they are waiting for the summer feasts of krill to commence. Of course, from the krill's standpoint, spreading out is a mechanism not just for finding more food but for starving out predators. But this process doesn't work on baleen whales, because they can wait until the krill swarms reform. Baleen whales are masters at fasting—they can probably starve for longer periods than any other mammal. They can wait patiently for eight months or more until the krill start their mating swarms again.[3] This gives baleen whales access to the greatest food blooms, the most abundant, concentrated, animal food resource on earth— the annual mating swarms of Antarctic Ocean krill.

The only way a small animal like a shrew or a mouse can starve for a long time is by allowing its body temperature to fall. An insectivorous bat living outside the tropics often has to reduce its body temperature to make it through a cold night. It also has to do so to get through long, insectless winters (in a process known as hibernation).

A principal advantage of warm-bloodedness is that it allows an animal to keep its nervous system at a constant temperature and thus to keep its brain fully functional twenty-four hours a day. The owner of a warm brain can at all times see and hear and is alert enough to run away or pursue prey at a moment's notice—any hour of the day or night. On the other hand, an animal with a cold brain is torpid—while its brain is cool it is probably functionally blind and scarcely able to hear, and before it can perceive very well, or flee, or attack, or fight, it must warm up its body so as to warm up its brain. This it does either by shivering for several minutes or by sitting in the sun. But although warm-bloodedness confers wonderful advantages on mammals, they pay for the advantage by requiring more food to keep their metabolic fires burning.

But isn't there some way a mammal might starve for long periods without becoming semicomatose? The answer is yes, and the animals that do this best are whales, primarily because of their huge size. Being large is the only way a warm-blooded animal can starve for long periods. Being large makes whales the ultimate mammalian masters of fasting. The reason large size allows an animal to starve for a long time is that the cells in the body of a large mammal actually live at a slower pace than those cells in the body of a small mammal. Cells in large warm-blooded bodies require less sustenance per hour, whereas cells in a small animal such as a mouse burn their way through life—each cell requiring relatively enormous quantities of food to survive. If a shrew doesn't get roughly its own weight in food every twenty-four hours it may starve to death overnight. A piece of whale tissue the same size as a shrew doesn't need nearly as much nourishment over the same period.

The reason that keeping warm is harder for a mouse than a whale is due to a simple principle that is often misunderstood: the bigger an animal, the smaller its surface area in relation to its volume. Looking at a whale, it is hard to believe that its enormous skin surface area is actually much smaller in relation to its total volume than the skin of a mouse is to the mouse's body volume. This is, nevertheless, the case—and dramatically so. For example, a mouse with a body one inch in diameter and two inches long will have a body surface area roughly 4.5 times its body volume, while a whale that is fifty feet long and twelve feet in diameter has a body surface area roughly 0.025 times its body volume. Thus the surface-to-volume ratio of the mouse is more than 175 times greater than the surface-to-volume ratio of the whale[4]—the mouse has a relatively enormous skin surface area compared to its body, and the whale a relatively tiny skin surface area compared to its body.

Why is this important? Because an animal generates heat with its body (its furnace) and loses it through its skin (its radiators). A small animal has a small furnace in relation to a large bank of radiators and therefore cools off very rapidly. A large animal has a large furnace in relation to a small bank of radiators and therefore cools off very slowly.

If such is the case, then why do some whales have such thick blubber? Because contrary to popular opinion, blubber seems to be more for fuel storage than for warmth. Blubber is in fact what fuels whales throughout their long periods of starvation. It has been calculated that from its blubber a large whale can maintain its basal metabolism for a year or more without feeding. The primary function of a thick blubber coat is thus probably related to its potential as an energy reserve during lean times.[5]

Thus we see that two of the most obvious features of whales—their enormous size and their thick blubber—are simply adaptations enabling them to live slowly enough, keep warm enough, and swim far enough to gain access to the most enormous blooms of animal food on the planet—the annual swarms of krill in the icy Antarctic Ocean.

Once whales had adapted to the point where they were able to bide their time awaiting the appearance of krill concentrations, the krill had to develop countermeasures. Mating swarms of krill convene in unpredictable places—sometimes swarming hundreds of miles away from where there were major swarms last year. But I believe that whales have a response to this: they emit loud, low-frequency sounds that carry for hundreds, even thousands of miles—useful for announcing the location of large krill swarms when they find them.

Although it has not been demonstrated that whales use their low sounds to share information on food finds, I find it hard to see how evolution would select against their doing so, particularly in the case of a species like krill that collects in swarms far too large for even the largest whale (often, even ten thousand of the largest whales) to eat alone.

I suspect that whales divide up the resources of the sea by fanning out all over the ocean, sharing information about the food sources that lucky ones stumble across. A whale that found food last year but so far none this year might survive by hearing other whales calling about newly discovered feasts—perhaps even the very whales that it helped last year. I believe that whales cooperate in widely scattered societies and that these societies are held together by calls that can carry hundreds of miles. I further believe that these societies exist for the purpose of sharing information on food finds and that they are probably maintained by reciprocal altruism.

By this line of reasoning we may see that the entire social structure of whales' lives may simply be a consequence of the strategies they must employ in order to find food. In other words, not just the great size of their bodies, but their blubber, their loud voices, and the very fabric of their social structure are probably founded on the predator-avoidance mechanisms of krill.

One of the thorniest questions about the migrations of whales is why many of them bother to migrate at all. The usual supposition is that, for the most part, winter is a time of starvation during which whales don't get much to eat at the low latitudes of their breeding grounds—the occasional snack, sure, but nothing like the staggeringly productive food bloom in polar seas (called the polar food pulse) from which they derive most of their year's sustenance. It is also assumed that the reason whales migrate is because the young don't have much blubber to keep them warm and must therefore be born in warm waters rather than in cold polar seas. This theory ignores the fact that the young of the largest whale species are born with ample insulation for the coldest oceans and that the layer of blubber in which the adults are wrapped is far more than is necessary for protection against heat loss.[6]

Not surprisingly, many blue and fin whale calves are apparently born in the high latitudes of polar seas. This evidence comes from whaling—data collected about the length and sex of the fetuses of pregnant females killed in the Antarctic. In the case of the 21,450 fetuses of female fin whales killed in the Antarctic between 1925 and 1948, the lengths of 90 percent of their fetuses indicated they would have been born in warmer latitudes. However, 10 percent of the fetuses were near term, indicating that had their mothers survived, these calves would almost certainly have been born in the Antarctic Ocean.[7]

We don't know whether there is a difference in mortality rates between blue and fin whale calves born in higher versus lower latitudes, but presumably lower-latitude calves would do better. However, the great emphasis often given to the need for calves to be born in warm water may well be incorrect, for as we shall see later, the real problem faced by large whales, even the young of large whales, in ice-cold seas is probably not keeping warm but staying cool when they are vigorously exercising. It is my suspicion that while a need to find warm water may be a factor in some species, it may not be as important as finding *calm* waters, which even in high latitudes may be encountered in the lee of islands or large icebergs (whaling ships often use the lee of icebergs to weather antarctic storms). There is one population of right whales that appears around Campbell, an island on the fringes of the

Antarctic Ocean at the "wrong" time of year. Campbell Island waters are cold, but they don't freeze over. It is possible that these whales are using the lee of Campbell as a way of escaping the full force of winter storms and are thereby avoiding a long migration. However, as we shall see, there is another intriguing possibility to explain the presence of these animals so far south in winter.

For someone who has never seen the full force of a storm in the open sea there can be no real understanding of the magnitude of its potential for devastation (I have a friend who claims that the only reason sailors ever return to the sea after surviving a major storm is that the human brain is incapable of storing images of such violence). Southern Hemisphere whales feed in some of the roughest seas in the world, latitudes known unaffectionately to seamen as the "Roaring Forties," "Frantic Fifties," and "Screaming Sixties." Whales also have the lowest reproductive rates of any marine mammals. The time it takes a female baleen whale to reach sexual maturity and give birth to her first calf is also very long. These facts, coupled with the vulnerability of whale calves in their first few weeks of life, make me comfortable in assuming that because their investment in their young is so high, female whales probably face strong pressures to migrate into calm or sheltered waters, so their calves aren't trying to learn to breathe in the chaos of an open ocean storm. I have witnessed humpback whales trying to breathe in thirty-foot seas created by sixty knots of wind (just barely a full winter storm) when there was no definite line of demarcation between air and water but a continuum of spray as the surface of the sea was whipped into a frenzy. The way the whales avoided accidentally inhaling this half-air, half-water interface was by waiting until the steepest face of a major wave had formed and then grabbing a breath while launching themselves out through it horizontally and then crashing back into the trough of the wave. They then expelled their breath and grabbed the next inhalation so forcefully that the sounds of their breaths were clearly audible above the shrieking of the wind. It remains in my mind the most spectacular thing I have ever witnessed in all my time at sea. Although the adults seemed to be experiencing no great problem in breathing this way, they were timing things with great accuracy. I suspect that a calf might well have been in deep trouble had it mistimed its emergences as it tried to breathe. It certainly seemed to me to be no fit place for a weak or inexperienced animal.

Besides finding calmer waters for her calf, I can also see the advantage to a mother whale that shallow waters afford when it comes to protecting her calf from attacks by predators like killer whales and large sharks (see chapter 3, page 103).

Such assumptions could explain why pregnant females who are near term would migrate, and it might also explain why mature males migrate—that is, in order to get a chance to mate with those females once they have given birth and are ready to mate again. But even if calm, shallow waters are the best place for bearing a calf, it doesn't explain why animals of both sexes should migrate when they are not yet sexually mature or are past their breeding ages, or why females who are resting between pregnancies should migrate. For such animals, why not just remain in the Antarctic, skip all those thousands of miles of swimming, and let spring and summer come to you, bringing with them the polar food bloom?

It seems likely that there *are* advantages to subadults in migrating—for example, to learn the migratory route, or perhaps to assist in the defense of their siblings or half siblings (though we have no evidence they do such a thing). Subadult males may develop skills in competing for females by watching mating groups, and for whale species in which there is no pair bond between males and females (e.g., right whales) it may be important for subadults to know who their brothers and sisters are—something they can do by migrating and being on hand when their mother gives birth to her next calf (see chapter 3). In some cases it may also help subadult females to form associations with other females and to learn who their sisters are, and by watching other, more experienced females do it, how to rear calves, how to stay out of trouble from other whales, etc. These advantages could be very important and might be expected to help offset the enormous cost of migration for subadults. But that still gives us no satisfactory explanation for why whales that have passed their reproductive years should swim all those thousands of miles to the breeding areas and then turn around and swim all those thousands of miles back.

We are probably not wrong in assuming that very old whales migrate. The ages of whales of some species can be determined by counting growth rings in a wax plug that fills the ear canal. There are whaling industry records of old whales that were killed on the breeding grounds whose age was determined by this means. In the case of right whales, we have found direct evidence that the old whales do participate in migrations; we see animals in the calving bays at Península Valdés which, by their lack of calves, large size, wrinkled skin, markedly slow movements, and socially aloof behavior appear to be very old. As the years go by, this assumption will be proven or disproven by noting whether whales we recognize return to the breeding bays when they are very old.

There is good evidence that killer whales kill the calves and sometimes the subadults of large whales—even the blue whale, though there is no evidence that these smaller whales represent a significant threat to fully grown adult blues. So a large whale, even if it is old, is probably relatively immune to attack from killer whales and sharks and therefore gains no important advantage in avoiding predators by staying around other whales so as to be overlooked in the crowd. Besides, species that predate on migratory animals typically follow the main herds during migration, dining off the slower and weaker individuals. An old whale, like an old African buffalo, may do better by becoming antisocial and avoiding herds—further reason not to join the migration.

Although it may seem counterintuitive, once an animal is past its reproductive years, unless it is making an important contribution to the welfare of the next generation, there is no way evolution can work on it to change it (or its behavior) either for the better or the worse. And there is no evidence as yet that old whales make a significant contribution to the welfare of the next generation. (Our studies of right whales show no obvious contribution from very old whales to the younger generation.)

Though none has been demonstrated for these species, it is easy enough to imagine ways in which they could make a contribution. For example, in the case of blue and fin whales, it might be of some advantage to the younger whales if the old whales stayed close to the polar feeding grounds during the winter. For, as we shall see, the very low frequency sounds of these species are capable of carrying for enormous distances, and if it stayed close to the feeding grounds, an old whale would be likely during the following spring to find the big food blooms first. Having found them, if an old whale made its loud, low calls, it could act as a beacon to guide younger relatives to the food. In this way the elderly would be making a significant contribution to younger animals, and the selective pressures of evolution would work to help old whales survive for more years, by selecting behaviors that tended to keep them alive longer. (As we shall see, although there is no question that the sounds of fin and blue whales carry such distances, it has yet to be demonstrated that they are used by the whales in this way.)

This line of reasoning suggests that for very old whales, participation in the annual migration could just be a matter of habit; they've migrated all their lives and they're too set in their ways not to do it again. Although habit does not seem to be a very satisfactory explanation for why an old whale might join a migration, it is, in fact, a perfectly valid one should it turn out that the success of their descendants is not affected by whether or not old whales remain alive after they have reached the end of their reproductive years. However, I am still unwilling to believe that in the case of old whales it all comes down to that. I believe there must be another explanation that is applicable not just to the oldest whales but to all whales.

Because the densities of zooplankton are so high during the annual food pulse in arctic and antarctic seas, one tends to forget that the time period of food availability is also very compressed and that there is a very long and hungry wait between the big annual food pulses. It is also easy to overlook the fact that at lower latitudes, there is still a great deal of food available in specific productive areas even though these can't match the concentrations of the polar food pulses. These lesser concentrations, however, are available over a much longer time span than the polar pulses, which may more than compensate for their reduced amount.

Our own observations that Southern Hemisphere right whales feed at Península Valdés in late winter and spring indicate that at least this species does not require the food pulses of the southern oceans in order to make it worth the effort to feed. Charles Mayo, who has studied the feeding of Northern Hemisphere right whales at comparable latitudes during late winter and early spring, has clearly demonstrated that there are large enough plankton concentrations in these nonpolar latitudes to offer this species substantial quantities of food.[8] The same is probably true of species like fin and blue whales, which rely heavily on plankton and small fish for food.

If whales remained at high latitudes in the polar seas during winter and spring in order to await the local blooms of food, they would continue to starve until the slowly lengthening days finally brought the spring food blooms. In both Southern and Northern hemispheres, spring advances northward or southward at a rate of about eighteen miles per day.

Spring hits Península Valdés in Argentina (forty-two degrees south latitude) about eighty days before it reaches the main areas of krill blooms in the Antarctic. Conversely, winter arrives in those Antarctic areas about eighty days before it arrives at Península Valdés. It is clear that by migrating northward for the winter and southward for the spring, a Southern Hemisphere whale can cut off some significant portion of 160 days (i.e., about half the year) of complete starvation in return for what are probably modest meals (or at least heavy snacking) compared with what it will find at higher latitudes in summer. By joining the migration to the breeding grounds, even the oldest whales only have to wait until spring arrives at their milder ocean climes and then follow its advance into higher latitudes, picking up at least a little sustenance from whatever planktonic blooms they encounter, as life turns on along the way. However, it is by no means clear that whales get more out of such snacking than they expend in swimming the hundreds of miles they migrate, and the books are not yet shut on the question of why whales ever leave their higher feeding latitudes for lower ones. As I have mentioned earlier, one group of right whales is reported to overwinter at Campbell Island, which is at the same latitude as the South Georgia feeding area in which we believe Península Valdés right whales gorge themselves in summer. The migrations of bowhead whales result in hardly any change in latitude. Instead, they spend their entire lives in ice water.

There can, of course, be other advantages to migrating besides getting a bit more food and finding a good place to raise one's young. While we know quite a lot about the migratory destinations of humpback whales in the North Pacific, their compelling reason for swimming to Hawaii from Alaska—a distance of some thirty-five hundred miles each way—is not completely obvious. The fabled clear waters of Hawaii are an indication of lack of productivity (the coral reefs being an exception—but not one particularly accessible to a humpback whale, since there are abundant hiding places for the fish they might otherwise catch in coral reefs). However, there is a curious possible second reason why humpbacks might swim to tropical waters. Humpback whales carry a species of barnacle called coronula on their heads, flippers, and tails—one of the larger barnacle species, and one which has never been found attached to any other animal or, indeed, any other surface. (Paul Struhsaker, a fisheries biologist working in Hawaii, once told me that when collecting samples of bottom-living organisms in areas frequented by humpbacks he had several times dredged up dead coronula barnacles from the Hawaiian seabed.)

It is important for whales to rid themselves of barnacles, because unless barnacle populations are somehow controlled they can become a serious drag—something true not just of whales but of ships. Barnacle loads on whales can be enormous; barnacles attached to the head of one humpback whale weighed a thousand pounds.[9]

The fight between a barnacle and a whale is not a spirited struggle involving parries and thrusts. The battlefield is growth rates: the barnacle racing to grow the base of its shell into the whale's skin faster than the whale can slough off that skin. And the rate at which whales grow and lose their skin is extraordinarily high—cell division in cetacean skin being up to 290 times as rapid as it is in human skin.[10] When we wanted skin samples from right whales for determining their sex (by examining chromosomes in the skin cells) we discovered we had only to swim for a few yards behind any right whale before we encountered a piece of floating skin. Large whales leave wakes of bits of skin in the water, rather like a car driving through a pile of dead leaves. When a right whale breaches, it loses even more sloughing skin, some of it in large sections. In Argentina, gulls of two species relish whale skin and have apparently cottoned on to the fact that a breaching whale means food. When a right whale starts a sequence of breaches, these gulls race out and search eagerly in the splash zones left after each breach, snatching up and swallowing the largest bits of sloughed skin. (There's often a lot of skin available, because breaches loosen lots of skin, and breach sequences often contain dozens of breaches.)

There is a curious twist to this pattern which I find delightful. The tail of a whale harbors the least amount of barnacles and other ectoparasites, probably because it moves fastest through the water and is therefore the hardest to hang on to if you are a sessile animal like a barnacle. For this reason there is no need for a whale to spend as much energy and stored resources growing new skin on its tail, particularly at a time when it is starving, as it must spend in growing fresh skin on other parts of its body.

Whales often engage in long bouts of "lobtailing," where they thrash the water repeatedly with their tails (sometimes over fifty slaps). There is little skin to be found in the splash zones caused by this activity and gulls don't fly out in search of skin when a whale starts lobtailing (even though the splashes from vigorous lobtailing may look every bit as large as the splashes from the last few breaches in a bout of breaching). It looks as if the gulls recognize the difference between breaching and lobtailing and know from experience it's not going to be worth the effort to search the splash zones of a lobtailer.

As an example of just how fast a right whale can grow skin: we have filmed the same individual twice within a twenty-four-hour period during a time it was undergoing massive peeling. Both photographs show skin condition clearly. In the first the entire skin is grossly blotched and patched, with large areas of peeling. The next day the same whale is covered in new skin, its entire body shiny and all but perfect. (Aside from one or two tiny zones which look like mild sloughing, there is almost no sign of yesterday's peeling.)

Presumably all this skin sloughing serves to get rid of the larval stages of parasites like barnacles which, as adults, cannot transfer to a whale. Barnacles transfer hosts as tiny, free-swimming larvae. A larva is adapted to growing fast once it has attached to a whale, so the pressure is on the whale to grow skin even faster and thereby slough the barnacle off along with the skin. The antifouling bottom paint used on boats employs a similar principle. Part of the efficacy of this paint is that it is toxic to larvae, but an equally important feature is that since it never really dries it is constantly sloughing off, taking the early growth stages of young barnacles, corals, and seaweeds with it.

When he told me about finding barnacles on the bottom around Hawaii, Paul Struhsaker suggested the interesting possibility that the water in Hawaii might be unfavorable for the growth of coronula on humpbacks (i.e., perhaps it is too warm or too devoid of their food, or too something-or-other else). If so, one reason humpbacks may migrate is to reduce their barnacle loads; rather like sailors who haul their boats once a year to remove the buildup of fouling organisms. Even though the truth of this intriguing speculation has not been demonstrated, I offer it as a means of underlining how less than obvious the real reasons for migration by whales may turn out to be.

There is some evidence, though, against Struhsaker's interesting suggestion. For example, although barnacles are usually described as parasites, we know that when humpback whales fight, their barnacles become weapons, inflicting scratches and wounds on their opponents. We also know that coronula barnacles are found in greatest number on the heads, flippers, and fluke tips of humpbacks, the same surfaces that male humpbacks use to strike their opponents. This may mean that rather than being parasites, barnacles are symbiotic with humpbacks. In return for a surface on which to live and ride to food that would otherwise be entirely inaccessible to them, they may provide the whale with weapons. Also, the periods when humpback whales most need their barnacles for fighting are presumably the winter months, when they are in places like Hawaii. It would seem a poor strategy for the whale to lose its barnacles during such times. It is possible, therefore, that conditions for coronula are just fine in Hawaiian waters—that maybe the reason they are lost is because as the whales fight they get knocked off and rain down on the sea floor.

While on the subject of barnacles and migration, I would be remiss not to note an interesting study that was made on the barnacles that grow on gray whales. As barnacles grow, they lay down their shells in successive bands, reminiscent of the way trees form rings. It happens that the chemical ratio of two isotopes of oxygen in the material of each band is different, depending upon the temperature of the water in which the barnacle is growing. If the water is warm when a band is being laid down, the band will have a different ratio of isotopes of oxygen in it than it will have if the water is cold. Thus, by examining the oxygen isotopes in its growth bands, you can deduce the temperature of the water in which the barnacle was feeding when each ring was formed. Like Madame LaFarge in *A Tale of Two Cities* the barnacle knits into the successive bands of its shell a record of the water temperatures to which it is exposed during its life.

Thus, when it is riding on the back of a whale, the barnacle will lay down in the layers of its shell a temperature record of the whale's migration from warmer to colder seas and back again each year. The demonstration that this record can be read was made by analysis of growth bands in the shells of barnacles from a gray whale—a species whose migratory route along the coast of North America is well known.

As I have mentioned earlier, coronula is confined in its distribution to the bodies of humpback whales. It has shared its fate with this species for millions of years; fossil coronula from gray whales appear in the fossil record of the Miocene.[11] Oxygen isotope ratios should be interpretable in specimens that are millions of years old. By applying to the growth bands of fossil coronula the same analysis techniques that are used on modern gray whale barnacles, we could find out whether the long-dead host whales, to which, presumably, the fossil coronula were attached, had migrated as their descendants do. This may be one area where the often-stated premise that behavior cannot be determined from the fossil record will prove untrue.

It is often possible to discover the main areas between which whales migrate (their migratory destinations), but their routes between these destinations are much more difficult to elucidate. The one species for which migratory routes are probably best known is the gray whale. Their route seems to follow a path pretty much along the western margin of the North American continent, between Baja California and Alaska (making it the longest mammalian migration known). The route followed by one of the four populations of bowhead whales (the population that frequents the Bering, Beaufort, and Chukchi seas) seems fairly well known. In winter we find bowheads in the Bering Sea near the ice edge, from the Gulf of Anadyr to St. Matthew Island to St. Lawrence Island. Their northward migration begins in April and continues into June. During this time they move up through the Bering Strait, through the Chukchi Sea, and past the northernmost point of Alaska, Point Barrow, then east into the Beaufort Sea. It is here that they feed between June and August in areas to the south and southwest of Banks Island and along the coast of northern Canada from Amundsen Gulf to a bit west of Herschel Island. Between August and November they are on the move again, proceeding along the Canadian and Alaskan coasts to Point Barrow. But then a strange thing happens: rather than turning south and heading back out of the Arctic through the Bering Strait, they head west across the Chukchi Sea to Herald and Wrangel islands, where they feed again. Finally, with winter truly threatening, they drive south and by following the coast of the Chukotsk Peninsula to the south and east leave the high Arctic through the Bering Strait—back to their wintering grounds in the Bering Sea.

I have gone into these details to make the point that the migration route of bowheads is as much east and west as it is north and south. In fact the movement east and west is greater. More and more studies of whale migrations are demonstrating a similar phenomenon. It now looks as though many species cover as much ocean to the east and west each year as they do to the north and south. In the case of the Bering, Beaufort, and Chukchi Sea population of bowheads this is not so surprising since they have only one means of entry to the arctic seas (the Bering Strait), and the summer ice edge is pressing them from the north, thereby confining most of their motion to east–west travel.

In the case of humpback whales, however, there are no such restrictions, yet they seem to be the greatest east–west migrators of them all. Back when the Japanese were shooting numbered tags into humpback whales and recovering the tags when the whale was killed elsewhere (in the cookers on their factory ships), eight humpback whales were marked off the Aleutian Islands and recovered near Japan thirty-seven hundred miles away. Of that huge journey, nine hundred miles of it were to the south and three thousand miles to the west.[12] Modern studies of humpbacks rely on natural black-and-white color patterns on the undersides of humpback tails to identify individual whales. By this means thousands can be followed. At the moment there are over 250 whales that have been seen both in Hawaii and in southeast Alaska. More of this migration is east and west than north and south.

In fact, if you look at the classic evidence demonstrating that whales migrate mostly north and south, you find that it comes from some often quoted work back in the 1950s and 1960s on humpback whales in the Southern Hemisphere. At the time people were tagging humpbacks in their wintering grounds off Australia, while most of the catches (and thus tag recoveries) of these whales were taking place in the Antarctic.[13]

The whaling effort in polar regions in those years was principally concentrated in one area of the Antarctic Ocean. But as the years went by and antarctic factory ships reduced the populations of whales in each sector of the ocean, they moved to the next. Scientists who were marking humpback whales far to the north near Australia, New Zealand, and several South Pacific islands realized that the whaling ships were moving away from areas due south of them, and since they expected whales were migrating north and south, they decided to move their marking operations to breeding grounds due north of where the effort of the factory ships in the Antarctic was concentrated. They knew from experience that the number of recaptures was small compared to the number of whales marked, and they wanted to make sure they would have enough marked whales for there to be at least some recoveries.

Unfortunately this practice confounded the conclusion because (1) most whaling was directly south of most tagging, and (2) most returns occurred shortly after tagging since, as we now know, many tags get lost.

This proved to be an unfortunate decision, as it loaded the dice to favor the conclusion that most whales were migrating due north and south and made it very difficult to detect an east–west migration if there was one, and no chance at all to detect animals that might be doing unexpected things like going farther to the north rather than to the south during the summers. Of course, if whales were migrating significantly to the east or west, this pattern might have been expected to have been picked up some years later, when an entire whaling operation had moved farther east or west. Still, this would require that tags stayed put for a long time, which some assuredly do. However, we know now that tags often fall out—a result of tissue rejection—a serious drawback of this technique. Besides, these whalers were killing most of their tagged animals within a few days, weeks, or months of tagging them. So the longer they had to wait to get a good indication of an east–west shift, the fewer whales they had that could demonstrate such a shift. Their data was thus biased badly toward the demonstration of north–south migrations.

In spite of such problems mitigating against the discovery of east–west migrations, the scientists doing this work did manage to demonstrate some extraordinary east–west migrations. Three animals were marked on the eastern and captured on the western coast of Australia—a distance requiring a minimum swim of about twenty-eight hundred miles. Another was marked in eastern Australia and captured in Fiji—a direct line distance of about two thousand miles.[14] A due-south swim to the nearest coast of Antarctica from these areas would be about eighteen hundred miles. However, these long east–west shifts were mostly dismissed as possibly aberrant. What we now know indicates that North Pacific humpback whales may migrate as much if not more to the east and west as they do to the north and south, and if this is a species trait it presumably holds true for Southern Hemisphere humpbacks as well.

There are now much better ways to study the migratory patterns of humpback whales than by firing the easily rejectable marks into them (benign studies that are based on photographing the natural markings on humpbacks' tails). My guess is that when this technique has been applied more widely to humpbacks feeding in the Antarctic, it will be seen that in addition to a large north–south shift, there is a large east–west shift as well. I also suspect that as time goes by and better sampling protocols are tried, we will see that migrations not just by bowheads and humpbacks but by many other whale species are more nearly giant traverses along curved and complex paths than they are a simple north–south shift.

The baleen plates that hang from the upper jaws of a baleen whale are used as giant strainers with which to strain the seas. They are lined with hairs that mat together and retain prey as the water in the mouth is expelled through them. Broadly speaking, there are two options: 1) to swim the strainer through the water slowly, the way humans pull a plankton net behind a boat; and 2) to lunge forward with the mouth wide open, engulfing tons of water (along with the prey) in the ventral pouch, later expelling it through the baleen, leaving the prey behind in the mouth. There is a third and unexpected method of feeding practiced by a few baleen whales, such as gray whales—sucking in bottom mud and straining it through very coarse baleen to retain the burrowing creatures (mostly worms and crustaceans) for food.

Gray whales have a profound effect on the ecosystem with this practice. It has been estimated that the amount of mud that the world's gray whale population puts into suspension each year is more than the annual sediment discharge of the Mississippi River in the same period. However, this method of mud processing seems to be practiced by only three species: the gray, the bowhead, and the right whale. The latter two species probably don't intentionally suck up mud but rather are skimming so close to the bottom that mud is accidently taken in along with water. Mud filtering is rare; the more common technique of feeding involves the processing of enormous quantities of water.

It seems obvious that a whale needs an enormous mouth, but the question of exactly why becomes a bit more complex if mouth size is considered from the point of view of the prey that is trying to escape it. It is in relation to the strategies of avoidance developed by their prey that both the jaws of whales and their strategies of catching food have been shaped.

It is obvious that the amount of water a whale can process depends on the size of its mouth. Skimming whales—whales that swim forward holding their mouths open and pushing their baleen strainers through the water—may process water for as long as they like, whereas blue, fin, sei, Bryde's, minke, and humpback whales usually lunge forward and fill their giant pleated ventral pouches with water before closing their mouths and stopping to strain out the prey they have included with the water (a process called lunge feeding). The water is held in a sac that the whale apparently opens by turning its tongue inside out.[15] When so everted, the tongue is stretched enormously and becomes a thin lining to the rear wall of the pouch reaching not just down the whale's throat but almost to its navel—a pouch that stretches to encompass a volume of water that some biologists have estimated at seventy tons in a blue whale and that appears in some cases to be even larger than the whale's body.[16] The filling of this prodigious sac is achieved by the whale rushing forward with its mouth opened wide during lunge feeding. Once the ventral sac is full, the pressure for expelling the water back out through the baleen (leaving the prey stranded against the inside lining of it) appears to be assisted by the whale contracting the muscles in its tongue and turning its tongue right side out again.

When you and I say the whale opens its mouth "wide" we may have a kind of mental picture about the process to which I'm referring. But in this case I can assure you that no one is ever properly prepared for the degree to which a humpback whale can open its mouth. I have witnessed a humpback repeatedly open its mouth more than ninety degrees. And I have, by making an off-the-cuff calculation, satisfied myself that it could have comfortably engulfed a medium-sized car in the cavern of its gape. I have a friend who was studying humpbacks in Alaska when one of them rose beneath his boat. The next thing he knew he and the boat were inside its widely opened mouth, a situation that only lasted for a second as the whale was apparently as surprised as he and instantly backed off. But he observed that when his Zodiac was in the whale's mouth it was not grounded on the whale's jaws but was floating freely, with water under its keel.

From the first moment that the prey perceives the horror of the approach of the whale's open maw, its only chance to escape lies in swimming either directly away from the whale or on a course that will take it sideways to the whale's line of approach and thereby out of the path of the mouth. Many animals on which whales feed are so tiny there is no chance they can get out of the way by outswimming the whale, particularly not if the whale is lunge feeding—a strategy employed by rorquals (the blue, fin, sei, Bryde's, minke, and humpback whales).

As for darting sideways out of harm's way, the larger the whale's mouth, the longer the distance the prey has to swim before it is clear of the lips. This means that the bigger the whale's mouth, the bigger the patch of prey it can engulf; the higher percentage of the shoal of prey it will get without losing significant amounts from the perimeter of its mouth; and the faster that prey can be (which usually means also the bigger it can be) before the whale is unable to catch it. A big mouth thus gives a whale access to faster kinds of prey, which means a wider variety of species on which to feed and a chance to eat bigger prey at higher levels of the food chain.

The techniques by which humpback whales feed are as interesting as their songs. Many of their techniques involve releasing air underwater. In the simplest of these cases the whale blows out a huge cloud of finely divided air bubbles—as though a seltzer bottle had exploded underwater. As the cloud of bubbles rises, the whale either races through it with its mouth open, skims across the top of it, or appears to drive fish against it and catch them as they turn back (the fish seemingly hesitant to enter the cloud).

The exact mechanism by which such bubble clouds work is not clearly understood, but there is another technique involving the release of air, the functioning of which seems more obvious. This is the technique of bubble netting: the setting of a cylindrical net made of columns of rising air bubbles around a school of fish and then coming up from below to catch them. Bubble nets are not made of continuous streams of bubbles but of bursts of air released by the whale to form separate columns of bubbles around the perimeter of a net. A whale engaging in such activity sounds like a steam engine. Once a whale starts making bubble nets, it may go on making them for hours at a time, making a new net every two to ten minutes.

Bubble net feeding was referred to in a passing way with North Atlantic humpbacks in the early 1920s but was first described in detail for Alaskan humpback whales by Charles Jurasz. Humpbacks encircle schools of krill and other plankton with "nets" made out of air bubbles, that is, air which rises and creates a wall through which their prey will not pass (even though there seems to be no reason why it cannot). The whale circles at an unknown depth. Judging from the delay between hearing the air expelled and seeing the first bubbles at the surface air is probably released at a depth of between fifty and one hundred feet. The whale then swims up inside the cylindrical walls of rising bubbles to engulf its prey as it crowds (and thus concentrates) against the water's surface. On several occasions when working in Alaska with Jurasz and others I have managed to record the sounds of air being released as a whale spun its net. There were no social or vocal noises, only the sounds of escaping air. This suggests that bubble netting is something more than just a manifestation of excitement by a whale which is swimming circles around its prey (i.e., the sounds aren't just excited noises like dogs yapping while pursuing rabbits). Apparently it is a deliberate act—in effect, the whale methodically deploying its net, that is, setting a trap. Thus humpbacks appear to be a tool-making as well as tool-using species.

Timing the sounds of the release of air underwater and the formation of the bubble ring at the surface reveals another curious fact. The time required to spin the net is longer than the time it takes for the bubbles to form a ring at the surface. The whale must therefore be swimming upward in a spiraling path while releasing air. Based on calculations of the speed at which bubbles of a given dimension rise, it appears that by spiraling upward more or less steeply whales may be able to adjust the "mesh size" (size of bubbles and distances between them) of their nets at will. This intriguing possibility is now under study. This much is already clear, however: whales use different-sized bubbles for different-sized prey. For example, when whales corral fish in bubble nets they use larger bubbles than those they generate to entrap krill.

Sometimes two humpbacks will cooperate, each making half of a larger net, then joining the ends of their two semicircles into a single oval net, and then rising together side by side within it.

It is not surprising that whales blow bubbles the patterns in which leave us guessing about their method and purpose. One of these techniques produces what look like giant smoke rings about three feet in diameter that rise rapidly to the surface. These madly spinning doughnut-shaped clouds probably wreak havoc as they pass through shoals of small prey, leaving confused and disoriented victims in their wake for the whale to retrieve and eat. This is the most distinctive humpback feeding strategy of which I'm aware, but we are still only guessing at how it works and what its real purpose is.

Only one particular whale has been known to engage in this activity, and even she seldom does it. However, once she gets going, the process becomes very obvious and is done vigorously. For example, she may blow twenty bubble "smoke rings" in a row during a bout lasting half an hour.

But by far the most sensational feeding method I have ever seen is one involving groups of humpback whales that hunt together routinely. There is obvious cooperation in these groups, in that specific individuals take specific roles. In this form of cooperative bubble netting the entire group of whales erupts through the surface at the same moment, mouths wide open and spray exploding into the air.

This may look like haphazard mayhem but it's not. By watching hundreds of such breaches, Cynthia De Vincent and Russ Nielsen have shown that it is usually the same animal (generally a female) who leads the charge, flanked by the same group of individuals that comes up on the same side of her and in the same order in relation to each other—like people playing positions on a team. Of perhaps even greater interest is the sound that precedes these breaches, a continuous whining buzz (Charles Jurasz evocatively describes it as "like a bee in a bottle") that lasts for at least thirty seconds. At the very end it inflects upward. This upward inflection is followed immediately by the whole group of whales bursting through the surface at the same moment. Although there is not yet proof that the whales use this sound to coordinate their communal breach, it is obvious that something must coordinate it so that each whale will emerge at the same moment. Because the whole cooperative maneuver is set up and achieved in the murky, nearly opaque waters of southeast Alaska, the method of coordinating has to be nonvisual. Sound seems the most obvious candidate, and this bee-in-a-bottle sound the most likely signal.

In all these instances one might wonder why the victims of these bubble techniques don't simply swim through the walls of underwater bubbles to their freedom. In 1990 we studied this question by placing schools of fish the size of a humpback's prey into an aquarium eight feet long on board the schooner *Crusader* and watching their reaction to rising columns of air such as the ones released by the feeding humpbacks.

The fish attempted to avoid the rising air bubbles. They shunned them, even when in order to do so, they were forced closer to disturbances (like us) outside the tank. Part of their apparent fright reaction was to group together tightly—very handy for a whale who wishes to herd them into the most concentrated possible clusters for convenience of engulfing.

We tested the reaction of fish to a pipe under two different conditions: motion across the tank while bubbles of air poured out of it alternating with identical sweeps of the pipe with no escaping air bubbles. We found that, not surprisingly, the fish passed more freely over the pipe when it was not emitting air.

Why do the fish have reactions that seem so ill adapted to this trick that the whales play so successfully on them? I suppose it is because throughout a fish's life, its best strategy when encountering bubbles underwater is to turn back. Presumably the kinds of circumstances under which fish are likely to come across bubbles naturally is in regions of strong turbulence like breaking surface waves or surf. These are not healthy places for small fish to spend time; their best strategy would always be to turn back rather than chance a passage through such bubbles. Thus, on the one occasion they turn away from bubbles which turn out to be generated by whales, they get caught.

Small fish have another strategy to avoid predation. They hide at the interface between air and water. It normally works well as a means of confusing their predators whether the predators dive on them from above, like a tern, or attack from below, as larger fish do. However, this technique fails with whales. When a tern is trying to see into the water, or a fish to see out of it, both are looking through a circular window subtended by an angle of about ninety degrees. As the bird approaches the surface, the window becomes smaller until at the last moment the opening is no bigger than a tiny fish. If a small fish living near the surface sees a tern diving on it, waits until the last possible second, when the tern is almost on it, and then darts sideways, it will seem to the tern to disappear past the edges of the tern's shrinking circular window. If the same prey being attacked from below by a larger fish waits until the last moment and jumps out of the water, it will also disappear for a moment beyond the periphery of the submerged predator's shrinking window. Such antics must cause a momentary confusion in the predator, since from its standpoint the little fish it was chasing will have vanished for a moment, only to reappear at some unexpected location.

I believe that the reason why wading birds have such long bills is because the closer they are to the water surface the smaller their window will be for looking for underwater prey. Having a long bill keeps their eyes a bit higher above the water so that at the moment of grabbing their prey the circular window they are watching it through will be large enough to allow them to adjust their aim right up to the last possible moment.

In order to see how this kind of strategy can serve a fish, imagine that you are chasing your cat and each time you are about to grab it, it disappears for half a second. If it could combine a sudden change of direction with a moment of being invisible, you might never be able to catch it. That's what a tiny fish accomplishes by jumping through the water's surface at the last possible moment when the tern comes from above or the predatory fish from below.

But a whale is not a fish from below; it is a creature so large that it can collect fish across an area too large for the fish to jump out of. When a humpback whale lunges forward with its mouth prized hugely open, collecting everything both above and below the surface, the normal strategy of the little fish (to dart sideways or jump through the surface) doesn't work at all. Just by being so enormous, a whale defeats these avoidance mechanisms of its prey.

The reason small fish cluster together when confronted by a predator is usually considered to be just another way to confuse it. Since the vast majority of predators pursue and catch fish one at a time, the strategy of clustering together in a dense mass, waiting until the predator charges, and then scattering in every direction seems to throw it off and cause it to miss its chance, thus giving each fish a better chance than it would have if it encountered the predator alone. I once watched from a circling plane as a tern dived repeatedly on a small shoal of fish. Before the dive the fish were clustered together into a little dark cloud. As the tern dived, they darted away in all directions so that the whole school of fish appeared to transform suddenly into a perfect ring with the tern always in the center, the dense black cloud quickly reforming each time the tern rose above the school. The whole time I watched, the tern never caught a fish. I suspect that this is also what a large fish experiences when attacking a school of tiny fish. However, I couldn't help feeling that when it was tightly formed, the school looked like a perfect whale-sized bite.

While I was observing sperm whales from a helicopter in Kaikoura, New Zealand, I noticed one day a vast disturbance at the surface that resembled a tide rip. It turned out to be a group of large fish of staggering proportions feeding on smaller fish by driving them toward the surface—a trick that both concentrated the prey and stopped its flight so it could be caught. The predatory fish formed a virtual mat of mouths, so that whenever a small fish darted away from one open mouth it found itself headed toward another. This technique resembled that of the whales in two ways: first, it echoed the way whales drive small fish against surfaces, whether a bubble cloud, an underwater cliff, or the surface of the water. Second, it was reminiscent of something called echelon feeding, in which the whales line up so that any fish trying to dart sideways and escape the jaws of one whale are caught by the whale next to it.

Clustering together is a terrible strategy if one is fleeing a predator like a whale, whose mouth opens unimaginably wide and is large enough to swallow an entire shoal. By doing so the fish are simply giving the whale a single target—the whole group—to attack and swallow.

When faced with a whale three aspects of the behavior of little fish defeat them: their normal reaction of turning away from bubbles, their tendency to hide at the interface, and their normal reaction to cluster in the face of predators. It is ever thus in life; some strategy that works well 999 times out of 1,000 is fatal on the thousandth occasion. Our species itself appears to be caught right now in just such a trap. Many of the most basic strategies that we have employed and that have worked well for millennia for our ancestors are suddenly fatally inappropriate as we confront situations that seem so similar to ones with which we have easily dealt thousands of times before but that are definitely not the same. In that sense we are like the little fish—used to encountering an ordinary predator or a few bubbles in the water caused by surf. But now the underlying conditions are different for us (like the underlying whale for the fish), and we are finding that our old strategies are entirely inappropriate—are in fact fatal—and that that error is about to swallow us up.

As an example of what I mean, throughout the ages something on which all humanity could agree was the universal goodness of motherhood. But we are now overreproducing to such an extent that every resource on earth is becoming stressed to the limit and beyond. Motherhood has gotten completely out of hand in this century. We now realize that our view of the benefits of unlimited human reproduction needs revising. This and many other of our normal, timeworn ways of responding to life are no longer appropriate and may indeed prove fatal.

Certainly unbridled human motherhood has been fatal to whales, a group that has suffered at human hands to a degree that has left some species extinct in large portions of their former range and teetering on the brink of extinction in others.

Of all the remarkable attributes of whales and their near relatives, the porpoises, I have always thought their ability to give birth to an air-breathing infant in the open sea was the most remarkable. As far as we know, no other animal except the manatees and dugongs has ever achieved this. But if we look even deeper into the miracle of development and birth, to the period when the unborn calf is in its mother's womb, the mystery deepens.

Enveloped in the flexible aqualung that is its mother, lying within her inland sea, an unborn calf must have the sensation that it can dive and hold its breath forever. As the mother descends the calf should have no sensation of pressure at all since it has no air in its body (the oxygen in its blood is replenished from that in its mother's—the calf itself is not breathing). Were the calf breathing on its own, it would have to equalize its ears and/or its sinuses from time to time as it descended. Unless calf and mother were exactly synchronized in this process, the calf would find it both awkward and painful not to be able to linger long enough to equalize its ears while they were descending together. Small wonder that the best way for a marine mammal to carry a calf is for the mother to do the breathing for both. Of course not just the lungs and respiratory tract would have air in them, the digestive tract might as well, but only if there was food in it to generate gas during digestion. Since the calf is not feeding, no food exists in the digestive tract and this problem is circumvented as well.

The reason that neither the calf's lungs nor its digestive system are working is because it receives neither of the natural substrates with which these systems deal—air and food. However, there is another system, the kidneys, which presumably could get right to work without having to wait until the calf is born since the material it is designed to process, the blood, is available before birth. As blood passes through the calf's kidneys, they would be able to clear it of metabolic poisons and pass them as urine into the amniotic fluid in which the calf is immersed. However, urine is not a viable substitute for amniotic fluid, so evolution has selected the strategy of using the mother's kidneys for clearing the calf's blood of urine. The calf's kidneys usually don't come on line and start producing urine until just after (sometimes just before) the calf is born.

Once born, if a calf had trouble clearing its sinuses (we have no idea if this is a potential problem to whales) it might find it hard to keep up with its mother as she dived. Sperm whale calves often stay at the surface while their parents dive, one or more adults from the group remaining behind to act as baby-sitters. But more than likely it is not the problem of clearing its sinuses that keeps the calf from diving deep, but the fact that it cannot hold its breath nearly as long as an adult, and the depths to which the adults must descend in order to feed are therefore inaccessible to it. It is interesting that this otherwise insoluble problem of what to do with one's calf during a long dive is resolved by living in a close-knit social group. Simply by becoming social enough to live in such groups an entire unexploited food niche in the deep ocean—benthic fish and large squid of several species—was opened up to sperm whales. John Kanwisher showed just how big this food bonanza is by calculating that the benthic squid and fish eaten each year by the world's sperm whales is about the same as the annual consumption of ocean fish by humans. That would be quite a resource to have to miss out on if you were so antisocial no one would baby-sit for you and you were unable to leave your vulnerable calf at the surface in safety while you dived deep enough to feed. For whales as for the other animals, this provides a nice example of the value of conforming to society's rules, whether those rules are cast by whales or humans.

The amniotic fluid of all mammals is remarkably similar to seawater; both fluids contain the same salts in almost exactly the same proportions. Amniotic fluid mimics the seas that nourished our ancient ancestors. Mammalian mothers reconfect it in their bodies in order to brew for their embryos the best conditions to foster life. It is this ancestral sea that is lost when a pregnant woman's waters burst shortly before the birth of her child. At birth, we humans reenact life's transition from water to land as we are born from the ancient seas of our mother's amnion to the dry land of our terrestrial existence. A school of psychology professes that much of human anguish has its genesis in the sense of loss that comes with leaving the womb. Over such a loss a whale need not mourn, for it is born out of the amnion of its mother into the amnion of the sea.

Thus generations of whales are like those pictures within pictures, forever recreating their origin from an ancient singularity of life, each nestled within the next amnion awaiting birth, all of them suspended within the earth's vaster amnion, the seas, out of which they will never be born but in which they will live out their lives. When a whale strands and expires, is its death not its first real birth out of the sea? As it lies beached and dying, does it not feel for the first time what it is to be like a human infant wailing in rage as it is stranded on dry ground out of its mother's womb? Does the anger that terrestrials show to each other and to the rest of life have its origins in the loss of our marine oneness—a regret for the mistake made by our ancestors who chose to be born out of the sea? And is that sense of oneness with life in the sea the thing to which people are keying when for the first time they swim alongside a whale, their hearts in their mouths, and discover that rather than killing them with a single swipe of its tail this huge creature greets them with a deep and ancient ocean peace?

CHAPTER 2

Living Among Whales in Patagonia

In 1970 I read a brief account in the *Antarctic Research Journal* by a friend, Ray Gilmore, who had seen several right whales along a little-traveled section of the Argentine coastline. The sighting was newsworthy because right whales are the most endangered baleen whale species on earth, and in 1969 there was nowhere near the interest in whales that there is today, so receiving a report of several together was a very rare event. Ray was traveling aboard the research vessel *Hero* and the place he saw whales was Península Valdés (about halfway between Buenos Aires and Cape Horn).

I had never heard of Península Valdés, but when I looked it up in an atlas I was struck by the fact that it was the same latitude south of the equator that Cape Cod is north. My family and I had always lived in New England, with Cape Cod virtually in our backyard. Two of my colleagues had seen right whales every year in Cape Cod Bay during the same season as Ray's Península Valdés sightings. Sometimes they saw them in numbers that were surprisingly large, given that North Atlantic right whales had been so utterly decimated before all right whales received significant protection in 1937.

I wondered whether it could be that Península Valdés was the Southern Hemisphere equivalent of Cape Cod Bay—that Ray Gilmore's sightings were not just freak luck but that right whales were still visiting Península Valdés every year. That possibility was made even more interesting by the fact that the landforms of Península Valdés, when compared to Cape Cod Bay and its associated islands, are surprisingly similar. Península Valdés is the same size as the area of Cape Cod and the islands, and encloses two nearly landlocked bays: Golfo San José on the north side and Golfo Nuevo on the south. The parallels were too inviting, and I yearned to go investigate.

At the time I was working at the New York Zoological Society, and by lucky coincidence the director, Bill Conway, knew the area well. He had visited the peninsula repeatedly, starting in the early 1960s, and knew some of the local naturalists. Most of his time had been spent studying and photographing birds, but he had never been present during the whale season, nor had anyone bothered to mention to him whether whales visited the area in winter and spring. He gave me the names of three residents to write to. Two of them replied to my letters: Antonio Torrejón (then head of the Department of Tourism of the State of Chubut), and Pablo Korchenewsky, an amateur naturalist and anthropologist who lived in the area. Both reported seeing lots of whales each year, but no one seemed to know what species they were.

Along with his letter, Korchenewsky enclosed two photographs of the whales that came each year. They were quite far away in the photographs but I could see the edge of one flipper held partly above the water.

By what now seems a rather remarkable chance we had in that same spring of 1970 come across two right whales, the only two I had ever seen, near the island of Bermuda where we were recording humpback whale songs. We had watched them for most of an hour, until it was too dark to see. I later learned just how lucky we had been; this was the first reported sighting of right whales off Bermuda in fifty years and as of this writing, no one has seen them there since. During much of the hour that we were watching, one of the Bermuda right whales raised its flipper into the air several times to stroke the other whale with it. So I got to see what right whale flippers look like, and I was struck by their distinctive shape. It was clear that the flipper of the whale visible in Korchenewsky's photograph was that of a right whale.

It was a great moment, and I began to wonder whether without knowing it my friend Ray might not have struck the mother lode of right whales. Information available in 1970 was quite different from what we have today—photographs of whales that showed their flippers were rare and hard to come by—and there were no clear underwater photographs of right whales the way there are now. Illustrations of species like the humpback, with whose appearance I was already intimately familiar, were usually so bad they looked more like blimps than whales (we used to call drawings of them "Goodyear Whales"). As a result, it was hard to be sure what was and was not an accurate drawing of a right whale, and the safest guess was that all the drawings were wrong.

But because of the right whales that had strayed into Bermuda waters that year I did know what a right whale flipper looked like, and when I realized the possible implications, the New York Zoological Society came forward with funds so I could go look. If the peculiar coincidence of my having seen right whales off Bermuda hadn't occurred, I'm not sure I would have been able to raise the funds to go looking for them that same summer. But in late September 1970 I went to Argentina to investigate, accompanied by an old friend, Oliver Brazier, and by my then-wife Katharine Payne. Katy, Ollie, and I drove from Buenos Aires on a narrow road (now a paved highway) that at times became a dirt track. Much of it went through nearly deserted land. In the north it linked cities like Bahía Blanca and Mar del Plata with Buenos Aires, but as we proceeded south, the population thinned out, and distances between small towns increased.

On the third day we passed the Río Negro, the northern boundary of Patagonia. South of this river, the land was very flat and arid, and the sea, though never more than a few miles from our road, was usually hidden behind high coastal dunes. Now the road narrowed and became rough for hundreds of miles, and between the small towns the distances were so great we sometimes traveled for hours without seeing a house.

To clear up any confusion: "Patagonia" is the name for a region whose borders differ depending on who is describing it. It has no definitely agreed limits nor even an agreed name—being called by many "the Patagonia" (something which has always seemed a bit affected to me). Basically, however, it comprises the southern cone of South America, which is to say all of South America south of the Río Negro (both Chile and Argentina). It therefore lies between the latitudes of about thirty-eight and fifty-seven degrees south—the "Roaring Forties" and "Frantic Fifties."

The South American continent is relatively narrow throughout Patagonia. For example, even though Península Valdés is on the east coast and at nearly the widest point of Patagonia, its climate is largely maritime, because it is so strongly influenced by the prevailing westerlies that come from the Pacific across a relatively narrow strip of continent. When these winds first hit Chile, they have been traveling for thousands of miles across the broad Pacific. By comparison, the overland passage that they next make, across Patagonia to the South Atlantic, is only 450 miles. This is also why Península Valdés winters are so much milder than Cape Cod winters, even though both regions lie at the same latitude. For instance, Cape Cod snowfalls can be fifty times deeper (and the temperatures forty degrees Fahrenheit colder) than they ever get in Península Valdés. To the west of Cape Cod lie not 450 miles of land before one reaches the Pacific, but 2,800 miles. In winter this is 2,800 miles of cold ground, since soil or rock loses its heat to the black night sky far more readily than does the ocean. By the time the air crossing North America has reached the Atlantic Ocean, the continental land mass has drained much more of the heat out of it.

The fact that the winds over Patagonia prevail from the west also means that the moisture in them gets stripped off by the Andes as they pass above that mountain chain. It is for this reason that Península Valdés is a semidesert even though it is on the coast. It feels the effects of the Andes even though they are invisible and three hundred miles away. The same is true of the water, for even though most people who live on the peninsula have to truck their drinking water from a town one hundred miles away, it originates in the Andes and arrives via the Chubut River—Valdés Penínsulianos drink last year's Andean snow and the last millennium's glacial meltwater.

On our fourth day out of Buenos Aires, we arrived at Puerto Madryn on the shores of Golfo Nuevo, the southernmost bay of Península Valdés. At the time it was a quiet little village by the sea, one of the more charming towns I'd ever seen. (It has since become one of the two biggest industrial and manufacturing centers in Patagonia and as of this writing is the fastest-growing city in Argentina.)

Three days later we stood overlooking the open sea at Punta Norte—the northeast point of the peninsula. Three right whales were playing in the surf not fifty feet off the beach. I was simply stunned. I dashed back to the car and in my haste to get at my recording gear threw all the suitcases on the ground. I then rushed back to the shore and hurled the hydrophones into the sea. All I wanted was to hear the whales and to find out if they were singing. My Argentine hosts, all of whom were intimately familiar with this same place as they had worked at it as game wardens at some time or other, were surprised at my haste since, as they explained, "The whales are always here." They claimed they would be there tomorrow too, and the next day—in fact all the time I was planning to stay. I remember thinking, "Sure, sure, maybe that's what you think, but I'm damned if I'm going to rely on the thin hope that these whales will stay around when I've just come six thousand miles and have a chance to make the first recordings of a southern right whale."

But three hours later, when I was frozen stiff and had my first recordings, the whales had still not moved more than a hundred yards. And as the days rolled by and I noticed that each morning it never took us more than ten minutes to locate the whales along the shore, and that we never saw them farther than a half mile off the beach (and usually within fifty or one hundred feet of it), I was slowly forced to admit that although they may not have known what species they were looking at, the local game wardens certainly knew a lot more about the habits of these whales than I did. It was an important lesson that I've never forgotten: any observant local knows more than any visiting scientist. Always. No exceptions.

In the days that followed we had a chance to get to know the peninsula. It was clear that it was just as Bill Conway had described it: "one of the greatest comings-together of land, sea, and wildlife on earth." Península Valdés has colonies of sea lions in several places, some of them containing over five hundred animals. Magellanic penguins are scattered along the beach, and there is another enormous penguin rookery at Punta Tombo a few miles to the south. Albatrosses, petrels, shearwaters, fulmars, terns, and gulls ride the winds of the Roaring Forties. Along the edge of the tidal wrack hundreds of elephant seal harems stretch in a line down the whole length of a forty-mile beach until they dissolve into the heat shimmer.

For the most part the females in these harems lie asleep in every imaginable posture of indolence, scattered about on the strand like cushions, each with a throw pillow—a small black pup—alongside. If you approach too closely, you will discover that she has been observing you through partly closed eyes. She now opens her eyes wide, lifts her head, and produces a series of long, shockingly rude belches designed to make you go away. The harem master bulls are much larger and far more aggressive. They make the same noise the females make only louder, lower, and ruder—gargantuan eructations designed to intimidate any intruder; an after-dinner noise of such exquisite vulgarity that even the most hardened eleven-year-old boy could not fail to be stunned with delight by the endless possibilities offered by such extravagantly crude sounds.

Mature bull elephant seals ride the tidal currents that scour along the beach face. These marauders stop every half mile or so to challenge the resident bulls and wake them up. The resident bulls then make their way down to the water's edge (progressing like someone humping along in a sleeping bag) while emitting loud belches to drive the intruder away.

The tidal currents, which can reach six knots, are generated by a tide whose amplitude is said to be second only to that of the Bay of Fundy. It rises and falls as much as thirty-three feet. The currents generated by such a vast quantity of water entering and leaving the narrow mouths of Golfos San José and Nuevo are the most violent ocean currents I have ever seen, and when storm winds are blowing opposite to their direction of flow, the resulting waves are appalling.

That first year in Argentina we were guests of the Chubut Tourism Office and were treated with great courtesy. Juan Olazabal ("Juancito") was put at our disposal. He chauffeured us around and carried out with quiet confidence and good cheer every job that none of the rest of us showed any inclination to perform. He had once worked as a letter carrier on the peninsula and knew it intimately. One morning while driving Katy into town from

Punta Norte to buy groceries, he mentioned that on his rounds he had often stopped at a small bay to eat his lunch and watch the whales, which were usually gathered there just offshore. The track to the bay was very rough but would she like to see it?

And thus it was that Katy returned in the early afternoon full of enthusiasm about the lovely place she had seen. Later that evening we stood on the beach at "Lote 39" (many properties are known only by their real estate lot numbers) overlooking a perfectly placid scene. A dozen whales were scattered about like drifting logs in the near, middle, and far distance. The beach itself was about two thirds of a mile long and flanked by tall cliffs that bordered the sea and stretched away along the coast to the north and west. I climbed the western cliffs and walked out to a nearby headland so I could look around the corner to see if there were more whales beyond. It was a much longer walk than I had expected, but by the time I finally reached the headland the wind had long since died and the sun was setting in a spectacular display of dark reds that reflected in the calm water and painted the whole bay a kind of pink-purple. As I sat quaffing great drafts of this view a whale started breaching far out in the bay, followed in the next few minutes by two others closer to shore. I stood transfixed. Slowly it dawned on me that I had never before borne witness to such a tranquil and beautiful scene. This place seemed to have the power to heal the soul, and perhaps to transform one's life.

It was September 18, 1970. I was thirty-five at the time, married and the father of four children, ages five to nine. For the first time I could see my life spread before me. Though I was breathless with excitement, my thoughts were steady and focused. I felt as if fate were giving me instructions. I realized that we had discovered Eden. Here was a place where the whales came so close to shore we could work from land and thereby learn about their lives without disturbing them and without the crippling expense of large boats. It was as far from cities as one could get and thus a place to which I could bring my young family without worry, knowing that here, in the wilderness, they would be perfectly safe.

By the time I got back to the car it was nearly dark. I asked Juancito if he knew the owner of this beach—these cliffs. He replied, "Antonio Torrejón." It seemed to be another of those extraordinary coincidences, for it was Antonio to whom I had first written; and Antonio who, because he was running the Tourism Department at that time, was our overall host—the Antonio for whom Juancito worked.

We returned to the United States and by the following fall the New York Zoological Society had given me the funds to go back to Lote 39. We would establish a camp there from which to study the whales for three and a half months. We later built a research station on this site, but it is probably because we camped in our first full season that the research station has always been known as "Whale Camp."

In the interim we had also figured out that the head of each right whale was distinct in appearance, owing to the fact that each was adorned with a different pattern of the raised, thickened patches of skin called "callosities." We had flown that first year in a small plane over the whales and photographed one whale well enough to see its callosity pattern clearly. I guessed that by photographing the heads of all the whales from the air we could create a "head catalog" of known callosity patterns and thereby keep track of individual whales over long periods. In 1971 we demonstrated that this was indeed feasible but more time had to pass before we were finally sure that the patterns were constant enough to be used in identifying right whales throughout their lives.

I felt that in 1971 we had spent too much of our time and energy camping and so wanted to build a permanent field station at Lote 39. In the following year, 1972, the New York Zoological Society provided half the funds for the first building—a house and lab (Katy and I raised the other half by renting our house in Massachusetts). The field station was finished in time for our arrival. As it turned out, its final position was selected by a whale. It happened this way: in 1969 a dead right whale washed ashore along the beach just below the spot where the field station now stands. Someone in Puerto Madryn had the idea of selling its oil and came out from town to cut up the carcass and "try it out." How much oil was tried out is not recorded, nor many details about what happened. But this I do know; a truck was driven all the way down to the back of the beach where the whale lay, thus creating a very crude track to the site where the field station now stands—a track which is now the driveway.

On the first day of our visit in 1971 it was this track down which I walked, backward, waving hand directions to the driver of a truck loaded with all our gear (we had shipped it to Buenos Aires by boat). When I reached the end of the trail, the driver threw everything off the truck until the ground was littered with crates and bags. It is in this same spot that the field station now stands. Thus, in a very real sense, the site of Whale Camp was chosen by a whale, in league with the winds and the currents that deposited it there. I was too green at that time and probably would not have had the chutzpa to ask for a road to be built—I had no idea how easy it is to build roads in Patagonia. No, we had to reach this place for taking large steps by taking a series of small ones. We had to evolve our way here (just as the ancestors of whales had to evolve their way back to the seas) even down to such seemingly unimportant details as having a ready-made track we could recognize leading to a paradise we could afford.

In the same year that we built the camp (1972) the New York Zoological Society and the National Geographic Society together provided enough money for a study of two more years. In late August of 1972—late winter in Argentina—I returned with my family for a twenty-two-month study. These were the most formative years of my children's lives and our happiest as a family. It was the longest I ever lived continuously in the wild and therefore the longest truce I ever made with my soul. As a result, Argentina is my heart's home—a place which by day fills my mind so full of images that they spill over into my dreams at night. The New York Zoological Society has operated the station continuously since then, and I have returned to Lote 39 in many Southern Hemisphere springs, often with my family, in order to study the right whales. As a result we now know over twelve hundred individual right whales, and ours is the longest continuous study of any whale species based on known individuals recognizable in the wild.

The land east of the Andes, south of the Río Negro, and north of Isla Grande is flat—very flat and very dry. Unless they have been planted or maintained by humans, there are no trees. The ground is lightly mantled by thin, steely bushes. It is almost constantly swept by a strong, arid wind, which has shaped the landscape and all life on it. It seems to be more the wind than people and animals that lives here. Patagonia is the home of the wind.

It was to this desolate, beautiful land called Patagonia that I brought my first family. And because my former wife and I lived in that enchanted place with our own children I have felt that an interesting bond between humans and whales grew up there as well—a bond which if it didn't affect the whales, did, at least, affect my family and me.

I feel a strong sense of kinship to the whales, for they raise their young there too. And since our two species live for roughly comparable periods, I feel a personal connection to the calves that were there when my own children were young. The calves have matured and are now having calves of their own—not unlike my own children who are now marrying and starting families.

And when the parents of those calves swim back into the bay for yet another spring, I greet them in a way that only we who had our children through the seventies understand. And thus, though I mourn the scattering of my own family, which is now spread about the world, I feel in Argentina that I am living in a larger, extended family that includes people of the sea as well as of the land.

Many authors have written about Patagonia. However, I feel they have all gotten it wrong. Patagonia is usually depicted as a mercilessly dry, harsh land—an ogre of inconvenience, dust, and discomfort. But that is not true; Patagonia is an incredibly subtle and shy beauty who hides behind her veil, offering only occasional glimpses of her sparkling blue eyes. Above the land stretches a magnificent blue sky whose sun burns down from the hot north, fading everything to a uniform dust color, twisting and curling boards like crisping bacon, and giving plastic the look of chalk. The sky is usually clear by day and brimming with stars by night. There is the upside-down moon and the Southern Cross and the Magellanic Clouds (our two nearest galaxies) and Scorpio riding high above the bay.

The beaches are deeply heaped dunes of tiny pebbles, mostly brown but also containing a few of every possible color. The area is alive with wildlife— not just right whales and seabirds, but Mora eagles, kestrels, falcons, sea lions, and elephant seals. The soil is strewn with fragments of fossil shells and scattered with almost invisibly shy spring flowers with odors so pungent they stop you in your tracks to search among the thorny bushes and armadillo burrows for the source. The sea has its own clear, clean, cintered smell— pristine and slightly acid. The mud on the roads when it rains is unpassable for a day or two—sucking and deliciously oozly-goozly.

The Tehuelches, a now-extinct tribe of indigenous peoples, once lived in Patagonia until we "civilized" Europeans dispossessed them from the area, put sheep on it, and returned to our cities, leaving the land largely empty of anyone to enjoy it. The Tehuelches were thought by the early settlers to be deprived savages. Deprived? I would say they were luckier than I. I was deprived. I was raised in a city—in the alien world of New York City. I suffocated in the confinement of its apartments, its canyon streets, its airless and lightless rooms. It was the sky that saved me throughout my youth in New York. I walked to school each morning looking up—looking for birds, but really, I suppose, avoiding looking at buildings (the way strangers in an elevator avoid eye contact by staring at the ceiling). Each day I saw hawks above the city. It was only years later, when I was a savvier bird-watcher, that I realized my childhood hawks had been gulls. But those mythical hawks still turn and wheel in my imagination—as real as the true hawks I have seen since. It is mythic hawks that pulled me through my life in New York.

One reason I appreciate Argentines is because they, more than any other people I have known, love open spaces, open horizons. It is built into Argentines to yearn for sky. The pampas are in their blood, and they too are forever looking up. The ethos of gauchos seems roofed with a broad and overarching firmament, and when they search the vault of the sky it seems to be with a lover's eyes.

In Lote 39 it was the winds that filled our days. The following is an entry from my diary:

> During the night a great wind has risen but at too slow a rate to enter our consciousness and wake me earlier. But now I am propped up in bed listening as the whole house is roaring, creaking, slatting, trembling and rumbling, and while flying sand, like sleet, gusts in waves across the tin roof. The tide is full and the sledgehammer sea pounds directly against the beach face along the kilometer-long anvil of Camp Bay. Along this entire extent there is at every moment some place receiving the full power of the blows so the sound seems to be continuous. It conducts back through the ground and through the house, making a deep note, so low as to be more felt than heard—like the bass pedal on a church organ. It is a note that runs through every-thing, every sound, every thought, every severed thread of sleep as the forbearing house stands resignedly in the darkness receiving its batter-ing from the wind.
>
> I awoke only slowly and became conscious only gradually of the full presence of this storm. Now that I'm listening more attentively to it I find that the roar of the wind is not a constant thing but a series of long rhythms which come and go slowly. And there are moments when a door which has long stood quiet in its frame suddenly becomes agi-tated and starts striking between latch and frame for 10 or 20 curiously spaced blows and then returns, trembling, to silence.
>
> Like a cat the wind is rubbing against the house, pressing against its corners—causing the rafters to creak and the steel-framed windows to bow and bend. Out in the darkness a piece of loose wire, perhaps one of the gutter hangers, scrapes against the tin of the roof when the hard-est gusts strike it, adding its scritch to the clatter of the rest of the per-cussion section.
>
> It is a wonderful thing to wake in a strong house surrounded by such a sense of siege. It is like awakening in the New England winter to find a storm has come in the night and brought snow, or like awaken-ing aboard a great ship which, though it dwarfed us yesterday as we boarded her in harbor, we now find fully at sea—a tiny speck in an infinite tumult, rolling and heaving and shuddering along through ris-

ing swells. Our house is a ship underway in a storm at sea with whales snuffling about our portals.

Or this from another day:

> We are in the third day of a temporal—a strong wind from the west that comes on after a front passes through and then blows without let for up to a week, sometimes even more. At the start of this one we had a flood which almost washed out the house, yet within less than an hour dust was blowing in some places. Even though it had just rained as hard as I have ever seen it rain, the wind which followed had dried out the surface of the ground that quickly. One can normally tell at a glance whether the tide is rising or falling by looking at whether the beach is wet (tide falling) or dry (tide rising). But in the winds of a temporal even on a falling tide the beach is dry. Today the whole beach is bone-dry.

We had a wind generator mounted on the roof to charge batteries (the camp's source of power). On most mornings I would awaken to hear the whole house humming with its familiar and welcome sound. As I listened to the major gusts strike the building, I knew that everyone was lying in their beds listening too—snuggling down deeper beneath their blankets. No boats would be launched today. The gusts were often accompanied by not just the sound of the generator surging to a frantic whine but by the sounds of pebbles and bits of shell rattling along the tin roof—carried there by a wind strong enough to loft them all the way from the beach fifty yards to the west. When the wind was more from the northeast, many of the bits of shell that hit the roof were coming from inland. These shells were fossils, tens of millions of years old—remnants of the once-fauna of this once-seabed, now uplifted and become a coastal desert. When you are a biologist, it is a special kind of thrill to be wakened by the sound of fossils hitting your roof.

The wind dissects fossilized shells from out of the now-dry and transformed sediments of this ancient ocean bed. In the cliff faces, one sees that each distinct layer of highly concentrated shells is separated from other such layers by relatively shell-less earth a few feet thick—the layering being plainly visible as broad horizontal bands in a three-hundred-foot cliff face. In some areas where the soil in the cliffs has been blasted by the wind for many years, the heavier fossils have been left behind, leaving entire screes of giant oyster shells of a species long extinct. So large are these oysters that had humans coexisted with them a single oyster could have fed a family.

On windy days our main place of study was the "cliff hut." It is two-thirds of a mile from camp, and on the nearest headland—one which overlooks the bay and gives protection from the wind. On windy days I sometimes arose before the others, breakfasted quietly alone in the kitchen, and started for the cliff hut, with a pack on my back. When we had been away for a while and no one had used the path to the cliff hut its surface would be pristine and untrodden—the powdered soil skimmed over by an eighth-inch crust of hardened mud, which was normally crushed by our footsteps, exposing the loose sand beneath to the scouring wind. The few times I have walked this path after lapses of weeks or months I have always been moved by its exquisite tracklessness.

Untrodden paths, like silent places, are rare things and are, to my mind, strong releasers of a sense of peace and well-being. I suspect they touch a very ancient chord in humans, for it must always have been a deep relief to our cave-dwelling ancestors not to see or hear any evidence that neighboring bands were encroaching on their territory—the news getting better and better the farther they hunted from the home cave without encountering tracks. I believe strongly that untrodden paths and silence have a far greater restorative effect on the human mind than we have yet acknowledged—that they are the source of a most ancient inner peace. (Could silence and tracklessness be the kind of peace which people imagine to exist in heaven?)

For the first steep pitch of cliffs I would be climbing in a lee, only ruffled by occasional stray fingers of turbulence touching down here and there, like fronds, in the gullies of the cliff. But as I reached the last and steepest bit and came up onto the steppe above, I would be hit and knocked staggering partway back by the pure joyous blast of it—my first true taste of the storm. In the cliff-protected glen in which the house is nestled there is some shielding from west winds (always the strongest), but on the tableland above one is in the pure slipstream of it all—winds that were typically sweeping half a continent—an inexorable force bundling everything before it.

There is to me no other such thrill as a windstorm. It sets all the country alive and springing, creating a whole new appearance to the land. The familiar cliffs fringing the bay generate giant wind palisades—pure, tactile columns—curtains of fluid air sweeping upward for thousands of feet—a curtain of wind which, if we could see it, might be shaped like the aurora australis. The modest arroyos and badlands behind camp induce massive erosive turbulences that sometimes thunder and snap audibly as they enfold the land in maelstroms of air wheeling wildly out of control.

The level plains are clear sheets of flat, moving air as featureless to most people as the plains they scour. But like that lovely, subtle desert that offers only clues to its underlying intricacy, the plains' windscapes also have little hidden areas, tiny whorls, minute regions of calm where even in the most roaring tempest one can take refuge and, while basking in the sun, listen to the storm.

In such protectories, dried flower husks lie in little wind-collected clusters like hailstones after a violent storm. These little piles eddy in the alleyways between bushes or lie trembling in dense little flocks like sheep in a fold, making little indecisive false starts, first in one direction, then in another, as the fingertips of the wind bat them about—like a cat playing with a mouse. In order to see their behavior you must watch from a distance, for to walk up to them is to scatter them everywhere as the turbulence that flows about your feet upsets the delicate balances in the micro windscape contours that are holding them in their invisible corral.

This same effect frustrated my attempt to observe ants at close range during the Patagonian winds, because when I bent over to look more closely at them, they vanished. They had been successfully picking their way carefully among the wind features in their vicinity until the larger eddies spilling from my body disrupted their local windscape, blowing them away. I found I couldn't even pick up an ant because the eddies shed by my approaching fingers broke through the thin boundary layer in which they lived, letting in the main slipstream of the storm so that it instantly broadcast them all over the surrounding country.

Unlike the lush forests I am used to, which noisily lash and sweep about in the wind, the windswept steppe of Patagonia seems strangely quiet during windstorms. I could hear the wind buffeting about my ears but no whoosh of vegetation. The bushes are stiff and bear scalelike leaves that don't make the rushing, sighing, soughing, whispering sounds of the trees in my familiar New England. Instead they have a high, steely hiss, very faint, even in a strong wind. When they are lashed by the wind, they do not weave and bow, sweeping their trailing branches like long hair from side to side. Rather, they vibrate and tremble—tight, hard, thorny, and inflexible.

The sound of the bushes maps the terrain so that during a strong blow you can hear their placement as you walk past. By listening carefully, one might, I suppose, walk blindfolded in a wind through Patagonia by threading one's way among the faintly hissing shrubbery. Standing in a hollow out of the wind even in a strong blow one hears silence but for the scattered bushes fringing it, announcing their positions in synchrony with the gusts.

It is not just dried flower husks and ants that are affected by the wind. Windstorms sweep the land and humble everything before them. I once saw a lizard I had frightened from a clear patch in which it had been sunning itself trying to make the cover of the bush next to me. Clearly panicked, it ran with its legs and lashed with its whole body, but each time it was about to reach safety it collided with an invisible wall of wind bending around the base of the bush and was blown backward a foot or two. At first the lizard landed running—heading right back in the direction of the bush—but after the third or fourth failure it halted to cock its head and to eye me before resuming its struggle. I noted that its pauses became longer—apparently it was growing habituated to this total frustration or maybe it had decided I was not threat enough to warrant such an all-out effort. As I left the lizard tilting at the wind it occurred to me that this strange country lives under the despotic rule of a wind so strong it can blow a lizard off its feet.

Fringing the cliffs are large sand dunes composed of material lifted from the cliff faces by violent updrafts during fierce onshore blows and deposited just behind the cliff verges. Millions of years ago the wind brought the whole peninsula from afar, dropping it as sediments in a shallow sea whose bed was later uplifted to form the present land. The same wind will give the land its new shape, carving its cliffs, polishing its stones, stunting its plants, smothering them with soil, burying them alive, unburying them, desiccating them, and tumbling their carcasses about until, stark naked, they fetch up against some fence. The wind plays with life, messes about with it in careless and destructive ways. What chance does a lizard have here? How can it hide from a hawk if the wind won't even let it reach safety?

The existence of the updrafts along the edge of the cliffs provides a continuous line of lift—a "wind road" used by kestrels and other hawks to hunt for lizards. The kestrels nest in the cliffs and search for lizards by hanging motionless in the updrafts while glancing about for their prey. When they catch a lizard, they even eat it on the wind, holding station in an updraft while wrenching off bits, and between bites tucking the partly eaten corpse within their belly feathers where it nestles so sweetly as to be entirely streamlined, offering when outside the kestrel's body no more wind resistance than it will when inside (or than it will when, still later, it becomes incorporated into the substance of the kestrel).

Mora eagles are broad-winged, soaring birds with a five-foot wingspan and characteristics that are both hawklike and eaglelike. They use the wind road as a means of patrolling miles of coast in search of snakes and other small animals among the dunes. They hunt in pairs and when a Mora eagle passes too close to the much smaller but cheekier kestrels, the kestrels attack and chase it off. My son John noticed that they only do this if the Mora eagles are using the wind road. Kestrels leave Mora eagles alone if they pass outside the line of updrafts—even if in doing so their flight path carries them closer to the kestrels' nests. What John discovered was fascinating: the kestrels fight for the wind—they own the wind.

The very cliffs themselves are changed daily by the winds and after each storm show striae that are gouged out like deep glacial scratches, vaned in the direction from which the wind last blew. The raised ridges of these striae are remnants of substrate protected at one end by being in the lee of some small but harder objects that protrude above the surface. Thus there is even a wind-created topography to the land, much as the constantly changing topography of the ocean's surface (the waves) is fashioned by the wind. On land the topography changes more slowly, but the changes are no less profound. The faces of the soft cliffs are eroded and sculpted by the wind, which brings out the underlying strata by cutting deeply into the softest layers and leaving the edges of the harder ones behind. This gives the cliff face a stratified appearance except in places where some portion of the cliff has collapsed and exposed a fresh face too recently for the wind to have yet performed its dissections.

Not just in cliffs and sand dunes, but in the live plants themselves one sees the effects of the wind. The bushes along the edges of the cliffs are suffocated—packed in dirt—not just the roots but the whole plant. The winds that eddy about the crests of the cliffs are laden with dirt, and the branches and leaves of the bushes that abound in the area are, unfortunately for them, so effective in capturing it that the entire structure of the plants—stems, branches, and twigs—gets buried almost completely, embedded in earth, with only the leaves on the outermost tips of the outermost twigs exposed. Fighting for its life, the plant hurriedly sends out more twigs through the dirt, which produce more tiny leaves, until the entire mound of earth appears to be covered with moss—only in this case the "moss" is a minutely ivied carpet of stunted leaves projecting from the dirt, making the plant into a soccer-ball-sized mound of earth covered over with a layer of tiny leaves. In spite of the incredible odds, the plant has not given up. It is still fighting—each leaf bears a spine at its tip.

Such spines are a defense against browsing animals. Because the entire area has been browsed by guanacos and sheep for so long the only kind of plants that survive are those with defenses against them. Thorns of every size, shape, and description protrude from every possible plant surface—there are even plants made of nothing but thorns—no leaves, no stems, just interconnected green thorns.

Virtually every bush hurts. The plants seem to take two basic approaches. One is to grow thorns so tough that they tear the sturdiest clothes without suffering any damage to themselves. The strongest of these will puncture car tires. I discovered this when I suffered two flat tires at once when I pulled off the road to make way for other vehicles (each tire had ten punctures in it).

The second strategy that thorns have is to produce tiny, fragile tips which break off in the skin when brushed against, causing lasting irritation and/or mild infection. In Península Valdés we got used to living with thorns in our knees, ankles, and shins, and were reminded of them every time a trousers leg brushed against their protruding bases. One never seems to have fewer than ten to fifteen such thorns in one's knees, hands, and feet, but it seems a small price to pay for living in such a beautiful place.

It is not just the bushes that hurt; many of the grasses do too. I have several times placed my open palm on some lush-looking tuft of pastel-green grass prior to sitting down comfortably on a tuft next to it only to discover that it was as sharp as a pincushion. There is even one species of grass (called "flecha," or arrow grass) which has a particularly cruel mechanism for dispersing its seeds. Each seed is tipped with an exquisitely sharp and multiply barbed point. When the seed gets picked up in a sheep's wool, every motion by the sheep causes adjacent wool fibers to slide back and forth a tiny bit along each other's length. This motion against the barbs on the arrow grass seeds moves the barbs deeper into the pile of the fleece. When a sharp-tipped seed reaches the sheep's skin, it penetrates both skin and underlying body wall musculature. Once inside the sheep's body cavity, it penetrates the sheep's internal organs, eventually killing it—the sheep's decomposing body suffocating competing vegetation beneath it and also providing, I suppose, an excellent bed of fertilizer for the next generation of arrow grass.

In many places the tops of the cliffs are dissected by the wind into fantastic cuts and scoops, reminiscent of the ways in which icebergs melt and decay. This carving by the wind is on a grand scale and means that the wind flow patterns among the dunes change over time so that once-protected areas move into the direct line of the blast when a dune that was sheltering them gets carved away.

The dunes of the cliff edge are thus a never-never land, a kind of plant limbo filled with slowly dying vegetation of such obstinacy that it is clear to everyone but the plants themselves they have lost the struggle for life. But failing to comprehend that, they persist, fighting on against hopeless odds. In many the roots have been exposed by the wind and are so dry it seems impossible they could be in contact with any moisture. Yet somehow the plant keeps going. Some hover near death's door for decades, refusing to cross the last threshold.

The healthiest-looking bushes in this worst of all wind zones are about 80 percent dead. Most of them are no more than dry twigs, once buried but now exposed, having been dissected out after their long burial by some capricious change in the wind currents blowing through their immediate vicinity—the result, perhaps, of the destruction of some hillock or grass-covered sand dune that had protected them for the past twenty years. Sometimes these bushes hold delicate fossil shells or bits of fossil whalebones in their upper branches—fossils which blew there. The first time I found one of these bushes decorated like a Christmas tree with fossil shells I thought that one of the lone gauchos I had seen passing far in the distance each week, patrolling the sheep fences, might be celebrating some private rite of Christmas here by the cliffs.

Only when the rain comes and washes the land and makes the leaves and pebbles shine and the bark of the bushes darker can you see the land become, for just a few hours, clear of the dust that otherwise coats it. But even after the rain has passed and the land has dried, the stain of the dust remains.

The sand in very wind eroded areas is surfaced with a layer of bits of fossil shells, twigs, and pebbles whose edges all touch—an imaginative and intricate natural paving which when chanced upon after a rain appears to be some newly washed terrazzo floor laid whimsically across the sand dunes. This minute paving is also the wind's work. The sand dunes are richly embedded with small stones and twigs and bits of fossil shell. As the wind blows endlessly on, it finds these natural tesserae and scours the dirt from around each one. They do not blow away but descend slowly as the entire surface of the dune sinks. In places where the wind has been carving for years, it has slowly lowered all the pebbles and twigs and bits of shell from their many levels within the dune, with the result that they now lie on the present, subsided surface of the ground in a continuous cover, somewhat protecting the underlying sand from further erosion by the wind, minute mosaics wind-laid into an undulating floor that covers the dunes.

When the wind is up, the dirt plumes off the cliff face and arcs high overhead, sifting down from above to fill my eyes and pack my hair so utterly that after only a few minutes it is standing on end, stiff and bristly. For me, part of the feeling of living in Patagonia is having dirt in my eyes, and my hair standing on end, and my hands polished with dust. Other than the wind, I think it is the patina of dust more than any other thing that I associate with Patagonia. It covers hands, faces, clothes, cars, tires, windows, houses, roads, bushes, leaves, grass—everything that exists or lives here. It is the great leveler, the great equalizer, making everything Patagonian. Nothing escapes its touch; it settles upon everything even when the wind is still. If you leave a clean black cloth on the ground during a perfect calm, when you return a minute later it will be covered with the finest scattering of minute beige dust particles, while anything that has lain on a shelf for several weeks or months, no matter how well you may think it was protected from draft, will be covered with a beige patina that puffs into a cloud of dust when you pick it up to shake it. Like many other such minor annoyances in life, you eventually get used to it and then you grow to like it, to expect it as a part of life—and, yes, to miss it when you are far away and it is no longer there.

I've seen water buffalo in Sri Lanka rising from the rice paddies, covered but for their eyes with a thin slick of mud. So much do they appear like the land it is as if they *were* the land. If patches of mud in the paddies formed themselves into buffalo before your eyes and went ambling off chewing the sweet grass of their cuds, their minds lost in other worlds, they would look no different. There is a similar sense about the egalitarian dust of Patagonia, which blesses everything equally, coating it finely, rendering it the same color and patina. This stark land marks everything as its own ("We were the land's before the land was ours") and everything that walks or creeps or hops on the soil of Patagonia is as if formed of the substance of the land. It is this dust that informs me that I am back in this place I love so much.

Much guff has been written about the winds of Patagonia, stressing the misery and inconvenience they bring. But this is true only if one expects it to be true. The winds can seem awkward when you are getting to know them, but awkward moments follow any introduction. Once we grew familiar with the winds we began to look forward to their visits because they were so wonderfully exhilarating. The windscapes and wind topographies that the Patagonian winds brought to our lives were worth more than the things they prevented us from doing, many of which were simply activities we longed for because we had grown used to expecting them in the different climates in which we were raised.

Sure, the winds can be unpleasant, but I prefer to recall the moments when I have sat in the lee of a bush, dirt sifting down on me like snow through hemlocks (so badly that one has to write in pencil because dirt clogs a ballpoint pen), watching the whales beneath me roll and wallow in the most relaxed way, while all the winds from all the quadrants conspire to whip the sea into a frenzy—a chaos of which the whales seem to take not the least notice. I have seen at such times the Mora eagles go rocketing by on half-furled wings traveling like arrows in flight. On calm days they progress slowly, flapping often, wobbling badly and appearing to expand all their feathers to the fullest so as to catch the smallest, most fragile bubble of rising air—anything to keep aloft. But on windy days energy is abundant and they are like gray projectiles.

These are the vistas one sees when approaching the cliff hut. Having arrived there I would wedge my way in through the door, using all my force to hold it against the wind (and feeling fearful lest I break off the handle). We lived with this same danger in camp, where the porch door was threatened by the same forces. It opened outward and we had to lock it in storms to keep from losing it by having it ripped from the opener's hands (or the opener catapulted across the porch). It seemed about the same as trying to open the door of an airplane in flight.

Once inside the cliff hut I would find that no matter how recently I had swept the hut, dirt covered everything. Even my binoculars would immediately be sprinkled with dust, though I put them on the desk only long enough to remove my pack and set out the telescopes, tripods, theodolites and notebooks I would use for the rest of the day. The windows, just washed yesterday, would already have a haze of specks and streaks on them. (On close inspection one could see that the glass was deeply pitted—sand-and-pebble-blasted by past storms.) As I looked out over the heaving, quaking sea below, marvelously scoured and foamed with cresting waves and spray, I could see several tiny reefs outlined by slow bursting seas—but I knew from the past that there were no such reefs in the bay. These were not reefs but whales. Some would have their flukes aloft for a moment, a flipper raised here, a head there, with spouts springing all around. They appeared as content in their soft bed as I in my aerie. It seemed that the storm that was so exasperating the sea was merely serving to keep them awake and bustling about the day's activities.

The idea was to choose one whale and to watch it for as long as possible, hopefully also photographing its head when it came close enough so as to identify it. On some days I spent up to sixteen hours gazing at a single group while talking my notes on their behavior into a tape recorder. Sometimes I have eaten my lunch while gazing through a telescope, unable to afford to take my eyes off some group for fear I might lose track of who was who.

When you are watching a group of right whales, 90 percent of the job is figuring out who is doing what to whom. This requires that you know who's underwater at any given time. To take your eyes away for even a moment could terminate a description on which you had already invested many hours' work. Sometimes it was exhausting, but that was the way we learned about the whales' lives, and though I had headaches at the ends of some days, I also experienced the joy of whatever small thing we had learned. But our lives were not all watching whales. When one is in the presence of a grand and sovereign wind, it is fitting that the ultimate sailors should be there to ride it, and by any account this planet's ultimate sailors are albatrosses—sailors not just in two dimensions but in three. Albatrosses use an exquisitely clever process to capture energy from the wind called dynamic soaring. It depends on the difference in speed at which wind blows close to the surface of the sea and ten or more feet up. It's a trick we humans can never hope to perform, for even the smallest of our flying machines are too large to make the kinds of tight turns necessary to exploit this kind of wind energy. But no matter: that doesn't prevent you from experiencing the delight of taking a comfortable seat and watching as albatrosses perform their continuous miracle. There is no better place to do this than Patagonia, for although the antipodes is usually thought of as being the hemisphere of penguins, of the Southern Cross, or the Magellanic Clouds, it is most of all the hemisphere of albatrosses.

I would not like to live for many years without seeing albatrosses. If you have never seen one, there is no use in trying to explain why they are so magnificent; they simply are. One must see them in their element, as they glide on motionless wings, sometimes without flapping for half an hour, moving across a hazy, wind-streaked, white-capped ocean—weaving, soaring, wheeling effortlessly by the hour, the day, or for all one knows, the week—in any case as long as there is wind. Their sustained flight requires a strong wind—they are creatures of the wind more than any other animal on earth. They use it, ride it, live in it, knit their way across it with complex but graceful stitches—weaving the woof and warp of their lives through it. The air they breathe while performing their miracles of flight is of the utmost delicate moistness, sprinkled with ocean spray—great rivers of air sinuously flowing, cool, fresh, and clear, over endless miles of open sea.

A curious thing has emerged from my many hundreds of happy hours watching albatrosses: it finally occurred to me that except for one special circumstance, I had never ever seen an albatross descend to the water's surface and pick up anything. That special circumstance happens when dusky dolphins[1] surround a school of anchoetas, a sardine-sized fish, to feed on them. Competition is at its height where the dolphins have corralled several barrelsful of anchoetas into a tight group and have driven them up to the surface. Here the gulls collect so thickly there is no room for later arrivals to land on the water, so they just land on the backs of the earlier arrivals, stabbing at fish between the shoulders of the birds on whose bodies they are standing. Such "feeding swarms," as we called them, usually contain a collection of bird species—actually a progression of species. Terns fly along above the dolphin schools by tracking the shallowest individuals, so it is the terns who get to fish first. They are followed a few seconds later by gulls of three species who kick out the terns and take over. In a few more minutes, cormorants, penguins, skuas, and finally black-browed albatrosses arrive.

The albatrosses are bigger than all the other species and so drive everyone else away.

It is not just albatrosses that supplant smaller birds; every species visiting the swarms does so as well. This means that each bird species really only gets a few minutes or seconds in which to feed before it is supplanted and has to move off and search for the next swarm (fortunately for the birds, once the dolphins start feeding on anchoetas they often corral several swarms of them in the course of an hour, so the smaller species get several chances). Given that this was the only circumstance in which we ever saw them feeding, it seemed that albatrosses might be dependent on the dolphins for creating feeding opportunities. There is no doubt albatrosses are successful in catching fish in feeding swarms; if you approach them in a fast boat, albatrosses lounging about on the surface where a swarm has just broken up will regurgitate their catch as they take off.

There are many days on which the albatrosses are not visible from the cliff hut. The same is true of the dusky dolphins. We are now keeping track of days in which we see dolphins and days in which we see albatrosses. So far it looks as though the presence of albatrosses is highly correlated with the presence of dolphins. Because black-browed albatrosses cover long distances when soaring, they are often several miles from their dolphins. However, they do appear to keep their eyes on them and to streak off in their direction when the dolphins start corralling fish and the terns start diving for them. Be that as it may, it appears that around Península Valdés black-browed albatrosses are dependent in winter on dusky dolphins to find their food. I haven't much doubt that if something happened to the dolphins it would fare very badly with the albatrosses.

Given that they never drop down to the surface unless the wind dies or until their school of dolphins creates a feeding opportunity, one might ask why albatrosses soar. The answer becomes particularly tricky when we try to explain why in winter albatrosses sometimes soar overland at Península Valdés. (This is rare but sometimes goes on for minutes or even hours at a time.) There is presumably nothing of any possible interest to a black-browed albatross on the semideserts of Península Valdés. They nest nowhere near Valdés (the season is wrong anyway), they don't need freshwater and they have never been reported feeding on land. It is hard to avoid the conclusion that they simply reside in the air, passing their time there waiting aloft for the dolphins to find fish, meanwhile living their lives on high. Perhaps they do this because it is safer for them there than on the surface. They truly seem to live in the air, soaring in order to remain airborne, like the Red Queen in *Alice in Wonderland*, needing to keep moving even if they wish to stay in one place. When the wind comes up after a spell of calm weather and albatrosses can be seen taking to the air once again (to resume their endless gliding about—but never alighting), I have had the same feeling one gets among a crowd of surfers when someone yells, "Surf's up." All of these points make it very tempting to conclude that albatrosses simply soar for the sport of it.

I have diverted to this side alley because it is a conclusion that arose as a direct result of our study of right whales—and is, in that sense, a part of the right whale research and will serve, I hope, to point out that the study of whales need not entirely concern only whales.

While in the cliff hut there were other diversions besides albatrosses. The best of these were visits from the children. They would watch for a while but when they got bored would go out to play near the cliff hut in the "elf-homes"—or in a section of cliff dunes that they carved with dried sticks into fantastic palaces and secret rooms. They later connected these chambers into open-sided galleries through which they then ran mouse races with mice they caught in box traps, gave names, entered in the races, and which to everyone's relief always got away (except for Santi José de San Martín Fierro Caliente, who got stepped on by mistake). However, one of the more memorable diversions occurred the day Holly and Laura (aged ten and nine respectively) decided to go camping.

It was late in the afternoon when the idea struck them; they would take a tent and pitch it over at Punta los Conos (Cone Point, a peninsula about three miles from camp named for several perfectly conical former seamounts standing on it). Holly's older brother John had taken her on a similar trip and Holly wanted to repeat the adventure—this time as leader. They rushed to pack their food and camping equipment and with the sun sinking fast set out. They could make good time because the tide was out and they could walk along the beach below the high cliffs between Camp Bay and Flechero Beach—a process that saved them having to climb up through some very rough arroyos and badlands behind the cliffs. (Flechero Beach—meaning "place of arrows," referring in this case to the dunes behind the beach, which was once a favored campground of the Techuelches and is therefore a place where many arrowheads have been found—is a vast beach stretching between the cliffs and the Punta los Conos.)

Because of the late getaway time, Katy and I insisted they take a walkie-talkie and report back to camp on the hour. The whole time they were packing I treated them to one of my paternal Gothic orations (complete with sage counsel, lessons on social responsibility, wise admonitions, notes of caution, and several somewhat unrelated but nevertheless deeply relevant afterthoughts). The main body of the lecture concerned the importance of not rambling on on the walkie-talkie so that its ancient batteries would still have some oomph left in case they really needed to use it. The area they were headed toward was even more remote than camp, but both girls were careful with things like fire and boiling water, and neither Katy nor I was seriously worried about them getting hurt. As far as anyone molesting them went, we were ten miles from our nearest neighbors (whom we knew and liked) and the only people they might encounter would be gauchos riding the fences. Not only did we know all the local gauchos to be excellent people, we also knew that they were incredibly shy about trying to communicate with someone they couldn't understand easily—using any stratagem they could think up to avoid such scary confrontations as having to make light conversation with blonde nine-year-olds and ten-year-olds. They were also very concerned for the welfare of our remote-living family and we used to see one of them come to the top of the cliffs in the distance—a man silhouetted on a horse—looking down benevolently for a moment on Whale Camp and then turning away. We supposed they were checking to make sure there were still signs of life around our house. It was the neighborly thing to do—a distant courtesy which gave us a good feeling.

The girls set out filled with confidence, cracking jokes and making a great show of staggering under their heavy packs, and were soon tiny specks inching along in the distance, all but invisible on the vast pebbly beach that stretches between Camp Beach and Flechero Bay. I was worried about their possible concern when they couldn't contact us on our unreliable walkie-talkies once they got around the bend in the cliffs, so I decided to go up to the cliff hut where I could get on with my work but have good line-of-sight communication wherever they might call from. I would have an excellent telescope with me in the cliff hut and might be able to see them if they got into trouble. As things turned out, it was a good decision.

The late afternoon and early evening proceeded smoothly enough and every hour Holly called in:

HOLLY: "Dad."
ME: "Hi Holl, how are things going?"
HOLLY: "Fine. Over and out."

I began to wonder whether I might not have overdone the admonition part a bit. I caught sight of them through my telescope once or twice, and they seemed to be moving along well, but by sunset I could no longer find them. However, I could hear them on the radio well enough, and as darkness came on they were being a bit more communicative—at least enough to say they had found a good place to camp. Unfortunately, however, they added that they were having trouble pitching the tent and lighting a fire because of the wind, which was now roaring. I could imagine they were and because I so much wanted them to have a good time, it made me sad to think of them creeping into a sagging badly pitched tent later on.

The girls ate their dinner, and about two hours after sunset I said a final good-night to them. I could see there was a major thunderstorm, crackling with lightning and distant booming thunder, bearing down on them from across the bay. Such storms usually accompanied a cold front in which the temperature could drop thirty degrees, and I began to wonder how that might affect them if their drooping tent leaked and got their sleeping bags wet. It was long past my normal hour to return to camp, but Katy and I had been in constant contact and as she reported that she couldn't always hear Holly and Laura's radio from camp I decided to stay in the cliff hut where they could contact us if they needed to. I planned to leave once the storm had done whatever it was going to do and I could be pretty sure the girls were asleep. Our final communication was scheduled for twenty minutes later. They called precisely on time.

"How are things going?" I asked.

"Oh, okay . . . I think," came Holly's voice—not quite as certain as before.

"What are your plans, Holl?"

"We're going to go right to sleep, we don't have much flashlight left."

"Sounds like a good idea to me. How's the tent?"

"Not so great. We had *a lot* of trouble setting it up. It's very floppy. [Pause] Dad, do you know where we are?"

"Well no, Holl, where are you?"

"About halfway along Punta los Conos."

"When you were pitching the tent could you see the cliff hut?"

"No, it's too far away to see but I could see where it is."

"Holly, I once heard that if you shone a flashlight toward earth from the moon that you could see it from your backyard with a small telescope. I have a telescope here. I'll train it at the place I think you are, and when I'm all set I'll ask you to shine your flashlight toward where you think the cliff hut is."

"Okay, Dad," came the reply.

I fumbled about as I opened the window of the cliff hut and positioned the telescope on its tripod, directing it at what I thought was the right part of the peninsula of Punta los Conos (not hard to do since it was so far away about half of the peninsula was in my field of view). Through the telescope the high hills behind the cliffs edging Punta los Conos loomed in darkness in a brooding and ominous way—the horizon beyond them only just perceptibly lighter than the dark hills themselves. I could see no details of any kind, only the menacing nighttime presence of the hills indicated by a dark, barely perceived texture that was presumably vegetation. Balancing my walkie-talkie precariously on a chair next to me, I fumbled for the transmit button and said, "Okay, I'm ready, Holl, shine your flashlight."

A moment later, from the lowest part of my field of view, came a minuscule pinprick of light, the faintest star one might ever imagine being able to see. It flickered for a moment and went out—a tiny scintilla of light appearing for just a moment only to vanish again, swallowed by the howling infinite of the ominous black hill that beetled and loomed behind it—a star more precious than any in the firmament.

Again, Holly's voice came up on the radio: "Did you see it, Dad?"

"Yes, darling, I saw it," I said, trying to sound as cheerful as might be. "It looks like an excellent place to camp. Now you and Laura go to sleep, rest well, and we'll see you tomorrow afternoon when you get back."

I put down the radio and sat gazing at the dark peninsula, exhorting it under my breath to take care of my daughters. I sat for a long time watching the thunderstorm. It flashed and rumbled as it slowly bore down on them. I could see it might just miss them, and I prayed that it would. But there was another bigger storm behind it, and I suspected they might not be so lucky with that one. As I sat wondering about these things Holly's voice suddenly came up on the radio: "Daddy?"

"Yes, Holl."

"We don't like it very much here. We think we want to come home."

My heart sank. "Just a minute, Holl," I said. "I need to think." It was 11:00 P.M. The tide was now high, so that the route along the beach at the foot of the cliffs that they had used on their way out was now under at least ten feet of water. They'd have to climb the cliffs in the dark and come through an area of badly eroded arroyos and canyon badlands lying behind the cliffs on the tableland above—something that could be dangerous in the dark since some of the canyon edges were deeply undercut or were hidden in vegetation. Falling in and breaking a leg was a real possibility. To avoid that they would have to go way inland around the entire eroded area and this would add a mile to their trip home and subject them to the possibility of getting lost. I wasn't worried about them being scared of the dark, because they had camped many times and weren't afraid of the sweet Patagonian nights. But there was no path on any of this route and a storm was bearing down on them. Their flashlight wouldn't possibly last all that way, so they would mostly be walking in the dark, reserving the light for occasional quick checks of the most difficult bits, some of which were scary even in daylight, and they would be saving it most for the badlands.

It seemed to me someone would have to go get them. As the cliff hut was in the opposite direction from the girls, I was a lot farther from them than Katy. I would need to stay where I was so I could talk with them if they needed help as they passed through the arroyos, an area of radio shadow for calls directly to camp. Someone would have to stay with Sam, the youngest (John, his eldest brother, was away at school in Buenos Aires). That left Lysa Leland, a friend who was living with us. I called Katy to confer. She and Lysa discussed it, and Lysa volunteered at once to walk toward the girls and meet them on their side of the cliffs and escort them home through the badlands. Now the question was where could Lysa rendezvous with them? It had to be a place that both parties knew and could find in the dark. On a recent family outing we had all seen a dead porpoise lying at the high-tide line on Flechero Beach. I called Holly: "Holl, do you remember the dead porpoise on Flechero Beach?"

"Yes."

"Do you think you could find it in the dark?"

"Yes, I think so." (I breathed a huge sigh of relief and thought, *That's my girl, Holl.*)

"If you have any trouble finding it, all you have to do is walk along the high-tide line and that will lead you to it. I think you'll be able to see it without a flashlight, and you must save your flashlight for times when you really need it."

"No, I know."

"Leave your things there except for a poncho, because I think rain is coming and you may need it—we can pick everything up with the boat tomorrow. Wait by the dead porpoise for Lysa; she's on her way to meet you and will walk home with you through the arroyos above the cliffs. Mum and I don't want you to try to walk that bit alone. I'll stand by here so we can talk if we need to."

"Okay, Daddy, we'll leave right away. Over and out." (Her voice was clear and without fear, and full of resolve again.)

The only radio we could give Lysa had problem batteries and was unreliable but she would stand by on it in case we needed to contact her. Katy and she packed a thermos of hot tea and a snack for everyone for when Lysa got to the girls, and Lysa set off with a fluorescent lantern that we knew to be good and whose batteries we expected would last the distance.

About an hour and a half later Holly called in, triumphant. She and Laura had found the dead porpoise and were waiting by it. Lysa was still not there, but I assured them that if it was turned on, they would be able to see her lantern any minute.

For the next two hours things went from bad to worse. There was no Lysa and no radio contact with her. Thinking that she might have lost radio contact by being down in some arroyo I kept calling her but never received an answer. The storm was passing close, the wind had come up and was blowing really hard, and it was raining in fits and starts and threatening to pour in a deluge. The girls were getting cold, and on my last contact had reported that they were lying on the ground under the poncho next to the dead porpoise trying to avoid the wind and watching the rain beat on the beach next to them. (Holly later told us that the porpoise stank so much that she and Laura got the giggles about it and that laughing about it cheered Laura up. The irony of their situation was not lost on either of them, and their response to it made me proud of them.) We were communicating every fifteen minutes. Their spirits never lagged, though all of us were worried about what might have happened to Lysa. Katy was on the radio too but she couldn't hear the girls and had to rely on my reports. She said that Sam was so worried about his sisters that he hadn't gone to sleep at all.

It was a bad moment. My heart ached as I thought of my daughters huddling together under a poncho in the rain as that howling wind swept over them, two minute specks lost in the enormous expanse of a vast beach, in the middle of the night, waiting in a storm by the body of a dead porpoise for someone to come get them. I longed to be that person but knew that it would take me at least three hours to reach them, and if I left the cliff hut area they would have no one to talk to during the time I was out of radio contact and that might be harder on them in the long run. I wasn't worried for their lives; they were strong, and brave, and smart beyond their years about the wild world, but I was pretty sure they were in for some rather awful hours of cold until the tide fell enough for them to make it back to camp along the beach. And what could have happened to Lysa? These thoughts were swirling in my mind when Holly's voice, full of cheer, came up on the radio. "Daddy, guess what we just saw."

"What did you see?"

"We saw a fox. It was running along the beach with its tail blowing in the wind and its fur all pushed up backward. It came really close."

"Holly, that's wonderful. You two have all the luck, I really envy you. How're you both doing?"

"Oh, we're *fine*." It was Laura's voice sounding very worried. "We're just a little cold. Do you think anything bad has happened to Lysa?"

"I don't think so, darling, and I certainly hope not," I replied.

About fifteen minutes later Holly was back on the radio, her voice bursting with excitement. "Daddy, we think we see Lysa's light. She's very far away though and way, way inland."

"Shine your light right at her," I said.

A moment later Holly's voice said, "She saw us, I know she saw us."

"Okay, Holl, do you think you can go toward her without losing sight of her?"

"Yes, we can."

"Go for it, but call me if you have any trouble. And call in any case when you reach her."

Half an hour later Holly's voice was back. "We found Lysa! She's fine. She just got a little lost, and her radio isn't working, but we know where we are and we're going home. Over and out."

I waited in the cliff hut to talk to them in case they needed help on their return past the arroyos. But it all went well and in about two and a half hours Katy called to say that they were safely back. All that time the wind had been dying and the clouds dispersing. The drama was over, the foundlings recovered, the storm past, and the sky clear. It was 4:00 A.M. I packed my things and walked back through the soft night under a canopy of stars toward home. The Magellanic Clouds were still visible, but Scorpio had set completely—only the stinger above the horizon. When I got back Katy was up waiting. She said had been a grand reunion as the girls came triumphantly in from the dark, blinking in the bright light from the pressure lamps. It turned out that Lysa had gotten lost in the very section I was afraid the girls might get lost in, and though she couldn't make us hear her on her radio she could hear us fine and had been agonizing the whole time as she listened to our worried conversations about what might have happened to her. Katy said that Sam had still been awake when the girls got in, had greeted them with wordless relief and long hugs, and was now fast asleep. Katy had given them hot cocoa, and now they were asleep too. I went to the door of their room, opened it a crack and looked at their sleeping faces surrounded by masses of tousled hair, silently thanking life that they were all right. And then I went to bed. The wind had dropped completely, and the sea had died down. I was lulled to sleep by a soft, suffusing sound of small waves washing the shore—as if the sea were breathing. Out in the bay I could hear the sounds of the whales, mixing their breaths with the breathing of the sea.

On my trips to the cliff hut I carried in my knapsack a thermos of hot water (coming across it in my pack each day was one of the day's small delights). I carried it so I could make mate (pronounced MAH-tay). Though drunk in many South American countries, mate is the national drink throughout Argentina and is intimately connected in my mind with Patagonia. It is favored by gauchos and thus revered by all Argentines, the same way Americans revere ten-gallon hats, blue jeans, and the other stuff of cowboys. Mate is a kind of very concentrated tea (ultrahigh in caffeine, technically, mateine), which is drunk several times a day, usually from a small gourd (*el mate*), old ones giving mate a better taste. It is sipped through a silver-plated straw (*la bombilla*) whose tip is expanded out into a strainer so that the leaves of the plant from which the mate is steeped, the yerba, remain behind. To make it, the gourd is washed, the straw placed in it, and the gourd filled entirely with coarsely ground leaves of the yerba plant while care is taken to hold the straw very still at all times (the trick being to reduce as much as possible the number of small leaf bits and yerba dust that enter the pores in the straw and clog it). When you are ready to drink mate, hot water is poured into the gourd from a little teapot, *la paba*, usually of enamelware (even battered, chipped and soot-stained *pabas* being greatly prized). There is so much yerba used for each mate that most of the water is retained by the leaves and the gourd holds only about two tablespoons of accessible mate. The person doing the pouring often sucks up the first mate and spits it onto the ground (it is too bitter [*amargo*] to swallow). The gourd is then filled again and passed to one of the people present. The recipient sucks the gourd dry through the straw. When finished, the gourd with the unmoved straw still in it is passed back into the center to the host (the one with the *paba*) for more water. Once refilled, it is handed out from the center to the next person in the circle, and so on round and round the group. The host, sitting at the fire and rebalancing the *paba* on the correct log between sips to maintain the temperature of the water, is the hub, and the people the spokes in this ceremonial wheel—a wheel that lies flat, beneath the stars, with the host and the mate situated in the center of the guests. At any moment there must be a thousand such wheels scattered across the campo of Argentina, each a part of the grand, overall ceremony of *el mate*.

The way you handle the gourd on your turn is an art. You must not hurry—it is good form to pause as you drink in order to add your opinion to the conversation between sips, preferably gesturing with the mate as you make some point. But it is bad form to keep the cup too long for yourself. When asked if you want more you say, "*Gracias*" if you do not, "*Bueno*" if you do, and "*Está rico*" when you receive it and have tasted it (for some reason this is hard for most foreigners to master).

If a group of the roughest gauchos are sitting by the side of the road and a group of the most elegantly dressed citified dandies stop to get directions, mate may be offered. If it is, it is usually accepted, even though everyone knows it will delay their affairs for quite a while. It is a wonderful trap, because it would be too ungenerous not to offer the mate, and too unfriendly not to accept it. Mate thus provides an unstressed and agreeable way to become acquainted with strangers. A fire is made, and water is heated. Getting the water to just the right temperature and keeping it there during the ceremony is diabolically difficult—is, in fact, a delicate art—one that makes whole groups of mate drinkers defer to the particular genius in their company who knows how to get the water temperature right and maintain it that way on an open fire. The mate gourd is then sent on its rounds, everyone taking their turns and passing it on. I know of no more natural circumstance in which to interact with total strangers. There is never any pressure. Like a peace pipe, the mate gourd provides its own perfect set of conditions for promoting the most civilized kinds of human interaction.

It is always the right moment to offer mate. It is a ritual with as many subtleties and as much dignity as the Japanese tea ceremony. I prefer the mate ceremony because the people who perform it best are the poorest and live in the harshest places, in the simplest manner, and with a kind of grace that has no equal among the rest of us whose lives sag with far too many material possessions to have the time to perfect anything so simple. Because mate is the only consistent luxury of the poorest people, they have had lifetimes to master its preparation. Thus it is that the best mate you will ever have will probably be served to you in the poorest surroundings by the poorest Argentine you ever meet.

Most Argentine city dwellers don't drink mate, but there is a group which does, including some of Argentina's most distinguished citizens. There is always a little pause, a kind of wink in the conversation, when you discover in some polished and dignified Buenos Aires office another drinker of mate like yourself. I have several times been served mate in such offices but under such circumstances the air is not as relaxed, and so the mate ceremony dictates less of the experience. But it always takes me back to Patagonia—perhaps to some evening when I sat with my family and Juan Gomés, an old gaucho, by his dying fire, passing the mate gourd around and listening to him playing the guitar and singing strange and moving songs.

Juan Gomés was a man who had spent his youth driving cattle across the Andes into Chile with only a woolen poncho on his back to protect him from the rain and his mate to cheer his spirits. He had learned that a person is happiest when they have swept the granary floor of their soul clean of the chaff of daily society and are living on their own mettle. He hadn't a dime and he lived in a discarded truck box on a deserted lot. He would sit outside it with perfect posture on a broken chair and as I passed indicate with a regal sweep of his hand the box next to him, inviting me to sit and "*Tomar un mate.*" On one such afternoon as we sat sipping mate and chatting he said to me with great pride, "People envy me. People envy me. They say, 'There is Don Juan Gomés who has lived his life on the pampa under the sun and the stars.'" He was right. Dead right. I envied him. I still do.

Mate, somehow, makes a subtle connection between the wind, the bitter taste of the yerba, and the aridity of Patagonia. It has a power to cut the dust in ways that nothing else can. When drunk *amargo* (bitter) it is the most refreshing and soothing drink I know. It is, I believe, the ultimate desert drink. I have spoken with others who say it is at its best in the moist tropics and subtropics where it is grown, but I have known it only in the dry lands of Patagonia, and it is in these semideserts that I find it, in its soothing, refreshing bitterness, to be the essence of that hard, pure land I love so much.

Except for the way the Argentines treated indigenous peoples (my European ancestors in North America were just as bad) I could wish I had been there at the creation of the present Argentina, at the beginning of ranching, the setting out of cattle on the pampas, the first days of the country. The mate represents in many ways the last vestige of yearning for the old Argentina. That is why, I suppose, old mate gourds are more prized than new silver cups, and why the tourist stores which sell the paraphernalia for making mate are also packed with all that is gaucho—the stirrups, the chaps, even editions of Martin Fierro's famous poem (a paean to the gaucho, sometimes bound in cowhide with the hair still on it), an account in verse of the old ways, the old values, in effect, the soul of Argentina, on which this most modern South American country is based. Someone once told me that Argentina is a European country that just happens to be located in South America. This might be true, were it not for the traditions of the gauchos—traditions like the ceremony of El Mate.

At the end of long days in the cliff hut alone, I would close up my notes, repack my knapsack, and head back along the edge of the cliffs toward home, the deepening dusk providing just enough light to pick my way among the thornbushes and find the faint track through the dunes. Once back at camp, I would find supper cooking and the windows steamed up, the sounds of the propane lamps hissing steadily, and the children in their rooms or at the table dressed in pajamas. Mealtimes were wonderful; during them, all the stories got told and the best bits saved for last. And at the end of dessert, there was reading aloud and then bed—the wind sighing its constant song as it had done all day, lulling our remote family to sleep.

But not all days were windy, and it was on the rare calm days that we did most of our work. Central to everything we did were aerial censuses in which we photographed the heads of all the whales in the area. We would fly along the coast in a small plane, lingering to circle over each whale or group of whales long enough to get a photograph of the pattern of callosities on their heads. The following entry on a census day, September 22, 1974, is from my diary.

Air-flight today. I was up late last night keeping up with my notes and overslept until 8:00. Now I am brought awake suddenly by the sound of a plane overhead. The girls in ground-length nightgowns are racing like autumn leaves through the house, leaving the doors flapping behind them. The wind is still—blessedly it is still. The plane roars over the house again and drones out over the bay and peace sifts down on us again like dust.

"Put your hands over your heads," I shout to them—our sign to the pilot we want an air-flight. As they race to do it, I stagger out of bed, belt on some sort of trousers and start rummaging through a chaos of equipment for our plane radio. No antenna. I recall that it packed up last time. I struggle with an improvised spare during which the drone of the impatient plane grows louder until with a whooshing roar it streaks directly overhead again, then back into abrupt silence as it passes over the cliff tops immediately behind the house (where it is now turning and stirring things up on the tableland above). Again profound silence. Even the sea is calm I now can hear, and that is rare—and very good for flying.

During this silence there is a distant birdsong, a wave lapping on the beach and then suddenly the plane is upon us once more, bursting in on the quiet bay and our patient house, hammering everything with its roaring. This time I'm prepared, and I contact the pilot. A brief discussion. He will land at La Anita, an estancia owned by our closest neighbors, about 40 minutes away by car; it has a modest airstrip well grazed by sheep.

After a brief breakfast, while packing cameras and gear, Bernd[2] and I leave. Katy comes with us to bring back the car so she can use it while we are flying.

At the airstrip we find Hugo[3] (the pilot) standing by my old adversary, the Cessna 182. It has 3,000 hours on the motor, which means it is ready for a major engine overhaul. We will fly in it anyway. I view the badly nicked propeller with alarm and recall Charlie Wallcott's[4] admonishments about not flying with nicked propellers because some nicks become cracks which allow bits of the propeller to fly off. The resulting imbalance of the prop sometimes causes vibrations so violent the engine tears itself out of its mounts (with its weight gone, the plane can no longer be controlled and you crash). I mention this to Hugo. He assures me this could only happen with the loss of a big piece of propellor and this prop seems destined to lose only small pieces. With this reassurance we grit our teeth and get on with it.

Flying here could be beautiful. The views are loveliness unfathomable and whales can best be seen and appreciated by looking into the water from above (a more all-inclusive view than seeing them from underwater). Were it not for my ungovernable distrust of machines (not Argentine machines, any machines) these censuses would be a pleasure. As it is they are all but wholly intolerable.

During this flight we find whales well concentrated in their principal areas, in places with names like "Children's Slide," "Whale Bay," "First Look," and "Windmill Farm Cattle Gate." In all we see 112 right whales today, one more than I have ever seen before in a single flight. The conditions for flying are perfect all day. The calm extends everywhere, even to Punta Norte, which is rare. As we try to cover all this, I take about 900 pictures while the world spins in slow motion beneath us—a slowly wheeling blue platter strewn with scattered bands of tiny whales. We see Alba, the white baby. The fourth year in a row that he's been here. We see old gray ones and new ones all mottled black and white unlike anything I have seen before. We also see the tiniest calf I have ever seen. Another large whale is white with a long black back—or is it black with a long white back? The pictures will tell. In addition they will tell us who is back this year and who is appearing for the first time. Bernd, who is recording data, is ill, but the grueling, endless circling has to continue all the same. He's such an incredibly good sport about it and so cheerful I never knew he wasn't feeling well.

In all the circling of this three-and-a-half-hour flight, there are only three level portions, and by the time we land back at La Anita we're all shot. Katy is there, and the sun shining and warm, and the world still and calm, with birds singing in scattered places nearby. Peace at last. We search for the hand radio which Katy misplaced while she was looking for a view to draw. Bernd finds it, and I go in search of a bush behind which to relieve myself, returning alone to the plane across a ground carpeted with tiny fragile plants bearing a lovely, fragrant purple flower. I first notice one, then two, then more and more until with eyes bent only to the ground I advance as if floating in some heavenly field of fragile stars. They are everywhere, more cheerful than seems possible for any such simple greeting from the earth. Soon there are so many I must place my feet carefully. I am wrapped up in the business of walking but feel as though I am floating on some enchanted veil, stretched loosely over the stony ground. A thought of cities enters my mind and with the next step there are no more flowers—not one flower. None. Nothing. Another step with no flowers. Another. I cast out the thought and a flower appears. I rejoice. Two flowers on the next step . . . Ah, I may recapture the feeling. The next four steps bring 5, 20, 100, 200 flowers. As an unprecedented abundance of them flows by I feel a pure pleasure, am lost in it, am oblivious of all my steps until with a bump I arrive at the plane and Katy. During all of this time both were standing quietly at the periphery of my revery.

We return home and find it all calm and bright and sun-warmed—light flooding in under the porch roof—the tide far out and the mud flats exposed. The children have gone to the Flechero in search of arrowheads and Mel has gone to the cliff hut. Soon everyone returns, radiant, and the children decide to go kayaking. Boxes are opened, gear tumbled out and much of it dragged down the beach toward the receding tide. Katy and I stay behind. With the calm afternoon slowly ticking on, we make love, and as I lie quietly in the late afternoon, wrapped in the warmth that all the circling of the day had torn from me, I hear each subtle sound—the children's distant voices—a tiny nearby bird—each embedded in its setting of profound stillness and peace.

The beauty and loveliness of this peace cannot be imagined by those who have never been quietly ushered into its presence. When it makes its appearance, it usually only insinuates itself in between the small sounds and scattered disturbances, which are always strung, beadlike, through a day. But if you let it alone, let it bloom fully—come out of hiding all the way—glance nervously at you and then from side to side, and then slowly ease itself from out of its shy retirement, you will find that the peace of Patagonia is the loveliest thing you can see or feel. Sometimes it has one appearance, at other times another. Sometimes it is a field of tiny scattered purple flowers that wait coyly to buoy you along by the pure power of their shy beauty.

In addition to the research we did there was something else I wanted our work with right whales to achieve. I wanted it to point toward a new way of being—to lead into, or at least reflect, a way of life—one in which science was the primary but not the sole end; where by combining living with studying whales we could straddle two worlds. In one of these worlds, the wild world, we would feel the least estrangement simply because the past four billion years of evolution has shaped humans to feel their most comfortable in such a world. In the other—the world of science—we would be living according to a set of rules that constitute the best way yet invented for understanding the cosmos. Thus, I suspected we would live a life circumscribed by truth (well, anyway, a better and better approximation of an unattainable truth) and every now and then we would be rewarded by answers to questions raised by our life in the wild.

In some way that I don't fully understand the wind and the mate are a part of achieving a resonance with the wildness of Patagonia. The beauty of some things is not obvious. To see it you must sometimes simply will that you love these things. Patagonia is like that. But when you will that you love it you find that you *do* love it—that you love it more than any other place. I believe that Alaskans fall in love with their winters through such a process. My mind was opened to Patagonia by learning to love two of the things that seem to have closed most people's minds to it—the constant winds, and the bitter mate.

I have always thought that the stories the old explorers brought back with them from the remote corners of the earth were wildly exaggerated with regard to the dangers they encountered. The places they visited often contained native populations complete with women and children and were in many instances safer and more agreeable than the places they had left. The image they had of far places was not a true image. It was colored by the fact that everything surrounding them was alien—everything they loved and that was kind to their sensibilities was far away. When they died, out of touch, remote from home and family, one of the contributing causes of their deaths must surely have been yearning—terminal yearning. They must have hated the remote places in which they died—often places you and I find exquisitely beautiful and which we sometimes spend years of our savings just to visit.

I was determined not to be estranged from the wild but to find my place in it. So when I decided to study the right whales of Patagonia, I was determined from the start to take my family with me. I knew that if they came, I would not be spending time worrying about them and could therefore work with better effect. I also reasoned that children might serve a uniquely important role on an expedition, becoming ports during the emotional storms of adults who are living in close quarters. In one two-year period my children had slept on the ground for more nights than they had slept in beds. And they were always cheerful about it. It is my belief that a good attitude is more important than any other aspect of a person's way of being. My children had the right attitude for expeditions.

It worked and is a thing of which I'm proud—a theory that turned out to be right. Having the family along gave our work a dimension that would have been sorely missed had they stayed at home. I have often been asked whether we weren't afraid of having our children in such a wild place? We were not. I feel that our years in Patagonia demonstrate that there is no major danger faced by children at the ends of the earth—certainly nothing to match the dangers of growing up in a city. At the end of each trip they were healthier in mind and body than when they left. It also seemed to me that they left standing in their tracks their friends who never got clear of the city. It demonstrated cleanly that some of the stories of those intrepid hunters and whalers were simply lies told by timid, homesick men—stories that never would have been written had their children been along ("Daddy, that's not what Sally said happened. She saw it too. Mommy told me. You could ask her about it if you want to, Daddy").

Our days in Argentina were the happiest I ever had with my first family and so it seems unaccountable to me that having discovered a means of continuing such an idyllic life I did not take up permanent residence in the Eden of Patagonia. I have often thought that the thing which prevents me from living a clement and unfeigned life in the wilderness is a kind of perverse obedience to the tenets of social responsibility that I am doomed to obey, slavishly, until I die. It is a kind of disruptive accountability, a maddened sense of duty, a self-imposed levy or tariff that I continue to wrest, like some deranged extortionist, from what might otherwise have been a quiet and amiable existence, immersed in science and in the serenity and healing that comes from the kind of life I once tasted, for twenty-two months, in Patagonia—in the peace and tranquility of wildness, safe among whales.

Having failed to escape the thrall of a social conscience, I now rely on the sea to save me from what would be the final degradation—dying in some city in the eye of the human storm. I pray that when my time comes, the sea will intercede on my behalf, negotiating for me an armistice with life, however brief, in which I can leave this world in peace. Camus must have had something of the same feeling about the sea, for in one of his notebooks is this passage:

> . . . if I were to die in the midst of cold mountains, unknown to the world, cast off by my own people, my strength at last exhausted, the sea would at the final moment flood into my cell, come to raise me above myself and help me to die without hatred.

CHAPTER 3

Behavior of Right Whales

The right whale is a huge whale, with a broad back that lacks a dorsal fin, a feature which, along with the presence of rough, thickened patches of skin on its head (the callosities) and a V-shaped spout, makes this an easy species to identify at sea. The V-shaped spout is the result of right whales having two nostrils. Sperm whales have but one blowhole, so their blows are single. This is important because there is no proper dorsal fin on the back of a sperm whale, which means a sperm whale may be confused with a right whale. However, as soon as one sees the blow, the difference is apparent. The two biggest remaining populations of right whales are the Argentine population that I have studied since 1970 and a slightly larger group living off the coast of South Africa.[1] They have a larger relative, the arctic bowhead whale, which grows to a length of sixty-five feet[2] and a more distantly related, smaller relative, the pygmy right whale, which gets no larger than twenty-one feet.[3]

The family of right whales (the *Balaenidae*) contains either two or three species depending on who you read (and who you believe). Nearly everyone agrees that bowheads are a single species, though some of the Inuit whalers who still hunt them believe there are two bowhead species—the bowhead and the Ingutuk.[4] This is an important point to Inuit hunters because the United States is a member of the International Whaling Commission, a body which controls whaling and sets quotas for all whales including whales in the national waters of those nation-states that have signed the articles of agreement of the Whaling Convention. This means that the Inuits have to abide by international law, and so if there were two species, the Inuits might be able to argue for two separate quotas. However, Inuit-sponsored research done jointly by Inuit hunters and biologists over several years has yet to yield evidence for a separate species in the annual Alaskan catch.

Bowhead whales live in the Northern Hemisphere. Indeed, they appear never to leave the icy waters of arctic latitudes. The species lacks the prominent raised patches of thickened white skin on their heads that right whales have.

Besides the bowhead there are either one or two species of right whales. Before they were reduced to their present precarious numbers (estimated at four thousand[5]) it is believed that there were more than eighty thousand right whales worldwide.[6] They were found in every ocean and off the western and eastern coasts of every continent—even off the coast of Antarctica. With adults up to 56 feet,[7] this is a slightly smaller species than the bowhead. On the basis of recent biochemical evidence comparing North Atlantic with South Atlantic right whales, some scientists now believe there are two species of right whales: the southern right whale, *Eubalaena australis* (in the Southern Hemisphere) and the northern right whale, *Eubalaena glacialis* (in the Northern Hemisphere).

The conclusion is based in major part on the genetic differences between the two populations. However, the evidence is inconclusive, since no one has yet looked at the genetic variance in widely separated right whale populations from the same hemisphere or even from different parts of the same ocean. Until they do so, it seems to me unwise to assign different species names to northern and southern right whales.

Taxonomy, the system of categorizing living forms, involves decisions that in the end come down to matters of judgment. It is very difficult to define a species, and even with the help of modern biochemical genetics, the determination of what constitutes separate species is a complex and vexed question. Until there is better evidence, I remain to be convinced that there are different species of right whales in the Northern and Southern hemispheres.

There is a much smaller species of right whale that goes by the name of the pygmy right whale but because of various peculiarities in its anatomy, it is assigned to a different family (the *Neobalaenidae*—the other right whales are the *Balaenidae*). Pygmy right whales look a lot like another small and much more abundant (but only very distantly related) whale species—the minke whale—with which they are probably often confused in the wild. Large minke whales can be thirty-five feet long,[8] whereas the largest pygmy right whale on record was twenty-one feet long.[9] Pygmy right whales are thus the smallest-known baleen whales. They are most abundant in those high latitudes of Southern Hemisphere seas that the early whalers almost never reached, and this species has, as far as we know, never been the target of a directed whaling industry. Because of the remoteness of the oceans it frequents, the pygmy right whale seldom crosses paths with humans. Even today, almost nothing is known about it. It is an entirely enigmatic species.

The name *right whale* is very old and dates back to the time when large whales were first hunted by Europeans. At the time, charts were still decorated with pictures of boats being menaced by krakens and sea monsters. It all reflected the near-total ignorance of humans about what was out there in the sea. One thing that people *had* started to realize was that there was more than one kind of whale and that any besides the right, bowhead and sperm whales was, in the words of Melville, an "unnearable brute" (e.g., he describes the fin whale as "belonging to the species of uncapturable whales, because of its incredible power of swimming"). Worse, even if you could catch and kill one, it was likely to sink and be lost.

In addition to their fat, whales were prized for their baleen, from which was made a variety of articles including umbrellas, buggy whips, corset stays, and other items that had to be springy. The whalers soon learned that the baleen of most kinds of whales was of little or no value because it was too brittle and too coarse. There was, however, one kind of whale that swam slowly, was so encased in precious fat that it floated after death, and whose baleen was fine and flexible and thus extremely valuable. Given the ignorance of the times about what swam in the sea, I suppose that whenever the early whalers saw a whale and were preparing to launch their boats and set off in hot pursuit, their first question would have been, "Is that the right kind of whale?" If it was, it was the "right whale." Of course we now know that there is more than one kind of right whale, but the whalers were in confusion about that and called both the bowhead and the right whale "right whales."

The populations of right whales that used to inhabit the seas off the eastern and western shores of every continent are either extinct or nearly so (e.g., the eastern North Atlantic and Pacific) or are represented by only a few hundred animals (western North Atlantic: estimated population, 300–350).[10] In spite of its extreme rarity and the fact that it is spread over an enormous area of ocean, the North Atlantic right whale is one of the better-known whale populations (owing to the dedicated efforts of several groups of North American researchers).

If you can recognize individual animals in the wild, you have the basis for making a long-term study of them. If the marks you use to recognize adults are also present when they are calves (as is the case with the right whale), you can follow the progress of known individuals of known age throughout their lifetimes. With every species to which it has been applied, the technique of using natural markings to recognize individuals over long periods has proven to be an exceptionally powerful procedure for learning about it, and studies with this basis have resulted in major insights.

Callosities, the patches of thickened skin present on right whale heads at birth, retain their form well enough over the years to enable us to identify individuals throughout their lives. As a result our study of right whales in Patagonia is, as I mentioned earlier, the longest continuous study of a whale species based on recognizable individuals. Although most people may think of calluses as thickened skin caused by wear, to a biologist "callus tissue" is simply thick tissue. Wear has nothing to do with it, just thickness (indeed, some plants have callus tissue). Once we began to use callosities to identify whales, others adopted the technique. Researchers working with Northern Hemisphere right whales found that although many individuals had callosities scattered over the same head areas as Southern Hemisphere right whales, many patterns were too alike to distinguish from aerial photographs. But we were lucky; we could use such photos, so that after making an aerial census and spending about three months of arduous work poring over the pictures and comparing them with those in our "Head Catalog" we could determine the identities of the individual whales we had seen, note where we had seen them, and with what other individuals they were consorting.

Every year since 1970 we have photographed the population of right whales around Península Valdés. At this writing we know over twelve hundred individuals. Some we have seen hundreds of times. Some we have never seen again—I suspect some of the single sightings were just passing through but that others were whales that have died in the meantime.

It is possible that right whales rely on callosities too as a means of recognizing each other. The way callosities are distributed on the top, front, and sides of the whales' heads makes every right whale recognizable by means of its callosities from all directions except below. But even from below, the identity of a right whale is visible. The bellies of most southern right whales have distinctive snow-white markings on them of highly irregular shapes that do not change significantly throughout the whales' lives. In most cases they are about half a square meter in area.

In many right whales the belly patches cover a major portion of the belly. When you are swimming with right whales in murky water these bright white markings look almost luminous and are clearly visible long before the rest of the whale looms into view.

One of the circumstances in which belly patches are probably of importance to right whales is during mating. Because the normal mating posture in this species is belly-to-belly, the significant approach by any male to another whale is toward its belly, and the uniqueness of the belly patch may help whales recognize each other. Mating in right whales usually takes place in groups containing several males and a single female (sometimes with more females). In such groups there is considerable competition among males, and the female frantically twists and turns, trying to avoid matings. The action is fast, difficult to follow, and sometimes violent. The water is often cloudier than usual since the bottom is stirred up by the prop wash from all those flukes during all that twisting and turning.

Let us imagine for a moment that you are an average male right whale trying to compete for a female in a group of other males. Because the water is so murky and you are so long, you, like the other whales, simply cannot see your whole body. This same problem makes it hard to see enough detail in the walls of black skin looming and moving around you in the murk to be able to orient yourself regarding who's who and what's what. And because of the terrible visibility, you're probably only very seldom going to get a glimpse of the genital slit of the female as she slips past you. But when you do see it, her belly patch will be in view as well so that you will subsequently know which one she is in the melee.

All female baleen whales are bigger than males (it is the opposite in most toothed whales). This means that maybe you could recognize the female just because she is larger than you. But let us not forget that you are just an average male—there may very well be other males bigger than you. So in these groups there will be two types of animals that are bigger than you: the female—she's who you want—and the bigger males—the ones you definitely don't want! It would not do to belly-up to a bigger male, thinking he was the female, particularly if, from any other view, you would have known perfectly well who he was (maybe even remembered that he was stronger than you). Equally, if you're too afraid of confusing bigger males with the female, you may lose your chance to mate by wasting too much time maneuvering around behind other whales in the group trying to check out their callosities to see who they are before you make your move. So once you have gotten used to using belly patches to recognize who you are approaching, you will have developed a technique that will prove of great importance to you.

One of the surprising things we discovered about right whales is that the callosities are more developed in males than they are in females (this is a statistical statement; there is considerable overlap). The really intriguing thing is that males use their callosities the way bulls use their horns—for fighting. In that sense callosities are like streamlined, underwater horns. There is no evidence that right whales can gouge an opponent with their callosities the way bulls can with their horns, but callosities are rough and can be used for rasping and scuffing against the skin of opponents. When a callosity with several tons of pressure behind it slides across a whale's skin, I suspect it is exquisitely painful. In any case, by the end of the season the skin of any male who has been consistently seen in mating groups is scuffed up and covered with scratches.

On most if not all calves, the natural color of the callosity tissue is white at birth but quickly becomes gray and stays that way throughout the lifetime of the whale. So why do the callosities of adults appear to be white? With very few exceptions they are covered with external parasites called cyamids (also called whale lice), most of which are white, thus making the callosities appear white. Cyamids spend their entire lives living aboard the whales—the only surface on which they are ever found. The cyamids get food by eating the thickened, dead skin of the callosities,[11] and in so doing carve the tissue into fanciful, sculptured forms.

This process sharpens the edges of the callosities, turning them into more effective weapons for the whales. It's like carrying around a whetstone to keep your sword sharp, only it's a living whetstone that works on its own, eating away with microscopic bites along the dull edge of the scraper blade and thus sharpening it. So it is not just the cyamids that benefit from this relationship; the whales appear to benefit as well.

Using the whales' callosity patterns to identify them, we now know mothers who have had as many as five calves over the years of our study. Wintra is such a mother. We first met her back in 1970. The tiny calf she had at that time is now as big as she is. We have followed her offspring's lives and know her to be several times a grandmother.

Aging right whales like Wintra are probably in their sixties, which means that she has probably swum about 175,000 miles[12] (equivalent to seven times around the world) just during migrations, has eaten at least ten thousand tons of food (that's twenty million pounds), has produced perhaps three hundred tons of milk (about 300,000 quarts), and somehow, through it all, has kept her unique dignity and aplomb.

Right whales make long migrations each year, which carry them between temperate/subtropical waters in winter and cold, boreal/subpolar waters in summer. Like most whale species that make long migrations, right whales are adapted to long periods of starvation. The pregnant females in the Argentine population who have been feasting on their feeding grounds in the southern oceans all summer and fall probably make the fourteen-hundred-mile swim up to their wintering grounds fasting all the way. They linger in the bays of Península Valdés for up to 170 days (the average is 77 days), during which time they give birth to a calf. (Though they may get an occasional snack, basically they are still fasting.) During the next few weeks and months the mother pumps massive quantities of rich, creamy milk into her calf, and in response, the calf, who is not otherwise feeding, probably adds at minimum 125 pounds a day (at least in the first few weeks) while also putting on a thick blubber coat. (All the while its mother is still fasting.) At the end of this period mother and calf leave the wintering grounds and swim all fourteen hundred miles back to their feeding grounds (she is still basically fasting). While nursing her calf the mother is its sole source of nourishment. It is only when mother and calf arrive on the feeding grounds that right whales start finding significant amounts to eat and at some point during this period the calf starts taking food in addition to its mother's milk.

Right whales are skim feeders, which means that they catch their prey by swimming along with their mouths open, often at the surface. Plankton nets dragged immediately behind a skimming whale collect more than seven and a half times as much plankton as nets dragged an equal distance at sampling stations in the same area but where whales aren't present and feeding.[13] So when a right whale swims along at the surface with its mouth open, it ought to be safe to assume that it is feeding. However, the picture may not be as simple as that, owing to the recent discovery by biologists Tom Ford and Scott Kraus of an interesting anatomical feature not previously described in this species—a band of tissue richly supplied with blood vessels covering the ridge that runs along the roof of a right whale's mouth.[14] Ford and Kraus postulate that this band is used as a heat exchange mechanism—a means by which the whale can cool itself. If their theory proves to be true, it may mean that at least some of the time right whales are swimming along with their mouths open they aren't feeding at all, just cooling off—a theory supported by the fact that the waters of their wintering grounds are the warmest of any that right whales experience.

But there are other indications that right whales are feeding, such as the fact that they zig and zag from side to side as they swim with their mouths open along sometimes tortuous courses. We also sometimes see copious feces from right whales when they are on their breeding grounds, which supports the idea that as spring advances there is at least heavy snacking going on at Península Valdés (more extensive data, particularly from plankton tows, support the same conclusion that North Atlantic right whales are feeding on their late winter/early spring grounds in Cape Cod Bay[15]). As food blooms increase, right whales appear to get a few solid meals just before they leave their wintering area for summer feeding grounds. However, it is in the summer feeding grounds that the real feasting, gorging, gormandizing, and surfeiting takes place.

Everywhere in this movable feast, the main course is copepods and krill—tiny shrimplike crustaceans, smaller than the smallest shrimp that you and I ever eat, even in the finest Sri Lankan restaurants. (The feast also includes minute quantities of things no whale would wish to eat if it knew what it was getting—but more of that in chapter 8.) It is hard to imagine building a whale out of copepods, something so small that it requires your full concentration and several tries just to pick up a single individual with your fingers (often a fatal experience for the individual, since they have such fragile bodies it is hard to hold them without crushing them).

I think of right whales as graceful harvesters, lined up side by side, rolling and lounging about at the surface in the presence of their helpless prey, then slowly subsiding beneath the waves to glide forward unhurriedly through the rich swarms of copepods whose million billion microagitations are unnoticed by the unhurried and serene whales, set by their enormous size into a unique and imperturbable world as they slowly scythe their way through the scattered silver showers of their prey, harvesting it the way fishing nets embrace whole schools of fish.

One of my great unfulfilled dreams in our study of the right whales has been to find their feeding grounds. We know about 68 percent of our population. Which means that should we ever encounter the Península Valdés right whales on their feeding grounds and manage to film their heads, our chances of recognizing a familiar animal, and thus of realizing that we had found our herd, would be about 68 percent. We have had, from colleagues who were working on the subantarctic island of South Georgia, a few reports and a few photographs of right whales they encountered near the island. Back in the late seventies an associate, Joe Jehl, took an especially clear photograph of the head of a right whale at South Georgia. Alas, it turned out to be a whale with the kind of callosity pattern we sometimes refer to as the "Plain Janes"—a small group of right whales whose heads have very simple and relatively nondistinctive patterns and are diabolically difficult to identify. With normal coverage in aerial photographs it is perfectly possible to recognize all Plain Janes—possible, that is, for Vicky Rowntree, my longtime associate and the person with the most years of experience in identifying individual right whales from aerial photos. (Vicky is an expert not just on right whales but also on their external parasites, the cyamids.) But this whale was photographed from a ship and at a low angle and the factor that made it invidiously difficult to identify was that the angle of the whale's head was just wrong enough in the pictures for us not to be able to be certain whether the distance between two partly obscured spots in the callosity pattern was correct (if it was it would have been identifiable as our whale from Península

Valdés for sure—if it wasn't, it would have been a stranger). So we were not able to say for certain that this was one of our whales even though all the things that we *can* measure about its head made it appear to be. It is ever thus in science: just when you think you have something dead to rights, you find you don't.

Then, in 1990, we received photographs from Ben Osborne of the British Antarctic Survey in South Georgia. Lo and behold, one of the whales pictured was definitely a Península Valdés whale. It is a little hard to describe how it feels to be poring over a set of photographs that have just come in and find a clear match with the Head Catalog. It is the kind of fix that sets you up for months, even years. The thrill is accompanied by an actual physical sensation. It rises, hot, up your back, lifting the hair along your neck, and then sweeps through your whole body like lava or a jolt of adrenaline (not surprising, I guess, since I suppose it *is* a jolt of adrenaline). And you get up from your chair and go swanning through the lab telling everyone else in the place—others like yourself whose days can be made by a thing as lovely as suddenly having solid evidence that the Argentine population of right whales may be feeding off the northern shore of South Georgia Island during the late Southern Hemisphere summer. And someone says, "Wow! You mean that picture we got yesterday was one of our whales! I want to see, I want to see!" And if they become convinced that the match is good, you beam in unconcealable delight. These are the moments that keep field biologists going during the long months of analyzing data indoors—the kind of thing that keeps researchers researching. Until you have experienced it, it may seem a trifle daft. But once you have, you never forget the feeling. Detectives must have similar feelings when they solve a crime.

But for a major whale population like ours one identified individual does not establish the feeding grounds. We're still not certain we've found the copepod and krill basket for Península Valdés right whales, though South Georgia does look like a good bet.

But back in 1989 the search had become more complicated. (Biological research always devolves in this way—the more you know, the more complicated you realize the final answer is going to be; living systems, whatever else they may be, are never simple.) One of the right whales in our research area was photographed off the coast of Tristan da Cunha. It was Jason, one of the males we have seen a lot, and an old friend. Jason is always easy to identify because he has a large white fleece-shaped mark on his back. He is a veteran of many mating groups at Península Valdés. Tristan da Cunha is a South Atlantic island about 2,800 miles east of Península Valdés which, along with its neighboring island, Gough, is the second most isolated island group in the world (the Hawaiian chain holds the record for being the most isolated). Even the old whalers must have known that the waters around Tristan da Cunha were a feeding ground for right whales—the logbooks of several old whaling ships show that they killed right whales near Tristan in the summer months. Apparently some of the whales that come to Península Valdés are feeding not only at South Georgia but near Tristan da Cunha too (and who knows, maybe several other places as well).

This simple fact speaks to me: I think of the right whales in Península Valdés easing themselves out through the entrance to Golfo San José as the season at Península Valdés nears its end, perhaps rendezvousing for a short while with companions and acquaintances at Punta Norte, and then setting out across the vast desert of the South Atlantic toward either South Georgia or Tristan da Cunha, reaching toward two island dots in that vast wilderness. I have been all over this planet, on every continent and every ocean— including both Arctic and Antarctic. There is only a handful of places that I would dearly like to go that I have never been (though there are many to which I would love to return). The two wild places that loom largest in my dreams are South Georgia and Tristan da Cunha.

As I write this I know that Jason and his gang are pitching up at Península Valdés, back from visiting those magical islands. In order to visit them they don't have to raise funds, secure boats, find the time, placate employers, and make detailed plans. All they have to do is want to go . . . and they're off. How enviable the life of a whale.

With the exception of four seasons (when others were present to do the work) I have returned each spring to Península Valdés since 1970 for several weeks or months in order to carry out research on the right whales. As I have noted earlier we now know over twelve hundred individual right whales. We are expecting our third generation of calves—descendants of mothers we first met back in 1970, many of whom are still alive and still in their calf-bearing years.

I know of no way to convey the feelings that overtake me when I encounter some old friend among the whales, back in the bay for the second, third, or nth time. In our very first year we frequently saw a female called Y-Spot (named for two prominent white marks on her back). By the fourth year of our study she had been missing for two years and we were worried that she had died.[16] Then, one afternoon, I was watching a female and calf way out in the bay through a telescope. They were inching their way toward me at a maddeningly slow rate. During one particularly exasperating hour while they played a lot they progressed no more than two whale lengths. As the long, slow afternoon wore on, I began to wonder whether the mother was ever going to come close enough so I could see who she was. And then, a wonderful thing happened: a thin veil of cloud shifted across the sun and at the same time the whale slightly changed her orientation. With the light reflecting just right off her back, I caught sight for the first time of the familiar pattern. "Y-Spot," I shouted. And I can remember tears starting to my eyes, and that I danced along the brink of the cliff waving my hat in the air—I was a lone mad figure lost under the infinite sky of Patagonia leaping and shouting and waving my arms—doing anything I could think of to greet this inirritable, intransmutable whale and to let her know how profoundly glad I was that she was still alive.

Our cliff hut, as I've mentioned, is quite far from camp. This is not in quest of further solitude but rather because it's located above the only place for miles where the cliffs plunge straight into the water. When the tide is halfway up or higher there is enough water right against the cliffs for whales to swim directly below the hut. And they do, because mothers with calves faithfully follow the five-meter depth contour at Península Valdés. Five meters is just enough water for a large mother to be clear of the bottom, but not enough to allow attacks on her calf from below by killer whales and sharks—probably a significant threat to newborn right whales. Because the water is so shallow it is not possible for a whale to dive out of view while it is directly below the cliff hut. So when the water below the cliffs is deeper than five meters, the whales, while following the five-meter contour, swim along almost touching the cliffs, which causes them to pass directly beneath the cliff hut as well. It is thus a perfect spot from which to watch right whales (even to get to see them underwater) without disturbing them. The day Y-Spot returned, she finally hit the five-meter contour and began following it. This brought her beneath the cliff hut, where she lay for about ten minutes. By now I was much quieted down, and I spent my time drinking in the sight of her graceful curves and silently welcoming her and her new calf back to the bay.

Since that time I have seen Y-Spot many times, once even during a flight when I was far from Península Valdés. On this occasion she was about three hundred miles from Lote 39—swimming resolutely toward it. I tried to film her but the filming conditions were so bad I couldn't get an unambiguous picture. So although I am 99 percent sure it was she I cannot prove it. It is therefore not entered in our data. It is, nevertheless, a memory I cherish—though I suppose it may be one that is in error—like the hawks I saw as a child in New York City.

There is another female, Troff, of whom I am inordinately fond but who certainly has no fealty to me. She is a successful mother and often hangs out in front of camp with her calf. I have spent a significant portion of my days in her company, watching her live her slow and deliberate life. But although I can say honestly that I love Troff, it is crystal clear that Troff does not harbor even the slightest affection for me, fleeing precipitously whenever I appear. In fact, I suspect that the worst I have ever shocked a whale was the first time I ever got close to her. In 1972 I silently paddled up next to Troff in a kayak as she lay, apparently asleep, in Camp Bay. She seemed to panic utterly (flinching as violently as if she had been kicked) and raced away, swimming flat out while I returned to the beach and watched her from higher ground. She kept going, just plunging along and without pause for three miles until she reached Flechero Bay—the bay next to Camp Bay. When she finally did stop, it was to whirl around and range back and forth, snorting and blowing loudly (so loudly that I could hear her clearly) as if in dread of what might be pursuing her.

But such setbacks are infrequent, and for the most part it is clear that every year the right whales of Península Valdés become braver and bolder toward people and boats. When we first came to Península Valdés most whales appeared to have no interest in boats and did not approach them. No more. Calves particularly are insatiably curious and often persist in following boats around in spite of their mothers' repeated efforts to intervene. It makes for a memorable experience when you have stopped to eat your lunch and a calf the size of an elephant comes over and gently bumps your quietly drifting boat (testing it out, I suppose) and its mother suddenly appears, steaming down on you and, with extraordinary contortions, interposes her own body (which is quite literally the size of a small herd of elephants) between your boat and her calf—in so doing creating the kind of currents and backwash that a large car ferry makes when easing into its slip.

We have learned a great deal about this rarest of the large whale species. We know, for example, that female right whales are creatures of habit and will swim to exactly the same area year after year. We commonly see right whales we know well swim past the same rock they passed on their previous visit, and they often return with their new calves to the same place in which they raised a previous calf.

Once they start having calves we see most adult female right whales returning to the bays of Península Valdés once every three years. Each time they come, they bring a new calf. By far the commonest interval between their calves is three years.[17] Given their low rate of reproduction, it is not surprising that the species is still so rare in spite of the fact that it has enjoyed some protection since 1935, and "full protection" since 1937.

The five-meter-deep water in which mother right whales keep their calves during the first few months of the calves' lives is, as I have mentioned, just deep enough to float the mother. Although she can roll over, the skin on the tips of her tail is often barked off, probably by repeatedly striking the bottom. Five meters is far too shallow for a mother to assume a vertical position, and even if she could somehow roll herself up into a ball she would never have enough room to do a forward somersault. Like a mother bear who withdraws into a narrow niche in a cave when it comes time to give birth and suckle her young, the mother right whale withdraws into narrow waters when her time has come. In its niche the bear is unapproachable except from the front, where its assailant faces an impregnable wall of bared teeth and long claws. As it happens, there are hundreds of whale-sized underwater niches in the eroded hardpan along the shores of Península Valdés, sea caves without roofs looking like perfect whale-sized ferry slips into which a right whale might back and thus gain protection from any attack from either side, bottom, top, or rear. However they never go into these places, which is not surprising since the front of a right whale is a toothless mouth, and their flippers are not equipped with menacing claws. Right whales defend themselves with their tails, which they sweep sideways presumably with stunning effect. In this sense they are like the "undefended" brontosaurus now believed to have fought off attackers by sweeping them off their feet with its massive tail—maybe even breaking or disjointing limbs in the process. So apparently it's an old trick: Tail Fighting—an ancient martial art taught in an ancient exclusive school, one that is steeped in tradition, but where you must be to the manor born: only pupils possessed of enormous tails need apply.

You cannot cripple an opponent with a blow from your tail in a confined space; you have to have sufficient room to swing it enough to get it up to speed if you are going to store enough energy in it for a truly crippling blow. Besides, imagine how painful and possibly disabling it would be to hit the rock wall with your tail if at the last moment your attacker dodged out of the way. No; the places chosen by mother right whales to defend their calves are ideal for that purpose—not sea caves but shallow water with soft, sandy bottoms and loads of room on every side from which to launch cataclysmic haymakers. When you think of what a lateral slash from the tail of a right whale might do, it gives you a soberingly fresh understanding of a motion often made by quiescent right whales. When approached by anything—a boat, a swimmer, another right whale, or a killer whale—they often flex their bodies laterally, holding the tail cocked for several seconds. It is an obvious threat display—readiness for a fight—like a person assuming a karate stance. Fortunately for unenlightened intruders like us it is a threat that right whales seem never yet to have carried out against humans. I suspect that if they did it would kill a diver instantly and if it didn't break him or her in two would, at the least, break every large bone in their bodies. A friend of mine once saw a large adult male killer whale about thirty feet long attacking a subadult right whale in shallow water. The subadult was lying at the surface in a submissive posture, its body motionless. The killer whale swam across its flipper, whereupon with a single stroke of that flipper the subadult lofted the male cleanly into the air. The entire body, even though it was being pushed broadside through the water, cleared the surface. If this was the blow from a subadult right whale using the flat of its flipper, imagine what the blow from an adult using a lateral slash from its tail might do.

The following story offers an idea of the effect of such a blow. One of the techniques we developed for studying right whales was to plot their exact positions in the bay using a surveyor's theodolite. This only works if you know how high the tide is; and as it turns out, the accuracy with which you know it is what sets the limit on the accuracy with which you can plot the whale's position. We therefore erected a single pole thirty-three feet high made out of 2½-inch steel pipe with its base embedded in a fifty-five gallon drum filled with concrete. At high tide its top was just visible, and at low tide it stood up as tall as a flagpole. It turned out to be perhaps the worst research idea I ever had. One day a mother came steaming along at high tide with her calf, and as they drew near the tide gauge pole the calf began breaching, brushing against one of the guy wires supporting it on its third breach. The mother turned and slashed at the pole with her tail, hitting it about three feet above the point where it entered the barrel—the very point along the pipe which would have been most resistant to displacement and bending, given that the barrel had sunk completely in the mud. The blow from the whale's tail bent the pole into a hairpin form and dislodged the fifty-five gallon drum of concrete, knocking it sideways several feet across the bottom. We launched a boat at once and followed the mother and calf to see if they were all right, but I could see no visible marks of any kind on either, and half an hour later the calf was once again breaching near its mother, and on the next air-flight we saw them calmly together as though nothing had happened. I decided that in order to have been bent so badly, the pipe must be very malleable and decided to test that theory by straightening it using a five-ton truck jack. But the jack broke without making any impression whatsoever on the pipe. It was a dramatic lesson about the power stored in the tail of a whale.

I later learned that some other animals apparently seem to have a good idea of the power in the tail of a right whale. For example, I once flew over a pack of killer whales for three hours as they moved along a line of female right whales and their calves. The killer whales approached each mother and calf in turn, but I never saw an attack. No wonder. What I did see was each mother flex her body, cocking her tail for a blow toward the closest killer whale. The killer whales paused, then left quietly, without further incident. It looked as if the mothers were unconcerned, but apparently that was not the case. As it happened, Katy was at the cliff hut watching a nearby group of mothers as the killer whales passed her. I was overhead in the plane and went on with them, circling above to watch. But after the killer whales and I had left, Katy saw signs of great concern. Several females came together and formed a ring with their heads directed toward its center, thrashing the water into a frenzy with their flukes. I would imagine that had any orca tried to get at a calf, it would probably have been killed outright. The female right whales maintained this star-shaped formation for about forty minutes.

When alone, it might behoove a mother right whale to hole up in a sea cave headfirst, leaving her tail exposed and ready to lash out at any threat. But though I have seen mothers lingering at the mouths of the Península Valdés sea caves, apparently looking them over (and have wondered what was going through their minds), they never get themselves into a tight corner. The closest they come is to move into the shallows—a strategy that leaves the option for lateral slashes wide open.

When they are in the shallows, the mothers spend much of their time sleeping. They float, motionless, at the surface for hours with their backs exposed—sometimes for periods so long their backs become dry. Their breathing rate is greatly suppressed, and when they do breathe, their breaths are very slow and quiet, quite different from "blows" under ordinary circumstances with active whales. The loudest in-air sound right whales make is a nearly pure tone reminiscent of a child bellowing "tooooot" through a mailing tube. Such sounds produce no visible reaction in other whales and several days may elapse between them. Though they're very un-whale-like there's always a whale in the direction from which a toot comes. The best bet seems to be that they're sneezes.

When mother right whales are floating at the surface apparently asleep they fail to close their blowholes tightly and the blowholes leak a bit of air (sometimes you can see a slow stream of bubbles forming in a little pool of water that invariably collects in a crease lying just behind the whales' nostrils). When the whale finally takes a breath, the nostrils may not close completely but remain slightly ajar. When the nostrils aren't opened and closed cleanly, you hear snores—wonderful noises that sound like deep growls (and at night can be very scary).

When they were very young, I was once standing with my children on the beach at Punta Norte photographing individual head markings when a whale began snoring right offshore. At the same moment a pair of large male elephant seals started angrily belching at each other. I looked over at my children to discover that all of them were looking at me, stifling their laughter. When they saw my face they fell in a row backward onto the beach, convulsed with the giggles, and lay rolling around on their backs for most of the next hour making the very rudest and longest snores and elephant seal belches they could manage. I stalked off to a quieter section of the beach trying to keep my departing shoulders from visibly shaking but inwardly cracking up at the exquisite impertinence of this wonderful gaggle of youth.

Even when we had all returned to the car sometime later to warm up and have our sandwiches, someone allowed a latent whale snore to escape. It caught me unprepared. No parent could have been serious under such circumstances. This time I lost control completely, erupting into laughter—which released the flood gates, and we all laughed until we were helpless. I sat in the front seat with my head thrown back, gasping for air, my children writhing around on the backseat in seizures of laughter, fighting for breath and holding their bellies. Although we were parked on a deserted road, at the height of it all an approaching pickup truck slowed to a crawl (undoubtedly to offer us help if we needed it—a local courtesy to stopped vehicles). They stared incredulously at a family helpless with laughter and then drove on. Gringos, gringos locos.

When mothers fall asleep in the shallows, the falling tide lowers them slowly toward the seabed. Often their flippers dig deep into the sand before they wake and move. This leaves obvious flipper impressions which, if the day is calm, survive the falling tides, so that you can later walk out dry-shod to where a whale was sleeping a few hours ago and admire the flipper prints of the mothers. As you stand between them looking around at the vast seeping and draining tide flats, the scale of these marks is an eloquent statement of just how big the mothers are.

Sometimes the mothers linger so long on a falling tide that their bodies are lightly grounded before they wake and move into deeper water. Even so, they move unwillingly, like a person disturbed in a deep sleep. This is another good reason for mothers to choose smooth, sandy bottoms. It wouldn't do to be over a sea floor covered with sharp objects if you occasionally overslept and had partly to drag your body into deeper water. Also, if the bottom had a slight hilliness to it and did not shelve continuously, by the time you woke up you might find that seaward of you there was a spot too shallow for you to pass over comfortably.

It is along the most extensive, most beautiful sandy beaches of the peninsula that long lines of mother right whales stretch out each day, like beads on an invisible chain. If you look at them in the morning, the whole group is stationary, a mother every half mile or so. But look again at lunchtime and you may find that the entire herd has moved, maybe three to six miles. The spacing between mothers is as it was in the morning, but the string of beads has slid along the coast. This is not just because of tidal currents. Even though the bay has prodigious tidal amplitudes, our study area is situated as far from the fierce currents that roar through the entrance as one can get. In our area the alongshore currents are not rapid enough to explain the movements of the mothers' herd. Besides, if you watch for an hour or so you will see that mothers do swim as a group, first one moving, then those adjacent to her, until everyone has progressed a bit down the coast—with their spacing still more or less intact.

This simple observation makes it look as though the mothers are avoiding each other—keeping their distance. But inasmuch as they stay within a half mile of their neighbors it can't be all avoidance—it must mean that they're also at least somewhat attracted to each other. That there is some strong attraction is also evidenced by the fact that mothers interact in twos and threes (and mores). Vicky Rowntree, who has studied this, has found that a common action is for one female to dominate another by putting her tail over the other's back. However there do not seem to be dominance hierarchies among mothers, as the females in a group initiate aggressive approaches toward each other equally often.

During early youth and puberty, young right whales seem to return every year to the area where they were raised. But after a few years, sons go off to live with other males, while daughters keep returning until the year they give birth to their first calf, at about nine years of age. At this point a daughter usually joins her mother's herd.

Although we have studied this species for twenty-four years, we still don't really know much about the life expectancy of right whales; we simply haven't been watching long enough. Scott Kraus of the New England Aquarium, who has been studying right whales in the North Atlantic, recently came across an old news photo of a female right whale taken on the occasion of the killing of her calf—the last right whale killed by whalers in North America. The year was 1935—the year a League of Nations' convention to regulate whaling came into force (it established the principle of protecting right whales but the protection only became significant two years later). This same group of researchers found that they themselves had photographed the same female four times, most recently in 1992. It would not surprise me if they keep seeing her for many years. Because the youngest mother ever encountered in right whales was five[18] at the time her first calf was born, this particular female must have been at least sixty-two years old in 1992.

Although I can thank God that no one has ever killed any of my children, I feel a particular affinity with this whale because I was born in 1935 and have lived through all the long years since her calf was killed. I wonder if in the last sixty years she has remembered her calf and the horror of seeing it murdered while she lay helplessly by. Do whales mourn? If they do, did she mourn for her calf? And if she did, does she still, or has she removed that chapter of her life from her thoughts? Does she remember the world the way it was when there were a fraction as many boats out there as there are now, and when the most powerful outboard motors were as nothing compared to the ones she now dodges, and when sailboats were everywhere? I would envy her if she ever saw a J Boat under sail, or watched the *Bluenose* racing against the *Gertrude Thibault*—for all those boats worked in her waters. Does she yearn for times when the water was cleaner and the sea around her teeming with life, when there was no pollution lurking in what she ate? All these questions are probably irrelevant because their genesis is from the human perspective, but although I have nothing to offer about the ways in which the minds of whales work, I believe emotions to be far older than our species and that it is more likely whales experience them than they do not. I suspect that it is not so much that she does or does not mourn (for those days, for her calf) as it is that such absences leave her life more vacant, more uninhabited. All I can say with certainty about her is that she has been out there, moving forward through the ocean for a very long time and must know more about the changes to the seas of New England during her lifetime and mine than I will ever know. And when she dies, will that perspective die with her? Or is she, even at sixty-two, a relatively young animal surrounded by much more elderly relatives whose perspectives are even older?

I will set aside all these questions and focus on a single much simpler one: I would just like to know how long right whales live. I always hope I will live long enough to find out. Of course if it turns out that right whales live significantly longer than we do, I will probably never know the answer.

I have discovered that when I am filled with hope and hotly trying to answer some question, it is very disquieting to stop and consider that there may indeed be no possibility of finding out the answer—that from the start, my entire quest has been in vain. I have had these feelings about many things I would love to know about whales but have decided to be grateful for the crumbs of truth—the minor insights—that whales deign to drop from time to time in front of scientists like me. The study of whales is a kind of a trial by fire in which one learns eventually (and at a not-inconsiderable cost) that it is enough to be a part of life on earth, rather than trying to control it. I cannot escape the conclusion that when we are trying to figure out how our own expected lifetime of seventy-five years relates to the 4.6 billion years that had to pass before the cooling planet earth could produce life as we know it, we might find it useful to affirm to ourselves that it is enough to be a part of the process rather than to continue our mad pursuit to become its ultimate beneficiary.

There is an interesting overall pattern to the way right whales distribute themselves in the bays. It is the females with calves who are at the center of wintering herds. Because they're bigger than the others,[19] females can help themselves to the best areas and kick everyone else out, which is just what they seem to do. The characteristics of a "best area" seem to be those I have just mentioned—a long beach, protected from the full force of storm waves, with a gently sloping sand bottom.

Surrounding the central core of mothers (central corps of mothers?) is an area in which adult males are common, some of whom drift in and out among the females from time to time. The females consort with each other and with females that don't have calves this year. Much of the behavior appears to be attempts at mating, but some of it is directed at sexually immature females. We have also seen sex-role reversals (where females take on the male role and vice versa), so it is clear that there is much more than procreation at stake. This area also includes scattered subadults—the adolescents. They are on the fringes of the band. Subadults are my favorites. They appear to be the bravest and most adventurous whales—the ones that approach boats and swimmers most closely.

Adults mostly ignore subadults. (We used to call subadults "The Inner Circle of Outcasts.") Subadults seem bored and ready for any kind of diversion, which is probably why they hang around people when they encounter them. It is subadults, also, that play with sea lions, and unsurprisingly, it is subadult sea lions that play with the subadult right whales.

As this is a book about whales, I've little chance to write about sea lions, but given what fertile examples of social values they provide I cannot be expected to resist all the time. Measured by how close they will approach swimmers and boats, the biggest cowards are the biggest sea lions—the fully mature males. After them come adult females, followed by the bravest of all—the subadults, which come right up to a swimmer or a boat and nose around, often nibbling gently at things that protrude, like oars or flippers. The very large and very macho males have huge, muscular bodies, aggressive temperaments, and enormous teeth. Yet they appear to be cowards. It's a little like human beings: those who arm themselves to the teeth are usually the most afraid—the most recreant, really—individuals for whom guns act more to compensate for the insecurity of their bearers than to protect the thing its bearers suppose themselves to be defending. I mean . . . Rambo? Brave? Does a man who needs to strap on a weapon to look impressive symbolize bravery? If before he sallied forth to investigate noises in the night my father strapped on a gun would I think him brave? Scared stiff, maybe, but brave? Give me a break. I admire the true bravery of a mother who investigates such noises unarmed, and I consider truly brave the man who confronts danger with enough self-confidence to believe that he can deal with the situation without a gun and without violence, and who, if he finds that he cannot, is unafraid to die, unarmed, defending *that* principle.

Because they are so brave, subadult whales are easy to swim with and observe underwater. But when your main interest is studying whales, swimming with them, though terribly impressive and perhaps the ultimate wild world thrill, is not all that enlightening. This is simply because as soon as it sees you, a whale stops whatever normal behavior it was involved in and either swims off or focuses all its attention on you. After that all you see is a whale circling you, coming in close to look you over, and then withdrawing faster than you can follow.

However, swimming with a whale can also offer valuable insights, for example, by allowing you to make observations of its overall health—something that usually cannot be otherwise observed benignly. (Swimming with whales is in most countries against the law [the USA is such a place] so if you wish to employ this technique in your work, you will need a special permit to do so.) Many adult whales exhibit no obvious curiosity toward humans in the water, so their condition is hard to assess. But subadults are different. They are friendly and curious and when they come across a swimmer they may hang around for hours. Sometimes when approaching divers they make repeated passes over them. It's an impressive moment if you're working underwater when an animal the size of a cloud temporarily blocks out the sun as it eases overhead, missing you by about a yard.

Getting any right whale to let you approach closely takes a while. But when one does so, it comes right up to look you up and down. Some people find it difficult to stand their ground and return a whale's close inspection (it took me a while to get used to doing so), but if you do stay put, you find that the whale remains courteous to the end. I think that the highest compliment a whale ever paid me was when I swam to within about a yard of the eye of a sleeping mother right whale. After about a minute, she opened her eye, looked me up and down for a few moments—her eye swiveling freely and broadly in its socket—breathed out in what seemed almost a sigh, closed her eye again and stayed put. I was in full view of her, and at point-blank range, yet she didn't move. She seemed to have the attitude: "Well, when you've seen one of these, you've seen them all." I was absolutely delighted. Sure, it wasn't what you'd call effusively friendly but at least it wasn't as unfriendly as Troff appeared to be when she fled into Flechero Bay the one time I approached her in a kayak.

It was in 1990, the twenty-first year of our study, that a mother closed her eye in my presence. It is one of the incidents that causes me to suspect that right whales may be becoming habituated to people. When we first maneuvered boats near right whales in 1970, they seemed less friendly than they do now. In 1971 I watched a right whale slam its head on the water repeatedly as it faced a diver at close range—a sure sign of aggression in toothed whales and something that certainly looked like aggression to me in that particular right whale. A few days later a calf breached onto a diver who was filming it, cracking two of his ribs and knocking the wind out of him. However, nothing like either of these incidents has ever happened to us since.

Overfriendliness seems more the norm now than aggression. Whales seem quicker to overcome their initial caution about boats, and when they do they start taking greater and greater liberties. We are still unsure about what their stopping point will eventually be, so from time to time we try to see how far things have progressed. In 1990 we let a whale that was playing with our boat continue to do so for a long time, to see how far it would go. The game started out calmly enough but things got pretty wild toward the end. For about forty-five minutes this subadult made long, slow circles under the boat, getting about an inch closer to us with each pass. At first its passes alternated with those of a chum who was with it. But after a while the chum appeared to lose interest. It pulled away a couple of whale lengths where it lay, patiently, apparently waiting for its friend to finish whatever it was doing and rejoin it. But the friend just kept on, getting closer and closer to our boat with each pass until finally it held its tail at right angles to the surface and hooked the boat with it, drawing us rather violently sideways through the water. The action appeared to be entirely deliberate, and though all of us wanted to keep going to see where things might end, we had left the water-proof cases for our tape recorders and cameras behind and would have lost everything including data, cameras, and pictures had the whale swamped or flipped the boat. So we got out our oars and paddled quietly away, started the outboard, and idled out of reach. The two whales rejoined each other and continued on their way.

On the same day as this incident, photographer Flip Nicklin was off in a different part of the bay swimming with a whale he was filming when it began making slow passes by him while rubbing its body along his (like a cat rubbing against your leg). When the tail came along, the whale deliberately used the flat of it to push Flip slowly underwater. Having experienced this on three passes, Flip decided this was not a great game and set off to rejoin the boat (he later told me he wasn't so sure he wanted to have his body clamped under the right whale's flipper and held underwater the way mothers punish their babies when they're naughty). But the whale seemed to be anxious not to lose its new companion and kept interposing its body between Flip and the Zodiac. It was only through the boatman's acting quickly to maneuver within Flip's reach while the whale was on the backside of its circle that Flip was able to get back to his boat. Even then he had to be quick, and as he hiked himself onto the pontoon, the whale swirled just beneath his feet, brushing against his flippers with its body. In Argentina there are strict laws protecting whales from harassment by people. Under circumstances like the ones Flip and I experienced that day, one might well ask, just who is harassing whom?

It is not just in Argentina that there is great concern about boats harassing whales. It makes groups of whale-watchers furious to see Sunday-afternoon boaters in their sports fishing palaces harassing some whale (and those who happen to know that in the United States there's a ten thousand dollar fine for doing it find themselves hoping the offender will get caught). But such boaters are probably the exception: the vast majority of people who are interested in taking their boats close to whales seem fairly cautious around them.

Over many years we have studied the structure and movements of the herd in our corner of the bay. It appears to be a single unit centered on females with calves, though it is not just these females that move during the day, but the whole herd of whales. It wanders back and forth with the females, covering up to ten or twelve miles in a day. The herd doesn't take up station at just any old point along the shore of a bay but oscillates back and forth along a fixed and relatively small stretch of the coastline. This stretch is of a different length depending on the bay, but once established the beat remains pretty much the same for years. There is something that these segments of coasts have in common; they are bounded at each end by the same kind of natural boundaries—points of land, that is, headlands, projecting out from the general contour of the coast.

The bounding points are seldom passed by the herd. Instead, the headlands almost invariably turn the whales back. Occasionally, one or two individuals may pass beyond them, but the rest of the herd does not and in a few hours the individuals that did pass come back to the same side of the point the herd is on. This strange behavior makes sense when one considers the underlying acoustics. Points of land cast underwater acoustic shadows, making it unlikely that a whale on one side of such a point would be able to hear companions close to shore on the other side. If they are to remain in contact, the whales must be on the same side of the point.

Bearing in mind that many right whales live close in against the coast, a long beach that is straight or concave will allow all the whales scattered along it to hear each other. But a convex shoreline will not. Because of the bulging land that gets in the way, animals that are right up against the beach but at opposite ends of it will be unable to hear each other. It is interesting in this regard that the beaches preferred by right whales are straight or concave. Though you may see herds passing them, you simply don't see herds lingering along convex beaches. This is true both in Argentina and in the South African bays where I have also seen right whales.

These rather simple observations provide at least some evidence in support of the theory that right whales use sound as a means of staying together in herds. Not that I suspect it is surprising to anyone to hear that whales may communicate using sound—but, believe me, it's comforting to have any evidence at all to support that commonly held belief.

If whales can communicate, what do they communicate to us? That depends on who you ask. Many people seem to wish to believe that whales are communicating with them at the deepest levels. But since the dawn of human history we have always greeted whales not by communicating with them but by killing them. This is particularly pertinent to the discussion of right whales because I suspect it is via this species that humans learned to kill baleen whales.

Although it is not known for sure which species of baleen whale humans first hunted, it seems likely that it was the right whale. Right whales frequently come so close to shore that it would be possible to strike them with a hand-thrown harpoon from the complete safety of a beach. If in an attempt to tether the whale, the harpoon were attached by a rope to, say, a driftwood log on the beach, the would-be whalers would have soon discovered that the right whale not only dragged all but the very largest logs off the beach but through the water as well until the whale exhausted itself. (It is easy to see how, by this means, the harpoon and drogue might have been invented.) If the whale died it might well have washed up farther down the coast, to be later found and the meat retrieved. It wouldn't take much of a step in imagination to sally forth in a boat with a spear (later a "lance") in order to finish off a wounded and nearly dead whale—perhaps as a means of marking it as one's own and thus keeping other competitors from claiming it; perhaps as a means of looking like a hero to watchers from a distant beach—a hero who has slain a monster—when in fact what one was really doing was stabbing an all-but-dead whale (who knows, perhaps even an already dead one—after all, whaling has always brought out the very best in everyone).

The reason right whales are so rare now is that during the nineteenth and early twentieth centuries they were brought close to extinction by whalers. Human beings have been the principal cause of the extinction of a minimum of seven hundred known species of animals and plants since 1600.[20] This includes species like the passenger pigeon—a dove that looked very like today's still-abundant mourning doves, only slightly larger and redder in hue. One hundred and fifty years ago passenger pigeons, like right whales, were very numerous. In fact they were the most numerous birds on the North American continent. Audubon described flocks of them darkening the sun in the lower Mississippi valley for periods of up to three days as they migrated past. When they established a roost for the night, their weight broke limbs off trees, which as they fell sometimes killed hundreds of birds perched on lower branches. People came to such roosts and shot into the trees just to see how many birds they could kill with one shot. The record was seventy-one pigeons killed with two bullets—not with a shotgun blast but just two rifle balls. The market hunters, who did use shotguns (as well as nets), sometimes killed many hundreds of passenger pigeons with one blast.

The last passenger pigeon, a female, died in the Chicago Zoo in 1914. She was thirty-five years old (Mozart was also thirty-five when he died). In less than a normal human lifetime, she had become the last of her kind and the last of what some biologists suppose to have been the most numerous warm-blooded animal species ever destroyed by *Homo sapiens* (the *thinking ape*).

We have also brought to extinction species that were very rare when we first encountered them: the Norfolk Island robin, for example, was rendered extinct by the unstinting efforts of a single individual—not *Homo sapiens* this time, but the lighthouse keeper's cat.

But in recent years we have become more proficient with extinctions. E. O. Wilson has estimated that as we destroy the rain forests, we are now bringing to extinction about twenty-seven thousand species each year, that is, seventy-four a day, or three every hour. Thus, human activity has increased extinctions by between one thousand and ten thousand times the estimated prehuman "background" extinction rate of one species per million per year. (The reason the calculated rates differ between one thousand and ten thousand times is because the estimates of how many species there are on earth differ by a factor of ten.)

Of all the thousands of animal species whose lives we have ended, there is not one which had a worldwide distribution when we started hunting it. We have only brought to extinction species whose distribution was limited: to an island, an archipelago, or sometimes, like the passenger pigeon, a continent (or, like the woolly mammoth, to two continents). As far as we know, no truly worldwide species has ever been lost owing to over-hunting by humans. The closest we have come to that new benchmark of madness is with the right whale. And we came vanishingly close.

When we started hunting them, right whales numbered about 80,000. They were abundant off the eastern and western coasts of every continent, including off the antarctic coast. It has been estimated that by 1850, almost two hundred thousand right whales had been killed by humans worldwide. At that time the species was considered commercially extinct. Even so, it was not until 1937, eighty-seven years later, that they were afforded any significant protection. What they got in 1937 was called "international" protection but enforcement was (and is) all but nonexistent and thousands have been killed and poached since then.

For example, even though the Soviet Union signed a protocol in 1947 protecting the critically endangered right whales, a Soviet factory ship while traveling between its home port in the Black Sea and the Antarctic Ocean during the 1960s killed right whales off Tristan da Cunha during a period when the inhabitants of that utterly isolated South Atlantic island had been evacuated due to an eruption of the island's volcano. In one year that they poached right whales off Tristan, unbeknownst to the Russian captain, there was a party of Tristanders on the island investigating with some volcanologists the seismic state of the volcano to see whether it was safe for the islanders to return.

It was the schoolteacher who saw catcher boats shooting whales and drove around the island in a motor skiff to investigate. The administrator for Tristan in those years told me that as he came around a small headland the schoolteacher saw a catcher boat its own length from shore with two harpoons in a female right whale who was wallowing in her own blood. Perceiving that he was being observed the captain of the catcher boat put it full astern, ripping both harpoons out of the female's back, and then steamed rapidly toward the horizon (where a cloud of diesel smoke announced what the schoolteacher assumed to be the factory ship). The female was still alive but very weak as the schoolteacher drove around her taking photographs. A formal letter of complaint from Tristan da Cunha to the USSR eventually received an apology for the catcher boat having "inadvertently strayed within the territorial waters of Tristan da Cunha." Every nation recognizes a three-mile limit, the vast majority recognize a twelve-mile limit, and most recognize a two-hundred mile Exclusive Economic Zone. All of those distances are quite a bit more than fifty meters from the coast. (For a discussion of recent revelations by the Russians about whaling under the Soviet Union see "Note Added in Proof" at the end of chapter 7.)

The particularly brutal destruction of right whales by the Soviets also affected right whales in the Península Valdés population. Several have terrible wounds, now healed, on their backs that are of the right size, form, and placement to have been made by harpoons. In the case of one of our whales, its spinal column is hideously deformed. In another, the wound has left a depression in the back large enough for a person to lie in. These old wounds become homes for huge colonies of parasitic cyamids (whale lice) which, because they consume the whales' skin, must be incredibly irritating to them.

There are several good reasons to suspect that the wounds in the whales were caused by harpoons: 1) they are near the places a harpooner tries to hit any whale—at the base of the skull or high on the back; 2) they have a central area of devastation (presumably caused by the head of the harpoon) with radiating gouges coming out from it (presumably the tines of the harpoon); 3) there is a single, much longer groove (presumably from the shaft of the harpoon) leading from behind into the center of the wound (harpooners usually approach whales from behind); 4) the blubber of right whales is harder than that of species which modern harpooners are used to hunting. The result is that you cannot shoot a right whale at the same low angle which you can shoot, say, a sei whale without the harpoon skipping off the right whale's back. The old whalers knew that and shot at higher angles (i.e., they only shot when closer to the whale), but because most modern harpooners haven't had experience in shooting right whales, they probably shoot at distances that are too great; 5) as mentioned earlier, we know that some of the Península Valdés right whales swim all the way to Tristan da Cunha.

By 1937 right whales were probably extinct in the eastern North Atlantic and eastern North Pacific (they may still be extinct or nearly so in those areas) and were down to a few dozen or a few hundred individuals in all other areas of their former range. Thus it is that first the passenger pigeon and now the right whale offer us the chance to see for ourselves just how entirely irrational we can be, even when our actions are considered acceptable by the overwhelming majority of "sane" and "normal" people. It is this sad history which made it noteworthy when my friend Ray Gilmore reported seeing right whales along the coast of Península Valdés in 1969.

When illustrating an article about whales, picture editors look for photographs that "read whale," by which they mean images that the lay reader will immediately recognize as being pictures of whales. If they have no underwater photograph, the best picture is usually a picture of a whale's tail—probably the whale's most distinctive feature. The tail of a whale is a singular structure and is used by whales not just for locomotion but for a variety of other purposes. In right whales, one of the most unexpected uses is as a sail. The whale holds its tail smartly up in a strong breeze for as long as twenty minutes at a time, so that the whale's body is pushed by the wind through the water. Sailing bouts may last for hours, but they only occur during winds of between nine and nineteen miles per hour. In lighter or stronger winds right whales do not attempt to sail. Sailing seems like a very good way for an animal to cruise about the ocean. Some jellyfish do it, and so do albatrosses (though as I have mentioned theirs is a very fancy form of three-dimensional sailing called dynamic soaring). All of the behavior that accompanies sailing in right whales is the kind of play behavior one sees between mothers and calves—it looks as though right whales do not use sailing to get around, but only as a diversion, a game.

Although they invented the wheel, it is said that the Incas used it only in toys, and never in so far as is known for practical things like carrying heavy loads over their long and exquisitely paved mountain highways. Before I saw my first whale I had often wondered why more animals don't use sailing to assist them in making their long passages. It seems an ideal means of going long distances—one simply sets the sails and steers. There is no need to expend any other energy. Just the thing for an animal like a whale, which migrates for thousands of kilometers without being able to refuel. How strange that when at last we encounter this behavior in mammals that it should be whales that perform it, but only in play. Incas, these whales.

It is curious that though tail sailing is not used for serious travel whales may use another means of extracting motive power from the wind. Waves are generated by wind, and whales appear able to use the energy in waves to assist propulsion. Whalers have traditionally cut off the fluke tips of every dead whale, claiming that during the time the catcher boat is off looking for more whales to kill the dead body will swim for miles unless the tail is cropped, often causing it to be lost (in the present day, corpses are marked with a radio beacon to assist in their recovery). Biologists traditionally pooh-poohed this as whalers' superstitions until recently when it has been shown mathematically that propulsive forces are indeed generated by ocean waves on the tails of whales. It appears to be a very significant assist.[21]

There are other things that right whales do with their tails besides sailing. One of the most impressive of these is lobtailing: striking the water with the tail to make a loud sound. This is a display of strength as well as a means used by the whale to signal to other whales. In order to lobtail, a whale has to stand on its head and hold the weight of its tail aloft (half a ton or more depending on how much of it is out of water) by sculling with its flippers (a whale's equivalent of arms). Some whales seem to get carried away and will smack the water up to a hundred times in a row, switching to their flippers and back to their tails, one form of water slapping melding into the other.

Flippering, lobtailing, and breaching are all ways of making a noise, and all seem to be used as a means of signaling to other whales. This seems to be one of their principal serious purposes. However, I have also wondered whether, when they are suspended upside down like that, or lying on their sides flippering, whales may not find it entertaining to see crystalline showers of backlit spray falling onto the water's surface. To see if this is so we note whether more strikes are made in succession on sunny rather than dull days or whether most blows are directed at preferred angles in relation to the sun. The data is still in its early stages. We must not expect too much, however, for even if whales do have preferred angles and weathers such preferences wouldn't prove the theory—though it *would* make it more beguiling.

Of course the ultimate way that whales have of making a disturbance at the surface is by breaching—a whale leaping from the sea in one vital column to crash back amidst an eruption of water and foam, like an iceberg calving from the face of a glacier. Of all the things animals have ever done, now or in the prehistoric past, I suppose that this display of pure force must outrank everything else. To witness any greater show than this I suspect that one must leave the animal kingdom and seek out the company of avalanches, storms, volcanos, or earthquakes. Breaching by right whales is not done for any single purpose but serves many functions: as a social display; as a display of strength; as a ritualized escape during courtship; as play between mothers and calves—during the excitement of which the calf gets much farther from its mother's side than normal, experiencing independence for the first time; as a challenge to other right whales; as a threat (e.g., chasing off porpoises); as just plain exercise; as a means of removing external parasites; as a means of creating a sound announcing the whereabouts of one whale to the next; and even, perhaps, for some unexpected functions like stunning shoals of small fish that otherwise could escape the right whales' slow jaws.[22] All species of large whales appear to breach, though some do so more often than others. (Fin whales breach very seldom, whereas for humpbacks and right whales breaching is a common activity.) The function of breaching has not been systematically studied in most other whale species so we don't know why they do it. However, it seems a good bet that breaching in other species is done for reasons similar to those for which right whales employ it.

Sometimes a right whale fails to hold its tail up smartly to catch the breeze effectively and instead lets it fall over limply until one tip trails in the water. This kind of tailing is done in any wind, even flat calms—in fact, particularly in flat calms. It is during calms that whales appear to sleep, and from the whale's low rate of breathing, its completely relaxed posture, its incompletely closed nostrils, snoring sounds, and subdued behavior, we believe that whales that hold their tails up in this careless manner are asleep.

When asleep, right whales often float high in the water with part of their backs exposed and their bodies on an even keel. But there are occasional head-heavy individuals who slowly pitch forward when apparently asleep until they are tilted so nearly vertically that their tails rather than their backs are in the air. Because they are asleep, however, the tail is completely relaxed, rather than being smartly held aloft to the wind the way it is when the wind is blowing and the same whale is sailing.

However, most right whales that have retained enough air to be sleeping at the surface appear to sleep on an even keel. (Some right whales apparently expel the air from their lungs when they sleep so that they tumble slowly to the bottom. From our plane we have seen them far underwater lying upside down or on their sides or at some oblique angle to the bottom for long periods—postures from which they rouse very slowly to return to the surface for air and then to fall slowly back down to the bottom, striking very gently in their original or some other equally indolent position, apparently asleep.)

Right whales appear to be active not just in the daylight but at night as well. Mornings are the favored times for sleeping. On a calm morning in Patagonia you can see many whales asleep, scattered around the bay like drifting crocodiles, with the sounds of their snores filling the air. When the morning is especially calm and sunny, the whales' backs get dried out in the sun and become sunburned. It is sunburn on a grand scale, followed by equally impressive peeling of skin—by the square meter. The peeling skin provides a food resource for two local species of gulls, the brown-hooded gull and the kelp gull.[23]

The kelp gull (which looks almost identical to the northern hemisphere lesser black-backed gull[24]) is a large species and has recently developed an unfortunate habit in some of the areas of Península Valdés populated by whales that appears to drive right whales frantic. Instead of limiting themselves to feeding on the loose sloughing skin caused by sunburn, kelp gulls gouge out pieces of live skin, creating crater-shaped wounds in the whales' backs.

Brown-hooded gulls don't do this, nor have kelp gulls always done so. This behavior first appeared in Golfo San José in the late 1970s but it has spread rapidly through the gull population until it is now a major source of harassment to the whales in San José, who writhe and twist to escape their tormentors. During the past twenty-four years of our study we have seen major, inexplicable shifts in the locations of two of the principal concentrations of the right whales at Península Valdés. It is not impossible that the gulls are a significant factor—perhaps causing the whales to shift away from areas where the populations of gulls have learned whale gouging into areas where the gulls haven't yet learned this trick (or where fewer know about it).

I can honestly say that with the exception of Troff's reaction to my kayak I have never seen anything that causes right whales such obvious disturbance as an attack by gulls; not killer whales, not helicopters, not planes, not boats, not divers, not other aggressive whales, not nearby shelling from the military—until recently there were annual military exercises in the middle of the right whale breeding ground in Golfo San José (the right whale breeding ground in South Africa is threatened by the construction of a missile-launching facility on one of the major calf-rearing beaches). But none of these things seem to bother right whales as much as gulls. They seem utterly defeated by gulls. Gulls that are really good at whale gouging fly along casually above their victim, dropping down for a bite whenever the whale surfaces, mercilessly keeping up their attack for long periods until the whale appears to be frantic, plunging along at the surface and diving, apparently before it has gotten a proper breath. However, in shallow water the whales aren't able to dive out of the gulls' sight in order to get some respite from the attacks, and this results in more merciless pursuit and what appear to be even more frantic efforts to escape.

It is also interesting to note that right whales have moved in increasing numbers into that very area of Golfo Nuevo where boat traffic is the densest. They have done this in spite of the fact that the bay they are leaving, Golfo San José, is now a right whale sanctuary where boating with whales is by scientific permit only, and where the whales are, as a result, very nearly undisturbed by boats. Not only have right whales shifted into the area of greatest boat traffic but also into the area of greatest whale-watching activity. Surprisingly, the whale-watch industry was set up and working actively before the whales moved into its area in large numbers. The industry now employs at least six boats at any given time, each of which daily makes several trips out to view the whales. It would be interesting to find out whether the whales seek out these unaggressive boats, which slow up and stop near them, because the gulls don't molest whales when there's a boat nearby.

If kelp gulls ultimately chase the right whales away from Península Valdés, the damage they do, though it may ultimately rob Península Valdés of a very lucrative whale-watch industry, should not last forever. I would expect that the whales would return to the area once all the gulls who had learned to feed in this way had died out, taking their pernicious knowledge with them. But since kelp gulls have life expectancies of about fifteen years[25] (some probably live much longer), if the whales ever do leave altogether it will be a long time in human terms before the last of the knowledgeable gulls has died off and the whales can safely return to their former haunts.

When we started our study of right whales, I would never have imagined that it might lead to such strange conclusions as the idea that gulls may be causing right whales to shift their breeding grounds periodically, and who can say that they may even be responsible for the redistribution of this species into new wintering areas around the world. One of the downfalls of right whales has been that they kept returning to their bays for several years in a row, even when there were whalers there killing them. It may seem strange that by driving whales from their chosen bays gulls may achieve what the whalers could not. However, a whaler bothers a whale only once, and the disturbance is usually fatal, offering the whale no chance to learn, whereas a gull pursues whales repeatedly, offering them a chance to avoid them.

There is, I believe, one other probable reason for the great shifts in distribution of right whales—the noise, vessel traffic, and pollution found in large harbors. Both we and right whales seek out the most sheltered coastal waters—we for harbors, right whales for their wintering grounds. This puts right whales in direct competition with people. In addition to Península Valdés there are still significant populations of right whales in Australia and South Africa—areas in which right whales were formerly abundant enough to support local whaling operations. In Argentina, Golfo Nuevo vessel traffic has increased at least tenfold in the last twenty years, but Argentina has strict laws protecting right whales, and in the two main harbors of Golfo Nuevo vessel traffic is especially benign toward them. Here the whales have become part of the lives of the local citizens, carrying out their normal behaviors a few yards from the main swimming and boating beach or cavorting with each other next to or even under the town dock.

One of the harbors in Golfo Nuevo, Puerto Pirámides, is seldom visited by ships. It is used extensively, however, by small boats. Most of the local boat operators are whale-watch captains who maneuver carefully near whales. Whale watching is the town's main industry, and visiting boaters are quickly informed about the need to leave right whales alone. The South African situation suggests that what keeps right whales away from some of their former haunts is lots of human activity and heavy vessel traffic. But the evidence in Argentina suggests that if vessels move slowly and cautiously among right whales, the whales can coexist peacefully with people.

I look forward to an enlightened world where right whales will slowly return to their former haunts in bays such as the Chesapeake and Delaware. Is such a scenario reasonable? It is not out of the question, I think, although to do so these whales will first have to survive the numerous other real dangers that arise from living close to centers of high human population such as oil spills, accidental entanglement in fishing gear, and being hit by passing vessel traffic that never even notices them.

As I have mentioned, the New England population of right whales is among the rarest of the remaining right whale populations, with current estimates putting their numbers at 300 to 350.[26] Scott Kraus has found that 57 percent of the New England right whales bear scars or other evidence on their bodies from entanglement in fishing gear, and that of twenty-five known right whale mortalities in New England waters, 32 percent were clearly caused by collisions or entanglement. Animals hit by a large ship can be cut to pieces by its propeller, and the corpses of right whales killed by ships are presumably seldom found, so Kraus's findings should be considered the lowest number of casualties. Clearly, some change is needed if right whales that live near people are to have much chance of survival. As I have mentioned, the centers of right whale concentration are often fairly predictable, and one change that could benefit them would be to adjust speed limits or move shipping lanes in areas where ships pass directly through right whale concentrations. Though no shipping lane has yet been moved, the dredging vessels used near Brunswick and St. Mary's Bay in Georgia and near Jacksonville, Florida, are now required to slow down to less than five miles per hour if a daily aerial census finds right whales within ten miles of where the vessels are working. The importance of this kind of law was underscored when an eighty-five-foot Coast Guard boat traveling at about fifteen knots accidentally struck and killed a right whale calf in that same area in 1993.

The final and most interesting form of tailing behavior which we have discovered is also the most curious. We have seen this strange behavior only in right whales, but other species may also perform it. In order to understand what its purpose is, it is important to know about right whale mating techniques. While there are several whale species in which females mate with just one male, male and female right whales form no obvious pair bond (mating being promiscuous and both males and females having several sexual partners in the same day).

Because females spend so much time in shallow water, there is usually not enough water under their keels for a male to get beneath them to mate. Indeed, one of the obvious strategies of females who wish to avoid males who are clasping them from underneath is to swim into shallow water and scrape the male off on the bottom. But I have seen a female in fairly shallow water, under which a male had managed to squeeze himself, flex her back dramatically so that her head and tail were lifted way out of the water. The result was, of course, that suddenly there were many tons of the female unsupported by the water, and these many tons came crushing down on top of the male. He left.

But there is another technique that some females use to avoid males which is subtler and requires skill and balance. Troff is a specialist in this technique. She uses it whenever she is being pursued by a single male. Instead of lying belly-up (the usual method of avoidance) she puts her tail in the air, holding it there for minutes at a time. In order for the male to get his body into mating position with hers, he must put his tail into the air alongside hers. But when he does so, his propeller (his tail) is out of the water, and he can't swim. He has to use his flippers to drag his whole body, held in a vertical, head-downward posture, around her as he tries to achieve a proper alignment with her. Meanwhile, she can easily keep avoiding him just by revolving slowly about her own long axis, keeping her back to him and her ventral slit just out of his reach. When she needs to breathe she slips off to one side and grabs a few breaths while he is trying to get back underwater and get his body in a horizontal position beneath her. And just as he does so she rolls forward and raises her tail into the air once again. He is always just a bit behind in this game, and one watches with fascination what appear to be manifestations of frustration in males who try, always unsuccessfully, to overcome this avoidance strategy of Troff and the other females who use it.

Although I have been describing attempts by one male to mate with a female, courtship and mating groups usually contain several males. Of all the behaviors at Península Valdés which involve three or more right whales, courtship is the most common.

In right whales, mating usually involves one or two females being pursued by several males who consort together in a group. There's a lot of rolling around, most of which appears to be efforts by the female to escape unwanted matings. The normal posture for mating is belly-to-belly, with the female on an even keel and the male upside down beneath her, holding his breath. Copulation attempts go on for hours but actual intromission appears to last only a few seconds.

Most of the time females are uncooperative with males who attempt to mate with them, and since they are slightly larger than males they can easily avoid mating attempts by single males. To males, overcoming this fact is the obvious main advantage of forming in groups when pursuing females; even though they have to share a female with other males, they have at least some chance of mating with a female if they are part of a group. Because each gets more chances to mate by cooperating with other males than he gets by competing with them, it is obviously of greater advantage to males to cooperate.

The basic mating unit appears to be a group of males that stays together for periods of at least six weeks. We aren't sure that they don't stay together much longer, nor are we sure how they are related or how they get together in the first place. However, these are questions we are studying. During the season they move from one female to another along chains of females with calves—female groups that linger in the same shallow-water areas.

The usual technique used by a female right whale to avoid unwanted matings is to lie belly-up at the surface so that her ventral groove is inaccessible to the male or males. To get around this, males working in groups of three or more array themselves around the female in a particular configuration: a male on each side of her, patiently waiting, with the third beneath her, lying upside down, holding his breath for prodigious lengths of time, also awaiting the moment when she begins to roll over in an attempt to get her blowholes in the air in order to take a breath. When she succeeds, her ventral groove will be rotated far enough toward him so that he may be able to mate with her while she is breathing. Since she must roll either to the left or right one of the other males is bound to get a better chance at her as she starts her roll. Males may have to wait for up to twenty-five minutes, but the moment the female stirs, each flanking male grabs a quick breath and dives, pushing and shoving somewhat, each obviously trying to be the one to mate. If there are three or more males they can virtually be assured that one of them will get a chance to mate every few times she rolls to breathe.

We assume that every time a male succeeds in mating with the female he can improve his chances of having his sperm fertilize her egg if he can produce enough sperm to wash out the sperm of the male who has mated with her just before him, replacing it with his own. The size of the testes of male right whales supports this assumption. Although the blue whale is the most massive animal that has ever lived, the testes of a male blue whale are not correspondingly the largest. A blue whale's testes weigh about seventy kilograms (about 150 pounds), while the testes of the much smaller right whale males weigh up to one metric ton, that is, 2,200 pounds—probably the largest testes ever to appear on earth. What could possibly be the importance of having such an extraordinarily large sperm-producing capacity? Presumably it is because right whales have a multiple-male mating system and the males are in sperm competition with each other—other things being equal, the one who gets the most sperm into the female will have the best chance of being the father of her calf.

Once males of any species are in extreme sperm competition, evolution will favor males with larger testes. The one-ton testes of the right whale indicate just how far this process can go. In courtship and mating bouts that stretch out over several hours, the best strategy for a male is probably to be the last to mate with a female, because then his sperm will be the most numerous in her. However, if he waits too long she may race off and escape the group before he can mate with her at all, or sperm from an earlier mating may already have had too much of a head start in reaching her single egg and fusing with it for the sperm of the male who is biding his time to stand any real chance. It must be a delicate strategy of timing.

The mating system of a species is a strong determinant of much of that species' behavior. The multiple-male mating system of right whales dictates many of the features of the social structure of this species. One such example concerns a peculiar feature of the schedule on which mature females visit Península Valdés: we often see females at Península Valdés in the year following the birth of their calves. However in the year before the birth of their second, third, fourth . . . calves we seldom see them.[27]

The reason this is surprising is that if, as is generally assumed to be the case, the length of their gestation period is one year, in order to mate, female right whales should be showing up at Península Valdés the year before they return with a newborn calf. Of course it is possible that the females are doing some of their mating elsewhere. However, if that were the case it would mean the many matings we see at Valdés do not result in impregnation of the females. I can think of no reason that males who were wasting their efforts this way would not have been replaced by natural selection long ago. They would have lost out to males who sought out impregnable females where they *were* hanging out and who spent their energies mating with them. It is a real mystery that we so seldom see females in the years before they give birth. However, as I have said, mating systems of species strongly affect their behavior, and I think we will solve the mystery by knowing a bit more about the right whales' mating system.

Even though females are bigger than males, they are easily overpowered by gangs of males (because so many matings appear to be forced it may be appropriate to refer to these groups of males as "rape gangs"). So if she is going to exert any mate choice at all, a female's best strategy, indeed perhaps her only strategy, is to wait until the male she prefers has mated with her and then leave the area at once, filled with his sperm. That way she will have the greatest chance that he will be the father of her calf.

If females do leave the area right after mating with the male of their choice, it could explain why it is that we fail to see females at Península Valdés the year before they give birth. We can only afford to fly a few aerial censuses each season (in recent years only one or two), and if females are leaving the area quickly we would be unlikely to see them during what are, of necessity, one or two brief annual census flights.

(This also means that if you are a male right whale participating in a mating group and see evidence that the female you are courting prefers some other male, your best strategy is probably to mate with her quickly, or else you may get no chance at all of being the parent of her offspring.)

I don't mean to leave the impression that females always avoid matings. We sometimes see females actively soliciting matings from males, and then it is the males that avoid the females by rolling belly-up. (Female porpoises are also capable of being very forward. Workers in Shark Bay in western Australia have seen male bottle-nosed dolphin swimming along apparently ignoring a female swimming beneath him stroking his genital area with her tail. The stroking can continue for several minutes.)

There is an interesting aside to this constant strategizing of the sexes: it turns out that by simply looking at the ratio of testes weight to body weight in a group of related species like whales, one can accurately predict what kind of mating system any given species in the group will have.[28] The evolution of large testes is presumably caused principally by the need for a relatively large amount of sperm—which is necessary if whales live in societies in which females mate with several males and where the males are therefore in sperm competition (so-called multiple-male mating systems). If whales have relatively small testes, it is because they have a social system in which a male can be relatively confident he is the only male mating with a given female (called a single-male mating system). Killer whales are an example of the latter. The male has to produce only enough sperm to fertilize the female's egg, not enough to be able to wash out or dilute sperm deposited in her by other males. Although the few species of whales whose social systems have been studied well enough obey these rules, our knowledge of the social systems of most whale species is still too rudimentary to know whether they have single- or multiple-male mating systems.

Primates are a group of closely related species for which the social systems of many species are well understood and for which the ratio of testes size to body weight is also well known. For example, chimpanzees have a multiple-male mating system. When she comes into estrus, a female chimpanzee mates with many males. Although the bodies of chimps are smaller than most human bodies, male chimpanzees have larger testes than we do. Gorillas have a single-male mating system. Once he has fought his way to ownership of a troupe of females, a silver-back male has sole access to females in his group. Even though they are much larger than chimpanzees, male gorillas have testes so small that during a dissection the testes are difficult to locate.

When the ratio is plotted of testes weight to body weight for the thirty-three primate species for which both the social systems and these ratios are known, one gets a cloud of points. When a median line is fitted through the cloud, the species above the line all have large testes in relation to their body size, and the species below small testes in relation to their body size.[28] A fascinating fact emerges: the primate species above the line have multiple-male mating systems, while those below it have single-male mating systems. Apparently the mating system determines how large a male's testes will be relative to his body size. The ratio of testes size to body weight thus provides a valuable clue to the breeding systems of primate species whose mating systems are not known.

Potentially, this result has social significance for humans, for we are primates and therefore our testes size should tell us which social system our ancestors favored: polyandry, in which a woman has several mates (the multiple-male mating system); or polygyny, in which a man has several mates (the single-male mating system). It turns out that in humans the ratio of testes size to body weight is neither high nor low. The human ratio lies practically on the line separating polyandrous mating systems from polygynous mating systems. How fascinating: it means that our species never made a clear choice of mating system that would have placed us unambiguously in one of the two systems. Given the shattering effects wrought on our lives throughout human history by this ambiguity, it is interesting that we still seem so undecided.

There exists yet another bizarre and unexpected feature to the mating systems of right whales; it involves another way in which males try to mate with females who are trying to avoid matings. When a female right whale is lying belly-up at the surface, she is inaccessible to most mating attempts. However if a male can succeed in pushing her under even a little bit, he *can* mate with her. The reason for this is that the erect penis of the male right whale is apparently under his control; he can sweep it from side to side, tapping about on the female's belly, apparently searching for her genital slit. When he encounters the slit, he enters her. A male right whale's erect penis is about nine feet long and he can achieve intromission when he is lying belly-up beside a female as long as she is belly-up with her belly awash or slightly beneath the surface. The surprising thing is that males help each other by pushing females underwater so their companions get a chance to mate with her.

When I first witnessed this I thought the males were being foolish, since it was obvious that the male who was making the effort to push the female under never got a chance to mate with her himself until much later, whereas his competitor, waiting patiently and quietly beside her, often seized the chance and *did* mate. It took several years until I finally realized that it was I who was being foolish and that what I was witnessing was something far more interesting than simple efforts to mate. I was seeing what appears to be reciprocal altruism—a system in which animals help each other in return for favors granted, a very common feature in species in which individuals are part of the same social group for a long time. Human societies are examples of long-lived social groups; so, apparently, are societies of whales and dolphins of several species. The reason this system can become established is that the reward an individual gets for making a small investment of effort can be immense. It's a simple system, but its possible consequences are very great.

For example: let us assume that you see someone drowning in a river. You reach down, pick up a stick, and extend it for them to grab, and then pull them to safety on the riverbank. But now they owe you their lives. They know it and you know it. You can expect a huge return on what was for you a trivial investment—leaning down, picking up a stick, extending it, and pulling. Humans might reason this through but in such a system it is not necessary for either the debtor or the creditor to think through the consequences or know how it works. When the debt is paid the recipient of the payment will benefit even if the payment is made for the most irrelevant reasons, simply because their fitness will be significantly improved. This will be the case each time any animal makes an investment in helping others in their group and receives a significantly larger return for doing so. Both debtor and creditor can even have some entirely unwarranted theory for doing as they do. For example, either might invent a heaven, believing that behaving in such-and-such a way will give them a reward in that heaven (even if their perception of heaven and God is diametrically opposite to someone else's perception). Evolution works blindly. It benefits snails and whales equally. The beneficiaries need not understand how what they do works. Those that prosper are the ones who behave the most adaptively—even though it may be for the most wrongheaded of reasons or for no "reason" at all if the ability to reason is lacking entirely, as in a plant.

There is a theory that the reason the human brain is so advanced and complex is because reciprocal altruism is one of the foundations of human societies. In order to work, it requires the ability to assess exchanges of favors and know whether what you are getting in return is fair. The argument goes that when a social system like reciprocal altruism becomes an important basis for the activities of a social group, cheating quickly follows. Once cheating appears, there will immediately be an advantage to any mutation that makes children of the cheated smarter enough to detect the kind of cheating that fooled their parents. The fight between both cheating and the detection of cheating pushes for better, more analytical brains in each successive generation.

But detection, in turn, gives the advantage to any genetic variations that give rise to a brain in the descendants of the cheaters that gives them greater guile and the ability to think up cleverer cheats . . . which in turn ups the advantage for a generation of smarter children in the same tribe that have genetic variations affecting the working of their brains such that they are better able to detect the newer, subtler forms of cheating . . . which gives the advantage back to children of cheaters, who have brains capable of inventing new kinds of cheating that are subtler and even more difficult to detect.

And so it goes, generation after generation, on and on, spiraling up and up with both sides of the equation—both the ability to cheat and the ability to defend yourself from cheating by detecting it—being favored by ever smarter and more complex brains. The push for smartness is the important point. The development of the brain is accelerated because the strategy that improves reproductive fitness for *both* the cheater and the cheated is the same: to have smarter children. Thus in a reciprocally altruistic social system all the selective pressures select for offspring with better brains. Most biological systems involve negative feedback where the production of an excess of anything (e.g., heat, offspring, hormones) triggers a mechanism to reduce its production, but in this case we are talking about a system running on positive feedback where more, or an excess, triggers a mechanism to produce even more—an example is the heat in a match that lights what quickly becomes a conflagration. All positive feedback systems move toward an extreme condition—what amounts to an explosion, as it were. The evidence points to an explosive development of the human brain. Not only did we get a big brain, we got it very fast—suggesting that its evolution was tied to a positive feedback system.

There is a further reason why it is appealing to think that reciprocal altruism may have shaped the human brain. It is the fact that reciprocal altruism succeeds best in social systems in which the associations between individual animals last for long periods—since it may take long periods for opportunities to arise by which individuals can pay off large social debts (a system based on reciprocal altruism is characterized by its many large debts). For example, if you save me from drowning it may be many years before a situation comes along in which we happen to be together and which is sufficiently momentous to provide me with an opportunity to discharge my debt to you—to return an appropriately large favor for which you have been waiting.

For example: imagine that you and I live in the same long-lived social group—we are members of the same foraging band—and that it is my life you saved when I was drowning in the river two years ago. Imagine also that you still haven't collected on your debt. We have fallen on hard times of late and have been starving for two weeks. As we are walking disconsolately along together looking for anything whatever to eat we come upon a bush full of berries. There is only enough for a decent meal for one of us. I say, "This bush is for you. You saved my life—this bush is *all* for you. This is the least I can do," and I walk off dejectedly. Only there's something wrong; we live in the same band, you know me very well, and you smell a rat. You think, "He doesn't usually act that way. He seemed a bit too eager as he left. He walked away a bit too quickly. I think he's faking." Your cheating detection system is working well—this is no real repayment of my debt to you. The truth of the matter is that I have noticed an even better berry bush in the distance that you haven't seen yet and if only I can fob you off on this lesser bush maybe I can make my way over to the new one and eat it in secret all by myself while you're engrossed in getting the berries from this lesser one.

The theory also states that reciprocal altruism cannot survive in a group of animals in which there is strong dominance by one class of individuals over another—a situation, for example, in which the strongest are strong enough simply to force the weaker members of the society to submit to them and give them what they want. Sea lions are an example of a society in which reciprocal altruism could probably not evolve, since the largest males are so big they dominate females and smaller males utterly, helping themselves to whatever they want whenever they want it.

Reciprocal altruism can only develop in a relatively egalitarian society. And in what species besides humans do we find individuals living in long-term associations and in relatively egalitarian societies? Porpoises and elephants are clear examples; I believe right whales will prove to be as well. All three are believed to have relatively sophisticated brains. It is perhaps less surprising therefore to find that porpoises (whose brain anatomy is well studied) have very complex brains. It may be that the same kinds of forces that shaped our brains shaped theirs. It is hard to know how to compare the relative intelligence of species whose anatomy and ecology are as profoundly different as whales and humans. However, inasmuch as reciprocal altruism appears to create a pressure toward fancy brains, maybe it would be worth looking to see whether the degree to which reciprocal altruism is developed in a species isn't a good indicator of intelligence. Maybe we should look for the most intense reciprocal altruists to judge with which species we are most intellectually akin.

As I have already implied, any social system, no matter how complicated or simple it may be, will be constantly tested by new strategies of cheating. A system will survive these constant challenges only by being slowly refined and fine-tuned to remove them or accommodate to them by detecting and punishing them.

A multiple-male mating system based on reciprocal altruism such as the one that right whales seem to possess will always support a percentage of cheaters. An example of such cheating would be when one male short-changes another in returning a favor (e.g., fails to push a female under for a male companion). This does not even require the intention of cheating. It can result, for example, from either male failing to assess properly the relative values of favors given and favors received. (Notice that it also takes a good brain to assess the relative value of favors—a further pressure pushing for complex brains in social systems based on reciprocal altruism.)

There is a simple overall mechanism that can greatly reduce the impact of cheating and allow a particular form of cheating to persist longer. The negative effects of cheating are reduced when a male mating group is closely related, for example, made up of fathers and sons. By being closely related, the individuals share many of the same genes, which means that even if one male in a group—say the father of two of the other males—is consistently able to get more than his rightful share of the successful matings (by receiving help from his sons and other group males more often than he gives help), he is nevertheless passing along roughly half of the same genes that his sons would have passed along had he not cheated them out of mating chances.

Because the father passes along so many of his son's genes it will take a lot longer for the process of evolution to remove the genes of the cheated males from the system if the animals in it have the habit of forming mating gangs that are consistently composed of closely related males. (The selective advantage of being the actual whale that mates rather than just the facilitator of mating is weaker in such groups.) As a result we would expect to see more cheating in species in which fathers and sons are competing for the same females. Another way to look at it is that if you are competing with your father or brother for matings, cheating is likely to be rampant.

However, in the case of right whales because they mate promiscuously there is no sure way that fathers and sons can join forces, because there is no obvious way that a father can recognize his son (it is not apparent how he could know for sure whose father he is), nor a son his father. There is, however, a male relative that a male right whale *can* identify, and that is his brother—or to be a bit more accurate, an older male can recognize his younger brother, though a younger brother cannot necessarily recognize his older brother without help from another relative, for example, his own mother. (This is, of course, true of humans as well.) Any male calf that another male finds accompanying his mother is sure to be at least his half brother and, if they both have the same father, a full brother.

This situation may explain our observation that every year for three years young males return to the same breeding areas where they were born and hang around for several months. After all it is here that a young male will encounter his mother when she returns three years after his birth accompanied by her next calf. If the newborn calf is a male, it is either a full brother or a half brother.

But there is another aspect of young males getting to know their newborn brothers that is even more interesting. It may explain a curious phenomenon we have observed several times: as I have mentioned, female right whales who have calves in any given year stick together in groups. This means that females who each have a calf bump into each other quite often. When this happens, everything is peaceful and quiet until the calves start to play. The moment play begins, one of the females breaks it up by interposing her body between the two calves and leading her own calf away. The distance she needs to lead it is usually no more than a couple of body lengths since during its first few months a calf normally does not stray farther from its mother than her body length. (I suspect that what it's doing is staying within view of its mother underwater.)

It is not surprising that females will not allow their calves to play with other calves when we recall that the female is the calf's sole source of sustenance and that during the time she is nursing it she herself is fasting. Every motion the calf makes is a motion its mother has to pay for—a payment that is made at a time when she is getting nothing, or next to nothing, to eat. She has swum a long way and has a long way to go before she finally gets what will be her first real meal in about five months. As we have mentioned, she sometimes gets a few snacks in transit or on the breeding grounds but it probably makes little real difference to the significant nutritional stress she experiences.

Even though mothers lead their calves away from play with other calves there is, curiously enough, one kind of playmate that a female *will* tolerate. She will tolerate play between her calf and some (but not all) subadults, even though such play sometimes becomes fairly rambunctious. It is my theory that such bouts of play will be allowed if the subadult is the female's offspring from a previous year, and that this is the moment when two related males can get to know each other, so that later, when both are sexually mature, they can become members of the same mating group.

This is a hard theory to test because it is very difficult for us to get photographs from the cliffs good enough to enable us to identify right whales that are farther away than about three quarters of a mile. Thus, if we witness a female with a calf that has started to play with a subadult, there is only the most slender chance we will be able to identify both the mother and the subadult before it stops and the subadult departs. But even if we do get the pictures, there is another problem working against us. Calves are covered for much of their first three months with heavy infestations of cyamids on their heads that unfortunately make them very difficult to identify. So, not only must we have the good luck to get an adequate photograph of the mother and subadult in one of these short-lived play groups, the subadult in the picture must be of one of the rare calves from the past two years that was photographed well enough to identify. We have not yet encountered such a situation, though we have a possible candidate.

There may be another reason that females break up play between their calf and other calves; it is one of the few forms of play over which they can exert control. When a calf is playing with the ocean by slapping the surface with a flipper, or breaching, or lobtailing, the only way the mother can stop it is to remove the calf's access to the water. This she sometimes does, by clamping the small of the calf's tail under her flipper and holding it there while the calf splutters and sneezes and coughs. Eventually the calf calms down and the mother lets it go, the two swimming decorously off together side by side with the calf docile and apparently chastened.

Mother right whales often avoid attempts by their calves to nurse. Two strategies are used. One is to roll belly-up so that their nipples are out of the calf's reach. The other is to lead the calf into shallow water where it can't get underneath her to nurse—just as she leads males into water too shallow for them to get underneath her to mate. When mothers do this their calves may butt and pester them for hours—apparently in order to get the mother to assume a nursing position. When the pestering goes on too long, the mother sometimes does an utterly charming thing. She will roll onto her back, easing in under the calf, and take it in her arms (her flippers). She then comes up from below until she has stranded it high and dry on her chest. She holds it like this, softly, in her arms, patting it now and again as if to calm it. Her rate of patting is ultraslow, something I imagine that only a mother of such vast size, patience, and gentleness could achieve. When I see mother right whales do this I wonder whether they are not the ultimate expressions of motherhood, of solace, of soothing calm—great, gentle, patient, wells of peace.

Because there is no pair bond among right whales, it is not surprising that males appear to show no contribution in raising or protecting the young. I have seen a mating group in which males continued actively pursuing a female while a group of killer whales was menancing a mother and calf less than three hundred feet away. The males in the mating group ignored all this extreme behavior and just kept on pursuing the female they had been after when the orcas arrived.

The fact that males appear to offer no protection to the calves makes me wonder what benefits, if any, a female gets from males during years in which she does not produce an egg requiring fertilization. There is plenty of disadvantage for the female in the persistent advances of males. For example, since gangs of males actively pursue females with calves, the calf often gets mixed up in the fray and may be struck hard by a male or partly crushed between two of them. Flip Nicklin once saw a calf that was all mixed up in a mating group get struck with such force by a male's tail that the sound was clearly audible underwater and the calf was driven into the bottom, raising a cloud of mud where it hit. He said that he felt he himself would not have survived the blow. Christopher Clark, who has recorded more right whales than anyone alive, heard on several occasions loud sounds that he guessed might be body blows coming from mating groups (he had a hydrophone array in the water on these occasions, which is how he knew where the sounds were coming from).

We cannot prove that the hardest of these blows are fatal but each year we find up to five dead calves on the beaches with no external marks on them to indicate an attack by sharks or orcas. (This by no means clinches the question, as there are, of course, many other possible explanations for the deaths of these very young calves.)

But there may also be advantages to the attentions males give to female right whales. Females with calves are found along the edge of the shore, almost never in the middle of the bays. Many other right whales, however, can be found scattered widely about in the middle of the bays, apparently doing nothing except for occasional bouts of furious breaching. When they start breaching, other whales respond by breaching as well—as does the group of males currently engaged in mating attempts with the females along the coast. It is clear that 1) breaching is sometimes used as a challenge; and 2) only one group of males at a time seems to get the chance to travel along the line of females in shallow water and attempt to mate with them. I suspect the males in this group have fought for that right, since other lone whales appear hesitant to approach them, instead remaining at a distance while occasionally initiating bouts of breaching that are answered by breaches from the group with access to the mothers with calves.

Although it seems that the whales in the center of the bay keep up the pressure against the successful gang of males (the ones with current access to estrous females and females with calves), we need more successful identifications of the central bay whales to be sure. We know that many of them appear to be males from observing that they sometimes move together in adult bands without calves (such assemblies are usually male groups); when we are lucky we occasionally get to see male ventral slits, and we also can see that the heads of many central bay individuals are heavily encrusted with callosities (a male characteristic). However, we need to identify by sex more individuals out in the bay before we can be sure of what is going on. (The prospect of finding the answer to this question is not made any easier by a prohibition against overflying the center of the bay in our survey plane.) If the theory is correct, it would suggest a possible benefit that gangs of males could be offering to a female with a calf: keeping other males away. They could be giving her protection from the advances of other males trying to mate with her. This protection would increase the chances that her calf could grow up enough to avoid an injury it might otherwise suffer during attempts by other males who linger in the center of the bay to mate with the calf's mother. It is true that the males do not protect females and calves from marauding orcas, but that is quite different from protecting their exclusive mating rights from other male right whales. If our suspicions prove to be true, this might offer another interesting explanation: namely, why females with calves ultimately *do* allow, in fact even cooperate with, mating attempts by males later in the season—even though they strongly repel them during the first weeks of their calf's life, and even though they are probably not impregnated during the same year they give birth to a calf. By offering matings to the dominant male group they may gain protection—reminiscent of protection rackets among humans.

Since a father's genes are carried by his offspring, evolution will select for fathers who protect their calves and who sometimes take heavy risks to do so. A male should, of course, only gain an advantage in coming to a calf's aid if he is the father—or is convinced he is. This does not imply that the male need have knowledge or understanding of what he is doing; I am simply using a convenient shortcut to say that males who have the inclination to protect the young of mothers with whom they have mated will leave more offspring than males who have the inclination to protect offspring of mothers with whom they have not mated. This tendency makes any male with whom she has mated the mother's best bet for helping her protect her much larger investment in a calf. Because she has such a large investment, it may pay her to make the effort to give males year-round sexual access to her, if it keeps them around and in a protective mood. She, of course, need not understand this principle. If she mates with lots of males over the year benefits will accrue to her even if she has no idea of what she is doing. For even though those matings do not result in pregnancies, she will have enlisted more males to protect her calves than females who mate with only one male each year—particularly given the fact that the mating system of these whales is promiscuous and that the males presumably have no way of being sure they are the parent of any offspring. The principle is that taking part in a promiscuous mating system is one way a female can ensure that she has the interest and help of a large number of males in protecting her young—a particularly crucial need for a female of any species with a low reproductive rate whose young have a long period of dependency.

One of the unusual aspects of the mating habits of right whales is that they mate throughout the year, even when on their feeding grounds.[29] Most animals concentrate their mating efforts during a rather short breeding season, but right whales, like humans, mate year-round. (Most unusual in the animal kingdom—we humans aren't aware of how oversexed even the most undersexed of us are.) In the case of humans this strange behavior is widely presumed to have evolved as a means by which a woman, by granting continuous sexual access to a male, can secure prolonged help from that male to rear their children.

We have not seen enough attacks by predators on right whale calves to know if males might go to the defense of some calves while ignoring the plights of others. It would be interesting to know the answer to this, because if it proved to be the case and if, like males of many other species, right whale males cannot tell when females are in estrus, then they will probably defend an infant if they have mated with the mother, even an infant that is not biologically theirs. Such a situation would mean that a good strategy for a female would be to mate with as many males as possible and at whatever time of year she encountered them, so as to recruit them later if necessary in defense of her offspring.

However, we have to stick with what we know for now, which is that male right whales don't appear to protect females that have calves from predators. This observation may well prove to be the norm, given that males probably have no way of knowing which calves, if any, are theirs. If female right whales are offering sex to males all through the year as well as in years in which they have a calf (years in which they may not be able to become impregnated), they must be seeking and getting some major advantage in return; the only thing that seems to make sense in our current state of ignorance is that they mate with dominant males to avoid being approached for unwanted matings by other males.

During the time right whales are on their breeding grounds they play with any floating object they come across, which gives the general impression that they are bored and looking for diversion. Nowhere is this more engagingly seen than in their slow-motion play with objects like seaweed. Because right whales have coexisted with seaweed ever since there were right whales, it is not surprising that their play with seaweed is stereotyped. When faced with a strand of free-floating seaweed, the first thing a right whale does is to maneuver its body under it so as to drape the seaweed over its head—usually over its blowholes. The skin in the area of the blowhole is richly endowed with nerves (not surprisingly, since the whale needs to be able to plot the progress of water as it washes toward its open blowholes when it is inhaling—so that they can be closed at the last possible moment). For a whale, having seaweed draped across its blowholes is probably a richly tactile sensation.

The whale's next move is to submerge just enough so that the seaweed strokes along its back (this may also produce a positive sensation). The whale then uses its tail to swish the seaweed to within reach of its flippers, whereupon it pats it with either flipper for a while before swimming back under the seaweed and repeating the cycle. Play with seaweed can go on for hours if there is no significant interruption.

Unfortunately the objects right whales play with are not limited to seaweed. We have found this tendency over the years to be an infernal nuisance. For example, when our efforts to erect the single tide gauge thirty-three feet high were foiled by the mother right whale who destroyed it, I decided to build instead a series of stakes along the steeply sloping beach face which we could use to determine the height of the tide. Of course by now we expected trouble. Sure enough it came. Right whales began to seek out our stakes and break them in such a way that it was obviously intentional. There was one mother who apparently found this kind of activity particularly diverting. She would ease up to one of our tide gauges, moving very, very slowly in the last few meters of her approach, and finally, pressing her head against it, would start beating her tail very slowly up and down, pressing against the stick and causing it to lean more and more until with a snap it gave way. She would then go galumphing off a short way, turn slowly back, search for the next gauge, and break it in exactly the same way. We were not amused.

Because we could not protect them from the right whales, we had to redesign our tide gauges so they were easy to repair. We would then post a TGS (tide gauge saver) on the beach, whose job it was to reerect the tide gauge posts as fast as the whales knocked them down or to rush out and save whatever boat had had its mooring broken or if its anchor had been dragged by a whale into water too deep for the anchor to reach bottom. On some days the saver had to rescue three boats in the course of a single afternoon.

Whales don't limit their play to inanimate objects; they also interact with other animals in their world. Young southern sea lions seem more or less incapable of passing a right whale without turning back to investigate and fool about near it. While most adult right whales seem unafraid of sea lions, the same is not true of calves. Young calves often wriggle partway out of the water and onto their mothers' backs when sea lions come along. But after a few months this apparent fright reaction often goes away and is replaced with rampant curiosity and rambunctious play.

One of the games we see young sea lions play is very curious. It is, I must confess, a complete mystery to me as to what is going on and what the sea lion is getting out of it. It consists of the sea lion doing loop-the-loops immediately behind the tail of a whale. During this activity, adult whales never seem to be bothered or to in any way enter into whatever it is that the young sea lion is doing (though subadult right whales may seem very nervous around young sea lions who are doing this—they keep turning around to face them whenever the sea lion approaches them from behind).

I have watched this behavior under ideal conditions (the young sea lion and the whale immediately below the cliff hut; me comfortably seated and looking through a fixed spotting scope) but no matter how hard I looked for it, I could not see the young sea lion catching and eating anything, or making any contact with the whale though it might once or twice in the course of half an hour of its wild loop-the-loops have touched the trailing edge of the whale's tail with its flipper as though pushing off from it. There was no visible reaction to this by the whale. But I once saw Troff slowly moving her flukes up and down in front of a young sea lion who was wildly whirling and twirling and loop-the-looping behind her tail. I have never before nor since seen such wild behavior of this kind by a sea lion. I noticed to my surprise that in spite of the motion of her tail, Troff's body was not moving through the water at all. I was able to observe this because she was very close to me, I was looking at her through a telescope, and it was held firmly on a tripod. Had she moved, her body would have drifted across the field of view of my fixed telescope. But it did not. And because Troff's tail motions did not result in any forward progress of her body, it appeared as though she might be making her tail motions for the benefit of the young sea lion. Eventually a small group of sea lions came by and the one I was watching left with them. The tide continued falling, and an hour later Troff began to touch bottom, as evidenced by clouds of mud around her flippers. She roused herself enough to swim off into deeper water, out of my view, followed by her calf, Troll. Such are the pleasant enigmas posed by right whales when you spend long and delightful afternoons watching them in the paradise of Patagonia.

CHAPTER 4

The Songs of Humpback Whales

Much of my life has been spent among whales. Above all I have tried to understand the messages that their songs and calls contain. Some of my happiest hours have been spent at night lying back in the cockpit of a sailboat, alone on watch, steering with one foot and gazing at the mast sweeping across vast fields of stars, while the songs of humpback whales poured up out of the sea, to fill my head, my heart, and finally my soul as well.

It was in 1967 that I saw my first humpback whales, off Bermuda where their migration carries them during passages between their North Atlantic feeding and breeding grounds. It was also then that I first heard their sounds. I had gone to Bermuda with Katy with the express aim of trying to see a whale. One perfect day we were guests aboard a sailboat when a whale was spotted blowing in the distance. We got into the boat's dinghy and eased nearer to the whale, which was by now lying at the surface blowing spout after spout of that delicate moisture with which whales announce their presence at the surface. As we approached, the whale turned slowly away from us as it started its slow dive, arching its back and lifting its massive tail high into the air until it towered above us. I sat in awe and fascination, transfixed by the deliberate grace of its departure and the implausible broadness of its back.

Even though this was the first whale I had ever seen, I had already decided to spend the rest of my life studying whales and working to secure their protection (back in 1967 the whaling industry was out of control). Since that time I have seen, I suppose, as many whales as anyone alive and have studied every species of large whale in all seven seas. I have seen whales in the midst of a gale, bursting through the faces of twenty-five-foot waves in which they were gamboling with porpoises; and I have had whales leap clear of the water so close to my boat I had to swerve to avoid getting soaked by the splash. I have seen mother whales on calm mornings rolling beneath their babes (so as to strand them on the vast shoal of their chests), and having taking them in their arms, pat them slowly, with a grace and delicacy possessed only by something of inconceivable strength. But in spite of all these vistas and delights, it is that simple first view of a humpback, in the morning, off Bermuda, arching its flukes and sliding beneath the sea, that remains for me a clear, unfaded image, as if it were my first, last, and only sight of a whale.

When breathing at the surface a humpback whale makes a series of shallow dives between breaths, but when it is preparing to dive more deeply it arches its back high. Although all whales flex somewhat when heading for the depths, the humpback bends and lifts its back higher than any other whale. And because a humpback's dorsal fin grows from a kind of fatty pad lying atop the most acutely curved portion of its back, the profile of pad and dorsal fin further exaggerates the effect of the bowing back and makes its hump during the predive flex even more prominent. This has earned the humpback its name, though a better name might have been the archback whale.

To anyone who has actually seen a humpback whale up close, the concept of giving such a magnificent and graceful creature such a pejorative name may seem unaccountable. But these animals were named by people who looked at them as blubber—and for whom the grace, power, and awesome beauty of the whale seems to have gone unnoticed.

Humpbacks are rorquals—that is, whales with pleated throats. The other five rorquals (blue, fin, sei, Bryde's, and minke whales) are closely related and are in their own genus (*Balaenoptera*). However, even though the pleated throat of the humpback whale gives it a superficial similarity to these other rorquals, humpbacks are actually in their own separate subfamily and are thus only rather distantly related to other rorquals.

A second obvious feature of the humpback (and a sure indication that you are looking at one when you see it) is its long, slender flippers. They can be fourteen feet long and are much narrower than a right whale's broader, squarer flippers. Sometimes your attention is caught from a great distance by a single flipper held aloft—a long, white, supple, bladelike appendage waving languorously from side to side high above the sea, like an immense palm frond bending slowly in the breeze. (Some fishermen say it is the whale beckoning to them.) Humpback whales have the largest flippers of any whale species, both relatively and absolutely. The whale's scientific name, *Megaptera novaeangliae,* means "large-winged New Englander," a name that gives a far better sense of the grace and power of this species.

These long flippers act as cooling planes through which the whale loses heat, making it possible for humpbacks to keep cool in waters too warm for other whales. This allows them to live closer to equatorial waters than other baleen whales. In fact we now know that alone among baleen whales, humpbacks can cross the equator between Northern and Southern hemispheres, and may do so routinely.[1]

Humpback whales make long migrations between their summer feeding areas in cold near-polar waters and their wintering grounds in the subtropics. There is no agreement as to why these whales—or indeed any whale species—migrate. It is usually assumed that, as their time draws near, females leave behind the winter storms on their rich polar feeding grounds and migrate to the calmer seas of lower latitudes to give birth, thus assuring that their newborn calves experience warm, calm seas in their first weeks of life. There is no definite evidence, however, that this is necessary, since mothers with very small calves are routinely seen in antarctic seas, and the fact that newborn calves are routinely seen in these high latitudes suggests that they were born there.

Though there is no direct evidence that humpback whales mate on the wintering grounds, it is known that many female humpback whales have a calf every year, and as gestation is believed to last twelve months, with most calves being born in winter, most mating must take place the winter before. Since births occur on wintering grounds, mating therefore probably occurs there too. The wintering areas are thus probably birthing as well as mating grounds. If females are sexually receptive on their wintering grounds, it would be of obvious advantage for adult males to swim the thousands of miles between feeding and wintering grounds each year.

There is no description of humpbacks mating in which hard evidence is offered that this was what was being observed. You can read wonderful, lurid accounts of their "mating" in the scientific literature, including one description by Nishiwaki and Hayashi[2] that has humpbacks charging toward each other and rising together out of the sea belly-to-belly for much of their length, then crashing back together in a welter of foam. Unfortunately, no evidence was offered by these scientists that what they were describing was mating—they just assumed it to be so. Because it sounds as if what they witnessed was more likely to have been fighting, for years whale biologists, including me, have been disdainful of this description of "mating" in humpbacks, feeling it was probably nonsense.

However, killer whales do apparently sometimes mate in a somewhat similar way. A killer whale trainer who watched two captive killer whales mating for several hours described to me repeated risings belly-to-belly, followed by topplings sideways back into the water together. There is no question this was mating, as she clearly saw intromission during several of the belly-to-belly encounters. However, this is apparently not the only mating posture of killer whales. I once circled for about two hours over a pair of killer whales while the male made repeated apparent attempts to mate with what I assumed was a female (it had a much shorter dorsal fin that swept backward in a curve). The male swam upside down beneath her, while she continued to swim very slowly and on an even keel at the surface.

Thus, even though it seems as though the mating technique described for humpbacks by Nishiwaki and Hayashi could be painful (or worse), killer whales apparently *do* at least sometimes rise together belly-to-belly above the water's surface while mating. This makes me less confident in discounting Nishiwaki and Hayashi's description entirely. Its main feature—the rising belly-to-belly partway above the water's surface—may someday be confirmed.

As interesting and unexpected as the anatomy and biology of humpback whales are, what captivates me most about them is their songs. During their breeding season, humpback whales produce long, complex sequences of sounds that can be heard by listening through a hydrophone. In 1967 Scott McVay and I discovered that these long sequences are repeated by the whales and are therefore properly called songs (just as the repeated utterances of birds, frogs and insects are also called songs).[3]

These songs are much longer than birdsongs and can last up to thirty minutes, though fifteen is nearer the norm. They are divided into repeating phrases called themes. When the phrase is heard to change (usually after a few minutes), it heralds the start of a new theme. Songs contain from two to nine themes and are strung together without pauses so that a long singing session is an exuberant, uninterrupted river of sound that can flow on for twenty-four hours or longer.

The pace of the song is very grand and extended and appears to me to be set by the slow rhythm of ocean swells—the rhythm of the sea. It is the beat most familiar to whales since they are immersed in it—are rocked gently by it. Throughout their lives they rise and fall with it. In storms the height of the swells is greater, but the pulse of the song persists. It would not be surprising to me if ocean swells set the rhythm of whale songs.

The first time I ever recorded the songs of humpback whales at night was off Bermuda. It was also the first time I had ever heard the abyss. Normally you don't hear the size of the ocean when you are listening, but I heard it that night. It was a bit like walking into a dark cave, dropping your flashlight, and hearing wave after wave of echoes cascading back from the darkness beyond, realizing for the first time that you are standing at the entrance to an enormous room. The cave has spoken to you. That's what whales do; they give the ocean its voice, and the voice they give it is ethereal and unearthly.

I once spent all night in New York's Cathedral of Saint John the Divine recording musician Paul Winter playing an ancient threnody on his saxophone. We were set up in the well-lit transept with Paul standing at the entrance to the bat-black nave, the extent of which was lost in impenetrable darkness. I didn't realize that the nave of that cathedral is the longest in the world until Paul played his first note and the nave roared back at him, half-burying him in a deluge of echoes. He seemed like some shepherd come to the mouth of a cave to beg an amnesty with his horn, who every time he played a note was drowned out by the roars of the dragon within. It is the same with the abyss. As you sit in your boat, lightly borne on the night sea, watching the weather and the stars and the sails, it all seems so simple, regular, ordinary, and you have no thought of how far beneath you the abyss extends. But then you put on headphones, and after a while a whale starts to sing, and the echoes from the abyss come tumbling and roaring back, and suddenly you are aware of the vastness of the mystery that underlies your boat.

Humpback whales adopt a head-down posture when they sing—might that allow the flow of blood to their heads to better perfuse their brains, helping them to remember their long and dauntingly complex songs? When you swim up next to a singing whale through the cool blue water, the song is so loud, so thundering in your chest and head, you feel as if someone is pressing you to a wall with their open palms, shaking you until your teeth rattle. When you swim close enough to touch the singer you doubt whether you will be able to stand the intensity of the sound. But you can.

The singer usually detects such an approach first, and when he does (I say "he" for it is the males that sing), he stops singing and slowly turns toward the intruder. At this point the entire ocean seems to be rearranging itself, and you are washed willy-nilly this way and that by the currents he stirs in his turning.

At such moments I have been made to feel smaller than I have ever felt otherwise. But such a feeling is a good thing for human beings to experience periodically, particularly when it is generated by some other nonhuman species, some fellow traveler on our mutual planet.

But although your heart may be trying to beat itself out through your chest, the singer means you no harm. He appears simply curious to see what it is that has taken it upon itself to interrupt his reverie. The disconcerting part is that he sometimes investigates such interruptions rather closely before going on his way.

Humpback whales and humans have been on separate but parallel paths of evolution since long before the appearance of our earliest hominid ancestors. During the past fifty-three million years there cannot have been, except for the briefest chance contacts, any significant possibility that humpbacks and our human ancestors were able to hear each other's songs and from that hearing to modify their laws of composition. Yet whales use many of the same laws of composition in their songs that we use in ours. Human music and whale songs are strikingly similar in many basic ways. For instance:

1) Whales employ similar rhythms. But why use rhythms in the first place? Why not free-form, rambling sounds? And having chosen rhythms, why should whales choose rhythms so reminiscent of some of the rhythms employed by humans in our music?

2) Whales use phrases of a similar length to ours—a few seconds—and create themes out of a few phrases before changing to a new theme. They could make a song have no repetitive phrases and themes, or have the song "grow" organically and not repeat material, wandering along like a constantly changing stream. But like human composers, humpback whales keep reiterating their material, sometimes also reiterating half a phrase by attaching it to a different beginning.

3) The length of humpback whale songs falls between the length of a modern ballad and a movement of a symphony. Why not a few seconds, like a birdsong? Why not several hours, as we might expect for an animal that lives such a slow life? Why choose the same kinds of lengths for performances that we do? Is it linked to their attention span? Is their attention span linked to the complexity of the vertebrate brain rather than to the metabolism of the brain's owner?

4) Even though they are capable of singing over a range of at least seven octaves, humpback whales use intervals between their notes similar to the intervals that we employ in our scales. Why don't humpback whale phrases leap about all over the place between widely spaced notes, or slide up and down through intervals so minute that the differences would hardly be audible to us? In other words, why don't they sing minute changes or make sudden jumps of several octaves? Indeed, humpbacks do sometimes include

four-octave leaps but usually only as a percussive element or at the start of several closely spaced notes which are separated by the same intervals that we use in our songs.

5) Humpbacks mix percussive or noisy elements in their songs with relatively pure tones, and mix them in ratios similar to the ratios humans use in symphonic music. In an orchestral score the percussion section is directed to put in occasional notes, more as an adornment really, while in most pieces the violins and other melodic instruments get far more notes. It is the same with whales, in whose songs percussive notes are much less frequent than tonal ones. Why don't whales parcel out their sounds in the opposite way and use more percussive than melodic material?

6) In some whale songs the overall song structure is similar to human compositions—a statement of theme, a section in which it is elaborated (the development section), and then a return to a slightly modified version of the original theme.

7) The quality of many whale notes is the same as the quality of human notes. With an infinitude of possible sounds to choose from, why don't whales use sounds we think of as unpleasant—like roars, or stutters, or grunts, or even the belches employed so effectively by elephant seals, or the brays used by asses, or the hideous calls of guinea fowls, or the hisses and rattles of rattlesnakes? Why should it be that all of the sounds humpback whales make are, if not pleasant to most human ears, at least not unpleasant?

8) Finally, and most surprising: humpbacks employ rhyme in their songs, a point to which I will return.

One of the most surprising features of humpback whale songs is a discovery Katy made—they are inveterate composers and tinkerers with their songs. This gives them yet another striking similarity with humans. Furthermore, the tendency to change songs is a trait that appears to be shared only by whales, people, and a few species of birds. Humpback whales change their songs continually so that after about five years they are singing an entirely new song and apparently do not ever again return to the original.

In order to discuss the ways in which humpback whales change their songs, we need to decide just how different two sounds must be before we will consider them to be different, and how much change we will ignore, deciding that it is an effort on behalf of the whale to make the same sound. The term "same" when applied to humpback songs refers to the rigor with which we demand that two songs be identical before we claim them to be the same song. Lacking any idea of what humpbacks consider to be a meaningful difference between two songs, the degree of identicalness is clearly a matter of personal opinion. At present we consider a song the same if successive renditions of it include the same themes in the same order, even though the numbers of repeated phrases in each theme may be different in successive renditions and even if some renditions of the song lack a theme or two. (If we demanded that all themes be always present and that the number of repeats of phrases within each theme be the same we would seldom find a humpback repeating its songs exactly.) To offer an analogy: if we were listening to someone singing a song with many verses and if in successive renditions of the song they left out one or more of the verses or put a varying number of *fa la la*s in the chorus we would not suddenly believe they were singing a different song.

This kind of reasoning may seem normal to us, but it invites an assumption: if the point at which we stop looking at the differences and declare two songs to be the same is at a level of analysis which is coarser than that at which a whale believes two songs to be the same, we may be ignoring differences between songs which are of great importance—for example, we might ignore the very aspects of the song that were loaded with practical information about, say, food and routes. Much of the structure in these songs varies highly from individual to individual—even between successive songs sung by the same individual. It is not out of the question that minor differences could have great significance so that, in effect, the song acts as a kind of carrier frequency for much more complicated messages which the whale subtly superimposes upon it. If that proves to be true, then the songs may carry meaning comparable to, or in excess of, anyone's most imaginative speculations.

As a plodding biologist, however, I suspect that the level at which we are analyzing the songs *is* significant and that those individual variations that whales demonstrate in rendering two successive songs are comparable to the kind of variability you hear when two human beings try to sing the same song: a series of differences that are obvious but that aren't intended to be different or to carry much specific additional information. But the most reassuring aspect of our assumptions of sameness is that when we make the kinds of assumptions we have made, the results we get are fascinating and significant—suggesting that the level at which we are looking at differences *is* meaningful.

There appears to be a fundamental difference between the way humpback whales invent new material in their songs and the way we humans do. When whales compose new songs they do so by making small adjustments in the existing phrases and themes of their current songs. Through this process they slowly change the form of the song until it becomes noticeably different. This differs from the human process: when two people set out to compose songs they produce songs that are entirely different. Each makes up melodies de novo, ones that are different from any they have heard before.

Inasmuch as whales dicker constantly with the phrases and themes of their songs, the changes they make accumulate until after about five years the song is completely different. At this point the fact that it ever bore any relation to the form in which it was first heard would not seem credible. But when you listen through the whole long process of changes during that period, you find that the song has reached its new state through a series of minor, accumulating modifications—that is, that it has *evolved* into its present form. In this respect, whales differ from humans. When we compose a song we create a whole new composition, and we create it all at once, generating it in conformation with a rather strict set of musical rules. Whales' songs also obey a strict set of rules; it's just that they make small, cumulative changes rather than large, discontinuous ones. Though the process takes place with nonverbal sounds, most of which have musical qualities, I will use words to draw an analogy to what is transpiring. Suppose we were singing the couplet:

> *Through the trees I sought the light*
> *Of rising dawn throughout the night*

and someone challenged us to write a different couplet. We might write:

> *Surprising things delight my thoughts*
> *And kindle dos and don'ts and oughts.*

Were whales able to speak and we heard a whale singing the same two couplets five years apart we might suppose that the couplets were unrelated. But if we listened all along the way we would find that they were derivative, and that the derivative intermediate versions were consistent with an underlying set of rules, and that they all made sense as compositions on their own. We might find that the whales moved between the above two couplets as follows:

> *Through the trees I sought the light*
> *Of rising dawn throughout the night*

to

> *The trees I thought would give me light*
> *But rising dawn threw out the night*

to

> *The unkind trees have caught my rising kite;*
> *How thrown my thoughts, how withdrawn my delight.*

to

> *The kindly seas when fraught and rising*
> *delight my thoughts . . . it is surprising.*

to

> *Surprising things delight my thoughts*
> *And kindle dos and don'ts and oughts.*

In both cases the opening and final couplets are the same; it is the route between them that differs.

In composing their songs humpback whales obey a large body of laws of composition that humans composing within such strictures would call musical conventions. These laws narrowly circumscribe what is apparently acceptable to each whale. When humpback whales introduce a new phrase, they sing it very rapidly, but as time goes by they stretch it out, singing it more and more slowly until finally it is dropped altogether and replaced by something derived either from it or from other material elsewhere in the song. The raw material from which the modifications are taken are embellishments to the existing material.

In the example of couplets I give above the changes are made according to laws of poetic conventions, but whales are singing, not speaking. If a whale's song contains a downward slide, the slide will be sung more and more slowly over time and eventually may be broken up into a series of distinct descending notes. As time passes, some of these notes may be dropped so that a descending chromatic slide has now become four notes in a descending arpeggio based on thirds. The whale might then drop the middle notes in the arpeggio, making it into a descending one-octave jump. Next, the whale might double the first note and treble the second, later adding a hum at the end. With time the hum might become louder and be repeated many times before the first of the two tonal notes. We see that what we started with was a descending slide—a glissando—and that what we have now is two quick notes followed by three quick notes an octave lower, followed by several humming sounds. It seems unrelated but by studying the process we are able to track it through all its intermediate forms. The whole process of change could take anything from a month or so to several years to achieve. But it would always be found to follow very simple rules and to include all of the intermediate stages.

In all the years we have studied the songs of whales at the Whale Conservation Institute, we have only once heard what appeared to be the abrupt introduction of a new song element. Even so, there is a chance that the introduction was gradual since the sound appeared at an unknown time during a two-week period for which neither we nor anyone else has recordings.

To my mind, one of the most interesting discoveries of recent years is that humpback whales employ rhyme in their songs. This discovery was made by Linda Guinee and Katy Payne. We have no difficulty in recognizing that a whale is using rhyme even though we don't understand what it is saying. After all, even if someone were speaking a language which you didn't understand, you would know when they were reciting poetry because you would hear a pattern of sounds at the end of a set of rhythmic utterances followed by a similar pattern at the end of an equal number of rhythmic beats. Even when you do understand the language, the words don't have to make sense for you to realize that they are intended to be rhymes. For example:

> Hey diddle, diddle
> The cat and the fiddle.

or

> Hickory dickory dock
> The mouse ran up the clock.

Linda and Katy also found that one of the reasons humpback whales use rhyme in their songs may parallel a use humans have employed since the dawn of history as a mnemonic device—a way of remembering what comes next when there is something long and complicated to memorize. Linda and Katy found that humpback whale songs with a lot of complex material often include rhyme. They also found that short, complex songs with lots of intricate material are more likely to rhyme than longer but simpler songs.

The changes in the songs are adopted by all males on the same breeding ground so that at any given moment all whales in the same area are singing the same updated version—all singers constantly modifying their songs to keep pace with the latest changes. Because male humpbacks may change breeding grounds, the males on different breeding grounds in the same ocean do lots of song swapping so that humpbacks in the same ocean sing songs that are very similar or are the same. However, males in different oceans sing songs that are different. This means that when we collect songs from the different oceans we are able to identify a whale's ocean and the year the song was recorded simply by comparing a tape of its song to our collection of song tapes. By listening to their songs we can easily distinguish a humpback that breeds in the North Atlantic Ocean from one that breeds in the North Pacific. The songs in different oceans drift apart until there are no similarities except for their overall structure. However, we also know that humpback whales improvise within a strict set of laws of composition, with the result that although the differences in the songs accumulate until the songs in different oceans are different, there remain many similarities of style.

This has resulted in some interesting discoveries. For example, all whales in the same ocean sing the same song. However, the songs of humpback whales whose breeding grounds lie in the Northern Hemisphere off the coast of Colombia in South America are different from other North Pacific songs. These animals are therefore probably from a different ocean and must have crossed the equator into the Northern Hemisphere—something that baleen whales were believed not to be able to do because the temperature of equatorial waters is so high the whales might die of overheating if they tried to cross them.

However, Lilian Flores, a Colombian whale scientist, along with two American biologists, Gregory Stone and Steve Katona, discovered two individual humpback whales among those that visit Lilian's study area off Isla Gorgona, three degrees north of the equator, that had also been seen in the Antarctic, fifty-eight hundred miles away (assuming that the whales follow the coast).[4] This is not only the first direct evidence that baleen whales can cross the equator but the second longest migration by any mammal yet discovered. (As noted earlier, what appears to be the longest is undertaken by the gray whale, which by migrating from Baja California to the Bering Sea may travel sixty-two hundred miles each way.)[5]

The way this discovery was made was by photographing the undersurfaces of the tails of humpback whales in both areas. Scott Kraus and Steve Katona of the College of the Atlantic demonstrated that the markings on the undersurfaces of the tails of humpback whales can be used to identify individual humpbacks. Every humpback whale tail is naturally marked with a different black and white pattern. By comparing lots of photographs of whale tails, one can show that the same individuals are visiting areas many miles apart. This makes it possible to learn about the migratory destinations of humpbacks.[6]

Such research techniques are benign inasmuch as they don't harm the animal. Benign research techniques are the most powerful tools for learning about whales yet developed; they have revolutionized our knowledge about every species of whale to which such methods have been applied. Some individual humpback whales have been photographically identified at least two thousand times.[7] A humpback whale named Salt is an example of this. She lives in New England and has probably been seen by at least three-quarters of a million people, making her one of the best-known, and now most-loved, wild animals on earth.

The old techniques of learning about whale migrations relied on shooting a steel tag into a whale and recovering it from the cooker when the whale was later killed in some other place and melted down for its oil. When using this technique scientists could only hope to discover two places where any given whale had been in its life—where it was marked and where it was later killed. Since the introduction of the technique of photographing tails, more data points about where humpback whales spend their time have been obtained from a single individual humpback than from all of the roughly two thousand whales from which tags have ever been recovered.

Although the technique of photoidentification has only recently been employed, it could have been adopted as a research tool back in the 1920s when the first major studies of humpback whales were made. The cameras, lenses, and film existed to do the work. The only thing lacking was the will to do it benignly. Nobody used it, simply, I suspect, because of the mind-set of the times: the major body of valid research had always involved examining dead animals—that was automatically the approach scientists took. It seems never to have seriously occurred to anyone that if the whole thing were done benignly it would also mean far more data per animal.

Since 1967 I have listened on and off to the songs of humpback whales—researching them, analyzing them, ransacking through them, beseeching them, always yearning to know what they mean. But they guard their secrets as effortlessly, as enigmatically, as they always have.

There are theories (there are always theories): one, that songs are sung to attract females; and a second that presumes their principal function to be a challenge directed by one male at other males; and finally, that they are a bit of both (as many birdsongs appear to be).

Biologist James Darling has proposed that the song is principally involved in competition between males and acts as a challenge—as a means by which males familiar with the voice of the singer could decide whether risking a fight was advisable. The fact that there is a great deal of fighting between males when competing for females could be considered support for this theory.

Darling has proposed an interesting annex to his theory; he suggests that the song is a means by which females might judge which male is able to hold his breath longest—something that might be a good indication of the male's overall fitness. Understanding how this works involves knowing a bit about the fascinating and unexpected ways in which sound travels underwater.

In the tropical and semitropical areas where humpback whales sing, the overlying layer of warm surface water bends sounds downward. This means that if you were a female listening from close to the surface to a singer also close to the surface, much of the sound would be bent downward so that most of it passed below you where you couldn't hear it. Only a bit of the stray energy would reach you, and so the song would sound faint. Since males continue singing while at the surface, a female could know simply by doing most of her listening from near the surface how often a male had to return to the surface for a breath. She could figure it out by noting how often the song got faint. Unless he sang all but the surface theme softly, there is no way a male could fake things so that she was not aware of his need to breathe, and therefore she would be able to make valid comparisons of the breath-holding abilities of the singing males around her and thereby choose (if so inclined) the male who could hold his breath longest. It is true that humpback whales sometimes sing especially long songs, but it is too early to know whether this interesting theory is correct.

But these theories about the song's function offer little explanation for the most unique feature of songs—their changeableness. Others have theorized that because songs appear to be loaded with information, they could be relating the whale's annual saga; singing, for example, about where the best feeding is to be found, and what fishing techniques work best this year. But if this were so, we would not always expect to hear different songs each year; we would expect to hear the old songs recur when the conditions they were describing recurred. But such is not the case. We have North Atlantic recordings spanning forty years, and although some of the sounds in old and new songs are the same, the old phrases are not ever repeated.

As regards the possible language content of humpback whale songs one can say with certainty only that no one knows whether they contain anything at all that we would equate with language. At the present state of knowledge, claims to the contrary are simply speculation.

It has also been proposed that humpback songs could be like a mantra and exert a similar effect—to induce a meditative state. But if this is so, then why do humpbacks only meditate for half the year, and why is it only males that meditate? Why don't females meditate too?

Another suggestion of interest is that the songs may be an effort by the whales to create every possible combination of the musical elements of which their phrases and themes are formed, rather like change ringing—a method of ringing bells in which every possible combination of eight bells is rung in succession according to a simple set of rules—not musical rules, but mathematical rules. (Some changes involve sixteen thousand combinations, and the effect produced is mostly discordant.) By this theory, since the whales' songs certainly have more than eight elements, it might take them a very long time to run through a complete change.

In assessing such a theory we must refer once more to the forty-year sample in which we detect no repetition of sequences. If humpback whales are singing a complete change, our long song sample shows that it is approaching a length which is longer than the presumed life expectancy of the singers. Quite apart from this evidence against the change ringing theory, I see no obvious way in which the singing of complete changes could confer an advantage on the whales should it turn out that they are doing so. I therefore fail to see how it could be selected for during the course of evolution. But then I also fail to see what advantage change ringing confers on humans and why some of our species continue in its practice.

Perhaps change ringing offers a chance to participate in a grand cacophony based on underlying set of simple rules—how curiously similar to a chorus of singing humpbacks. Could it be that there is something attractive about being part of a loud chaos—a tendency so old that it predates whales as well as humans? Are choruses of frogs, insects, whales, and people expressions of a single life force? Is mass hysteria simply an extension of this force? Do loud music and mass hysteria have a common genesis? Is that what drives human behavior during rock concerts? Is effective crowd control more a matter of conducting than of head bashing? Is it possible that there is something riot police could learn from chorusing frogs, humpback whales, and symphony conductors?

One can imagine that humpback whales might use their songs somewhat as Australian aborigines use theirs—as song lines: songs that store descriptions of way points and features needed to keep track of where one is, what landmarks to look for (however faint), and points at which to change course during a long journey. This would mean, however, that if the whales followed the same route every year, the song might be expected to remain the same. With the exception of gray whales (which have not yet been heard to sing), we do not know what routes migrating whales follow, but it again seems unlikely they would choose to swim anything but the shortest possible distance—a strategy which would dictate swimming a constant route and which would thus require an unchanging song to describe it. But even if there is some reason for choosing different routes in different years (fluctuating sources of food might be one), another factor makes it unlikely that humpback songs are like Aboriginal song lines: humpback whales from several different feeding grounds are present together on a single breeding ground. It is known that although individual humpback whales are faithful to a particular feeding area, they are not necessarily faithful to particular breeding grounds. Thus when several humpbacks leave the breeding ground where they have all been singing the same song, they head for several distinct feeding grounds—some of them in very different directions.

Thus, if humpback songs were describing journeys, whales on the same breeding ground that were bound for different feeding areas should sing different songs. But that is not what happens; all whales on the same breeding ground sing the same song. In fact every time we have made comparisons between humpback songs from different parts of the same ocean, we have found that they were the same and that as they changed they changed together. The only exception to this involves whales in the western and eastern North Pacific which sing related but not identical songs. However, the songs evolve in the same way. Because the distances between the two population for which this is the case are the greatest distances between humpback whale populations in any ocean, it is not surprising that changes should take longer to transfer between them and that differences should accumulate a bit more. Overall, it is clear that all whales in the same ocean sing basically the same song even though as changes get made on one side of an ocean they may take more or less time to transfer to the singers on the other side. This process argues for the need to have whales swimming between breeding grounds and bringing songs with them, rather than hearing their relatively high frequencies over oceanic distances, the way, as we shall see, the low-frequency moans in the songs of humpbacks and some other species can travel.

The song line possibility cannot be ruled out completely, however, since it is possible that the song includes directions not just between one breeding ground and one feeding ground in the same ocean but between all known breeding and feeding grounds in that ocean. I can see how such information could be of use to whales, but the theory seems to me a bit far-fetched—one for which there is no evidence one way or the other.

My own theory is more simple-minded: that the songs function as a vocal display by which the male intimidates other males and attracts a female, and that new material appears in the song when a male invents some slight variation that is attractive to females, thus giving him a temporary advantage over other males—an advantage that will last until the other males with which he competes, in whatever breeding area he is in at the present time, have learned his variations.

If he then leaves that breeding area and carries the new successful variations in the song to a different breeding area, he may enjoy a few days or weeks of advantage there until his competitors in that area have also learned the new variations. Of course for this to work a male must have some means of assessing how successful the new variations he invents or learns are.

There is a curious fact about humpback whale songs that could make it possible for a male humpback whale to recognize a successful song change when he heard it: the songs appear to obey some of the same laws that dictate success in the human fashion market. One of these laws is that unless a style is universally accepted in the marketplace it will have a very short life. If it is so accepted, it will last for a much longer time—relatively speaking, of course. Katy, Peter Tyack and I discovered that it is the same with new phrases in humpback whale songs: unless they appear in the songs of all the singers in a particular area, they are lost very quickly.

But once all singers adopt them, they last a long time. This means that a male whale could measure the success of a new song variation just by listening to how many other males around him are singing it. If all the males adopt it, it's a success and is going to last.

A young male might learn a new variant and hear that it was gaining broad acceptance in an area in which he was unable to compete. In such a case his best strategy might be to swim to a new breeding ground, bringing the "market-tested" variation with him. When he arrives at this new ground, he will have a brief advantage before others copy him. We know that males move about considerably between breeding areas in the same ocean even when the breeding grounds are very far apart. For example we know of a North Pacific humpback whale that swam thirty-two hundred miles between two different breeding grounds in the same season—a fact which supports, although it by no means proves, this theory.

Because of the extraordinary practical difficulties attending research on whales, a whale biologist reads with particular interest the results of work on any other species (even unrelated species) whose behavior is similar to that of whales. Such work often provides a useful check on one's conclusions about whales. That such checks have meaning is one of the major conclusions of the past forty years of studies of evolutionary biology and animal behavior. The large body of work on many species as different as insects and mammals has shown that a given social system brings to bear the same constraints on species practicing it whether they are closely or distantly related, so that once they start down the road of the same social system even very distantly related species often end up developing many of the same behaviors.

The parallels between the sage grouse and the humpback whale are a case in point. These two species have been utterly out of contact since the ancestors of whales entered the seas at least fifty-three million years ago. The thing that makes the comparison between sage grouse and humpback whales so interesting is that each of these two species appears to have a similar and rather uncommon social system—the lek system.

A lek is an area of high concentration of males of breeding age all showing off and posturing and making noise and strutting their stuff. When a female is ready to mate, she seeks out one of the crowded leks in her area where she selects a male from among the contenders that are present. A humpback whale singing ground appears to be a lek—a broad area to which male humpback whales come in order to display. Unlike the leks of land animals, however, there is no evidence that a particular male humpback whale defends a particular place in the lek area from day to day. However, in other ways the parallels with the leks of land animals are striking. The lek behavior of the sage grouse has been the subject of considerable study. The leks of grouse are in the open prairie with the males closely crowded together. When females come to these leks to find males, the males intensify their displays, posturing and showing off vigorously. This gives each female a wide selection from which to choose. One basis for her choice appears to be a tendency to select the male that is the healthiest, fittest, or most popular with other females. It has recently been shown that on days when a lot of females come, not only does the most popular male get to mate with more females, he also gets to mate with a higher percentage of the females that appear.

The inescapable conclusion is that at least part of the female's basis for judging which of the males on the lek will make the best father for her offspring is by noting which male is the most popular with other females. Presumably this behavior is selected for because the offspring of a female who mates with a popular male will resemble many offspring in the next generation (a disproportionately high number of local offspring in the next generation will have been sired by the same popular male in our example). This increases the odds that the genes of her offspring will be in fashion among offspring in the next generation. This situation will favor selection of her offspring and explains why popular males not only get to mate with more females when more females come, but why they get to mate with a disproportionate number of those females.

This means that once a male's popularity has been established, he will not only do better than any other male but will mate with a higher percentage of the females present. (One wonders whether this law might not govern the reproductive success of rock musicians in human society—females get to see droves of other females expressing their attraction to them, even though many of them certainly don't appear to be very fit, may carry sexually transmitted diseases, or show visible signs of having sustained damage from substance abuse.)

If female humpback whales really do judge a male by his song, then what the sage grouse could alert us to look for is whether it would make sense for humpback males to copy the song changes of those males who get matings more often, not just as a means of mating more frequently but of mating with a higher *percentage* of all receptive females as more and more females show up. In fact it might even behoove a male to learn the new song variation himself, even if he can't really hope to compete with the larger males, if for no other reason than as a means of making sure that the other more successful whales who introduced the variation won't enjoy a runaway popularity with the females that would cut the less successful male out of even the slim chances he has.

With all this in mind, let us look once again at the humpback males who spend a significant part of the breeding season swimming from one breeding area to another, bringing with them a new and successful variation of a song. Even if they only enjoyed a brief advantage in attracting females on the new breeding ground before other males learned their new song variant, the advantage it would give them, as regards how many matings they got, might be significant (if humpback whale societies obey the same laws that sage grouse societies do) and might easily repay them for swimming all those thousands of miles between breeding areas.

Before leaving the question of what function humpback whale songs serve I want to reiterate that the theories I have mentioned are simply theories and are offered more to stimulate discussion and further investigation rather than with any deep conviction that I think understand the true function of the songs.

No one knows how humpback whales make their songs. We don't even know where in their bodies to look for the sound-making apparatus. It seems reasonable to assume that humpbacks must use air to make sounds, yet they release no air while singing. It is quite possible that they may some-how shunt air around inside their respiratory systems and in the sinuses in their heads—we know that it is not necessary for a whale to open its mouth to be heard underwater. Since the bodies of whales are 95 percent water, most sounds made by a whale pass straight through the watery medium of the whale into the water of the sea without the whale having to open its mouth. Humpback whales can therefore be heard just fine when they sing with their mouths closed. (We have to open our mouths to be heard because the human body also being 95 percent water is relatively opaque to airborne sound, and sounds have to be conducted from their place of origin in the lar-ynx out through the air in the throat and mouth and into the sea of air that envelops us.)

When you are very close to a singing whale you can hear it singing right through the hull of a quiet boat. The boat's hull acts as a kind of sounding board to help the sound pass from water to air. (See the appendix for more on this). Back in the days of quiet boats, sailors told stories about strange and haunting sounds coming from the sea. Perhaps the most famous of these is the myth from the *Odyssey* in which the deadly Sirens used their fatally beau-tiful songs to lure sailors to their deaths.

When he encountered the Sirens, Odysseus had his men's ears stopped with wax so they couldn't hear the singing but left his own unplugged. He also took precautions to avoid getting himself into too much trouble by ordering his men to ignore him even if he begged them to row toward the Sirens. And he also had himself tied to the mast—just in case. In this way Odysseus was able to hear the Sirens' singing and survive.

I've long suspected that the sailors' stories of the Sirens had their origins in humpback whale songs. When sailors heard humpback whales sing, it seems to me it would have been exceedingly unlikely that they would have realized that it was a whale making the sound. This is because when a whale is underwater singing you cannot see it, and when it is at the surface alter-nating breathing with singing, you hear nothing whatever of the song through the air. In order for you to hear even the faintest rendition of a song, the whale must be submerged and your boat stationed almost directly above the singer. But in that position you are actually hearing the sound coming through the hull of the boat, which gives you no indication at all of the direc-tion of the source. When you are swimming you will hear the song loudly through the water, even though you may be quite far from a singing hump-back. But because human ears are nondirectional when underwater, you get no indication of the direction from which the sound is coming no matter how close you are to the singer. I suspect that our generation is the first to swim up to whales underwater, but even if earlier generations had done so, they wouldn't have been able to see the whales clearly without goggles. And even if they somehow mastered that and could see a singing whale clearly, a singing whale shows no movement whatever of its mouth or throat, unlike a bird, which opens its beak to sing, and so you cannot see that it is singing—and to make matters worse, as you approach a singing whale it goes silent.

Whenever sailors heard the "Sirens'" songs through the bottoms of their boats, there would always have been humpback whales nearby, but the chance that these sailors would connect the two things—whales and songs—is in my opinion unlikely. Besides, before whaling, sailors were typically afraid of whales and whenever they saw them sailed or rowed hard away from them. But, as I have pointed out, you must be directly over a humpback and in a quiet boat to hear it singing—you won't hear it if you're racing away from it. Besides, there was no reliable information at that time about just what a whale was. Whales were sea monsters and were, to boot, bigger than most boats. It's a fair bet that the person who could make the most lurid fabrications and claim most unshakably that whales were frightful agents of destruction would have been the one whose opinion held sway—even with those who didn't want to believe it. And after all, what better thing for conjuring up a terrifying myth than strange and beautiful voices heard while in the company of terrifying sea monsters? Homer would surely have appreciated the value of stories containing that vivid combination. It is also possible that since humpback whales continually change their songs, the songs the sailors described to Homer were, indeed, stunningly beautiful. In the late 1960s I heard North Atlantic humpback songs that could best be described that way.

But the best argument for humpbacks being the Sirens rises, I feel, from the peculiar way in which sounds get from the water into the air when one is in a small, quiet, wooden boat. In modern boats with a motor or generator running all the time you cannot hear a whale singing through the hull. But in a boat powered by oars, whenever the singer is very close to the boat you are able to hear the singing right through the body of the boat. And, because the water in which the boat is floating is vibrating, the entire hull is being excited to vibrate. This means that sounds are being broadcast at you from all points of the hull. Essentially you are sitting in the middle of a loudspeaker with sound coming at you from all directions simultaneously. This is, for any human being, ancient or modern, an entirely unique experience. We always think we know the direction from which every sound we hear is coming. To make the determination we may have had to listen carefully, and our opinion about the direction may have ended up being wrong, but we always think we know. However, since a boat's hull acts as it does, it is impossible to determine the direction from which a whale song is originating. As a result, the song takes on an unfamiliar and otherworldly nature. The way most people's brains resolve this dilemma of directionless sound is by deciding that the whale song is originating from inside their heads; something that would have been entirely inexplicable to ancient sailors (or to ancient scientists for that matter)—just the thing from which to create resoundingly memorable myths.

We are not sure just *where* in the Mediterranean the Sirens lived (for it was in the Mediterranean that Odysseus had his great adventure), but we know that humpback whales do exist there now.[8]

Of course we cannot be certain they have always been in the Mediterranean; in fact the oceanographic literature of the Vatican library offers evidence that they were absent. It comes from a wonderful theory that involved whales. The Vatican was concerned about a theory of tides that was developing at the time and that conflicted with the Vatican notion of planetary motion. To get around this, a new theory was presented: it was whales that caused the tides. Everyone knew there are no tides in the Mediterranean and everyone knew there were no whales in the Mediterranean—which proved the theory.

Homer fails to situate the Sirens accurately, but since the sailors of his day didn't really know very precisely where they had been, he can be forgiven (I suppose that the sailors of those days had to be content to wave their arms a lot when explaining their whereabouts, since they seldom had any clear idea of where they had been, where they were going, or, for that matter, where they were). There is a sixteenth-century print showing whales being flensed on the shores of the Strait of Messina (between Sicily and Italy—one place thought by some scholars to have been the home of the Sirens). Although you cannot tell what the species is from the engraving, charts of the strait reveal areas that have bottom topography at an ideal depth to serve as a humpback whale singing ground. The sea floor around places where whales were dragged into shallow water for flensing is always littered with sunken bones. For many years I have wanted to find the point on Sicily where the scene in the print is taking place (the engraving is so carefully done it looks as though it might be possible to find it by lining up the mountains in the scene), and having found it, to search the seabed for whale bones. If one found humpback bones, it would prove that humpbacks once came here and would make the Siren myth a more intriguing mystery.

Given that the lineages of whales and humans have been absolutely separate for so many tens of millions of years, there is, as I have mentioned earlier, good reason to expect that the sounds that people and whales make would be totally different and entirely unrelated in the two species—particularly when these two species are very distantly related and live in two such different environments. After all, the choices open to any noise-making system are in effect infinite, and whenever animals have totally different evolutionary paths, they tend to diverge (the longer the evolutionary time period the wider the divergence), since each is being affected by independent, random mutations. The laws of chance dictate that these mutations are unrelated in the two groups—hence the divergence. When this concerns sounds, what we would expect to hear is a greater and greater difference in the sounds produced. But so similar are the songs of humpbacks to some human music—particularly to some of the music of the Orient—that many people are struck by the parallels.

Animals that look very similar even though they are distantly related are said to be examples of convergent evolution—a situation in which the forces that shape animals are apparently so strong with regard to what will work in a given niche that there is really only a very narrow range of body plans that will fill the bill. Evolution slowly shapes the bodies of any animal that can occupy that niche until it ends up looking like other species elsewhere that are occupying an equivalent niche. When two such species encounter each other, one will have a slight advantage and will replace the other.

When animals have been isolated for millions of years, the convergence can become very pronounced indeed. An example is the marsupial mice of Australia and the mice of the rest of the world. The former carry their young in a pouch like minute kangaroos, while the latter include the familiar house and field mice. (Australian mammals have been out of contact with the rest of mammalian evolution since the continent of Australia sailed off on its own about forty-five million years ago.) Although they are no more closely related than a kangaroo and an antelope, the two mouse species look so similar most people would have to examine them closely enough to note the pouch in one of them before they noticed that they were different. The reason they look so identical is that the forces that control the mouse lifestyle are so stringent and so universal that only a small number of viable body plans can fill the bill.

If whale songs and human songs are examples of convergent evolution, what is the major force affecting the lives of humpback whales and people that has made their songs so similar? Presumably it must concern the brains of these species—yet the brains of humans had not begun to evolve into anything like their present form until long after baleen whales had large brains with large acoustic areas and had entered what has proven to be a long period of relative stability. It must be that whatever is shaping the songs of whales and people is older than we thought.

The strange parallels between the laws of song composition in humpbacks and people suggest to me that the vertebrate brain finds relatively few sounds attractive, so that when, in the course of evolution, we and whales were selecting from among all the possible sounds we could make (we with voices and instruments and whales with whatever it is that they use to make their sounds—presumably valves and sinuses inside their heads) that our two species independently selected the same sounds as well as the same basic laws of musical composition (of course whales probably would have selected them millions of years before we did).

In 1989 I worked with musicians Paul Halley and Paul Winter on a record album called *Whales Alive*—a series of compositions taken from whale songs. When we were making the album my job was to transcribe whale songs by writing out the notes of which they were composed. To achieve this I first found on my cello (the only musical instrument I can play at all) the note the whale was singing. What resulted were wonderfully bizarre tone rows that pianist/organist Paul Halley (who can score anything) would harmonize. In so doing he succeeded in embedding whale songs into the last five hundred years of Western musical tradition. He and Paul Winter then played them together with whale sounds, breaking off from the whale line from time to time to improvise on the whale themes in jazz style. This had the effect of placing the songs in a more current musical context.

Thus what we created were pieces composed by whales but arranged and played by humans. Before we made *Whales Alive* together I had always been a purist about whale songs, feeling loath to mix them with anything—a process I viewed as gilding the lily. But bravery is attractive in all enterprises, even musical composition. So I opened my mind and went along with the two Pauls. Some of the cuts on the album have a profound impact on human audiences—particularly on Japanese audiences, where the record has enjoyed its greatest popularity.

To my knowledge no one has yet tried playing the compositions in *Whales Alive* to humpback whales, so I have nothing to offer about how or whether they react to them. Biologist Christopher Clark once played Handel's *Water Music* to the far less musical-sounding right whales of Argentina but saw no visible reaction either to that composition or to humpback whale songs (the right whales did, however, turn immediately toward his underwater loudspeaker whenever it was broadcasting either right whale sounds or Chris's voice imitating them).

When the two Pauls and I were making the *Whales Alive* album, we found that no matter how we manipulated it everything we created was reminiscent of the music of the twentieth-century composer Messiaen. Messiaen had one of the earliest collections of recorded birdsongs and used it as the basis for some of his most famous compositions. I had discovered at the start of my research on whales that if you speed up humpback songs they sound like birdsongs, just as slowing down the songs of melodious birds (e.g., the Carolina wren or the wood thrush of the eastern United States)[9] makes them sound uncannily similar to humpback whale songs. I suspect that even if they were not particularly taken by them, anyone who spent an afternoon listening to the music of Messiaen, slowed-down birdsongs, *Whales Alive*, and *Songs of the Humpback Whale* would see strong similarities between the sounds of each of these "musical" traditions and might get the feeling that they had been sampling the music of some unfamiliar human culture.

I have spent such an afternoon; it gave me the unmistakable impression that whales, birds, and humans share peculiarly similar laws of musical composition. I get the feeling that the main difference between the songs of humpbacks and songbirds is their pace and pitch—a consequence of each animal's size. As I noted earlier, the metabolism of any warm-blooded animal is slower or faster depending on its size (fast for small animals, slow for large ones). As a general rule, the larger the structures involved in sound production, the lower pitched the sounds made. It makes sense that whales should sing slower and lower than birds do, simply as a consequence of their enormous size. However, what *is* surprising is that the notes whales and humans sing are similarly melodious and that some of the laws of song composition that we and they use should be so similar. To me it suggests strongly that the vertebrate brain, whether located in the head of a humpback whale, a songbird, or a human, may only find a relatively small array of manipulations of acoustic material attractive—which suggests that there may be a single acoustic aesthetic shared by vertebrates, even vertebrates as distantly related as humans, whales, and birds.

It must be only recently that whales have become aware of humans. The vast majority of them still probably have no knowledge of our existence—of our boats, yes, but of us? Unlikely. It would be hard to imagine a more total barrier to contact and mutual understanding than that which exists between animals like whales which live entirely in the sea, and ourselves, living almost entirely on land. Therefore prior to the appearance of ships just a few hundred years ago it is no more likely that whales heard us singing than that we heard them singing. It might, I suppose, have happened very occasionally under very exceptional circumstances, but not very often and not to many individuals from either species. Before humanity had achieved even the most primitive means of moving upon the sea—a log, a bundle of reeds—there was no way a whale could have had anything but the most rudimentary hint that we even existed. If whales saw us at all we would have appeared dim and indistinct—ectoparasites clinging to some large, floating object or a dimly perceived shape moving along a distant shore, viewed fleetingly, once in a lifetime, through eyes designed for seeing underwater.

By the time our earliest hominid ancestors appeared, the whale species already in existence looked so much like their modern counterparts do that any one of us might have trouble distinguishing them from modern whales. Modern whales had been in command of the seas for twenty-six million years—eighty-five times longer than modern humans have existed and two to four times longer than the entire hominid lineage. And what of the twenty-seven-million year history of whales before that? Even then the marine ancestors of whales were, to quote Polonius, "very like a whale." During the entire fifty-three million years that intervened between ancient and modern whales there is no chance of any significant acoustic contact having occurred between whales and our primate lineage.

Given all this, why should there be such intriguing similarities between the songs of whales and our own songs? Why should they sound so similar to our ears? And why should whale songs and human songs use such similar laws of composition to achieve their effects on listeners?

To me the most striking affinity between the musical traditions of humans and humpbacks is the impact whale songs have on human emotions. Many people are moved to tears when they hear them—as though something unaccountably ancient was overmastering them. This commonality of aesthetic suggests to me that the traditions of singing may date back so far they were already present in some ancestor common to whales and us. If this is true it says that the selective advantage of singing and of the laws upon which we humans base our musical compositions (laws which we fancy to be of our own invention) are so ancient they predate our species . . . are tens if not hundreds of millions of years old . . . are thousands of times older than we are.

Music is fluctuating patterns of energy. When music is played, everything is affected and shaped: the drum, the drum skin, the wood of the drum, air, ears, walls, floors. The physicist Brian Swimme notes that "We think of the drummer as playing the drum only; in truth, the drummer is playing the world." Swimme points out that galaxies come from music—that what organized both galaxies and their clustering must have been the patterns of energy, the music, that permeated the original fireball at the beginning of time. The fireball was not flame, but of a density greater than anything on earth. "Chords of energy resonated throughout [it] like music vibrating through a great cosmic bell. These patterns of music organized the fireball into complex forms—forms that would receive the name, some fifteen billion years later, 'galaxy.' A galaxy is a chord of music from the fireball, now expressed in a new form. . . . The music of the fireball becomes galaxies, becomes stars, becomes meadowlarks, humans and whales."[10]

In mathematics there is an unproven (and probably unprovable) concept called mathematical Platonism that supposes there to be a universal mathematics awaiting discovery. Is there a universal music awaiting discovery, or is all music just a construct of whatever mind is making it—human, bird, or whale? The similarity of music in humans and whales tempts one to speculate that the Platonic alternative does exist—that there *is* a universal music awaiting discovery. (If so, have whales, with their jump on us of tens of millions of years, come closer to it than we?) Is it possible that those who believe that whales have a profound message about the universe to deliver to humankind may actually turn out to be right? And that when we have discovered the universal music we will finally understand what whales have been trying to tell us?

There is not enough evidence to determine how ancient singing is. But if it is as ancient as I believe, it would perhaps explain why it is that we find so much meaning and emotion in music and yet cannot explain why it makes us feel the way it does. Such an impenetrable vagueness about such a basic part of our lives seems to be a sign of something whose roots lie closer to our ancient lizard brain than to our recent reasoning cortex—something with a more ancient origin than human language, which is, after all, the quintessential invention of that most recent and most prominent human trait, the cerebral cortex.

If there is a truth hidden here, might it not suggest that the depth of emotion evoked by the music of a Bach or a Mozart owes its effect to laws of composition, laws of ordering, laws of symmetry that are in fact older than our species and that exert their effect beneath our consciousness? Might they not, in fact, be as old as the universe? Might they not, in fact, as Swimme suggests comprise the very order of that universe? That order to which we respond with such longing? Is it possible that the universe sings? Is it possible that God is the song of the universe?

CHAPTER 5

A Heard of Whales

If we wish to understand the social behavior of a species, it is fundamental to find out how many individuals of that species are in contact at any one time and are thus affecting one another's behavior. At the simplest level, this comes down to the knowledge of how large the species' social units are (in the case of whales, their herds). In this chapter I will explore the question of herd size in whales, the sense modality whales must be using to keep the herd together, and how widely they might be scattered about the sea and still stay in contact. In other words, how do whales maintain their herds and what is the maximum herd size? The chapter avoids some of the headier details of ocean acoustics (which are summarized in the appendix), as I have tried to keep it all as nontechnical as possible.

Consider the following statement: With very few exceptions, whales are social animals. If sociality can be measured by the number of animals in a herd, then toothed whales, sometimes forming herds of a thousand or more animals, are the most social of all. Baleen whale herds, on the other hand, usually contain less than ten individuals. They do sometimes get much larger—the biggest of which I'm aware being a herd of fin whales near Norway, estimated to contain at least a thousand individuals.

There is an assumption in the previous paragraph that makes the entire paragraph nonsense, and that stems from the way in which we define "herd." The word is usually used to describe a group of animals of the same species whose behavior is linked—so far, so good, but how do we determine that their behavior is linked? We do so by watching, and we *see* that they are, for example, moving or resting or feeding more or less together. The word "see" presents the problem. For if we are using vision to make a judgment of who's in the herd, and the whales are using some other sense besides vision to keep together, our conclusions will almost certainly have no bearing on what the whales consider to be their herd, and our thoughts about herds and herding behavior will therefore have no relevance at all. So the first thing we need to know is which sense modality (or modalities) whales use to maintain their herd structure. Let us first ask what senses whales *could* find useful as a means of maintaining contact with each other. What would the sense of vision do for them?

In clear, midocean waters near the equator at midday, it is possible when diving in a submersible to sense light from the surface down to about 1,600 feet. The depth at which you can truly say it is dark varies. In waters offshore major cities such as New York, Tokyo, or Rio, the sea is a kind of grayish, greenish brown because of plankton and suspended mud combined with effluents from the city. In such water half the light striking the surface is gone at less than 10 feet, and 90 percent by 25 feet. In the very clearest midocean waters, we find that for every 230 to 250 feet of depth, the intensity of sunlight falls to about one-tenth of what it was. Thus, at around 1,800 feet, the light intensity is only a hundred-millionth of what it is at the surface, and you probably won't see it. By 2,000 feet, however, we can safely assume that we would not see any light at all, even on a day of blazing sunshine.

The greatest distance at which anyone has ever reported being able to see an image underwater is about a thousand feet (about four city blocks). This occurred under shore-fast antarctic ice—a place where the sea is so still that most of the suspended matter in it has settled out, leaving crystal-clear water behind. Under most circumstances a hundred-foot visibility is extraordinarily good. I have experienced such clarity of water only four times in my life: in Hawaii, the Seychelles, Sri Lanka, and in the eastern tropical Pacific.

So I conclude that even under the best circumstances, vision won't render useful images beyond a hundred feet, and under most circumstances a whale can't even see its own tail—it's simply too far away from its eye through the murk.

One might presume that the sense of smell is as important to whales as it is to sharks, which can detect the odor of their prey far farther than they can see it, even in the clearest water. The olfactory areas of the brains of whales and dolphins, however, are poorly developed, though all of the typical mammalian olfactory regions of the brain are known to be present in dolphins. There are also small depressions at the base of the tongue which seem to be involved in taste. For a long time there was speculation that a pair of grooves on the undersurface of the tip of the upper lip of baleen whales was being used for chemical sensing. However, its microscopic anatomy suggests that it is some kind of touch receptor. The thing that made these grooves so tempting as chemoreceptors is that they are believed to be derived from Jacobsen's organ, a sense organ that appears to be used in ungulates like stallions, for example, to sample the urine of females so as to assess their state of estrus. (In horses it is believed to come into play during the so-called flehmen display in which the stallion lifts his head high after sampling the mare's urine—presumably to allow the urine to run over his Jacobsen's organ.) I have twice seen a female right whale urinate copiously while being vigorously pursued by males in a mating group, though this by no means demonstrates that it had any significance.

There are consistent reports by reliable observers of what seems an entirely baffling observation: for example, when they wander into an area where another beluga whale has been killed several hours before, belugas flee. The same species has been seen fleeing abruptly when startled by a fisherman's gun. After some time a new herd appeared and when it arrived at the same spot from which the first herd had fled to the open sea it fled as well though there was no visible sign of any disturbance. People also report very widely spaced bowhead whales moving through almost continuous ice cover where there are only occasional leads but where a series of whales use exactly the same breathing holes even though they may visit them as much as an hour after the previous visit from another whale. This suggests that a scent trail may have been laid down. The Glockner-Ferraris (along with S. Atkinson) have reported[1] mucous secretions being released into the water from the genital slit of female humpback whales which on analysis were found to contain female hormones but no male hormones. It has recently been demonstrated that gray whales have an anal gland (something used by many mammals for scent marking). However, there is still no definite proof that whales are using any chemical sense they may have for anything other than tasting their food (captive cetaceans reject food contaminated with various chemicals). Neither the behavior of belugas nor my observation of right whale females urinating while in mating groups nor the mysterious use of breathing holes by bowheads nor the evidence of glands and secretions can be said to demonstrate clearly a chemical sense in whales. In spite of this failure to demonstrate that olfaction is a useful sense to whales I remain to be convinced that it is not of greater use than is generally believed. I await the work of others. But even if evidence finally appears I am betting that the chemical sense will prove to be of little use to whales in maintaining herds over any but quite short distances.

There is always the possibility that some electric sense could be used by whales for herd maintenance. Sharks and a variety of other fish are exquisitely sensitive to electric fields, enabling some species to find prey completely hidden in the sand by detecting the faint electrical currents associated with the animal's muscle action potentials (such as its beating heart). I must emphasize, however, that no electric sense has ever been detected in either whales or porpoises.

There are muddy-river-dwelling porpoise species whose eyes are no more than vestigial organs, like those of cavefish. Some of the fish who share their muddy rivers have organs that emit electric fields that the fish then use for setting up territories, attracting mates, and detecting objects a few centimeters away. If the river dolphins could detect the electric fields of these fish, they could catch them. Although it is not entirely out of the question that blind river dolphins may turn out to have some degree of electrical sensitivity, it would seem hardly necessary since, as we shall see, they—like all dolphins and porpoises that have been studied in more than the most passing way—have a far more powerful method of examining objects, even in opaque water—their exquisite sense of hearing and their highly evolved sonar. This includes species like the spotted dolphin, which has been filmed attacking fish apparently well hidden under a thin layer of sand.

No, I am forced to conclude that whales would not find it possible to use either vision, smell, or some electrical sense to maintain the large herds in which they are often encountered. The only sense that seems a likely candidate for whales is sound. We know that whales make a great variety of sounds and we know (from experimental evidence) that bottle-nosed dolphins have exquisitely sensitive hearing extending to frequencies three octaves higher than those we humans can hear. We also know (from anatomical evidence) that large whales have well-developed inner ears and exceptionally well-developed acoustic areas in their brains.

This suggests that sound is important to them. The primary reason that sound would be so useful to cetaceans is that it penetrates ocean water so superbly well. Make a loud bang in the ocean, and it illuminates all the black water beneath the boat, piercing right through to the sea floor, then ricocheting back to the surface, twinkling, acoustically, off everything in its path. The ensuing cascade of echoes—if we only knew how to interpret them— would enable us to image things in the sea as well as the major features of the sea floor. This is known to be what sonar does for a dolphin, and everything we know points to dolphins being masters at it.

Because we observe the world with eyes, our most vivid impressions are stored as visual images: the first time we flew above the clouds in a plane; our first sight of a waterfall; the time we dropped a casserole of baked beans on the white rug. For whales, vision is useful only for close-up examination of objects. Sound is much more useful for middle and distant "views," and therefore I suspect that many of their most lasting impressions are stored not as visual but as acoustic images.

One of my longest ongoing preoccupations is simply trying to imagine what it would be like to be a whale, to observe the world around me primarily through the interpretation of sound waves rather than light waves. What must a whale's acoustic impression of its first breach be like? What about the sound of an approaching pack of killer whales or the sensation the whale feels when a killer whale's sonar locks onto it for the first time? Or that moonlit night when, swimming in deep ocean, a whale passes a dead companion floating motionless at the surface—no sound of breath but only the lapping of waves against its body, a strange sound out here where normally the waves lap against the moving, steaming flanks of live whales? I imagine the whale slowly circling and examining the corpse in the moonlight, and then moving on. What will its feelings be each time it hears that same lapping sound again?

What are a sperm whale's sensations on its first truly deep dive into the unknown abyss where, for the first time, it pursues and then bites into something that has hitherto been nothing but a furtive, withdrawing echo? Forever after, that echo will evoke the sensations of scales, and a definite texture, and a violent struggle leading to an evocative crunch, followed by submission and a flood of delicious taste—the echo from it never again being impersonal but now given substance—enriched, imbued with reality, texture, and anticipation.

And what about the impact on a male of the image of an "acoustically beautiful" female when he has deduced for the first time the sensuous echoes of her shape?

Because we may not be familiar with the concept of underwater sound, it is well to get a bit calibrated. Sound moves through any substance whether gaseous, liquid, or solid. In fact the medium through which it propagates least well is the gaseous kind with which we are most familiar—air. It propagates far better through water, and better still through rock. The only thing through which it will not propagate is a vacuum—for example, the vacuum of space—which is a good thing; otherwise we might be deafened by the roaring of the nuclear holocaust taking place on the sun.

Sounds sound exactly the same whether carried through water, air, or even the rock mantle of the earth—it's only that they sound softer when made in one medium and heard in another. If you were lying quietly underwater in a swimming pool, holding your breath and listening as your friend shouted to you from dry land, you would hear exactly what your friend was saying and you would know at once that it was your friend's voice and not someone else's. Your friend's voice would sound exactly the same as it sounded in the air, only much fainter. There are two reasons for this: 1) your ears are suited for listening to airborne sounds, not waterborne sounds, and are therefore more sensitive to sounds with the characteristics of airborne sounds; and 2) a sound wave loses a lot of energy whenever it passes from air to water or water to air.

When you want to listen to sounds underwater you lower a hydrophone into the water, attach it to an amplifier, and listen to it through headphones or a loudspeaker. If you had a hydrophone in the water and a microphone in the air and were recording the sounds of ocean waves, your two recordings would sound almost identical except that in the underwater recording you would also be able to hear ocean noise along with echoes from the bottom. If there were boats nearby, you could also hear the sounds of their propellers while the in-air microphone would also pick up voices, the cries of gulls, and other sounds in the air. If you take a very sensitive hydrophone, hold it in the air, and speak into it, you will hear your voice clearly, although it will sound very faint compared to using a microphone in the same setup. However, even though they may sound the same, there are important differences in the characteristics of sounds traveling through the air and sounds traveling through water. But these differences are not intuitively obvious.[2]

Whales live their whole lives in visual conditions that would seem like a perpetual fog to us. Swimming along underwater, a whale usually cannot see its herd mates, but it can hear them and it undoubtedly knows they are only a few hundred yards away to the left, just as in a thick fog we can hear the foghorn or bell from the ship just to our left but cannot see it. When the ship looms out of the fog practically on top of us, the passengers on both ships only survive if both captains have been proceeding with great caution. But with radar both captains can move their ships along faster because the radar sees through fogs and allows the captains to detect ships and determine their movements long before they are close enough to pose any danger. Whales use sonar to see through water that light cannot penetrate. They get from sonar the same advantage we get from radar. Sonar enables them to swim faster in safety, even in opaque seas.

Fast-swimming animals living in tightly knit social groups in a relatively opaque medium like seawater are, in effect, partly or wholly blind. A group of whales each weighing fifty tons and traveling together in a tightly knit herd must run the same risk of collisions that a convoy of ships does when navigating in a thick fog—only whales face the added complication of having collisions in the third dimension as well. For whales collisions in any dimension could be disastrous.

The skin of a whale appears to be very tender; you can rub off the outer layers with your thumb. Even much thicker skin would be damaged in a collision between animals this size. A collision even at moderate speeds between animals the size of baleen whales could disable both parties.

When I was a child growing up in New York City, I used to take the ferry between Manhattan and Staten Island and during the tricky crosscurrent landing at Staten Island watch as the ferry sometimes missed its slip slightly. The ferry berths were flanked by two large clusters of wooden pilings deeply sunk in the mud and tightly bound together with thick steel cables. They loomed above the deck of the ferry, yet when the ferry nudged against them they would bend like a bundle of reeds. As they groaned and shrieked with the force of the impact, the zone of contact between ferry and pilings would become so heated that tar on the pilings would melt (I can still remember the acrid smell of the smoke). Ferries of the time were only a little heavier than the biggest blue whales. This leads me to guess that even though the impact would be greatly padded and absorbed by the blubber, a collision between large whales might do real damage.

If, instead of diving and surfacing in synchrony, each whale in a tightly packed herd left the group and returned to the surface to breathe any time it felt like it, there might be disastrous collisions like those which sometimes occur in convoys when ships move asynchronously. Even though all the ships in a modern convoy are equipped with radar and radios, synchronous maneuvers in formation are still strictly observed—in order to avoid collisions. The fact that small herds of large whales breathe in rough synchrony may simply be a means of maintaining a strict formation in order to avoid collisions. I assume that if animals as large as whales are to live in social groups for a lifetime of several decades that they must surely require some form of rudimentary acoustic signaling if only to avoid serious collisions.

It may seem overly simplistic to wonder whether whales moving in groups communicate such rudimentary information as, for example, the direction of an intended turn (a message no more complex than that sent via turn indicators on a car). As I have noted before, there is surprisingly little evidence that whales communicate by any means—including acoustically. This doesn't imply they don't communicate, it just means that we don't have much evidence that they do. It seems to me that swimming in herds is an example of a situation in which communication might well be crucial.

When they have been out of sight of each other for a long time and wish to come together it is of obvious advantage to marine animals to be able to locate each other acoustically. It seems logical that the evolution of an acoustic communication system in whales probably started with simple signals for staying together and avoiding collisions and went on to the development of louder sounds so that herds could be spread out over wider areas and still maintain contact.

If we know how far away one whale can hear another, then we know how large an area another whale can be in and still be contacted by its friend. The area within which a whale can contact another is a circle with a radius equal to the maximum distance its voice can carry and still be heard. Because the *area* of a circle increases in proportion to the square of its radius, it follows that if a whale could amplify its voice to carry twice the distance, it could quadruple the effective area in which it could be heard. From this simple mathematical law we see that if it is important for whales to communicate, the selective pressures for speaking louder must be very great. It's as if the effects on the whales' fitness of each small improvement in how loud it can shout were squared.

As a freshman at Cornell University, my younger daughter, Laura, won the "Primal Scream Contest." Ever since it's been a great family story with which to impress newcomers, as well as the source of a lot of laughter between Laura and her siblings. However, had she, like a whale, derived some major benefit out of being able to contact others at longer distances, a stentorian voice like Laura's might be of great significance to her lineage (after all, with less extraordinary abilities major dynasties have been founded).

If, as we have surmised, sound is the only sense modality available to whales for purposes of staying in touch over distances greater than a few meters, then aren't all whales that are in acoustic contact members of the same herd? If we talked about a whale "heard," might we not be describing more accurately what whales consider to be their herd?

Though we may not know how big a herd is, we can be absolutely confident of one thing: if whale herds are held together acoustically and we judge their size on the basis of visual evidence, the chance that we are wrong will be almost 100 percent. If, after watching a group of whales, we decide that they constitute the whole herd, and if it later turns out that we were right, it will only be by chance that we were so. For, as I have pointed out, you cannot assess an acoustic phenomenon visually any more than you can judge a visual phenomenon acoustically—if you decide that the brightest rainbows accompany the loudest thunder you will sometimes be right of course, but only by chance. Most of the time you will be wrong.

Which is to say that our currently held beliefs regarding what constitutes a herd of whales are nonsense—just pure guesswork. As this chapter attempts to demonstrate, it is possible that the truth about herd size in whales is exactly the opposite of current beliefs—that it may be toothed whales that live in herds with the smallest number of herd mates, and baleen whales that live in herds with the largest number.

If the term "herd" must accommodate a species in which each member is in communication with all adjacent members and those in turn with all adjacent to them, then it may follow that all porpoises are, indeed, members of one herd. The truth is probably that porpoise herds *are* much larger than we have thought them to be but are still discrete entities.

I once traveled for four hundred miles across the eastern tropical Pacific by square-rigger, stopping every three hours to listen through a hydrophone. Though we seldom saw porpoises, at every stop we heard at least a few porpoise cries. Sometimes they were very far away but they were always there. Their calls were like some vast net cast across the sea. The cries of porpoises, as it turns out, are too high pitched to travel very far,[3] so each animal probably could only hear a few of the animals closest to it. To keep together as a herd, porpoises in the open ocean would have to pass information along by repeating it. Given what one learns by playing the game of "Telegraph," any system which relies on the repetition of messages from individual to individual is bound to be plagued with errors. (Query: "Where are the fish?" Perceived reply [misheard]: "Over here by Sue." Real reply: "Over there by you." Result: the recipient sets off in precisely the wrong direction.) I suspect that herds can only function effectively if the signals that organize them are loud enough to be audible across the whole extent of the herd by every animal in the herd. Therefore what I will take as a herd is a group of whales, all of whose members can hear all other members under average wind conditions most of the time. I feel safe in assuming that however simplistic such a definition may be, it is likely to be a great deal better than calling a group of whales that is visibly moving together in some united purpose a herd. I suspect that in the latter case there is a very large chance that all one is seeing is a part of the herd.

As I have mentioned, the cries of porpoises are too high pitched to travel very far. Sounds that are lower pitched and louder, such as those produced by the larger whales, travel much farther. The sounds made in rhythmic, repeated patterns by fin whales and their near relatives the blue whales are both the loudest and the lowest sounds yet attributed to any animal. At what distance can fin and blue whales hear each other? It was with that question in mind that I became interested, many years ago, in calculating the distance that fin whale sounds can be heard. I will explore the question here in some depth (I have explored it in greater detail in the appendix) for, as we shall see, the sounds of fin and blue whales travel for astonishingly long distances.

As I have said, the sounds made by fin and blue whales are both the loudest and the lowest sounds yet attributed to any animal. Because these sounds are rhythmically repeated patterns of sounds they are properly called songs—

very slow, very simple songs you might say, but songs nevertheless. In the case of fin whales, the songs are in the form of slow, measured sequences of sounds, which when they were first seen on the very slow moving paper recorders of the early sixties (the paper moved about an inch each hour) were called "blips" because they looked like brief spikes instead of the second-long moans that they are.

It is hard to imagine a less apt term than "blip" for a twenty-hertz, deep-throated moan lasting a second. However, by being such an entirely inappropriate term it becomes memorable—rather like a dalmatian I once knew named Stripe—so I will refer here to the moans of fin whales as "blips." For inappropriateness the term "blip" need not feel alone: naval acousticians routinely call fin whales "seismic profilers" or similar names indicating that it is only recently that they have become aware that it is whales who author many of the loud, rhythmic sounds in the sea.

Blips are nearly pure tones centered at about twenty hertz. Twenty hertz lies at the very bottom of the range of sounds we humans could once hear when we were young and when our hearing was at its best—if you're old enough to be reading this, you can probably forget about hearing twenty hertz anymore. Each blip lasts for about a second and is repeated at very regular intervals several times each minute. Sometimes it is hours before the whale either stops or modifies its patterns of blips, and starts blipping at some different interblip interval.

Fin whales make trains of blips for about fifteen minutes followed by a silence of about two and one-half minutes, a pause that suggests that the whale has come to the surface and is breathing. The most common spacing of blip trains is about twelve seconds, but fin whales also produce "doublets," which consist of a loud blip followed by a softer one, the pair repeating every few seconds. Doublets are named for their interblip and interpair intervals. This gives them names like the "22–15 second type," or "9–12 second type," etc.

Blue whales make sounds that are about as loud and as low in frequency as fin whale sounds but that last much longer, some of them about thirty seconds. Some of the sounds blue whales make are long, continuous tones ending in a slow upsweep or downsweep of frequency, but because they sweep in frequency it is a bit more difficult to calculate the distance they travel. Although this chapter is mostly concerned with the very low frequency sounds made by fin whales (simply because most is known about them), all the other members of its genus except the sei whale are known to make some low, loud sounds potentially useful for long-range communication. The general conclusions I present here are potentially applicable to the loud, low notes made by any large whale—blue, Bryde's, minke, humpback, bowhead, gray, and right whales—as well as any other species that is found in the future to make loud, low-frequency utterances.

Before it was shown that fin whales were the authors of the blips, no one could take seriously the idea that such regular, loud, low, and relatively pure frequency tones were coming from within the ocean, let alone from whales. The sounds were first thought to be a simple malfunction in the amplifier— something causing its volume control to oscillate. But when it became obvious that there was nothing wrong with the amplifiers, it was postulated that the sounds were artifacts from geophysical sources located outside the ocean. It was suggested that sources like geomagnetic anomalies, airborne sounds, or seismic signals from inside the earth were responsible. Accordingly, recorders were set up to monitor the same frequency band in these media. But even with the hydrophone recorders overloading on the twenty-hertz acoustic signals, the other monitors showed no signals above background noise, forcing the conclusion that the sounds originated from within the sea and were not—in the words of one of the engineers at the time— "from deep within the earth nor from the action of breaking surf on continental shorelines." Even so, there was still great reluctance to believe that such loud and regular sounds could be coming from whales.

Then someone suggested that the sounds might be a scheme by the Russians to fill the oceans with very low frequency sounds that would establish standing wave patterns in the sea—the idea being that when a U.S. submarine moved it would interrupt the pattern and the sub's position could be determined—a kind of grand expansion of the same technique behind those sonic burglar alarms that insonify a room with a high-frequency sound so that when an intruder moves through it the standing wave pattern is interrupted (or in later versions a Doppler shift created) and an alarm bell activated. With the Russians as a possible cause of blips, there was suddenly lots of money available to study the mysterious twenty-hertz noises. But biologists William Schevill and William Watkins soon showed that the sounds were coming from fin whales, and as soon as it was obvious whales were responsible, the party was over and the funds dried up.

Every now and then paranoia pays a small dividend. This was such an occasion. Such dividends are usually based on some plausible but erroneous assumption; this is such a case.

So, as we can see, we are dealing here with a sound so loud it was first thought to have its origin in everything from faulty electronics to surf on distant shorelines to sources not even in the ocean. Just how loud are these whale sounds? The average of a careful series of measurements gives their loudness at about 155 decibels[4] (where 0 decibels is the human threshold of hearing). One hundred fifty-five decibels is a sound louder than that heard in the front row of a stadium while listening to a rock band, a sound as loud as being a yard from a jet with its engine at full power—a sound so loud that if twenty hertz lay in the middle of the frequencies humans hear well, it would not only be painful, it would cause permanent deafness to twenty hertz tones. Some whales make twenty-hertz sounds at this intensity some of the time, but some make softer as well as even louder sounds. There is some as yet unidentified species of mystery whale that is out there producing sounds even lower than twenty hertz, maybe as low as four hertz. It behaves like a whale, but we don't yet know which species.

In 1971 Douglas Webb and I calculated that before ship traffic noise permeated the oceans, fin whale blips could have traveled as far as four thousand miles and still be heard against the normal background noise of the sea, and that on a quiet day in the pre-ship-propeller oceans they would only have fallen to the level of background noise after traveling thirteen thousand miles![5]

When Webb and I published our theory in 1971 we had no direct evidence that it was true. At the time Doug was essentially alone in the non-military exploitation of long-distance signaling in the ocean and had carried out low-power, long-range signaling experiments in the deep sound channel using pure tones that gave results in good agreement with our predicted propagation distances. However, in the past two years biologist Christopher Clark has managed to track whales using hydrophones located in deep ocean over a thousand miles from the whales.

It is hard to describe the thrill I felt when Chris told me about his work. We were seated by an ancient millstream in an even more ancient churchyard in Bosham, West Sussex, on a sunny June day. A scene in the Bayeux tapestry shows Prince Harold stopping at the church in Bosham to pray for victory (on his way to defeat) at the battle of Hastings in 1066. (The church was already over a thousand years old by then.) The stream we sat by is thought to be the one in which King Canute's eight-year-old daughter was drowned. King Canute ruled Britain from 1016 to 1035. It was he who, in order to prove to his courtiers that they were wrong when they claimed him to be all-powerful, set up a chair at the edge of the sea in Bosham and commanded the advancing tide to turn back. And then smiled when it kept coming.

I felt the advancing tide too when on that summer's day Chris and I sat by the same stream. In his earliest career with whales Chris had worked with me and my first family. He came to Argentina for several years when we were in residence there. Everything in my world was young then and Chris became a part of the family. But then we grew apart for a while. Now he was coming back, to sit on a bench beside an ancient stream and tell me of a wonderful discovery he had made.

When Doug Webb and I first came out with the theory that fin and blue whales could be heard across oceans, it got a very chilly reception among whale biologists. (I suspect that my career was held back significantly because of the way people responded to the theory of long-range communication.) Most of the criticism came from those who knew nothing about the Jules Verne world of ocean acoustics.

However, just before he died, I explained the theory to Maurice Ewing (codiscoverer of the deep sound channel, although better known for his central role in establishing the theory of plate tectonics, the modern explanation for continental drift). When I told him of my trouble getting colleagues in the whale world to take our theory of long-range communication seriously, Ewing's response was heartwarming. He smiled and said, "But it's so obviously true; it could have been predicted ten years ago."

There is a symposium on applied mathematics every summer at Dartmouth University. In 1979 the topic was underwater sound, and I was offered a chance to explain the theory of long-range communication to the participants. Since the symposium had attracted some of the brightest minds in underwater acoustics, I knew it would be the best-informed audience I had faced with the theory. During my lecture I was interrupted every few minutes for questions (it took five hours to get through). However, the only real criticism our theory sustained was that Webb and I had probably been too conservative—that even in the ocean noise of the present day, fin and blue whales ought to have no trouble at all hearing each other across deep oceans. The remarks both by Ewing and the seminar participants certainly were encouraging but only demonstrated that at least someone else agreed with us. They did nothing to change the fact that all we had to offer was a theory.

Thus, when Chris Clark said to me, "Roger, I have tracked a blue whale from over a thousand miles away," the feeling that came over me is one I may never again recapture. The fact that he had not only heard them but had also been able to track them was an off-scale delight.

For me, however, the most moving thing about the moment was that it was Chris, the prodigal son, who had gone out and done what I could not do and was coming back in triumph to tell me. A feeling of amity swept over me, bringing me almost to tears. I felt as though I were bearing witness as the future passed to the next generation. Like old King Canute I smiled as the tide of time washed over me and I felt my gray hairs bending with the eel grass. And yes, I also mourned for the allegorical drowned daughter of my youth—mourned for the passing of those golden years when my first family with Chris as a part of it was young and when, for a brief Camelot, we lived beside whales in Argentina.

When they got to listening through the navy's hydrophone arrays, Chris and several navy acousticians managed to track a blue whale with a particularly recognizable voice for forty-three days, during which time it traveled fifteen hundred miles, starting its journey about three hundred miles northeast of Bermuda and progressing south toward Bermuda and beyond it, then turning west until it was about two hundred miles northeast of Cuba and cutting back northeast to a point about a hundred miles south of where it started, where Chris lost it when it went silent.

Why did the whale become silent? What goal had it reached? Another whale? A seamount of interest? With repeated observations of this nature it should be possible to learn more about the behavior patterns of these whales.

To me, the most intriguing thing Chris discovered was that while still three hundred miles from Bermuda, this whale set off in a perfectly straight line for the island, suggesting that it had either heard another whale there and was traveling toward it or that it had echolocated the Bermuda rise from three hundred miles away—a distance in good agreement with Clark's and Ellison's calculations that three hundred miles represents the distance from which whales should be able to get a useful echo off an island.

In future it ought to be possible to discover whether there is another blue whale vocalizing in the right place next to an island when a blue whale starts to make a beeline for that island. It would be even more interesting to see a whale continuously correct its course to maintain its aim on a second vocalizing whale as that whale moved around. In the near future, Chris will direct our Whale Conservation Institute's boat, *Odyssey*, at a blue whale that he can hear vocalizing in order to see if we can find and record the same whale. If we became adept at doing this, we might get a chance to determine whether it is male blue whales or females or both that make the loudest, lowest sounds. It should also be possible to determine whether the nature of the sounds made by two whales changes when and if their moans start alternating—suggesting a possible exchange of information between them. Of course it now seems very possible to use acoustic censusing to monitor the recovery or the decline of the populations of any whale species that makes low sounds (blue, fin, Bryde's, minke, bowhead, right, and gray whales are known to do so). Commercial whaling is now resuming. If we had a good means of acoustic censusing it ought to be possible to use it to blow the whistle on the whalers when they start to reduce a population of whales they are hunting. It would also be a useful means of defusing two of their most common arguments: that there are plenty of whales just across the horizon; and that some area they have just decimated is only a tiny fraction of the total pool of whales of that species. Ship surveys for whales normally cover a strip only about two miles wide (planes give strips about four miles wide but are hampered by the fact that the plane is moving so fast it only sees about half as many whales as a ship does for the same miles traveled). A ship towing an array of hydrophones can effectively hear whales in a strip 150 miles wide— an improvement of seventy-five times. Once we knew the percentage of silent to moaning whales, a ship that was both carrying an observer and towing an array would have the potential of "sighting" seventy-five times as many whales for every mile steamed.

Visual censuses represent such a small sample of what's out there that they invite irresponsible extrapolation of estimates of whale abundance from a tiny base, resulting in estimates with very wide limits. This situation is invariably exploited by the scientists of whaling nations, who argue for quotas based on the upper end of the estimates, sometimes refusing to accept less than the mean even though they are fully aware that this estimate is just as likely to be above the true value as below it. Having seventy-five times as many "sightings" for every mile steamed would do wonders to alleviate this problem.

The future for this line of research is extraordinarily bright. However, there's a hitch. It will not happen unless the underwater network of hydrophones used by Chris is maintained. It is a network called the Sosus array that was set up over the past forty years at a cost of billions of dollars in order to monitor Soviet submarines. Thanks to the end of the Cold War, this network is no longer necessary and the navy, which mans it, is considering mothballing it. It's a little like giving an astronomer a space telescope and just as its full potential becomes apparent, taking it away. The real problem at issue seems to be security since the sounds of our submarines will be audible over the array. However, it should be at least as easy to screen scientists who are potential users of the system as it was to screen personnel who used it to gather military data. The use of this extraordinary tool seems to be in danger of being lost for irrational reasons. The security issue urgently needs solving. Once the Sosus array is closed down the highly specialized personnel who know how to run it will spread to the four winds, and though it may once more be put on line for military purposes it may never again be available to scientists outside the military. The funds needed to keep it working amount to about twenty million dollars a year. Ten million annually would keep it just ticking over. The ten million dollars cannot seriously be considered a problem, as it is less than one one hundred thousandth of the U.S. tax bill, or one penny on each thousand dollars of tax paid by the average U.S. taxpayer—an annual drain on the average person of about a penny a month. If we could only find the will to make the decision to keep the Sosus array working not only would it cause an unprecedented leap forward in our knowledge about whales, it would also provide another important service.

As I write this in the summer of 1994, ATOC, a major experiment using the Sosus array, is underway. By using underwater sound it should finally be possible to measure whether global warming is taking place and if so the rate at which the earth's temperature is rising. This can be done by measuring the speed of conduction of sound across oceans—the warmer the water, the faster the sound arrives at its destination. Because the arrival time is affected by the entire sound path, local regions of hot and cold ocean don't throw off the measurement if one is listening across an entire ocean. In this way the overall temperature of the earth's surface can be accurately assessed. It would be hard to imagine a result that was likely to have a more profound effect on future policy regarding the release of the combustion products from fossil fuels, as well as other greenhouse gases.

If we could explain this to the whales, I believe they would also wish to see the experiment carried out, even though the noises made during the measurements will constitute yet more noise of human origin in the ocean. As I write this I am, nevertheless, trying to persuade those doing the experiment to change two of the places in which they intend to locate their underwater loudspeakers—Monterey Bay in California, and the Hawaiian Islands. Both of these areas are important habitats for whales. It seems to me that they could hardly represent worse sites for loudspeakers releasing the loudest pure tones ever made by humans. Many conservation groups are opposed to these two sites—many being opposed to having the experiment happen at all, there being other ways in which global warming can be measured which do not involve putting such loud sounds into the ocean over many years. My worry is that information on global warming is desperately needed by humanity (whales would benefit by it as well) and that no one seems to be pursuing the alternative experiments with the same vigor of those who wish to do it with sound. The whole project scenario presents a major dilemma. I think that if something could be done to put the loudspeakers in better areas that the benefits of this experiment would probably outweigh the costs, though the results might be gained at a heavy price for a number of whales. Whatever one's view, the benefits of just these two programs (there are other good reasons to maintain the arrays) seem worth at least a penny a month. Or are we not even willing to pay that much to know about global warming or to learn enough about whales to protect them from whaling?

Chris's discovery provides evidence that the sounds of whales propagate to great distances but doesn't yet prove that they pay any attention to these sounds at long distances. I fully expect that he will soon have evidence bearing on that question as well, but in the meantime, the only evidence that fin and blue whales hear each other over relatively long distances and do something about it is negative evidence. It is the fact that when mating is at its height and fin whales must somehow find each other, they are not concentrated in some known mating ground but thinly dispersed over millions of square miles of ocean. Unless we postulate communication over significant distances, how do fin whales find each other during the mating season? Fin whales do not show the usual marine mammal pattern of coming together at some rendezvous point to mate.

The fact that fin whales must get together for mating at a time when they are thinly dispersed over millions of square miles of ocean is supported by the failure of the whalers to find the breeding grounds for fin whales. Whalers have never found a breeding ground for blue and fin whales the way they have found the breeding grounds—probably all the major ones—for many other species (e.g., humpback, right, gray, and sperm whales).

This failure has not been for lack of trying. Because the economic rewards for finding these breeding grounds of the largest species would be so enormous, the Japanese whalers (particularly) have expended fortunes looking for them. Since the 1960s Japanese scouting boats with lookouts on board (constituting some of the most experienced whale spotters who have ever lived) have covered all the world's oceans looking for new whaling and fishing grounds. Virtually every ten-degree square of latitude and longitude has been thoroughly explored. All this data has been brought together in a map of the world that shows the numbers of sightings made per mile steamed. Although it has not yet been published, I have seen the data and it is clear that when fin whales are outside the Antarctic they are, for the most part, broadly scattered across the world's oceans rather than being concentrated in specific areas. The same is true of other *balaenopterid* species, except for the Bryde's whale, which shows a tendency to remain in relatively small areas throughout the year.

I believe the reason that whalers have never found a breeding ground for blue and fin whales is because none exists. I suspect that when blue and fin whales wish to find a mate—when "he" wishes to meet "she"—they simply start calling. Even if it takes several weeks of swimming to get there, getting together could be achieved by homing on the sounds of individuals or groups of whales. This would free fin whales from the necessity of having to meet on a specific breeding ground at a specific season—a necessity for the much softer voiced gray whales, who are tied to specific rendezvous lagoons in Baja California—a habit that made them very vulnerable to the old whalers.

Marine species that roam widely over huge expanses of ocean often rendezvous in vast numbers either annually or once in a lifetime at precise times and places (salmon, sea turtles, penguins, sea lions, seals, albatrosses, and many other species are examples). The main advantage of such congregations is that they bring members of the same species together in time and space during mating season when they need to choose a mate. An equally important advantage of having a fixed, annual or once-in-a-lifetime rendezvous site is that it makes it possible for the species *not to be together* at other times. This keeps them from competing so directly with each other and encourages the members of the species to spread out over the maximum possible area, exploiting resources whenever and wherever they are encountered. But there is a major disadvantage to the strategy of having a fixed rendezvous time and site: it means that if it is to join a breeding concentration, an animal may sometimes have to leave a feeding area it has discovered at a possibly inconvenient time. It also offers its prey a good opportunity to escape predation, for if its predators are in the habit of deserting their main feeding grounds at the same time each year in order to join a breeding concentration, the prey may be able to choose that time to congregate for breeding.

Another major disadvantage of assembling at some predetermined breeding site is that sometimes food supplies in the vicinity of the assembly site fail, with the consequent loss of a large proportion of the young in the population. This may occur even though food may be abundant in the area the participants left in order to join their breeding concentration. This latter problem, while it might affect dolphins and small whales that are unable to starve for protracted periods, is probably not as important to species like gray or right whales, both of which though they are known to feed outside their main summer feeding grounds are, as I have already discussed, probably capable of fasting for many months.

A system by which animals were able to come together at any time simply by calling to each other over vast tracts of ocean would circumvent the drawbacks of the rendezvous system while at the same time allowing individuals to wander at will over the maximum possible area of ocean, exploiting any food source they could find. It would be a great emancipation for a species to be able to locate potential mates at will without having to go to some mating site to do so.

If the call whales used to find each other was a repetitious signal containing a very simple, redundant message then it would not need to be detected all the time (or even a large fraction of the time) in order to do its job. In fact, for a whale seeking to rejoin a mate or a herd, a single detection, even if thousands of repeats had gone unheard, would be sufficient to indicate the general direction in which to swim. Of course, receipt of more than one signal would help confirm the decision.

There are two other lines of evidence pertinent to fin whales suggesting that they communicate over long distances. The first concerns the fact that migrants can have different feeding destinations in different years (as well as the fact that throughout the year there are at least some fin whales in every part of their range). The second of these involves the ability of fin whales to assemble in major concentrations at unexpected times and places.[6]

In the vast majority of cases the antarctic whaling industry found fin whales concentrated in food-rich areas. But as I have mentioned in chapter 1, the blooms of krill on which the whales feed shift widely from year to year, and fin whales must somehow find the krill in its new locations each year.

Fin whales are also frequently encountered feeding in areas that were covered with ice in other summers. Sometimes tens of thousands of square miles of ocean that were ice covered last year are quite clear of ice this year—and thus freshly accessible for exploitation by the whales.

Also, fin whales are not necessarily faithful to one food-rich area; the analysis of tag recoveries from marked animals reveals that some fin whales wander broadly even in summer, and as I have pointed out earlier (chapter 1), tagged whales are often recovered on feeding grounds far removed from those on which they were marked—as far away as the opposite side of the antarctic continent.

All of this is indicative of a species that freely roams over enormous areas yet somehow finds and mates with its own kind at very different places in different years. It would not be possible to hold a family reunion in a different state every year if you didn't have some means of communicating with your relatives about where to meet.

Fin whales sometimes collect into large herds at unpredictable locations and seasons, and when a group of five hundred to one thousand fin whales is seen in areas in which only a few animals are seen in other years, it seems unlikely that these whales independently stumbled on the same area at the same time. (In one instance a group of fin whales was observed near the Shetland Islands, with up to two hundred whales spouting at once.) It seems more reasonable to postulate some form of communication that enables these whales to assemble.

To summarize the evidence currently in support of the theory of long-range communication: Chris Clark has been able to track humpback whales acoustically at distances of one thousand miles. Doug Webb confirmed experimentally that simple sounds similar to those made by fin whales prop-agate to distances predicted by calculations such as those we used for fin whale sounds. Mating is known to be at a minimum during the one time of year when fin whales are most concentrated, and at a maximum during the time when they are thinly dispersed over millions of square miles of ocean. There are no known breeding concentrations for fin whales. Krill are notori-ous for appearing in unpredictable locations far from regions of previous high concentration, yet wherever krill form their concentrations in different years, fin whales assemble to feast on them. The overall picture of fin whale migrations is one of apparently disorderly movements in which the whales don't follow definite rules. The many exceptions to the stereotyped rules of migration show that fin whales are apparently able to come together at will, even during seasons when they are known to be broadly spread over the ocean. There are also reports of occasional large concentrations of fin whales in areas in which they are usually only sparsely distributed.

All these otherwise inexplicable observations would be explained by fin whales possessing a means of signaling to each other over long distances.

As loud as fin and blue whale sounds are, the power in their blips is really only about ten acoustic watts—about the same power as the light that radi-ates from a thirty-watt fluorescent bulb. I have said earlier that a fin whale is as loud as a rock band. But how could that be when rock band loudspeakers are rated at hundreds of watts? It is because loudspeakers are notoriously inefficient devices (about .1 percent to 1 percent for wideband speakers) and convert most of the watts they absorb from their amplifiers into heat rather than into sound. A speaker rated at a hundred watts doesn't produce anything approaching a hundred acoustic watts.

The thought that an animal other than ourselves might signal by sound over hundreds or even thousands of miles may seem unique, but it is really no more remarkable than the fact that it is possible to signal by means of a hand-held radio. A walkie-talkie putting out ten watts (the same power as the whales' vocalizations) can be heard half a world away . . . *sometimes*. This kind of transmission results from a phenomenon very similar to the kinds of sound channeling one finds in the ocean (see the appendix). The energy of the radio is not allowed to spread but is confined in a duct, in this case an atmospheric rather than a marine duct.

Every now and then when I was trying to communicate via walkie-talkie between the field station in Patagonia and our boat just a mile or two away, our signals would be jammed by some walkie-talkie in America. I remember hearing loud and clear someone in a shopping mall in Louisiana, forty-five hundred miles away, with the call sign "Bullfrog" talking with a friend. So strong was his signal I had to wait until he finished transmitting before I could continue talking to the Zodiac a mile away. I'm sure there must have been many days when Bullfrog's transmitter couldn't be heard more than ten blocks away—similar to days on which even very close whales fail to hear each other—simply because the conditions aren't favorable.

It is easy to be impressed by how loud the sounds of the fin whale are and how far they travel. But the surprising thing is not that they are loud but that sounds of such relatively little energy should be audible so far away in the sea. The fact that they propagate for long distances is a consequence of the strange characteristics of ocean acoustics. And the fact that they are still audible after such long journeys is a consequence of the exquisite sensitivity of the vertebrate ear.

If whales can hear each other over hundreds or thousands of miles, how might such an ability benefit them? Besides the benefit I have already discussed, of finding each other for mating and thus avoiding the necessity of coming together at rendezvous sites each year, it is my belief that fin and blue whales (and probably several other species of large whales) are in tenuous acoustic contact, that is, are communicating throughout relatively enormous volumes of ocean for purposes such as finding food, keeping together in widely dispersed herds, route finding in ice-covered seas, and navigating, both by being beacons for other whales to swim toward as well as echo-locating large underwater features like continental slopes, islands, and seamounts.

Back when I began this discourse about how far fin whales might hear each other, I pointed out that the reason this is an interesting question is because it will tell us how large a herd of whales can be. And I have pointed out that because they make such loud sounds, fin and blue whales are probably able to be in contact anywhere in the same ocean basin. If we accept as the definition of a herd that group of animals which are in contact with each other so that their behavior is in some sense linked, then a single deep-water ocean basin contains a single herd of fin whales. What I am postulating here is a new form of herd structure—a "deep ocean herd," that population which lives in tenuous acoustic contact throughout the deep water encompassing one or more ocean basins. The reason I emphasize basins and exclude the shallow perimeter of the ocean (the continental shelf) is that sound ducting of the kind necessary for long-range communication will not take place except in a deep-water basin. If a whale could signal to another whale anywhere in the same deep-ocean basin or in adjacent deep-ocean basins (such as between the Antarctic Ocean and the ocean basins adjacent to it), then all whales in that overall area could function as one herd—seeking out and utilizing resources scattered unpredictably throughout it.

The greatest potential use of communication for whales may be as a way to share information about the location of broadly scattered food resources. If whales share information about their food finds, then the greater the range over which two whales can detect each other, the greater the potential resources available to each. The simplicity of the fin whale sounds suggests that there might not be enough information in them to describe where the prey was, its relative abundance, and its type. (Sounds used to announce food would presumably have to contain such information in order to be of much use.) But if the whale could get information about the direction and distance to a sound from the characteristics of the sounds it hears (a discussion of how it might do so is coming up), then the information would not have to include direction and distance and need only contain a description of the food to be had.

In regard to finding food there could be many advantages to large herds. The most obvious is that it would give a species the chance to divide up the resources of the sea—a simple way to accomplish this being to have any whale that is hungry remain silent and any that is well fed start blipping. By following such a simple law, a hungry whale could listen for its fellows and swim toward the roar of the loudest summed blips. This strategy would carry it toward the area of best feeding.

Ice distribution is not the only factor that makes it difficult for whales to find food. Climate anomalies such as the El Niño affect ocean currents and dramatically change patterns of food distribution, as do a series of less well understood factors that cause local populations of the prey species of whales to go through cycles of boom and bust (such factors as diseases and the fluctuation of populations of species that predate on food sources important to whales are undoubtedly at work here). As I have mentioned already, for whales of several baleen whale species the concept of an individual being able to return to the same spot year after year and find food there is a relatively rare occurrence. Each year members of these species must surely have to search over relatively huge areas of ocean for food. It is not just krill that is unpredictable in its distribution, many species of potential prey species that must be highly concentrated to be worth a whale's effort to collect them are notoriously difficult to predict as to when their concentrations will occur. Being able to communicate over great distances must be of great value for finding such species. But by spreading out over the entire ocean to search for food, a "heard" of whales could vastly improve the chances of animals in it finding food no matter how unpredictable its occurrence.

Winter is the time of year when fin whales seem to make most of their sounds, a time when little food is available and when their mating season appears to be in progress. (Though this has been far less studied in the Southern than in the Northern hemisphere.) But my reason for emphasizing the possible use of sounds as a means of finding food is to point out that when a species has the ability to be heard across oceans it is hard to imagine how that could be overlooked by evolution as a means for helping the species find food.

In order to operate a system based on sharing information about food finds, we need not require that the whales be closely related (i.e., it does not require kin selection although that is one mechanism that might select for it). The system can also work if it is based on reciprocal altruism (see chapter 3)—a system in which individuals exchange favors. Such a system is usually confined to members of long-lived social groups. Whales that are members of the same ocean herd throughout their lives would certainly meet the requirement of being long-term participants in the same social group. It is also obvious that the further apart they could be and still hear each other, the more chances whales would get to hear of food finds when they themselves had located nothing.

Fin and blue whales are found in deep water on all sides of pack ice, which can extend for hundreds of miles, particularly in the Antarctic Ocean in spring. When pack ice starts to close in, presumably whales must occasionally find it necessary to travel many miles to find a lead that will get them through it. (In 1988 daily news broadcasts about the fate of three gray whales caught in pack ice near Alaska reached the entire world. It was considered a major news event, even though it is highly probable that many whales become trapped in this way every year. Blue whales, for example, often strand on the southern coast of Newfoundland in early spring when wind swirls the floating pack ice ahead of them in an enormous gyre, pinning both ice and whales against the coast.)

When a whale finds itself getting increasingly boxed in by wind-drifted pack ice, it presumably could prove vital to the whale that is trying to choose an appropriate escape direction to be able to hear even quite distant companions toward which it could pick its way to safety before the pack ice became too compacted to afford suitable cracks for breathing. The ability to produce sounds at frequencies that are so peculiarly well suited to long-range transmission under ice seems of obvious advantage. Chris Clark and Bill Ellison observed bowheads avoiding large floes of multi-year ice (which is deep keeled and potentially dangerous) by detouring around them without ever getting close enough to the floes to see them.

Everyone is guessing when it comes to figuring out how whales find their way while migrating toward some isolated breeding bank. One theory is that they may stretch out in a phalanx, calling as they swim, so that the ones who find the breeding ground first stop and linger and in that way "share" their discovery with others near enough to hear that they are no longer moving. Though it is known that humpback whales do indeed sing throughout their long migrations, there is no convincing evidence that this theory is true.

Earlier I have mentioned that Chris Clark and Bill Ellison calculated the sound reflectivity of islands and sea mounts and found it is strong enough for whales to be able to echolocate such features at distances of hundreds of miles. They also calculated that the lowest blue whale sounds propagate far enough for the whale to get a useable echo from a distance of two to three hundred miles.

Over the years I have spent a lot of time thinking about how whales can possibly find distant islands when they must sometimes swim for thousands of miles from one end of a migration to the other—for example, how can humpbacks find their breeding grounds in Hawaii from Alaska when it involves a twenty-five-hundred-mile swim toward a target which from Alaska subtends an angle of less than five degrees? Clark and Ellison's calculation indicate that it may be a relatively simple thing for a whale to do.

One of the earliest theories of the origin of blips was that they were the heartbeats of whales, even though it seems unlikely that a whale's heart would stop beating for two and one-half minutes every fifteen the way the blips do, or that it might be silent for weeks at a time. But when it had been demonstrated that it was fin whales that made the sounds, attempts were made to record the sound of the heartbeats of a stranded fin whale. It was immediately apparent that no one could hear the beating of a fin whale's heart even at point-blank range, and the theory was abandoned.

We could also ask whether twenty-hertz sounds didn't evolve principally as a long-range sonar. There is no question that twenty-hertz sounds should prove useful to a whale for some kinds of echolocation, but their long wavelength would prevent them from providing a very detailed view of the ocean bottom and its inhabitants (except, perhaps, large schools of fish, the summed echoes from which would give the overall shape of the entire school, though not of the individual fish in it).[7] Such low sounds could also provide valuable information to a whale about the distance to the bottom (at least within 125 feet—since that is half of the wavelength of a twenty-hertz sound and thus the limit of possible accuracy for that frequency—see appendix). Presumably such deep sounds could only inform a whale about major features of the ocean like seamounts and canyons. However, the repetition rate of a singing fin whale seems much too fast for such a loud, low-frequency, long-wavelength sonar if one wished to argue that this is the principal use of blips.

It has been shown that animals producing twenty-hertz sounds often meander slowly about in a restricted area for long periods while vigorously blipping. If the blips were principally used as signals for sonar, it would mean that that sonar was a very long-range one, and for animals that are hardly moving what new information could be gained by such relatively rapid repetition rates in a sonar that can capture so little detail and that can echolocate objects hundreds of miles away? If there was not such good reason to believe that the sounds are omnidirectional, then one could believe in any blipping rate, however rapid, since it might represent the animal directing a beam of sound about in order to investigate in different directions—like someone glancing about in the dark with a flashlight. But I fail to see how there could be much to be gained by blipping loudly a hundred times above the same underwater canyon or abyssal plain at a frequency so low when all you can "see" of the topography is its very largest structures.

Also, the fact that the blip rate is unchanging would make these sounds differ from the sonar systems of other animals, which vary dramatically in pulse rate and pulse structure depending upon the animal's activity and the proximity of a target. However, if the twenty-hertz sounds are mainly for purposes of communication, it is easy to see how a steady repetition rate could evolve. For as soon as the animal stops advertising its presence and becomes silent, it "vanishes" from the rest of the herd.

•　•　•

We must realize that if whales are using long-range communication, they are doing so on a very crowded communication line—the entire ocean being one party line over which thousands of whales of every species capable of producing very low frequencies could be speaking at any given moment. This makes it seem highly unlikely that whales could find much use for the sound channel as a line over which to chat while sitting on opposite sides of an ocean basin. But even if they somehow could, the other factor which limits this channel's utility for short, pithy conversations is that the way sound is conducted through deep ocean (the deep sound channel—see the appendix) smears out sounds very badly. But as I keep mentioning, whales have large, complex brains and the reason they are so large is completely unknown. Perhaps they use them to help unsmear messages that the sound channel has smeared. Also, if you knew the characteristics of the sound you were expecting and could unsmear it, you would be able to infer a lot about the sound channel. It seems unlikely that this is the prime function for their large brains, however, since the largest brains belong to whales that do not make sounds of low enough frequency to be eligible for long-range communication. The losses at the high frequencies at which they speak are so great that high-pitched sounds will have died out completely long before they get very far.

Because of the way it smears out sounds, if fin whales use the sound channel they will, I suspect, only be able to send either very simple signals by it or, if they wish to transmit complex messages, will be limited to very slow transmission rates. This is another reason why a whale with a loud voice that can carry for a long way may be singing a simple song, whereas a whale like a humpback (whose higher song frequencies cannot possibly travel far enough to get scrambled by the deep sound channel) can afford to incorporate wonderful complexities in its song—features missing entirely from the songs of the deep-voiced fin and blue whales (although it is probably significant that the low frequencies in the songs of humpbacks travel for a hundred miles or more).

We might well ask why, if long-distance communicating is so good, more species don't use it? The answer is that small animals probably could not make loud enough and low enough sounds. Even if they could, they might not have sufficient ear separation to obtain a useful bearing on low frequency incoming sounds. But there is another potentially important reason: the signal an animal makes to contact others of its species must not also attract its predators. Long-distance signaling would only therefore be expected to evolve in animals with large heads and widely spaced ears that were reasonably independent of predators—animals such as large whales.

Of all the assumptions Doug Webb and I made in our calculations of the distances to which fin whales can be heard, the one that was probably the most unrealistic was that a whale can no longer hear a sound once it has fallen to the same loudness as the background noise. By making such an assumption, what we were saying is that whales are not nearly as good at acoustic analysis as we are. This fails to take into account the fact that baleen whales have well-developed ears and a large region of a large brain given over to acoustic function. They are probably at least as good at detecting a signal in noise as is a human being—an animal that presumably does not rely so much on ears for its livelihood as does a whale. It seems, in fact, much more probable that the whales are a great deal better at finding signals in noise than we are (since modern whales have been living in a very noisy environment three times as long as there has been anything in our ancestry that was even slightly humanoid).

The ears of humans may be at the theoretical threshold of sensitivity, but in other respects we're not very sophisticated acoustically. For example, we can't use echolocation to "look at" the world around us with sound—the way porpoises and bats can. We can't acoustically select a mealworm out of a chaff of twenty falling objects that all give very similar echoes, the way some bats can. We can't use echoes to distinguish acoustically between two cylinders that differ in dimension so little that the differences aren't visible to us, the way some porpoises can. All in all, we aren't a very acoustic animal; we are primarily visual and are probably only average (below average?) when it comes to analyzing sounds.

If you were blindfolded and ushered into a pitch-black room, and in the darkness you clapped your hands, you could probably tell next to nothing about the room except, perhaps, some very rough idea about its overall dimensions—for example, whether it was very large and cavernlike or very small and cozy. If a porpoise or a bat analyzed the same clap (appropriately raised in frequency to pitches that bats and porpoises hear best) I would not be surprised if either species could tell the room's dimensions accurately as well as the general size and position of the major objects in the room. Either might also be able to detect the dragon suspended silently from the ceiling, its mouth agape, its pilot light lit, poised to immolate the unwary.

But the question before us concerns a somewhat different skill: how well we can pull a signal out of noise. All of us have carried on conversations in very noisy surroundings—a party, a street corner with some diesel engine at full revs next to us, or while standing near a jackhammer. If we could measure the intensity of the noise at the position of our ears and compare it to the intensity of the voice of the person with whom we are conversing (being careful also to measure its loudness at the position of our ears), we would find their voice to be much fainter than the noise. We can actually detect a signal (the person's words) at intensities less than the noise (i.e., at a signal-to-noise ratio measured in negative decibels).[8]

How well we do this depends, not surprisingly, on how complicated the array of alternatives is from which we are trying to select. If you were an experienced telegraph operator listening to a chain of Morse code, you would only have to decide whether each sound was a dot or a dash. You would know you could discard anything that didn't sound like a dot or a dash—say, a hiss. You would also have lots of other clues to help you out. For example, you would know that there are only forty-three dot-dash patterns from which to select twenty-six letters, ten numbers, and seven shortcut symbols. In addition, the farther into the message—even into each word—you got, the more accurate your subsequent guesses would become as to what the dots and dashes that were obscured by noise were intended to mean.

Compare this task with trying against the same noise background to hear the name of some street in a foreign language that you don't know—your task being to be able to repeat it sometime later to a taxi driver with enough accuracy to ensure that you reach your business meeting. In this case, because you would have far fewer aids to getting it right, you could probably only hear the street name well enough if there was much less masking noise.

Many studies of the ability of humans to hear signals against noise under carefully controlled conditions have been made. In order to select a study applicable to the problem faced by a fin whale trying to hear the pattern of the two notes of another fin whale, we must look for studies where words had to be selected from a small number of possible alternatives. One such study involved a vocabulary of two, four, eight, sixteen, and thirty-two words that had to be detected against noise. In all cases the percentage of correct words chosen by participants in the study was at chance level or better for signal-to-noise ratios equal to or higher than minus eighteen decibels.

If we decide that a fin whale is able to do as well as the people in this study and detect the signal of another whale at a signal-to-noise ratio of minus eighteen decibels, and if with that new assumption we look at how far fin whale sounds could get before their signal-to-noise ratio was eighteen decibels less than the ocean noise values on which Webb and I based our calculations of the range to which fin whale sounds will travel, we would see that even today with ship traffic noise being as high as it is, one fin whale could hear another across oceans.

When we calculated the range over which whales could hear each other against noise, Webb and I assumed that background noise in the ocean is true noise ("white noise"). Such a noise is perfectly random mathematically and its source is therefore unidentifiable by any means. However, ocean noise is not white noise; it is the jumbled totality of discrete, familiar signals, some of which are very identifiable. From which it follows that if some animal is able to identify more sources in background noise than its fellows, it will be working at a lower noise background than they are.

Because ocean noise is that part of the total noise background not due to sources that the listener can identify (i.e., what is left over once all other sounds have been identified), it makes a huge difference what sort of brain is doing the identification of those other sounds. For example, there are species of shrimp that are known to hear well, but I would not expect them to be able to identify as many noise sources as a whale.

If the brains of whales are significantly better at analyzing sounds than ours, they may be listening for their signals against lower noise backgrounds than we. From which it follows that it may be just as misleading to assume that a whale is working against the same noise background we are as it once was to assume that bats were silent simply because we could not hear them.

Several new theories have arisen from this acoustical work. For one, if fin whales find their sounds useful for keeping track of each other, might we not use them for the same function? It might prove to be possible to estimate the numbers of fin whales in the sea by listening to their calls and counting them. It is a long-standing dream of many biologists that it ought to be possible to make an acoustic census of whales. It is a technique now being pursued by several investigators on several species (the work on sperm whales and harbor porpoises seems particularly promising to me) and one which with time might prove useful for monitoring the recovery (or decline?) of several species. Chris Clark has done it for bowheads off Alaska and has demonstrated in the process an increase of 1 to 3 percent in the population. Of course, the ultimate would be to discover a sound to which all whales would respond by making a sound of their own—then you could drive around the ocean making that sound and writing down the responses, not unlike a teacher taking attendance in class.

Another possibility that grows out of the ability of whales to hear for long distances occurs to me as a nice example of how bizarre some of the consequences may be of hearing sounds that have traveled for a long way.

As I have mentioned in chapter 1, without upwellings the ocean is depauperate in the minerals needed for life because there is no mechanism to lift them back to the surface. Another thing that can enrich ocean water (though to a lesser extent than upwellings caused by deep-ocean currents rising when they hit a continental shelf) is the stirring up of water by storms. The major ocean storms that rip through the Antarctic Ocean in winter leave mineral-enriched water in their wakes. There is evidence that the areas over which the tracks of these storms pass often later become regions in which microscopic algae flourishes and in which krill later thrives.[9]

Such storms are also great generators of sound in the same frequency band in which fin and blue whales speak. The deeps of the Antarctic Ocean are continuous with deep water in all the oceans that abut it (the South Atlantic, South Pacific, and South Indian oceans). The sounds of major storms should therefore propagate well beyond the borders of the Antarctic Ocean right up into the latitudes toward which fin and blue whales have moved in winter. If these whales simply listened from their warm winter latitudes for the sounds of distant Antarctic winter storms and, some months later, during their return migration were to swim in the remembered direction of the storm that they had heard, this could eventually put them into areas where their chances of finding krill would be better.

Having entered this argument, I don't wish to miss the magnitude of its potential by looking at it from too narrow a viewpoint. Everything a sound touches as it transmits for long distances underwater, whether the bottom, the surface, a seamount, internal waves, or an ocean ridge, leaves its fingerprints on that sound. Storms reveal themselves not only by the noise generated at the surface but by the fingerprints of surface roughness from which it is probably even possible to estimate wave direction. Humans are now learning to read those fingerprints; I suspect that whales have probably been able to do so for millions of years.

I have emphasized that the two principal means by which whales can improve their chances of hearing each other at greater distances are to make louder sounds and to process noise better. However, there is another interesting feature of underwater sound that probably benefits whales by adding to the range at which they can hear each other.

The differences in path length along which sounds propagate mean that a single sound arrives at a listener along several paths that are spread out over time (called multipath propagation in the time domain). This occurs when the earliest arrivals of the final soundwaves in a single utterance overlap with the most delayed arrivals of the first soundwaves from the same utterance and their energy is summed at the point in the ocean at which another whale is listening. At long distances this can be expected to make a significant difference to the loudness of sounds heard by a whale. Whales that can hear distant whales at all ought to be able to estimate their distance by several means. In the appendix I consider one such way of knowing distance—by noting the rate of build-up to the loudest final sound in smeared-out transmissions of discrete sounds that are traveling via the sound channel. Because higher frequencies are absorbed by water faster than lower frequencies, at closer distances a whale could note what percentage of the higher frequencies in a familiar signal was missing—the farther away, the fewer the high frequencies.

Humans have recently taken to using an interesting strategy in order to be able to listen for signals of ships and submarines deeper into background noise. It involves listening through hydrophones many miles apart and works like this: a group of widely separated hydrophones is set out on the ocean bottom, and wires carrying the signals from each hydrophone are brought to the same place so that the signals from the various hydrophones can be compared. Each ship's propeller generates a different sound—called the propeller's "signature." If the signature of a ship you know is present in the traffic noise audible to the hydrophones in your array, it will probably be present on several of them. If you are listening for a ship at twenty hertz, once you have determined the directions from which the many twenty-hertz ship noise sources are arriving at each of your hydrophones, you can discard noise that comes from directions not of interest to you. In this way the ship's signal is heard against a lesser noise background. If you are listening for a whale, and your hydrophones are widely enough spaced compared with the distance to the whale to which you are listening, the whale's position can be determined by comparing directional information from two or more hydrophones. Chris Clark has been following a process very similar to this using naval hydrophones. It was by this means that he was finally able to offer hard evidence that fin whale sounds can travel at useful intensities for hundreds of miles and those of blue whales for a thousand miles. Is there some way a fin whale might use the same strategy to hear the twenty-hertz sounds of other fin whales that would otherwise be too deeply buried in ocean noise? Can a fin whale use the technique Chris uses? At first glance it seems most unlikely, since a whale cannot be in several places at the same time like the hydrophones in an array.

But let us recklessly assume for a moment that fin whales might have another ability—the ability to store detailed records several seconds long of their sounds. If they could do so, they might be able to swim a few miles, stop, listen, memorize a few seconds of sound with great precision, swim a few more miles, stop, listen again, store another sample, and so on until they had made a collection of detailed sound records. If the whale could then compare these records, using directional information derived from them to discard noise from inappropriate directions, it might be able to diminish considerably the noise against which it was listening for distant companions.

A relatively recent trick to improve the accuracy with which the direction to a sound source can be determined is the use of a towed array of hydrophones to generate what is called a "synthetic aperture." Suppose you have the simplest of arrays, a dipole array, composed of two hydrophones (say, two ears). And suppose that you "tow" this array through the ocean at a fixed speed while listening at systematic intervals for extended periods of time (i.e., distance). What you are doing is the equivalent of having a much larger fixed array in which the number of sensors is the number of times you have listened, multiplied by the number of elements in your array (in this case your two ears). Such an array will work only as long as the ocean water remains unmixed, that is, coherent, in the frequency band of interest during the time you are collecting samples. However, for twenty hertz that's at least twenty minutes (and probably more like forty).

A fin whale traveling between four and five miles an hour would generate an array aperture of about three miles before the water mixed significantly, which would provide it with a bearing resolution of less than one degree— meaning that it would know to within one degree or less its angle with relation to another whale (very good accuracy indeed).

There is a step of elegance that a whale might add to this: if the whale which was listening through a synthetic aperture took careful note of the repetition rate of a friend it was trying to locate (let us not forget that fin whale repetition rates are *very* precise), and if it listened to that friend again several hours later (by swimming along and generating another synthetic aperture), it could determine the range to the other whale and thereby, perhaps, decide whether swimming over for a visit would be worth the effort. All of this requires a very good onboard chronometer—that is, a good clock— in the central nervous system. But judging from the precision with which fin and blue whales turn out their sounds, they seem to possess chronometers that are very good indeed.

But there is a chance that the situation could prove even more fanciful. If the whale "knows" the characteristics of the sound channel intimately, it might, theoretically, determine the position (in three dimensions) of a friend calling from as far away as six hundred miles, even when it was listening to that friend from one place. As Chris Clark, who drew my attention to these possibilities, put it, "It's computationally very intense—but heck, what's that to a bit of gray matter!"

I like it, I like it. How welcome it is to be given another possible reason for why whales might conceivably have big brains. In addition to requiring great computational ability, the ability to store acoustic information in enough detail to hear a distant whale signal deeply buried in noise and to figure out the direction to it almost certainly requires a very significant data acquisition and storage capacity, as well as an especially sophisticated analytical network—that is, a large brain.

I want to emphasize that this outrageous hypothesis comes to you with no evidence at all that fin whales can do any such thing. So why do I so recklessly present it? There are two reasons: 1) primarily in hopes of stimulating further research about it, and 2) because of what it implies about a fin whale's brain. As regards the second, I have spent a significant portion of my life trying to think of things a whale might be doing with its large brain that would be important enough to justify the huge metabolic expense of maintaining such a structure (in the first few weeks of life, for instance, about a third of the metabolism of a young porpoise is devoted simply to maintaining its brain). In spite of years of listening to the theories of many others about how whales use their big brains, I have neither encountered nor thought up any theory that seemed very plausible to me.

The usual problem with the theories I hear is that the advantage to the whale of each scheme is never very convincing. Often it is impossible to imagine useful intermediate benefits for which plausible selective pressures might have existed during the time the whales' brains were evolving toward the postulated function that requires the modern brain size. That is why I welcome the theory I have just presented; I can see the advantage to the whale and why every intermediate step, as well as every decibel of improvement in finding a signal in noise, would have strongly benefited the ancestors of modern whales. All of this forcefully suggests to me that the sizable brains of whales may in large part be concerned with improving their ability to pull sounds out of the cacophony of the oceans.

Evolutionary arguments such as this one are sometimes of value in testing the plausibility of a theory. There are several other such arguments that bear on the theory of long-distance communication.

Let us look at how strong the selective pressures may be for a whale to make even very small improvements in its ability to hear another whale's signal in noise, and what dividends it would pay both to the whale in which such an ability first appears and to its offspring.

There are two ways in which low-frequency sounds can propagate in the ocean—by spherical spreading which does not carry very far, and by cylindrical spreading—a sound which by avoiding reflections from surface and bottom can travel for enormous distances (see the appendix for an explanation of the differences between these two kinds of propagation). As I have pointed out before, because the area of a circle increases as the square of its radius, if a whale can hear another whale twice as far away it would find that its friend could wander about in an area four times as large and still remain in contact. Because the decibel scale is exponential, if a whale could improve by only six decibels its ability to hear a signal in noise, it would double the fifty-mile, spherical spreading range at which it can be heard in modern times. This hundred-mile radius would mean that instead of only being able to hear another fin whale within an area of 7,850 square miles, it would now be able to hear it anywhere within 31,400 square miles—an area four times as big. (The six decibel improvement has added 23,550 square miles to the "hearing zone.")

Consider a sound propagating through the deep-sound channel; any fin whale born with an adaptation that allowed it to hear signals just one decibel deeper into the noise than its fellows would extend by 25 percent the distance at which it could hear other whales. Consider a fin whale like the ones in the above calculations whose sounds are already known to propagate at useful intensities out to four thousand miles. Such a whale would be audible anywhere in a fifty-million-square-mile area of deep ocean (the total area of the Atlantic Ocean is thirty-two million square miles). If some fin whale developed an adaptation that enabled it to detect our fin whale's signal just one decibel deeper in the noise, that whale would now be able to hear ours at a distance of five thousand miles. This adds another twenty-eight million square miles of ocean to the area in which our whale can be heard. Twenty-eight million square miles is four million square miles less than the area of the entire Atlantic Ocean (Atlantic meaning both North and South Atlantic). Thus, by being able to find its signal in a noise background which is only one more decibel louder, this listener has added an area of ocean in which it can hear another whale almost equal to the area of the Atlantic. Recalling that even under the best of listening conditions the difference in loudness between two sounds that differ in intensity by only one decibel is barely detectable, it becomes apparent how strong must be the selective pressures operating on the ability of whales to make loud sounds and to hear those signals deeper in ocean noise.

I suspect that two of the selective pressures that have operated most strongly on whales are their ability to make loud noises and their ability to hear signals in noise.

As I have already pointed out, any adaptation that improves the maximum effective signaling distance should be strongly favored by natural selection. There seems to be nothing that would limit this process, that is, nothing that would select against an improvement in signaling range, for surely the wider the herd can be spread and still be in contact, the fewer the constraints it will face in encountering and exploiting every possible food source in every shifting and unpredictable location. Thus the trend to improve range would be limited only when the boundaries of the inhabitable range had been reached. Beyond that there would be no selective pressure to favor an increased ability to signal over greater ranges, and the system would reach equilibrium. It is interesting in this regard that our calculations of the maximum range to which twenty-hertz sounds can be heard is about thirteen thousand miles. There are no deep-water paths following great circle routes that are longer than about thirteen thousand miles. The coincidence may be no more than a coincidence or it may be meaningful. After all, once a whale has managed to communicate over the longest possible deep-water path, there would be no selective pressure to select for louder sounds or for the ability to hear sounds that originated farther away.

Unless, of course, the whale could hear another whale not just through the sea, but through the rock of the earth's mantle. This is perhaps the strangest of all of the possible consequences of the peculiar characteristics of speaking at a frequency as low as twenty hertz, but it may not be as mad a speculation as it seems. Sounds of the same intensity and frequency as whale calls are known to propagate through the earth's mantle. (This is known from their times of arrival—they arrive too rapidly to have been waterborne yet are on schedule for their conduction to have occurred via the mantle.) It is not impossible that whales utilize the same sound transmission route.

Inasmuch as the sounds of whales can safely be assumed to propagate through whatever contiguous media will conduct them, it is hard to see how whale sounds could avoid being conducted through the earth's mantle. If they effectively transmitted through the rock of the ocean bottom in the vicinity of a listening whale to the seawater surrounding it, it is hard to see how the whale could be prevented from hearing them.

Having lived through the reception by my colleagues of my theory regarding long-range communication via the sea, I do not expect to make many friends with this newest suggestion. Nevertheless it is seriously offered.

Having so vigorously followed the line of argument that some whales may be able to communicate over long distances, I wish to make it clear that I do not believe the only function of the low-frequency sounds of fin and other whales is for long-range signaling. If these sounds were, for instance, useful as a means of assessing the depth of the ocean, or of echolocating underwater landmarks, or large schools of fish, or for navigating, I would think it less likely that they replaced other sonar and navigational systems than that they simply augmented them. By the same token I do not feel that very low frequency sounds are the only means by which whales maintain contact, or navigate, but rather one of several means—the one working at greatest range.

The overall conclusion I draw about the possibility of long-range communication between fin whales is that, as with so much else in the study of whales, we have probably had things backward and that for many years we've had no idea what we were talking about when we referred to herds of baleen whales. What long-range communication implies is that it is not the relatively high-voiced toothed whales (porpoises, killer whales, belugas, dolphins, etc.) that live in the largest herds, but the baleen whales. I suspect this is particularly likely to be the case for blues and fins and probably for others as well (with the exception of the relatively soft-voiced gray whale). Before the whalers decimated them, single fin whale herds might have contained as many as tens, and perhaps even hundreds, of thousands of individuals (in the Southern Hemisphere particularly). The main reason porpoises are limited to much smaller herds is that their sound frequencies are too high to allow them to maintain contact over more than a few miles.

If the theory of long-range communication by whales is the wrong explanation for the function of their very low frequency sounds, a better theory will have to explain:

1) Why twenty-hertz sounds are so loud, so constant in repetition rate, so pure in frequency, and so narrowband.

2) Why they may go on for many hours at a time, even though the animal producing them is simply meandering around in a relatively small area.

3) How an individual rejoins a herd after time spent feeding elsewhere.

4) How five hundred to one thousand fin whales ever happen to come together at one place and time when normally they are found widely scattered as singles or in small groups.

5) How whales find each other when, at the height of the mating season, they are, inconveniently, most widely spread.

I suppose, however, that one of the main reasons I am inclined to believe that twenty-hertz sounds are designed for long-range communication is because the characteristics of the sounds are so ideally suited for transmission over great range. If one was to ask an engineer to come up with a relatively low-power acoustic pulse that could propagate for a few thousand miles through pre-propeller-driven-ship ocean and be heard well in ice-covered waters by the ears of a whale, he or she would probably come up with something sharing many of the basic characteristics of a fin whale blip. I refer to the fact that twenty hertz has an extremely low attenuation with range, has almost no losses in reflecting off the bottom, is the highest frequency that would be relatively independent of wind-generated noise, and is that frequency which has particularly low transmission losses under ice.

As this chapter deals mainly with the herding behavior of whales, I might leave it at this point. However, as I have demonstrated, it is not possible to talk about herds of whales without talking about sounds. Therefore having joined a discussion about sounds, I will review in the most sketchy manner some of the other sounds produced by whales—sounds that may still have something to do with maintaining herds but that are not as highly implicated in that process as the twenty-hertz sounds of fin whales.

There is a vast assortment of sounds made by whales. There are the wild songs sung by humpback whales that I discussed in chapter 4. The right whale makes an astonishing assortment of sounds: moans, growls, shrieks, ratchets, motor boat noises, chortles, chuckles, whinnies, snarls, whoops, caterwauls, howls, sighs, bawls, brays, wails, roars, bellows, trills, toots, whistles, barks, yaps, yelps, yips, and on and on. Essentially, you name it, they make it. To listen to all these sounds makes it all very suggestive that right whales may have a very complicated vocabulary and may be communicating relatively complex information among themselves. But in spite of a noble effort by Chris Clark while he was a graduate student working in Argentina to elucidate just what all of those sounds meant he was still only able to tease out the probable meaning of a handful of them—for example, a noise made by a mother to call her calf; the sound made by a right whale when porpoises are about (perhaps, though by no means surely, to chase them away); a sound made by an excited male as it joins a mating group, etc.

None of the meanings that Chris was able to ascribe to right whale sounds are what all of us (Chris most particularly included) so much want to know: to wit, do these animals have the ability to carry on anything we might recognize as even a rudimentary conversation—for example, a change in the kinds of information one whale gives another in response to what it hears from the other?

The big breakthroughs have yet to be made. It is a maddeningly difficult field to crack, since just to tell which cetacean in a group is vocalizing is a major undertaking. As I have mentioned, unlike birds or land mammals, which conveniently open and close their mouths while making sounds, whales give no evidence at all that they are producing sounds. No air escapes, and there is no change in their expressions or any obvious motion of muscles anywhere, except in the melons of some porpoises, which appears to be only to focus or defocus the sounds. In fact whales appear to be completely impassive while making even the most extraordinarily complex and vigorous noises. Biologist Peter Tyack has invented a clever apparatus that he attaches to the heads of all porpoises in a captive group with suction cups. The device turns on a light on the head of the porpoise that is vocalizing. When everyone is wearing their lights, it is finally possible to tell which porpoise in the pod is vocalizing and which individual, if any, is responding. Peter was able by this means to demonstrate that when one porpoise made a sound, others would answer it. However it will probably be a long time before we can in any sense eavesdrop intelligently on their conversations (if that is an appropriate term for their vocal interactions).

Given how much we have learned about whales in recent years, I am simply miffed when I reflect on how robustly ignorant we are about some of the questions that everyone is most interested in seeing answered. I frequently get asked to comment on the mental abilities and communication skills of large whales and have to invent new ways to explain that we simply have no evidence one way or the other with which to answer these questions. Whales may be the most skilled and subtle communicators ever, possessing the most complex and sophisticated brains that have ever existed in the known visible universe—or they may be somewhat slow mentally and have only a few gruntlike and very simple dispatches to offer. Or (as seems most likely) somewhere in between. We simply don't know. There isn't the evidence to know—to guess, yes, but to know? No.

There is some interesting ongoing work by psychologist Louis Herman concerning the abilities of bottle-nosed dolphins to respond correctly to strings of visual commands that function like words in simple sentences. In these experiments, hand signals are used as subjects, verbs, and objects. The results show, among other things, that a dolphin can make the correct distinction between a sentence that says "put the stick on the ring" and one saying "put the ring on the stick"—in other words, that dolphins can manage sentence syntax correctly. The work is cleanly and carefully done and with appropriate controls, but the critics of this kind of research still question whether the ability demonstrated by Herman's dolphins is truly analogous to human language capability.

Besides, "put the stick on the ring" is a country mile from what everyone wants to know about the language ability of porpoises. Much more effort will have to be made before people who love porpoises will feel either vindicated in their beliefs about the mental abilities of these animals or defeated by evidence that they are cognitively intractable. It seems clear to me from the contentiousness of the work on ape language that even if the language capability of dolphins turns out to be on a par with human language, neither Herman nor anyone else will ever be able to convince all comers that it is so. There seems to be an inborn refusal in many humans to accept the possibility that the mental abilities of our species might be in any way unremarkable in comparison to others.

Having said all this, I must register my current belief that the dolphins' aptitude for language is probably *not* on a par with that of humans. However, I freely acknowledge that the jury is still out on this most interesting question. In the meantime I suspect that the brains of cetaceans have evolved for some very important reason about which we haven't a clue, and that dolphins must do some crucially important thing with them, though heaven knows what it is.

Given that the problem of comparing language abilities between dolphins and people is such an intractable one, I feel we could take better advantage of the work of scientists like Lou Herman and his team by ceasing to worry about whether porpoises have a language ability comparable to ours and instead use Herman's techniques to interview porpoises about things that might be more interesting to us, and to them, than "put the stick on the ring." I have followed up on this suggestion in chapter 6.

In this chapter I have been talking about whales and porpoises listening to sounds made by others of their species for their benefit—to contact them— or sounds made by storms or other things in the whales' environment from which a whale might infer information. This is passive listening. But there is an entire other world of sounds that whales make that are not primarily intended to be heard by another whale, but to be heard by the maker of the sounds itself—sounds for which the echoes of the sound are the crucial element. I am referring, of course, to sonar.

Experiments with dolphins have shown them to be capable of echolocating. Echolocation is just a fancy way of referring to the practice of directing a beam of sound around like a flashlight and by listening to the echoes that return from objects in the path of the sound, interpreting the underwater world around the sound maker—using its ears to "look" at things reflected in its sounds, the way we use our eyes to look at things reflected in light. You shine the flashlight beam on something so you can cause it to reflect some of the light back to your eye and thus see what it is. You find it necessary to illuminate an object because it doesn't emit light of its own, just the way a whale finds it necessary to "illuminate" a silent fish with sound because it doesn't emit sounds of its own.

Most sounds used by animals to echolocate contain very high frequencies; porpoises produce frequencies as high as two hundred thousand hertz (two hundred kilohertz). The wavelength of such a sound in seawater is about one-quarter of an inch, suggesting that the smallest object detectable in the sonar of a porpoise is about one-quarter inch in diameter (see the appendix). The reason that porpoises have evolved such high frequencies is probably because it makes it possible to "see" the world acoustically at a relatively fine grain. After all, such short wavelengths also open the possibility of focusing sounds into a beam even when the structures to do that focusing are limited in size to what can fit in the head of small species.

Also, let us not forget that the higher the frequency, the less interference from background noise in the sea, so that if it is relatively easy for a porpoise to make its sounds very high pitched, it will be listening for echoes against a relatively quiet noise background.

The strength of an echo returning from a target is inversely proportional not to the square of range (as is the case for animals listening for sounds made by their companions) but inversely proportional to the fourth power of range—the inverse square law acts on echolocation clicks, both on their way out to their target and on their return as echoes from it. This means that if the distance between animal and target is doubled, the echo returning is one-sixteenth of what it was before ($2 \cdot 2 \cdot 2 \cdot 2 = 16$). Thus, for an animal to increase significantly the distance over which it can detect prey, it must shout louder or focus its beam of sound (so as to pack more energy into a smaller beam cross section). However, listening more acutely to hear its echo buried deeper in the noise is not so critical as the first two, simply because there is so little background noise at very high frequencies.

Making louder, more focused beams of sound could have an unexpected consequence for a whale. If it could form a beam of sound loud enough and tightly focused enough, a whale might theoretically achieve sound intensities capable of disorienting or even stunning its prey at least long enough for the whale to swim up and grab it—the sci-fi dream of a ray gun (well, at least a ray gun with its setting on "stun"). If this interesting possibility (first suggested by Kenneth Norris and Bertil Möhl[10]) proves to be true, we can guess that it would have been no less surprising to the first whale who achieved such beam intensities than it would be to us if we discovered we could stun an animal by shouting at it.

I once spent two weeks in Sri Lankan waters with biologist Hal Whitehead. Hal had heard what he described as "gunshots," which all of us guessed might be the paralyzingly loud sounds predicted by Norris and Möhl. I was anxious to hear them. During my days on Hal's boat I spent as much time as I could listening through headphones to the constant clicks of sperm whales being picked up through a hydrophone we towed behind the boat. I ate with headphones on, sometimes stood my watch while listening through them, and even slept with them on my head—all in hopes of hearing gunshots. But I never heard one. (Maybe those sperm whales weren't hunting during that period—if they starve for several months at a time, it could be difficult to hear a "gunshot.") I have since heard recordings thought to be of sperm whale gunshots but I am not all that sure they are what Hal was referring to—as he also pointed out, they could simply be artifacts, a sound which by chance was recorded extra loud when the whale happened to direct its beam exactly at the hydrophone for a click or two.

Sperm whale biologist Jonathan Gordon is also less convinced that sperm whales make sounds loud enough to stun prey, particularly after making many days of recordings of large male sperm whales near Kaikoura in New Zealand without hearing gunshots. (The evidence that sperm whales feed in this area is very good.) Nevertheless I find the evolutionary argument underlying the theory of Norris and Möhl compelling and would not be surprised to find that they are correct. For this reason I am anxious to test it. As a result the Whale Conservation Institute's research vessel *Odyssey* is now in Galapagos Islands' waters where sperm whales abound, trying to see whether Norris and Möhl are right.

Biologist Fernando Ugarte was recently able to film an extraordinary behavior in very clear Norwegian waters showing a killer whale circling around a shoal of fish until the fish were tightly bunched and then slashing its tail sideways, creating a sound like a very loud gunshot. Though I, like many other biologists, had always assumed that a whale would not be able to move its tail fast enough to cause cavitation of the water (i.e., to create a momentary vacuum behind the tail into which water vapor explosively expands), this orca seemed to be doing just that. The result was that several of the fish rained down through the water as though stunned (presumably from the intense sound), whereupon the orca swam back around and collected them, repeating the behavior several times. This isolated observation would be less convincing were it not for the observation of biologist John Ford, who has heard gunshotlike sounds from orcas as they were suddenly accelerating.

Other biologists have reported such sounds from baleen whales of several species. For example, Chris Clark has heard right whales and bowheads making gunshotlike sounds which were "intense and painful to the ear." William Watkins describes similar sounds from fin whales and Gregory Silber from humpbacks. I remain to be convinced that an animal as big as these baleen whales could move an appendage fast enough to cause cavitation and I suspect that these sounds come from animals hitting each other with their flippers and tails underwater. Clark has suggested as much for right whales and notes that aggressive behavior was going on when he heard these sounds from them, as well as from bowheads.

I want to end this discourse on the strange ways in which whales and porpoises may use sounds by pointing out the curious consequence of the fact that the body of a whale is more transparent than it is opaque to sound, because like us whales are 65 percent water—which means that sounds propagate through the oceans and through the tissues of whales in much the same way. (The reason we don't hear them well is because our ears are specialized for hearing in air.) This has a fascinating consequence for an unborn whale.

A near-term fetus ought to be able hear its mother's voice clearly right through her body. Whenever the mother whale makes a sound, it must be for her fetus roughly the same experience a human fetus would have if we shone a light in its face.

For humans, sounds heard in utero are not, of course, accompanied by the possibilities of acoustic images the way they are in porpoises, and therefore probably have little meaning beyond being generally comforting (or for some sounds perhaps disquieting). However, an unborn calf should hear not only its mother's voice but everything else going on in the water around it: the noisier fish and snapping shrimp living in its neighborhood, its uncles and aunts quarreling, its cousins calling back and forth—in effect inviting it out to play. If it's a dolphin, its relatives may even take a peek at it with their sonar while it is still inside its mother's body (although we know that porpoises seldom point their sonar beams directly at each other—doing so probably carries aggressive implications).

I see no inescapable reason why a mother whale could not direct comments to her infant in utero—nor why the infant couldn't have clearly heard its mother's voice long before it first sees the light of day, having heard right through its mother as she hurried along, seeking out the shallow, protected waters in which her calf is to be born. If it had the mental development to learn while still in utero (we have no idea whether it does), an animal like a whale with a gestation period longer than ours might have an excellent potential for learning as it awaits its transition to the slightly noisier world outside its mother's dark, internal ocean, where, for the first time, it will be able to see with its eyes and be responsible for taking its own breaths.

If while in utero an infant dolphin could learn the meaning of any of the communication sounds used by its mother, it is conceivable that it could be born with a head start in communicating—having only lacked air before its birth with which to make sounds. This, of course, assumes that it is air with which whales make their noises, and although the evidence is good that such is the case with porpoises, we are not altogether sure that it is the case with baleen whales.

If we could record a different set of sounds from a pregnant female than we get from a lone adult female, one possible explanation for that fact would be that the different noises were coming from the calf. From this we would be able to conclude that air was not required by baleen whales to make sounds. However, nowhere near enough is known about the sounds made by female baleen whales at any stage of their development for us to be able to say with any confidence what is her sound and what is possibly a sound from the fetus within her. Even after the calf has been born it is hard to get recordings from a mother and her calf—mothers and calves are all but quiet—which makes sense when you consider that calves are far more vulnerable to predators like killer whales and large sharks than are large adults. Even though I would be very surprised if baleen whales did not use air to make at least some of their sounds, the bottom line is that our knowledge of baleen whale sounds is still rudimentary.

One way baleen whales could make sounds without air would be by vibrating some muscle very fast—a distinct possibility for the low frequencies made by many baleen whales. Because such sounds would not be limited by how much air was in the bellows behind the whales' noisemaker (the bellows being their lungs or some sinus cavity in their heads), a baleen whale would be able to make very long sounds. With the exception of the blue whale, which makes a very low sound lasting about thirty seconds, no whale is known to make sounds longer than about eight seconds, which suggests that they make their sounds with air. So little do we know about the mechanisms by which baleen whales make their sounds that at this stage of our ignorance we welcome even such indirect and negative evidence as that.

Although I am unsure of it I will assume that because the unborn calf has no air available to it in utero, it cannot use its voice and therefore cannot answer its mother. For a whale fetal life is that unrealistically exemplary time when an infant is all ears—where the mother gets to tell her offspring anything she likes, and it can't talk back or sass her. Of course this idyll would all end when the calf was born and had the air with which to express itself. To an infant whale, as with any mammal, birth would also bring its first sensation of shortness of breath, its first chance to experience the sensation of drowning.

But for cetaceans that are capable of echolocation, there is a still more remarkable possibility. Even though an unborn dolphin cannot make sounds of its own, it may be able to "see" the world around it by paying attention to the echoes from its mother's sounds—for example, it might be able to "see" the bottom by hearing its mother's sounds echo off it. If it has been paying attention to the echoes that its mother gets off the fish she pursues as well as off other targets at which she aims her sonar, it could also know much about how the world around it "looks" ("sounds") acoustically before it is born. Frog eggs are transparent, which means that the developing tadpoles while still in their eggs can see their world clearly. Porpoises and bats are probably the first animals to come along since frogs with the capability of "seeing" the world (this time acoustically) through the walls of their birth chambers. For all these reasons, bats, porpoises, whales, and dolphins truly reside in a "womb with a view."

One imagines the frustration of the infant porpoise waiting for its mother to make the next sound as she dives so it can see how far beneath both of them the bottom is now. ("Mother, are we nearly there?") Some human mothers report that they can stop their fetus from wiggling by singing to it. Looked at from the fetus's point of view, the fetus has trained its mother to sing for it by wiggling. Presumably if your only way of communicating with your mother is by wiggling in her womb, you'll quickly learn to wiggle. Perhaps a porpoise fetus learns to move in such a way as to signal its mother so that she will make a sound and it can "see." The porpoise equivalent of "Quick, Ma, shine your light over there."

CHAPTER 6

Making Friends with Whales: Laying Our Fears to Rest

When you stop to think about it, going swimming with a whale ought to be the scariest thing you could imagine doing. Talk about being vulnerable! The first thing that makes it so is that having pulled alongside a creature that could kill you with a single swipe of its tail (the way we might casually swat a fly), you then get into the water with it—into a medium in which it is entirely at home and in which you are entirely at odds. To make matters worse, you put on a heavy wet suit and strap on a lot of cumbersome gear (including lead weights), which makes you clumsier and which might, should anything malfunction, easily kill you regardless of what the whale does. And in this hopelessly blundering outfit, you swim up to the whale. When I first did it, it seemed rather like putting on a straitjacket and rolling around on the ground in front of a polar bear.

Your companion is with you, but should the whale be surprised at something your companion does, it might carelessly blunder into you as it is shying away from your friend, like some skittish horse, knocking you senseless long enough for you to drown. It's crazy; you get in the water with an animal which is at least four thousand times more powerful than you,[1] which is far more maneuverable than you, and which can dive to depths that would crush you and which can hold its breath twenty times as long as the average person.

The wonderful thing, of course, is that the whale does not take advantage of your condition. It doesn't blunder into you, or smash you against the bottom even when it is in fifteen feet of water and you are below it. Instead, it maneuvers with consummate skill—sometimes missing you only by inches with its flippers or tail—and no matter how sure you are that it has not seen you and is about to knock you senseless or wipe off your mask, at the last minute it lifts its flukes over your head so as not to touch you. It is a miracle, and like all miracles, must be experienced to be believed. It is, I feel, the most valuable thing the whales have given us—the knowledge that these largest of "monsters" are gentle.

It is curious how different are the customs of land animals from those of sea animals. There seems to be something like a general amnesty in the sea. It would be courting disaster to enter into the same proximity with any number of large land animals that one can enjoy when swimming with the largest seals, sea lions, porpoises, or whales. The rules of the sea appear to be different; there are people who even swim with wild killer whales and who claim that the only reaction of the whales seems to be a mild curiosity.

If you think you might feel apprehensive about swimming with whales, consider the work of a remarkable Canadian scientist, Jon Lien. Jon has made it his special task to help Newfoundland fishermen by removing humpback whales from their nets without serious damage to either whale or net. Before he came on the scene, the fishermen dealt with the problem by killing the whale, and the whale returned the favor by destroying the net as it died—a blow to the fishermen hardly less severe than the one they had dealt to the whale. It was what you might call a lose-lose situation.

The Newfoundland herring and capelin seasons are short and intense, and when the fish are running, up to three hundred billion capelin come inshore each summer.[2] To catch them, Newfoundlanders put out fish traps—basically huge, box-shaped nets set out in shallow water about a hundred yards from shore, with an opening on the landward side. A long "leader" coming out from the beach at right angles to the shore enters the opening of the box-shaped net. When a shoal of fish swimming along the coast encounters the leader, they turn and follow it seaward, which leads them into the net, out of which they usually cannot find their way.

Unfortunately, such a fish trap is also an excellent trap for humpback whales. Up to 156 of the humpbacks that gather each year to do some fishing of their own have been caught during the brief Newfoundland fishing season. It is these animals that Lien sets free. The community in which the fishing takes place is poor, and the catch from their nets during the brief season may provide those with fish with a third or more of their year's income. If a whale gets into a net, it's a disaster. If it destroys the net, it may ruin the owner. A whale getting into a net can be the cause of someone's children going without clothing for a year—or worse. So it was a blessing both to the whales and to those whose lives depend on fishing when Jon came out and began to disentangle the whales without cutting the nets—something he and his team have now done with over a thousand humpbacks.

During the capelin fishing season, this man works as hard as I have ever seen anyone work, often getting little or no sleep for days at a time. When he approaches a whale in a net, the whale may have been in it for thirty-six hours or more. All that time it has been struggling with the net, presumably getting more and more frantic, frustrated, exhausted, and out of sorts. When Jon pulls up he is in a rubber boat with a tiny but noisy outboard motor. There is no way he can do anything which the whale might perceive as being of any possible use to it without first getting practically on top of the whale—sometimes his boat is literally on top of it. In order to figure out exactly how the whale is tangled and how to proceed, Jon puts on a face mask and leans over the side of his boat to look about, ducking his head into water so cold there are often icebergs floating nearby. He must immerse his head repeatedly. Each time when he sits back up, the water carried in his hair pours down his neck and soaks his clothes (he doesn't wear a wet suit or a dry suit; he has found them to be too constricting). By now he may have made the boat fast to the net or pulled several broken net lines into the boat and tied them to it, so that if the whale chose to apply its full strength it could capsize the boat or pull Jon under and drown him. Often the lines cut deeply into the whale's flesh—sometimes into its mouth, sometimes right across the blowholes or the genital slits. The motions Jon makes in pulling on them must hurt the whale, for it often flinches when he's doing so. Nevertheless, if Jon is going to be able to free the whale, he must sometimes pull hard enough to actually tow the whale a short distance (for example, out of the net) by these very ropes that are cutting into it.

During all this time, Jon is totally vulnerable, at the mercy of what must by now be an entirely exasperated and panicked animal, which in spite of Jon's best efforts he is sometimes inadvertently hurting. At any moment, he and his assistant might become entangled in a line and be injured or drown. Yet in spite of all this—in spite of their experience in rescuing over a thousand whales—no whale has ever hurt them. Not one. Not ever.

There have been times that whales have panicked, but they have not attacked Jon. At such times he pulls off to one side to let the animal thrash around on its own for a while. Jon says that if he can see the whale's eye well enough to determine whether there is a lot of white showing, or its pupils are widely dilated, he can tell a lot about its condition. He also says that even though his face is upside down and he is peering at the whale through a weird, tiny lens—the face mask—the whale will find his eye and make an "eye-catch."

It is interesting that even under these terrifying and painful circumstances, humpback whales can apparently discern that this strange creature in its noisy boat is trying to help them. This is especially remarkable given that Jon is often on the scene for a long time, often inflicting further pain on the whale long before any line is freed. Indeed, it would be perfectly logical for the whale to assume that Jon had come, like some giant spider, to truss up its catch and kill it, rather than free it. And having drawn such a conclusion, the whale might well be expected to await its chance and turn on Jon when the opportunity presented itself. But the whales don't do that.

I want to be clear on one point: Jon does not believe he has some sort of mystical rapport with the whales. He simply feels that of the two most likely interpretations of his behavior available to the whale, the whale apparently chooses to believe that Jon is there to help. Jon seems to regard what he does in much the same way someone else might view a job like tending cattle or unsnarling fishing line.

The story he told me which impressed me most, however, concerned a humpback whale that had been in a net for an especially long time and by the time Jon got there had a line cutting so tightly across its blowhole that it had worn a groove several inches deep. Jon managed to cut the rope on both sides of the blowhole, but because it was so deeply and firmly embedded in suppurating flesh, he still couldn't free it. He realized that the only way he was going to be able to remove the rope was to reach down inside the blowhole itself, grasp the rope, and draw it out of the wound. The muscles in the walls of a whale's blowhole are awesomely powerful. They must close the blowhole with enough force to prevent the entrance of water at depths where pressures are appalling. Jon knew all this, and he knew that if the whale chose to clamp down with its blowhole muscles, it would probably break every bone in his hand. Beyond that he knew that if the whale then submerged—a not unlikely thing for it to do under the circumstances—it would drag Jon under by his hand. Since he had neither compressed air nor a dive regulator with him, nothing could have saved him—unless the whale relaxed its blowhole muscles, something whales presumably never do underwater. Being Jon, he decided to go for it, reached slowly and with great care into the whale's nostril, grasped the rope, and wrested it out of the wound, an action that required his full strength. He said the whale flinched violently but that it did not close its blowhole on his hand. Nor did it loft him and his boat through the air with a toss of its head. (Whales fight by tossing their heads, so it would seem to have been a natural enough reaction for the whale to have made at that moment.)

The quiescent behavior I have described can't be said to occur because the whale is too exhausted by its struggles with the net to put up a fight. Immediately following their release, most whales leave little doubt as to their healthy state. They swim off fast, sometimes striking the water repeatedly with their tails—showing clearly that they still have abundant energy reserves they might have turned on Jon.

This man is engaged in maintaining the most fragile truce between the fishermen and the whales—a truce that greatly benefits both parties, but a truce nonetheless. If anything ever happens to him, heaven help both sides. To people who have never had to deal with the hatred that many fishermen feel toward whales, it may seem strange that anyone could hate these creatures. But some people do. The cavalier attitude that whalers have toward whales is bad enough—but I'm talking about people who aren't just careless about whales but who actively dislike them. Jon says that Newfoundland fishermen who have lost a season's pay because a whale blundered into one of their nets consider whales to be "a kind of marine rat." But this sentiment is shared by some fishermen who have not lost gear to whales but who see them as competitors for fish and distrust everything about them. There was a time when orcas (killer whales) were shot on sight as vermin that competed with salmon fishermen, literally (as it was then perceived) for their jobs. The U.S. navy considered killer whales so dangerous that whenever they were sighted, naval policy was to recall from the water immediately all personnel in small boats. When the first orca was taken into captivity, some of the people from the local fishing port near its site of capture denounced the man who trained it to eat fish from his hand. This was an animal they had long feared and often persecuted. They probably spoke for most people at that time. Like the U.S. navy, most people—including scientists, who should have known better—considered killer whales one of the most dangerous animals (to humans) in the sea.

Although I have not researched this point carefully, I know of only one authenticated death due to a whale attack in the wild, and one nonfatal instance of a whale breaching onto a boat.[3] On several occasions people have reported being seriously hurt by captive whales attacking them, and every now and then a boat collides with a whale at sea, which sometimes sinks the boat. Biologist Jonathan Gordon has been researching this, and it is already clear that whales collide with boats either accidentally or intentionally much more frequently than was hitherto suspected. In spite of these exceptions, the overwhelming rule seems to be that whales are peaceful toward humans even though we have been killing them for centuries with every means we could devise.

I have wondered whether the reason for this seeming amnesty in the sea is because there are just so few places to hide there. In the open sea one must get used to facing even the worst monsters of one's dreams. Of course there could also be some intrinsic difference between the reactions of land animals and those of sea animals to humans, but I think not. It seems to me more likely that because we have only recently had the technology to enter freely into the realm of large marine mammals, in their medium we are seldom seen and are unfamiliar to them. On land nonhuman life knows our ways well and has learned to fear and flee us—we provide for most land animals an abundance of opportunities to experience fear in our presence or in the presence of the things we devise. But at sea we are still a curiosity and so are met with less fear. And since fear leads to aggression, we see less aggression from animals in the sea. However, in spite of the fact that by now there must have been millions of close human approaches to whales that have passed without incident, it is not something anyone should try who cannot read a whale's behavior. In the U.S. (and several other countries) it should not be tried at all as it is against the law.

When in some rare, wild place we come upon an individual of some species—any species—which has never encountered humans before, it usually accepts us peacefully. This simple fact provides an important clue to one of the questions I am addressing in this book: what would our natural association to nature be if we chose not to exploit it? I have the feeling that where animals have not learned from firsthand experience to fear us, they are usually prepared to greet humanity in peace. This may be the most important thing I have learned about whales. It would seem to follow that the wildness of animals may well be a creation of our approach to them rather than of theirs to us. It is not necessarily a propensity with which they are born. From which it would follow that in order to live in peace with the wild world, we need only change how we present ourselves to it. If we could do that, I believe we would be shocked at how quickly the rest of life accepts us, for it has, I think, a strong natural inclination to do so.

In my view, we are on the threshold of a new connection between animals and people: an Age of Friendship during which a significant number of humans will extend a tentative hand to the rest of life. I expect that from this new approach extraordinary associations will develop.

In the past, humans have usually approached wild animals by totally dominating them; that is, by killing or enslaving them. Even animals we love are sometimes treated despicably. Trained elephants are examples: before training commences they must be "broken." The process of breaking is usually brutal, its purpose being to convince the elephant that it has no control over its own life—that humans are in complete command. When a human does this to another human, it's called "brainwashing."

Even when our association with another animal is based on love, as in adopting a family pet, we often exert virtually total control over even the most fundamental aspects of their lives. We make them adhere to human schedules rather than to their own, we control their comings and goings, decide on their food—including the time, menu, and the amount they eat— govern their chances to interact with their own kind—even their opportunities for sexual activity and sometimes even whether they are allowed to remain sexually functional—and in the end, when they grow old, it is we who decide whether they should be allowed to live longer or have their lives terminated.

But there is now a small cadre of people who are willing to adjust their lives to animals' lives rather than vice versa. Their main objective is not to subject animals to human will—not to train elephants to load teak logs, or whales to push barges around—but who approach such animals simply as companions, who want just to get to know them and spend their days near them, always working to build acceptance and trust with wild animals. They do it just to see what comes of such a friendship. It is not very different from the way the rest of us form friendships with other people.

Some of the earliest of these people were scientists—animal behaviorists for the most part—who loved animals and had a great curiosity about how they lived. They figured out ways to support their habits through grants and scientific research, living for prolonged periods in the wild with some species that fascinated them. They were joined by volunteer nonscientists who began to help them with their projects, assisting by taking notes and photographs or in analyzing data. Often, although they started as volunteers, they stayed on and, though only ever getting a pittance, became essential to the entire operation. In recent years however we have seen a new fraternity. Call it the Brotherhood of the Wild (perhaps it should be Sisterhood, since so many are young women). This cohort of young people increases annually. They are young Mowglis, some of whom live in society during the weeks but spend their time off in the wild among whales or dolphins or gorillas or other wild animals whenever they can scrape together enough time and money to be there. They are reacting deeply to their suburban upbringings—fulfilling a lifelong dream of the wild—a kind of irresistible tug from their genetic past. They aren't focused on doing science or working in eco-tourism, and they don't have plans to make what they do into a profession. To earn a living they wait on tables or work in offices at unrelated jobs, spending all their free time with whales or other wild animals.

The existence of these people offers a wonderful new window through which to view the lives of animals. There is no way of knowing where the new kinds of associations these people are building between humans and animals such as whales may lead. Some of them have demonstrated extraordinary and unexpected things about wild animals. In a few cases, they are on a sharper cutting edge than some of the established scientists in the field.

When Captain Scammon first discovered the entrance to the lagoon in Baja California now bearing his name (at least on English-language maps—its

Spanish name is Laguna Ojo de Liebre, meaning Rabbit's Eye Lagoon), he sailed his ship inside and discovered that the lagoon was filled with gray whales. Bonanza! He immediately lowered his boats and began killing whales left and right. The whales had a ready response and immediately began killing men and smashing boats left and right. This caused the Baja whalers to christen the species the "Devil Fish," because of the "viciousness" of its behavior. The name stuck for years but it has recently started to come unglued.

When whale-watching tourism began in the 1960s, one of the first subjects was the gray whale. Gray whales pass the California coast during their annual migration, and swim very close to shore where they are now seen by millions of people. However, for those interested in viewing more than distant spouts from a coast road there are day trips, and for those really interested, trips of several days' length to the gray whales' calving lagoons in Baja California. It was from these lagoons that reports soon began to spread of gray whales that appeared to be acting friendly—approaching boats to lie alongside them while tourists patted them and rubbed their backs and heads, then rolling over so the tourists could reach their sides and bellies as well. This behavior became known as the "friendly gray whale phenomenon."

It is in San Ignacio Lagoon in Baja that this behavior is now most developed. Though they cannot be corroborated, there were rumors in 1970 from fishermen in Ojo de Liebre (as well as from elsewhere) of what may have been "friendly" gray whale behavior.

The first documented and widely photographed friendly encounter occurred in San Ignacio Lagoon in the winter of 1975. It involved a whale named Nacho[4] who was interacting with the skiffs tied astern of a tourist boat from San Diego while the boat was anchored for the night. Some of the crew got into the skiffs and began stroking and patting Nacho, using oars and a long broom. The following year a San Diego veterinarian named Bruce Cauble witnessed similar behavior by gray whales. Once again this occurred at San Ignacio but this time involved two female-calf pairs. Two years later biologists Steve Swartz and Mary Lou Jones found "a few" friendly gray whales near the end of the season.[5] A camera crew was working in the area when Jones and Swartz encountered "Amazing Grace," a gray whale that "really warmed up" to them. During the next five years Swartz and Jones saw friendly gray whales increase in San Ignacio, and in 1982—their last full winter in the lagoon—friendly encounters "went from being a relatively rare event to a common daily occurrence." By the next season they noted that "you were more or less guaranteed to have your whale watching (or fishing, or research, or whatever) interrupted at least once by one or more gray whales."[6]

By the 1980 season Jones and Swartz found several gray whales coming to boats where occupants stroked and petted them. Because the lagoons of Baja California are often windy, the smaller inflatable boats that are launched from larger tourist boats and then filled with tourists are often blown briskly along the surface. Because the wind does not press directly on the whales, on windy days the whales are obliged to go through antic contortions in order to keep their position so that people can scratch them from the rapidly drifting boats. Modern tourist boats are not silently rowed as were Scammon's whaling boats. They have noisy outboard motors, which make a much more intrusive noise and which one might expect to disturb a whale more than oars. Nevertheless the whales continue to behave in a friendly manner. Hardly what we would expect from a "Devil Fish."

It seems clear enough that the natural inclination of this species is to greet in a nonaggressive manner other species that approach it in a nonaggressive way. We just never gave them a chance to exhibit this behavior to us before. For thousands of years we were as aggressive toward whales as we could manage. Now that we have changed our stance we are finally able to see for the first time what their normal approach to us is.

When the first gray whales befriended people, there were dozens of skiffs filled with tourists and only a few "friendly" gray whales. By now the situation has reversed, and there appear to be more friendly gray whales than there are boatloads of tourists. As a result it is now the tourist boats that are the limited resource—not the friendly gray whales. Under such circumstances I would expect to see competition for tourist boats among the whales. Many gray whales don't wait for the tourist boats to approach them but swim fairly rapidly toward them, sometimes even bumping them—at times this is not very gently done. I have wondered whether this is not competition over a scarce resource. It has led to some amusing misunderstandings: biologist Jim Darling told me about a gray whale that a policeman on Vancouver Island reported to him because it had "rammed" the policeman's boat. The waters off Vancouver Island are a major Canadian tourist area as well as a summer feeding ground for a few gray whales. The policeman was concerned as to whether he ought not do something about the whale, since it might represent a threat to boaters in the area. As they discussed the incident Jim asked the policeman whether the whale had rolled belly-up after ramming his boat, to which the man replied, "Why yes, as a matter fact it did." Jim suggested that there was nothing wrong with the whale. It probably just wanted to be patted.

Since gray whales are one of the only species that has been given an adequate chance to respond positively to us, I would not be particularly surprised if it turns out that this species is not any more friendly than some other whale species. In fact, I'm betting there are friendlier species out there. If there are, it could provide a valuable lesson to our species—that we will always receive the best treatment from the wild world when we approach it in ways that at least give it the *option* of responding positively toward us.

We already know that every species of whale with which anyone has swum is normally peaceful—is careful to avoid hitting the clumsy and helpless human swimmers around it with its flukes. Bumps and bruises occasionally do occur, but usually from calves, which are universally clumsy, and from the stories I have heard, they only collide with swimmers when the whale appears to be spooked and is moving fast to get out of a tight situation. If you were to compare whales to horses, you would find the horses dangerous beasts by comparison—lots of people have died from accidents with horses. And I am not referring here to wild horses but to tame, riding horses.

I look forward to a future in which people and whales have the chance to interact more and more and to the bonds that may grow between our species from such interactions. At the moment this interaction will not happen in U.S. waters, because it has been declared illegal in the United States. Harassment is defined as anything that causes a change in the behavior of the whales. Breaking this law brings with it a maximum fine of ten thousand dollars, a major deterrent to building bonds of friendship between our species. I recognize the original intent of the law (I had a minor role in creating part of it), and I am grateful that such a law exists to protect whales from fools (and vice versa). But I feel that those who interpret and enforce the law have done whales a grave disservice. As Sylvia Earle, biologist, diver and former chief scientist at NOAA (the National Oceanographic and Atmospheric Administration of the United States Department of Commerce), once pointed out, unless a diver attacks a whale, there is no way to significantly harass it, since when the whale chooses to leave, it simply does so: there is no way the diver can then keep up with it. In recent years the United States has often been a leader in the passage of laws to protect animals, but in its enforcement of the Marine Mammal Protection Act and the Endangered Species Act (both pieces of landmark legislation) the federal government has behaved in a way that I believe is not entirely in the best interests of the whales. Although it is obvious that underwater films of whales are one of the major positive influences on the public's growing interest in whales, and that they are therefore of the greatest benefit to whales, the branch of the government which grants permits for the filming of whales, the National Marine Fisheries Service, has made it very difficult even for serious scientists to film whales in the course of their research. Quite apart from any loss to science brought about by this policy, there is not the slightest evidence that such filming has ever resulted in any serious negative effect on a whale, whereas it is self-evident that the huge surge of interest in whales—which has benefited them in the most basic ways—is overwhelmingly due to the coverage they receive on television.

When I started studying them in 1967, there was practically no interest in whales. Tens of thousands were being killed by the whaling industry each year, and only a handful of people raised any kind of complaint. With the popularity of the *Flipper* series on television and the first underwater images showing how graceful whales are, all that changed. By the early seventies, the above-mentioned laws protecting marine mammals were passed. The blatantly obvious connection between beautiful images of whales and their improving state in relation to people seems to have all but escaped the law enforcement wing of the federal bureaucracy.

What seems to offend the enforcement division most is the prospect of anyone making money from films of whales. A recent case in which naturalist/photographer Lee Tepley filmed a woman being carried underwater by a wild pilot whale and who then sold the film to a commercial television channel resulted in a fine against the woman, Lisa Costello, of two thousand dollars and Lee for ten thousand dollars. (The case is being appealed.) The reason for Lee's fine being larger was stated explicitly: he indicated that he felt no remorse from having made money on the film of the incident and might again film such an unusual incident "if there was 'commercial value' to it." It is crystal clear from the circumstances that when the photographer went out that day he had no thought or expectation that he would ever get to film the kind of thing that happened. Only a neophyte with no experience at all could have believed he would have the chance to film what Tepley filmed that day. It is incredible to me that such a fine should be levied against either party and particularly offensive that his fine should have been so large for the reasons given. But this strange approach by the enforcers seems not to be limited to people filming whales, but to extend to the whale-watch industry.

Should we welcome the fact that the whale-watch industry now brings in more money every year than the world's whale-killing industry, or should we diminish its future impact by regulations that forbid close access to whales because we believe, on the basis of no evidence, that whale watch is seriously deleterious to whales and maintain that belief in the face of increasing evidence that it is not?

A study by Erich Hoyt has shown that in 1992, 3,431,250 Americans went whale watching, spending 46 million dollars on whale watch tickets and 225 million dollars on indirect costs (T-shirts, meals, travel, hotels, etc.). Hoyt estimated that in the same year a worldwide total of 4,480,000 people went whale watching, spending 75 million dollars on tickets and nearly 318 million in total revenues.[7] Japan has recently entered the arena, and the whale-watch industry there is exploding. In 1988 less than a hundred people went whale watching in Japan, but by 1992 more than nineteen thousand did so. The Japanese paid $782,000 for tickets and $8,119,000 in total revenues.[8]

In every country to which whale watching has been introduced, this tourist industry has grown rapidly. In today's world it turns out simply to make better economic sense to keep whales alive: they are worth more alive than they are dead. A single live whale can provide millions of dollars in revenue to a small community, since money changes hands every time someone visits a town, hires a boat, and goes out to look at a whale.

The philosopher Emerson once pointed out that if the stars only shone once each century, everyone would be out watching them for that entire night. Nature is extravagantly beautiful, and yet those who experience it daily become blasé about it, like guards in art museums who tire of the works they protect. That is why tourists make such good advocates for conserving endangered species. They may only see a whale once or twice, so they remain in awe of them. And that is why I feel it is so important to defend the opportunity for tourists to become awestruck by whales. In the long run it is they who will determine the fate of whales more than many of the scientists who get to spend their lives with them.

Recently a law has been under consideration by the National Marine Fisheries Service—hanging like a sword of Damocles over the whale-watch industry. This is the proposal that whale-watching boats not be allowed to approach whales closer than a hundred yards. The proposal is ill-advised, and without scientific merit (there being no evidence at all for the selection of this distance). Mercifully, at the time of this writing it has been tabled. From my own experience it is crystal clear that a distance of one hundred yards offers no real benefit to a whale but does wreck the experience for the tourists who wish to see it. It is much too far away to give the spectators any sense of being awed by a whale, which will leave them less satisfied and therefore less influenced in favor of whales.

What interests me far more than the economic success of the whale-watch industry is the change in attitude toward whales that whale watchers come away with and how that builds their interest in the rest of the wild world. The only reason whales should be asked to put up with the human voyeurism represented by whale watching is that it gets a message across to these people. If boats are kept too far from the whales to allow them to make a basic impact on the passengers then why should boats be allowed anywhere in the vicinity?

Before it was tabled, I had the feeling that this ill-considered minimum-distance law was being railroaded through in spite of the fact that in the course of public hearings the overwhelming advice from scientists was not to pass it. Scientist after scientist pointed out that in every place that a whale-watch industry has sprung up, the meaningful indicators of the well-being of the whales—such as the numbers of whales returning each year to the same area, and the numbers of calves being produced by them—demonstrate that the whales are thriving.

One gets the feeling that the work of scientists who study this kind of thing means little to federal enforcers—that it is instead their prejudgments on this matter that dictate their decisions. All who love whales probably assume that any human action that affects them will do so negatively. But the brutal facts are that where evidence exists, it indicates that such is not the case. I know how strong such prejudgments can be because they were my own when I started research. I was, for example, sure that the right whales at Península Valdés were being harassed by boat traffic, and when in 1972 I noticed what appeared to be a great falling off in population of whales in Golfo Nuevo, I assumed it was due to a large increase in vessel traffic that year. Fortunately I waited until the following year to confirm my theory, for in 1973, even though the boat traffic in Golfo Nuevo increased, again the number of whales there also increased, and Golfo Nuevo now has not just the heaviest vessel traffic but also the greatest population of right whales in the peninsula—far more than were there before, both relatively and absolutely.

Suppose you were one of those fishermen who hate whales and you were offered a contract for a million dollars to drive the whales out of some area, the deal being that you were not allowed to kill them but that you would be required to pay all your expenses yourself if you were unable to get rid of the whales for good (i.e., if they kept coming back season after season, you wouldn't get your million dollars). Would you sign such a contract? I wouldn't. Quite apart from the fact that chasing whales out of an area would be an outrage, I don't believe it could be done. The determination of whales to continue occupying areas in the face of the worst possible human molestation—killing them—is what has made it possible for the whaling industry to all but destroy them.

As I see it, the kinds of harassment the government sometimes punishes constitute no significant harassment at all. Are we to seriously believe that the fitness of the pilot whale that dragged the woman underwater for a few seconds was adversely affected by the experience of doing so? Did it fail to reproduce that year for that reason? Did it fail to find food? Did it fail to find a mate? Did it develop some sort of life-disfiguring neurosis because of its experience that morning?

I understand the deterrent value of making an example of someone, but when it is done for reasons like the ones in this case, it ends up making a mockery of the law, which weakens it rather than strengthening it.

I would strongly advocate coming down with the full force of the law on anyone who actually did what I am about to discuss doing, but I wish to present it as a point of discussion nevertheless. Suppose that someone drove their boat as fast as possible toward a whale, missing it only by inches. What result would that have on the whale? Twice in my life I have been narrowly missed by cars careening out of control. I certainly didn't like the experience, and one of them, in particular, resulted in occasional bad dreams, but I cannot see that it affected the richness of my other life experiences, or that it affected my reproductive (or overall) fitness. If you were coming to work this morning and stepped off the curb carelessly and almost got hit by a bus, would that ruin your life? Your morning? Your next five minutes? Should someone be fined ten thousand dollars for doing something for which there does not seem to be even a small likelihood that the whale involved suffered in any meaningful way and which was not an intended act on their part?

The point is not to approve of careless activities by boats around whales but to understand what we do when we use the law to punish people who are doing everything in their power *not* to harass whales as though they were deliberately molesting them in life-threatening ways. It is an important fact that both captains of whale-watching boats and photographers are fully aware that their livelihoods depend on not molesting the whales with which they interact. I once watched a very flirtatious young woman trying to persuade the handsome young captain of a whale-watching boat to bring his vessel closer to a whale so she could get a better picture. I had never met the captain, and he had no idea that a whale biologist was on board, so what followed was not done for my benefit. He simply wouldn't budge. She spent the rest of the trip coldly snubbing him for having stood his ground. I heard him mutter to one of his crew that he was damned if he was going mess up his business for anyone, even her.

There are, I realize, instances when whale-watching captains must be harassing whales, but in my experience they are rare. It is clear that the far more frequent culprits are recreational boaters who rush up to whales, occasionally even colliding with them. In 1989 there were two humpbacks on Stellwagen Bank off Boston carrying deep wounds, which from their size, form, and placement left no doubt that they had been caused by the propellers of power boats. The problem of enforcing against the harassment of whales by recreational boaters is clearly daunting to the federal authorities. I sympathize with both the need to do so and the difficulty of accomplishing such enforcement, but the response of federal government enforcers seems to be to put pressure on smaller targets—scientists and whale-watching boats. The honest thing to do would be to bite the bullet and pass legislation requiring that boat propellors should be protected by a wire cage. However, that's a political bombshell which no federal employee seems to have the courage to introduce. Therefore, rather than fulfilling their job—to protect whales from injury—they seem to prefer instead to give the appearance of doing so by bearing down on those who are least likely to be harassing whales. It's the old story: "If you can't kick the boss, kick the dog."

As for damage done by filmmakers: in the late 1960s I heard a story about two Hollywood photographers who went into Scammon's Lagoon and threw cherry bombs at gray whales in hopes of creating some kind of spectacular reaction they could film. They got nothing, of course, because the whales simply fled without surfacing. (The natural response of whales to a major disturbance is to flee underwater, simply, I suppose, because whales make their best time when they are submerged and are not wasting energy generating waves at the surface.) One is grateful that we now have laws to discourage this kind of madness. Thankfully, such outrages appear to be very rare.

The preconception that most people seem to have is that a photographer who is trying for a picture will rush in to get it, thus seriously disturbing the whale. I have probably worked with as many photographers filming whales underwater as anyone alive. I have never once seen a photographer rush in on a whale in an aggressive way to try for a better shot. Any photographer with any experience at all knows that to rush in is to assure that they will go home with nothing. It would be like bursting out of a bird blind to film some unique behavior of the bird on the nest; it just wouldn't work—and any photographer experienced enough to have landed a job filming whales knows better. The key to photographing all wildlife, whales included, is patience—being as quiet and unobtrusive as possible. The only instance I have seen of anything resembling clear harassment involved with photographing whales was a film showing television host Geraldo Rivera swimming aggressively up to a humpback whale in order to be filmed touching it. But Fate is not entirely without mercy: after all, there has only ever been one Geraldo Rivera.

It goes without saying that humans should take extra precautions to avoid harassing whales. But I feel there is a danger that in our zeal to protect them from harassment we may overprotect them, and thereby disallow even careful approaches by experienced people. If this occurs we will be stifling the kinds of friendships that might otherwise form between humans and whales. One of the payoffs of our new awareness of the wild world is going to be a whole new scale to the kinds of associations that we can form with wild animals. A law keeping people and whales apart that is blind to this kind of payoff (and the ones now in existence clearly are) will rob the world of what might otherwise turn out to be a rapport between species and whales that could change our lives in grand and unexpected ways (and secure a far better future for the whales into the bargain).

Federal laws notwithstanding, there is abundant evidence that porpoises often seek out boats. For instance there was the famous "Pelorus Jack" (probably a Risso's dolphin) who lived in Cook Strait, between the North and South islands of New Zealand, and for thirty-two years accompanied the ferry and many other ships passing through the strait. Pelorus Jack became such a national institution that a law was passed fining people up to one hundred pounds for hurting him. There was also a pod of killer whales hunting in the same strait. According to whalers who manned a whaling station there, the killer whales helped them by driving humpback whales toward their boats—the whalers then sharing their catch with the killer whales.

On the coast of Morocco, there is a group of dolphins who work with fishermen, appearing when the fishermen appear. The fishermen claim the dolphins come in response to a special call that is made to attract them, but it seems to me more probable that the dolphins simply come when they see the fishermen gathering on the beach with their nets. The dolphins drive fish into the fishermen's surf seines, working right among their legs. In return for this service, the fishermen share their catch with the dolphins.

Dolphins sometimes save people from drowning by pushing them toward shore. For those who have had their lives saved by dolphins it is difficult to dismiss such behavior as being anything besides the dolphin's natural interest in the welfare of people. As animal behaviorist and dolphin trainer Karen Pryor once remarked, "Of course you don't hear from the drowning people that the dolphins push *away* from shore." Laying aside that unanswerable objection, Karen interviewed several people who claimed to have been saved from drowning by dolphins and discovered that the details of their experiences were similar (e.g., the manner in which the dolphins had pushed them, what parts of their body they pushed against, how long each bout of pushing lasted, etc.), causing her to conclude that dolphins really do sometimes recognize the struggles of a drowning person and save them. What more could one ask of an animal?

It is clear that over the years there have been many efforts by dolphins to form bonds with humans. One of the earliest-known (and perhaps the most famous) of these is an association that occurred between a boy and a dolphin in Greece, two thousand years ago. The ancient Greeks had a loving attitude toward dolphins, who were part of the dramatis personae of their religion.

In the instance to which I refer, Pliny reports on a dolphin from the town of Hippo that came up to a boy who was swimming offshore and pushed him back to the beach. The following day the dolphin came back, this time in the company of another dolphin, but the boy and his friends fled from the sea to watch from the safety of the beach as the dolphins performed all sorts of antics. This went on for the next few days, until gradually the boys lost their fear of the dolphins. Eventually the boy that the dolphin had contacted first developed a deep friendship with it, riding to school each day across a bay on its back. The story of the boy on the dolphin spread, and its fame soon attracted visitors, until the resentment at the disruption of normal city life caused those in power in the town of Hippo to kill the dolphin in secret.

Records of encounters between humans and dolphins in the human written record were lost until recent times. I doubt they were especially rare. I suspect that the Western world may have rejected such tales as myths and legends because of the changes we were undergoing in the way we looked at nature. We went from being a society centered on a pantheon of gods inhabiting every field and wood and stream to a religion based on one God who created humans in His own image and gave them supremacy over everything in nature. As part of its effort to stamp out pagan religions, the Christian church connected the ability to communicate with animals with witchcraft. For a long, dark time it wasn't wise to say you had made friends with a dolphin.

In the present age it is no longer dangerous in most cultures to admit to a liking of wild animals, and it now seems that at any one moment there are a couple of dozen wild dolphins of several species scattered broadly around the world that are interacting with humans in obviously friendly encounters. A New Zealander, Wade Doak, has collected information on forty-four modern instances of close contact between humans and dolphins in the wild. Now that people are braver about approaching whales, I suspect that there will soon be enough material to make it worthwhile compiling records of human/whale encounters as well.

One of the first such encounters of which I am aware occurred in Argentina in 1972 between a remarkable young woman, Jane Frick, and a right whale she named Dulce. Dulce was a young female who seemed to seek out Jane's company (Dulce once left a mating group in which she appeared to be a willing participant to come over and be with Jane). Dulce's behavior was the same each time she approached Jane: if Jane stayed motionless treading water, Dulce would swim slowly up to her, rest her head against Jane's body, and allow Jane to stroke her head. This same behavior occurred at least three times before Jane left Argentina to return home. Other divers discovered "that tame whale," and two of them based the best sequences of their films on pictures of Dulce.

There is a famous humpback whale, Daisy (named by biologist Deborah Glockner-Ferrari), who has a very high threshold for annoyance by human swimmers. She returns each year to Hawaiian waters, bringing a new calf with her. Debbie recognizes Daisy by the pattern of lip creases on her lower jaw. She says that it is Daisy who appears in a disproportionate number of the many films about humpback whales which have been made in the Hawaiian area, simply because she is such a cooperative subject and seems to be completely relaxed about photographers.

Why is it that so many whales and dolphins are interacting with people? And just what it is that these animals get out of such encounters? Because these questions interest me, I decided to see for myself what some of the wild dolphins interacting with people were doing. I visited three different groups of bottle-nosed dolphins, starting with the captive bottle-nosed dolphins at the Dolphin Research Center (DRC) in Grassy Key, Florida. This group had been described to me as unwilling to leave their compounds even when the wire that barred them from the open bay was lowered to allow them to pass. The second group I visited was the famous dolphins in Monkey Mia, in Shark Bay, Australia, which are fed by hand several times each day by tourists. The third was just one of the many solitary dolphins in the world currently interacting with human swimmers—Fungie, who lives near the small fishing port of Dingle, Ireland.

At the Dolphin Research Center I swam with Aleta, Anessa, and Santini—all born there. At the time of my visit, these females were the principal dolphins in the DRC's Dolphin Swim Program. As soon as I entered the water, I took particular pains to make sure I never made any aggressive moves toward them, always trying to remember to hold my hands below them rather than over their heads and to move very slowly and as though I wasn't paying any attention to them. I resisted the temptation to reach out and touch them. They were obviously somewhat wary of me at first, but they gradually warmed up as time went on and I did nothing to harm them.

In the end my patience was rewarded in the most beguiling way. At one point Santini came over to me, lying on her side, swimming in a somewhat funny manner, coming very close, and waving (or should I say shivering) her flipper. "Oh," said the dolphin trainer, Linda, "that's a great idea; she's inviting you to hold on to her flipper and she'll give you a ride." (This was a command that Linda had not used all day and that Santini had come up with on her own.) And so I took hold of her flipper and Santini towed me smartly along. What was so appealing to me was that Santini had thought up this act on her own. Furthermore, it was immediately followed by her offering me her dorsal fin. Linda said, "She's getting really friendly. She's inviting you to take hold of her dorsal fin and she'll give you another ride."

The most touching thing about this is that Santini had scraped the skin off the tip of her dorsal fin and it was clearly sore. Although I took care to hold the fin without touching the wound, I supposed that I had finally won her trust enough to give me the chance to hold on to her wounded fin.

But there was another thing about all this that impressed me. By the time she offered me a ride, she had all but stopped taking fish—even though they were still being offered. She had been working with the other dolphins in front of the swim platform as they huddled together for pictures. During that time Linda mentioned that Santini was now showing almost no interest in fish. These dolphins are rewarded for interacting with people, and there was no question in my mind that at the start of my session they needed a reward in order to build up enough courage to come close to a large galoot like me. This means that in the end, when Santini came over to offer me her flipper, it was not some last-ditch effort to get another fish—she was all but surfeited with fish.

At the DRC these dolphins are held in fenced-off areas of the bay, and because I was curious to see firsthand what I had been told—that the dolphins would not flee to the open ocean—I asked for the fence to be lowered. Thus, the dolphins were entirely free to leave the fenced-in area anytime they wanted to, which they did many, many times—between thirty and fifty times during the course of the day. But most impressive to me was the fact that at lunchtime, when we went off to get something to eat, leaving the dolphins alone for about two hours, we did not raise the fence again but left them to do as they liked. This step was taken even though it was obvious that the dolphins were thoroughly sated with food and even though there was no one around to blow a whistle or give them any signs should they decide to leave for good. My last sight of them as we left for lunch was impressive: they were swimming at high speed seaward—out past the fence. I was worried lest they should be lost because of my request, but Linda was entirely unconcerned that they might defect. Sure enough, when we returned they were all back in their pen.

At the end of the day I stayed around long enough to see the fence reerected, a process that took about thirty minutes. As the young man who did the job swam over to it, the dolphins swam attentively along with him, staying very close, though he largely ignored them (they knew him well). When he got to the fence, he raised up the first piece, and from that moment on they ambled into the pen and lazed slowly around without the slightest effort to swim out past the fence again, even though it took him twenty-five minutes to close off their escape route, which was longer than the time between their previous sallies seaward. The man reerecting the fence never made any sounds or motions to chase them back into the pen or to direct them in any way. They seemed entirely content to be on the side of the fence that thirty minutes later would be inaccessible to the sea.

When I discussed this point, Linda said that she felt the main reason for the fence was not to keep the dolphins in but to keep predators out. But on a fence inspection in recent years, it was discovered that much of the underwater portions of another section had been storm damaged and that the dolphins had been freely coming and going through it for several days.

The behavior that the three dolphins showed as we worked with them throughout the day was reminiscent of the behavior of the Dingle dolphin that I was to meet. They would break off from working with me and go off a short distance outside the fence—for a little stroll on their own so to speak—and then swim right back into the fray and resume interacting with people (just as the Dingle dolphin would slip away for a moment on his own, returning to be with us after a few minutes). At no point did I feel that the dolphins were being driven hard against their wills. Rather, it seemed to me as though it was a form of work in which they participated freely.

The thing that makes it hard to assess the motivation of the DRC dolphins is the fact that so many of them have been born there and that all of them are fed there. I reasoned that it was at least conceivable that they didn't really like people (though I do not believe it for a moment given the kinds of subtle cues in their behaviors that strongly argue to the contrary). As a scientist, I wanted to investigate a situation where it was a little clearer that the dolphins might be approaching people entirely of their own accord. So I went to Monkey Mia—a resort on the shores of Shark Bay in western Australia—where a pod of wild dolphins comes in to shore to interact with tourists and to be fed several times a day.

This is a holiday trailer park with a few cabins and is just like any other such resort with one exception—there's a pod of wild dolphins swimming about among the bathers. A small strip of coast along which the dolphins come to be fed is marked off with buoys and there's a law against people entering this water—it's the dolphins' area—the idea being that this is a place the dolphins can go to get away from people while remaining in shallow water if they wish to. Although they appear in that area during feeding time, at other times they can also be seen along other stretches of beach, where they often mingle with people or beg alongside boats for fish. They do this by swimming with their heads raised above water, often touching the boats with their heads, and staying closest to that point of the boat where a person is sitting. They keep their mouths open and sometimes make noises, apparently to draw attention to themselves. They're obviously waiting to be fed, and if the person from whom they are begging has been successful while fishing, he or she may share the catch with the dolphins (though I was told that this is illegal), and the dolphins will eat what they are offered, leaving no doubt as to the function of this "begging" behavior.

There is an excellent long-term research program on bottle-nosed dolphins going on in this area, and although it focuses on the other wild bottle-nosed dolphins here (2,100 are estimated to be in the Shark Bay population), the researchers know quite a lot about the dolphins that beg fish from tourists. One of the most interesting findings is that the cohort of begging dolphins drives away other dolphins who try to get a share of the free fish. Thus they keep this unique feeding opportunity for themselves. They sometimes make quite strong attacks on possible interlopers, so it seems that they value this resource enough to fight for it. However, not all animals are driven away. For example, after a calf was born to Holey Fin, one of the begging cohort, she began to bring the calf to be fed. Thus, it appears that these dolphins guard their fish franchise and pass it on to their families, just as the human owners of the Monkey Mia dolphin franchise guard it from other humans and will presumably pass it on to their children when they retire. The whole thing looks like a proper transaction. Good business, really, between the two species.

But seeing the dolphins at Monkey Mia still didn't provide the insight I sought. It was hard to figure out whether the only thing that really attracted the dolphins to the area was the free fish, or whether they really chose to be with people.

The wild bottle-nosed dolphin that lived in Dingle Bay, Ireland, offered a clearer insight. I worked with a young couple, Sheila Stokes and Brian Holmes, who were among the small group of people responsible for taming this dolphin and habituating him to people.

I will tell the story from the point of view of Sheila Stokes, because it was with her that I spent the most time. Sheila worked as a legal assistant in a law office. A few years ago she and Brian decided they wanted to see a dolphin, but they didn't know where to go. They started traveling around Ireland asking fishermen if they ever saw dolphins. In County Kerry, in the tiny fishing port of Dingle, they finally found what they were looking for. The fishermen said there was a dolphin they saw daily in a very small area between Beenbawn Head and Reenbeg Point. Sheila and Brian are both divers and had bought a tiny eight-foot inflatable boat that they used on their long weekends to paddle around near the dolphin trying to get him to interact with them (they knew by now he was a male). They soon struck up a friendship with the local lighthouse keeper, who allowed them to camp on the lighthouse property. They would rise every morning at dawn and go out in the boat to spend the day with Fungie, as the dolphin had come to be known. He showed some interest in them but was very shy and never let them touch him. They tried feeding him fish but he was not interested. However, he did bring a fish to Sheila once or twice.

On the forty-second day of trying, Sheila was finally able to reach out and touch him. She can now take him in her arms, and whenever she goes to Dingle he comes to play with her by the hour and by the day. At the time she and Brian were doing this there were several other people working with Fungie as well; in particular two divers, John Allen and Ronnie Fitzgibbon.[9] Since that time Fungie has become a major attraction for tourists and hundreds of people have swum with him. I went when the weather was still cold and we were about the only people present.

In summer, however, people come out by the fishing boatload to see the dolphin, and there are often crowds of twenty or more boats surrounding him. Tourists fill the hotels, restaurants, and shops of Dingle, renting snorkels, flippers, and dive gear and buying film and souvenirs. Fungie has transformed the economy of this tiny town. Its only other economic shot in the arm this century was when it was used as the set for the film *Ryan's Daughter*.

It has been estimated that the money Fungie brings into Dingle is about a million pounds a year. However, this is a somewhat casual estimate that mostly covers hotel bills, meals, and the charter costs for boats. It doesn't take into account the less obvious kinds of revenues the town receives from Fungie tourists. But a phenomenon like Fungie pours money into an economy. If we could collect data on it, I suspect we would find that it's half again as much as the existing estimate. For example there are sales of postcards, and postage stamps, and sun cream, and souvenirs, and new batteries, and Guinness in the pub, and aspirin, and maps of the area, and gifts for the family, and taxis to and from the quay, and long-distance calls home, and a new sun hat because you forgot to pack the old one (ditto for new toothpaste), and a new fountain pen to replace the one you lost overboard, and a new T-shirt, because, well . . . and so on.

But even this is not all the money that changes hands because of Fungie. People come from far away, which generates sales in their hometowns, as well as en route. They buy new cameras (which trigger the need for new slide projectors "for best results"). They buy video recorders (also requiring adapters that fit Irish wall sockets). And they need tickets on Aer Lingus, and taxis to and from home (or tolls and parking fees if they take a car). And tips to porters at the terminal, and flight insurance, and commissions to banks on traveler's checks (as well as to money changers at both ends of the journey). And there are snacks and meals at the terminal, and last-minute rolls of film and reading material at the kiosk, and duty-free goods in both directions, and departure taxes, and rental headphones for the inflight movie, and drinks with dinner.

If there's an overnight stop en route there are hotel costs, and these give rise to tips for bellhops, and rental movies in the room, and six-dollar cans of peanuts from the minibar. On the way home there are more tips and cabs and departure taxes, as well as calls from the gate to say the plane is running late. And once home there are dry cleaning bills and replacement costs for the things the airlines lost as well as developing costs for slides (plus boxes in which to store them) and printing costs for prints (plus albums in which to display them). And copies of the best pictures for Grandma, and stamps to post them to her, and calls to invite friends to a party to see your Fungie slides, and snacks when they arrive, and so on and on.

Fungie is like a movie star in terms of the money he causes to change hands. And all that money shifts around simply because a couple of divers made friends with a dolphin.

As I watched Fungie's behavior during the days I was in Dingle, I realized that I was seeing striking similarities between this entirely wild and free dolphin and the three dolphins used by the Dolphin Research Center in the Dolphin Swim Program, suggesting that much of their behavior was the normal behavior of this species even though the DRC dolphins had been born in captivity.

On my first day in the water with Fungie, one of the things that intrigued me most about this dolphin was that on each approach by Sheila Stokes and me, he put himself in reach of her without making himself accessible to me. In fact the only way I was able to touch him was when she was stroking him and he had his eyes closed—as though in ecstasy. But after a while he appeared to become aware that there were hands in contact with him other than Sheila's, and he would open his eyes, look at me, and move out of my reach. My conclusion was that although this is indeed a wonderful dolphin, as dolphins go I suspect he is not necessarily a particularly friendly one. It dawned on me one morning that it might not be the dolphin that represented the breakthrough as much as it was the people. For Sheila and Brian had gone out looking for a dolphin, found one, and then had stuck with him for forty-two days of cold green water and bitter winds until he finally accepted them. I suspect that a braver dolphin might have accepted people in a shorter time—perhaps even initiated physical contact on its own. If there is anything to this theory, we may soon find out, for Sheila Stokes is planning to try someday to find and tame another dolphin at some undisclosed location along the Irish coast. But this time, she said, she might decide not to announce the location.

Although Fungie avoided me on the first day, by the second day he was much more relaxed around me, and throughout our swims with him he kept coming back to be petted. He did this in spite of the fact that he was receiving no food from us or from anybody else. I felt that apart from his just wanting human company, there was another possible attraction that people might hold.

Dolphins in captivity are very active sexually. They show sexual arousal to a wide variety of obviously inappropriate stimuli. For example, they hold their genital slits in underwater jets of water, or rub them against the corners of objects on the bottom. Because Fungie is a male, it would have been dead obvious if he was exhibiting sexual arousal. I had asked Sheila if that ever happened, but she said it never did. I was worried that she might not have wished to discuss such a thing with a stranger like me, but during the entire time I was there I never saw any hint of sexual arousal in Fungie. If he has never accepted food from people (which he has not) and if he is not sexually aroused by humans (which he evidently is not), it seems to me that we are more or less forced to conclude that he simply seeks human companionship. Such a theory fits exactly with the way he behaved when we first appeared each day; he leapt and leapt and swam wildly around Sheila as soon as she entered the water—reminiscent of some exuberant dog bouncing around like a rubber ball next to a family member who has just gotten home.

During the days that I was there, Fungie repeatedly interacted with swimmers, a kayak, and the fishing boats that passed us every few minutes. It was surprising to me that Fungie's interest in the kayak was even stronger than his interest in humans, and that his interest in fishing boats was stronger still. He would leave any person when the kayak came by, and leave a person or the kayak whenever a fishing boat appeared.

The people with whom we were working were convinced that Fungie liked to race boats. I was less convinced until one day when we were working with the captain of a very powerful boat that could go about forty knots. I was inshore when the boat first appeared, watching in disgust as he drove like a madman, roaring around Fungie, missing him by inches. When this tasteless display was over and he came ashore to pick us up, I scolded him harshly for behaving so irresponsibly. He was obviously chagrined and we set out at a sedate pace of about eight knots, a speed I suggested since it matched the speed of the fishing boats with which Fungie was most familiar. To my surprise and chagrin, for the next fifteen minutes Fungie stationed himself just behind the underwater unit of the 140-horsepower outboard motor, swimming steadily, with his head about two inches from the propeller—even closer at times. As I watched Fungie's behavior, it dawned on me that maybe it was I who was wrong. I had been so harsh on the captain that everyone in the boat was silent, and in an effort to make amends for having been so nasty and to relax the tension, I asked the captain how long he had been driving his boat around Fungie.

"Oh, for many months, sir," he replied.

"And is it your impression that Fungie likes the kind of driving you were doing before we got on board?" I asked.

"Oh, yes, sir, he seems really to like it," he replied.

I thought it over and then said, "Okay, since you've had more experience with this animal than I have, let's do it your way. Go ahead and do what you think Fungie likes."

He blushed, hiding his smile of relief, then slowly increased his engine power and soon arrived at top speed. What ensued was the most spectacular piece of swimming I have ever witnessed by any dolphin. As we gained speed, Fungie immediately pulled away from the rear of the boat and began swimming alongside us, leaping into the air as high as our heads (we were standing at the console), then diving beneath the boat to switch sides, then leaping to head height again. All this was done so fast that at first I thought we had been joined by a second dolphin. As the boat gained speed and Fungie could no longer keep up (though it was stunning how fast he could go), the captain began driving in broad circles. This was something Fungie knew all about. He immediately veered away from us and began swimming along chords of the curve, taking shortcuts and calculating his path so accurately he missed us by only inches as he shot in front of the boat on the back side of its curve. He would then rocket out of the water in repeated jumps at eye level beside us—all the while swimming at top speed. That is what he and the boat had been doing when I was standing onshore scowling. It was clear I was wrong about the captain; he wasn't showing off to us, he was entertaining Fungie. He and Fungie understood each other perfectly. It was the most animated that we saw Fungie during the entire time we were in Dingle.

After a few minutes it became apparent that Fungie was going a bit slower, something the captain noticed immediately. He slowed his speed at once, stopping for a few minutes so Fungie could rest. Although I still cannot accept the thought that driving a boat in this manner near a dolphin is right, I left feeling a bit sheepish. Once again I had seen proof of my own law: any observant local knows more than any visiting scientist. Always. No exceptions.

As I see it, this human/dolphin bond is a classic example of what humanity could gain simply by changing its attitude toward the wild world. I believe it shows that if we decide that the natural world—even the alien, wild, freely-swimming-in-the-sea, natural world—is desirable, attractive, or lovable that we can not only reach out to it and touch it but take it in our arms. I ask myself whether in the Greek tale it was the dolphin or the boy who was the more remarkable.

I would love to discover that in the year 2000 in every ocean people were bringing in the new year by swimming with wild dolphins and whales—all over the seas, everywhere, a hundred such friendships, each with its history and special attributes, so many such companionships that it would take much of the ensuing year just to tell their stories. Sure, I see all the obvious objections—any scientist would—but as George Bernard Shaw said, "Nothing was ever accomplished by a reasonable man." It is my suspicion that the wild world is waiting to be befriended by humanity.

There are two deeply contentious issues that I feel obligated to address in this chapter: whether people have the right to keep whales and dolphins in captivity, and whether whale watching should continue. More and more conservationists are coming down on the side of banning both captivity and whale watching. I am not so sure we are ready yet. I feel that the sight of a person riding on the back of a killer whale is in the deepest interest of killer whales. It destroys in one stroke their image as dangerous monsters and shows them as well-disposed toward humans. Opponents of captivity might concede that point but note that there are now plenty of photographs and films showing people riding killer whales, even balancing on their snouts as the whale performs a full breach, and that it is therefore no longer necessary for killer whales to be served up to the public in this way. I feel, however, that this overlooks an important point: most of what one sees on television is a shadow of the real experience. Anyone who goes to a dolphin show knows that it is only on film that the jumps of whales last long enough to be well scrutinized. So why do dolphin shows still attract so many visitors? Given that the images of dolphins are available on network television more times a year than the average person gets to go to a dolphin show, if the impact of television images is as powerful as watching a live animal perform, why are people's appetites for seeing porpoises jump not satisfied, even surfeited, by television—why is there any market at all for dolphin shows, particularly when they cost lots of money—and compete with images of dolphins that are free (at least on network television)? I suppose it is because television is such a neutral and third-hand experience, whereas even with all their hokeyness, dolphin shows contain at least some of the elements of a genuine experience. To someone who has seen many dolphins on television, seeing them in the flesh at an aquarium is, I suppose, a little like seeing some rock group live in concert after repeatedly watching their music videos. Even though producers do everything possible to make a video fascinating, it's not as interesting as being at a live performance, even in a bad seat, and even though live staging cannot approach the visual trickery possible in a video.

The same argument is true regarding whale watches. On a whale watch one is only rarely afforded views comparable to those available on television—and the views on whale watches are accompanied, for many observers, by seasickness. Nevertheless, whale watching is an incredibly successful industry and has enjoyed an explosive increase everywhere it has sprung up. I believe that this is because it provides a genuine experience and not a secondhand one. For instance, nothing on television can offer the real impact of being in a small boat and seeing a whale approaching you. Because you are so vulnerable, you fear that the whale may breach on the boat or with a flick of its tail capsize it and put you in the water, even closer to the whale. When none of these fears is realized and you are breathing with relief as the boat heads back to port with everyone safe and dry, you are finally free to experience the exultation of what you have just been through. Allowing whale watchers to successfully confront their fears is probably the main benefit whale watching has to offer.

The same is true of having the chance to pat a killer whale or a dolphin in a dolphinarium. Of course I realize that only a handful of people have had the experience—far fewer even than the very small number of people who have been on a whale watch or attended a dolphin show. But for those lucky few who have patted a killer whale on the head or massaged its tongue (something killer whales seem to like), the experience is absolutely riveting.

It is the kind of experience that can change one's life. Such opportunities, fortunately, *are* available to people like presidents of countries, cabinet ministers in charge of fixing policy on the environment or the oceans, and heads of whaling delegations to the International Whaling Commission (IWC), the international body that meets annually and is responsible for the orderly regulation of whaling (see chapter 7). Imagine an IWC commissioner on the way to an IWC meeting at which a vote was planned on the question of whether the IWC would accept the responsibility for controlling small whales and dolphins as well as the great whales. Suppose this commissioner was to have the experience of patting a killer whale and quietly interacting with it for a few minutes at some dolphinarium. It would, I suspect, make it far more difficult for that person to abandon orcas to an unregulated hunt such as the one the Soviets conducted in 1980 when they killed 916 killer whales in a single antarctic season. For many people an experience like patting a whale can be life changing—the kind of experience that might have a profound impact on policy, particularly when you realize that only a handful of the members of the roughly forty delegations from IWC countries have ever even seen a live whale. I suspect only one or two have ever patted one.

Something like that happened to me once. I used to harbor a deep distrust and fear of big cats. Then one day at the Bronx Zoo I was handed the bottle-fed cub of a snow leopard. I only held it in my arms for about five minutes, during which it was softly growling from time to time while assiduously avoiding looking at my face (making direct eye contact is a threat in much of the animal kingdom). From that moment on I lost my heart to big cats.

I want to examine the question of keeping whales in captivity. It is a moral question. In order to discuss it we have to decide whether cetaceans are proper objects for moral concern. The usual way of handling this is to examine the characteristics of something that is generally agreed to be worthy of moral concern and then to look at the attributes that make it so. Human beings are a good example. One moral view considers that as a minimum requirement for moral consideration something must be alive, have interests and needs of which it is aware, and that these interests must be advanced or denied by some other being capable of acting morally. But if we apply that definition rigorously to humans we soon find that we're no longer being logically consistent because we would have to exclude from the ranks of those worthy of moral concern human fetuses, the hopelessly insane, the comatose, and the senescent.

The point at which whales are differentiated from, say, cancer cells (which don't give us moral qualms when we deprive them of their rights) is that life matters to whales—that they are aware of their lives. Cancer cells are not seen as appropriate objects of moral concern since there is no basis for concluding that they are aware of any of their interests. Which is to say that although they presumably experience the stimuli that impinge on them, they do not experience their lives as such.

To see whether these criteria apply to whales, we need to see evidence that whales have enough neural sophistication to be aware of their lives and to take an interest in them. The brain anatomy of whales is complex in its cell structure and is in this complexity equal to or even greater than our own. Some think that morphological evidence in the structure of an organ is excellent evidence of function, perhaps even the best evidence. This would mean that if we are self-aware and find a brain quite similar to ours in another species, as we do with whales, that that species may be self-aware too. But anatomy doesn't prove self-awareness. People who are "brain dead" may have the same anatomy as normal people. However, we might feel confident that whales were self-aware if we were able to see evidence of this in their behavior. Many of us have sought to find clues to the mental capacities of whales by watching their behaviors for evidence of such abilities. But what we have been able to elucidate has clearly always fallen far short of resolving this issue.

The kinds of behaviors we see among whales indicate that most species live in highly social groupings, sometimes helping each other. Mothers and calves of all whale species form long-lasting, dependent bonds typical of animals in whose lives learning is important. Whales and dolphins also demonstrate classic signs of some emotions—for example, appearing to grieve when a companion dies. Captive whales who have suffered the loss of a companion have been seen to exhibit temporary depression of breathing, loss of appetite, dilated pupils, and a withdrawal from social situations.

There are other actions that seem to require (but do not prove) intelligence in whales: whales show complex forms of play behavior both with objects and with each other. Some species sing songs, as we have seen, and humpback whales change their songs, improvising within a complex set of rules and even applying rhyme to their phrases.

It is simply bad scientific procedure—a violation of Occam's razor[10]—to argue that a better explanation for complex behaviors like these lies in mental processes that are distinct and/or unrelated to the kinds of neural activity that take place in human brains when we are performing similar behaviors. And that is the point, for in a human being whose language you could not understand and whom you suspected not to be self-aware it would be just such behaviors as these that might convince you that they *were* self-aware. I conclude therefore that since we have no compelling evidence to the contrary, in order to apply Occam's razor, it is most probable to conclude that whales probably *are* aware of their lives and know to some extent what is in their interests. If so, they are thus fit objects for moral concern.

The inclusion of an animal in the collection of beings eligible for moral concern does not constitute an argument about the value of that moral system, either as applied to animals or to people. Regardless of the moral values to which one subscribes, logic demands that the criteria for deciding what constitutes an object worthy of moral concern be applied to any species, even nonhuman ones. What this means is that in our Western moral codes the casual killing of a whale or the taking away of its rights is immoral. How, therefore, can I argue for captivity under any circumstances?

My argument is pragmatic and assumes that the practice of keeping animals like whales in captivity should be discontinued as soon as practicable. I also recognize that keeping a few animals under the best possible conditions greatly favors the many (of the same and related species). What I am getting at, of course, is that one of the most important roles of the zoological park and aquarium industry is public education regarding the uniqueness and importance of cetaceans—and by extension, the importance of preserving them.

There is another function served by captive whales that I suspect is equally important. I see it best expressed as "The Child in the Window"—a certain child gazes through an underwater window at a whale or dolphin for a long time. I realize that the vast majority of children stay only a moment before going on to see what else is to be seen, but I was a city child, and I've watched my own children at such windows when we lived in New York City.

This is not necessarily a small effect. In countries with dolphinariums the vast majority of people live in cities. In the United States, the annual attendance at zoos and aquariums is greater than the paid annual attendance at all professional football, baseball, basketball, and hockey games combined.

Suppose there were no aquariums. How would whales and dolphins reach the public consciousness? One need only look at the businesses that compete successfully with zoological parks and aquariums for the public's entertainment and educational dollar but which nevertheless do not engage in the capture and confinement of cetaceans. Examples are whale watching, human-dolphin swim programs with wild dolphins, and educational television films, theatrical releases, and picture books featuring wild cetaceans. The degree to which these competitors succeed in modifying the public's views and sympathies toward cetaceans is, unfortunately, not known. If it were, it would constitute a measure of how well the basic aims of the zoological park and aquarium industry can be achieved short of capturing and exhibiting whales.

Since capturing and exhibiting any animal robs it of one of its most basic rights, it seems wrong to do so unless some unique justification exists. If we could attain the same results achieved by zoological parks and aquariums without confining cetaceans, then confining them would be not necessary but gratuitous and morally questionable.

I believe that at the moment we cannot pragmatically attain all the desirable end results achieved by zoological parks and aquariums without them and that they therefore *do* perform an important service which is in the interests of cetaceans as a whole. In assessing whether aquariums are worth the suffering they may be causing some *individual* cetaceans, we need to keep in mind the world in which successful zoological parks and aquariums operate. Most successful ones are in the centers of thoroughly urbanized areas. For the vast majority of the human occupants of such areas the animals with which they have most contact are the ones I knew when I was growing up: dogs, cats, pigeons, canaries, rats, mice, hamsters, cockroaches, guppies, and goldfish and an occasional horse with a policeman on it. It would, of course, be "speciesist" to claim that there is anything inferior about these animals. However, we must look at how they are perceived by most humans and whether they can inspire us the way cetaceans can.

Because it seems likely to me that they cannot, there is one major way in which aquariums may be benefiting their occupants and, by extension, the rest of life on earth. It is the example I have already given: a child standing transfixed before an underwater window, watching the grace and beauty of the animals swimming on the other side of the glass. What is she learning at that moment? How long will it affect her behavior toward whales, and by extension toward nature? How much are such moments worth to her? More importantly, how much are they worth to the whales?

We do not know the answers to these questions but until we do it seems irresponsible to support the concept that captive cetaceans are of no importance in educating the city-dwelling public about the need to conserve whales and the natural world. So how do we proceed until we know better? All we can do is decide for ourselves whether we believe that cetaceans in captivity can create more sympathetic and determined supporters for cetaceans in the wild than do television programs, theatrical releases, whale watching, and swims with wild dolphins. There are no studies demonstrating conclusively that this is the case, but common sense suggests that any first-hand experience is more compelling than a recorded image. Which do we remember more—the first underwater view of a dolphin in a dolphinarium or the first underwater sequence of a dolphin on television? It is likely that most people would find that the live animal stamped their feelings with a deeper impression. But there are also people who get to see live whales at sea, and that is probably the most memorable experience. Unfortunately, however, such experiences are only available to a small proportion of the human population. The majority of the world's urbanized populations only has access to live cetaceans in their zoological parks and aquariums.

Even those who criticize the use of orcas in shows must acknowledge that we and the orcas both owe a debt of thanks to aquariums for changing the killer whale's image in the collective human consciousness and building for it a new constituency—one that has grown from a handful of people to what must now be in the hundreds of millions. The first people claiming that orcas were not a threat to humans were voices crying in the wilderness— they were considered by hardened fishermen to be a sentimental bunch of crazies until the first orca shows came along to shore up their claims. Things have changed so entirely that we now see a constituency calling for the release of all orcas from captivity. Two organizations are mounting serious efforts to introduce, in cooperation with aquariums, the concept of borrowing marine mammals from the wild, limiting the time they are held in captivity. The gist of this idea is that after they have served for a year or two as ambassadors to our species, orcas and other marine mammals would be returned to their families in the sea to live out the rest of their lives in peace.

It shouldn't take aquariums long to catch on to the long-term benefits that might be gained by creating special celebrations on the anniversaries of the day some orca was returned to its family, to say nothing of the value of the free publicity from news media and TV documentaries, as well as from periodic news updates on how the orca was doing in the wild based on reports of people who had seen it. If the orca carried a satellite tag people who had known it when it was in the zoo could keep track of its whereabouts on a daily basis. The information might even get put onto the Information Highway for access by home computers and schools—the logo of the aquarium accompanying every report from the field.

There are now several species that are extinct in the wild and exist only in zoos—the wisent (the European bison), Père David's deer, and Przewalski's horse are examples. If we were able to ask the survivors of those species which they would prefer—life as they know it in captivity or a return to the wilds and certain extinction—there is little doubt that they would prefer their lives in captivity. With humans it is the same: inhabitants of death row typically exhaust every resource at their command to avoid losing their lives even when their only hope is to have their death sentences commuted to life imprisonment, a change which includes the absolute certainty that they will never again taste freedom. In the case of the most endangered cetaceans— the freshwater dolphins of China's Yangtze River—the only realistic hope they now appear to have for survival is to be taken into captivity. But this is itself a slim hope, given how little is known about how to care for their kind. The entire basis of any chance they might have of surviving captivity is the experience we have garnered to date from caring for their more-abundant relatives, principally the bottle-nosed dolphins and orcas. If more expertise and more funding and talent had been expended in keeping even more cetaceans in captivity, the Yangtze River dolphins might now have a better chance. As things stand I would guess that their hopes for survival are practically nil.

It would be nice to believe that the case of the Yangtze River dolphins is a special one, but judging from the rate at which humans are multiplying I expect that the earth will lose several more cetacean species from the wild— first the freshwater dolphins, then a few coastal species with very limited ranges like the tiny porpoise called the Vaquita in the Sea of Cortéz—before humanity gets its act together. It costs millions to keep cetaceans in captivity, but they are one of the few animals that can generate the capital to do so. Thus for them an argument of survival through captivity may be valid (much as it was the attraction that a few people felt for Père David's deer which paid the costs of keeping the species alive on estates and in zoos when their natural habitat became lethal to them). If we insist on ending captivity for all cetaceans now, we will in effect be making the decision to send those whose only hope is captivity to certain extinction and will bring to an end the possibility of developing further expertise for pulling critically endangered species through.

There is a strong counterargument that states that a whale or dolphin in captivity is not itself—not a wild, free thing—but our prisoner and therefore of no benefit to itself or to us. Let us assume that porpoises do suffer in captivity, but that they do not suffer as much as the most pessimistic among us might assume. Let us assume instead that they suffer far worse than such people claim, in fact worse than we can imagine—worse than the most pessimistic of us would ever dream they suffered. And then, having defined that amount of suffering, let us assume that they actually suffer ten times worse than that. Let us add to that assumption a second assumption: that as the last Yangtze River dolphins are taken into captivity, the wisest experts that can be assembled are asked to guess at the time it will take for a breeding program to produce enough animals to start returning them to the wild. For the sake of argument let us say that the figure they come up with is ten years. Let us further assume that these same experts also believe that by then there will be some river ready to receive those animals on whose banks lives an educated human population who will respect their presence in the waters and protect them when they are returned.

But let us also assume that in spite of their best estimations, these pundits are wrong—dead wrong—and that everything takes far longer than anyone had thought, and that the first Yangtze River dolphins are not returned to the wild for a hundred years (make it a thousand years if you like). All during this hundred years the line of Yangtze River dolphins will have been confined in captivity, suffering the mental tortures of the damned in spite of the best efforts of their captors to make them comfortable. But now let us imagine that we have come to the last day of those hundred years (or thousand years) and we are standing next to a stretcher on which is lying the first Yangtze River dolphin to be returned to the wilds. And because so much time has gone by, our sophistication has grown to the point where somehow we can now interview this animal, saying to it, "Given how horribly you tell us that you and your ancestors and your family have suffered in this facility during every generation since your great-great-great-great-great-grandparents were first put in here, and given that you are going to be released today, do you think that all that collective suffering has been worth it?" I suspect that the dolphin's answer would translate into something like, "Who knows? Who cares? All I can tell you is that I'm out of here."

The point is that unless and until someone is able to reconstitute extinct species from examples of their stored DNA, anything, no matter how intolerable you and I imagine it to be, is better than death or extinction—ask any prisoner on death row. However awful any alternative may be, extinction is worse. It is intolerable. All of which tells me that in spite of how much we may despise the idea of captivity for a species that is otherwise sure to become extinct, captivity beats death and extinction. Any day. And if we don't support trained people and facilities that are steadily evolving toward doing a better job, we are essentially abandoning these species in order to assuage our feelings of guilt about how we should otherwise be dealing with the consequences of problems *we* have created. It's like taking a bath in sentiment in order to cleanse our sensibilities. As I see it, it is not moral to give up on trying to save a species just because in doing so it makes us feel better about ourselves.

For someone of my own personal views it is hard to put forward this kind of argument, since my inclination is to release all animals that are held in cages and aquariums. I believe, however, that that is an irresponsible stand—a kind of easy way out, a chance to relieve one's sense of guilt without taking responsibility for the brutal consequences of one's actions. It is often of great value to base a course of action on sentiment but I feel that in this case it would ultimately prove deadly for several whale species.

However, I am a strong advocate for improvement in stress reduction for marine mammals held in aquariums. The holding and transport conditions for dolphins, porpoises, and whales is in many cases outrageous. We have been told that because it benefits the transporters to get their new captives to market in vigorous and healthy condition, they give them the very best care. But such is not the case, since it also benefits the owners to get them to market as cheaply as possible. In the beginning, when no one was looking, "cheap" was achieved by capturing more animals than were needed and tossing out the carcasses as they appeared en route to the dolphinariums. This attitude, the tolerance of appalling conditions of transport and temporary holding tanks, infuriated many people when it was brought to their attention. Also, "temporary" has sometimes stretched into many months (even years in extreme cases) while the owners try to get a higher price for their catch, during which time the captives are held in tiny tanks, sometimes with filthy water and inadequate care.

The money that zoological parks and aquariums now earn from exhibiting marine mammals is enough to erase all excuses for keeping animals in the conditions of the past during capture and transport. The public will soon demand—is already doing so in some cases—that those who profit from the marketing of dolphins and orcas be required to transport and house them with greater care. Until laws are in place worldwide to ensure this we will probably see more and more public opposition not just to the further capture of dolphins and whales for display but to keeping them in captivity in the first place. I feel that such opposition will increase the industry's appreciation of the value of taking better care of those animals (it has already done so in some cases). Meanwhile, it would behoove the aquarium industry to take the lead in pushing vigorously for the highest possible standards—*worldwide*—of capture, holding, and transport. Offstage the wrath of many people is building. If the industry continues to do little or nothing, those who are angry will take the initiative and will end up controlling the situation. The industry should also take the lead in establishing the principle of returning their captives to the wild after short periods.

Another area that I feel is in need of change is the reduction of echoes and underwater noises in aquariums and the boring nature of tanks used to hold cetaceans.

Although animal display facilities have, in general, shown an increasing sensitivity to the needs of terrestrial animals (in some cases the naturalness of new exhibits has apparently induced several species that were notorious in the past for not breeding in captivity to do so), they are still far behind when it comes to creating nonstressful habitats *below water*, where cetaceans spend most of their lives. Next time you turn off some noise that is annoying you and enjoy the peace that then descends, realize that this is the kind of relief a captive whale can never achieve, ever. With few exceptions, even the most modern dolphinaria, with well-designed displays above water, have brutal acoustic properties below and very little that is of interest to the cetaceans that live out the sentence of their lives there.

It has been suggested that the strong echoes from the cement walls of tanks may be a factor in the observed reduction of sound output by cetaceans living in captivity. The roar of the filters is heard underwater in most places twenty-four hours a day, 365 days a year by the inhabitants of even the fanciest new tanks. It seems probable that this is a serious potential stress-inducing feature for captive whales (loud, continuous sounds are known to produce stress in humans). It also seems self-evident that marine mammals should be able to find quiet for some part of their day—and not just through the turning off of water quality control facilities. Whales and dolphins are, of course, exposed to noise during storms in the oceans for days at a time, but our studies of right whales show that they sleep heavily in the calms that follow storms. For all whales there are many days of quiet, and for the populations of orcas that live in fjords, there are places they can go to escape noise.

Although some form of anechoic surfacing for these tanks (to stop the ricocheting about of sounds) might cost a lot to install, it might also reduce stress enough to have a major impact on the welfare of dolphins and whales in captivity—thus saving their owners money in the long run. One might start by treating just two adjacent walls of a rectangular tank. It is, of course, true that when close to a rocky shore whales and dolphins must experience loud echoes, but they do not normally pass very much time in such areas and some sound deadening would help their tanks imitate the natural surroundings in which the vast majority of their lives are lived (even right whales, which spend long periods very close to shore, do so along gradually shelving pebble or sand beaches that are notorious for not returning strong echoes).

Anechoic surfaces were developed for marine mammal tanks as long ago as the late sixties. Though they work well, they are very expensive to build and the first ones had a few inherent flaws such as the difficulty in cleaning dead fish and feces from the many wedges of material out of which they were constructed. These problems are sometimes emphasized by the aquarium industry in defending the kinds of deafening surroundings routinely installed in marine mammal tanks, but there are other more modern tricks involving new surfacing materials that might prove more attractive economically but which have never, to my knowledge, been tried in any serious way. Experimentation along these lines has only just started—more effort is needed.

As those who make their living from the sea well know, the ocean is not an empty environment but one filled with great variety. Even though there is no direct experimental evidence to demonstrate that variety and newness are qualities of importance to captive cetaceans, given what we do know about animals with large brains it is not reasonable to assume that such qualities are unimportant to them.

There may be several quite simple things that could be done to make the environments of captive dolphins more novel. For example, killer whales often go to special "rubbing rocks" against which they rub their bodies. Rubbing rocks could be provided in future for captive killer whales. It might also be interesting to provide an area of kelp in large tanks in which orcas are kept. If they tore it up, it could easily be replaced. Perhaps after a longer time the dislodging of kelp would become rarer and other uses of it would be available to the orcas.

I see no reason why toys might not also be introduced to help cetaceans pass their time more comfortably. It is well-known that captive cetaceans play in underwater jets of water or air. It might prove rewarding for them if they had access to some means of controlling such a jet—by pushing a lever to turn it on and off, for instance. A set of large revolving brushes such as those used in drive-through car washes might also prove diverting to captive cetaceans, allowing them to swim through them so that the immense, soft brushes stroked their flanks. A small cluster of anchored, air-filled plastic pipes in some corner of their tanks through which they could push their way, allowing the pipes to stroke and bump along their flanks, might also be popular with them.

Perhaps aquariums could work toward the principle of having an entire shed full of different and ingenious floating objects to be selected in random sequence each day by their keepers for dolphins and whales to play with (some of these objects might move slightly, others might make sounds). All of this would cost relatively little and might make a significant difference to the lives of the inhabitants of otherwise barren tanks.

One of the things that most offends people about dolphinariums is the nature of the tricks taught to dolphins in their shows. Deciding what is offensive and what is not is, of course, a bit like deciding what is pornography and what is art. However, at both ends of the spectrum are acts about which there should be near-enough universal agreement for us to be able safely to include them on a list of deeply offensive tricks. Brushing the teeth of a killer whale with an immense toothbrush or having a dolphin wear a straw hat spring to mind. At the other end of the spectrum are tricks that seem more acceptable—for example, high, arching leaps that demonstrate the power and grace of the animals.

It has occurred to me that one could turn the tables and put the degrading aspects of tricks onto the visitors rather than onto the whales. This might be done by letting the dolphins train the tourists. I'd like to see an aquarium in which a dolphin had access to a keyboard with keys that produced whole sentences which were then made visible to visitors at the aquarium. At a moment of its own choosing (and with a human subject of its own selection), the dolphin could hit a key that would display a message on a video screen outside its tank where tourists were watching through an underwater window. The sign might say, *Come over here*.

The tourist approaches. The dolphin hits another key and the sign says, *Point at me*. The tourist points at the dolphin. The next sign says, *Wave your right hand*. The tourist waves. The next sign: *Stretch your arms over your head*. The tourist does so. Next sign: *Jump up in the air*.

Next sign: *No, jump higher*.

Next sign: *No, no, no, really high. Jump high enough to touch that ball you see over your head*.

A ball has been lowered within reach of the tourist's highest jumps as determined from seeing how high they were able to jump on their second jump. The tourist jumps really high and touches the ball. The dolphin slaps the water to congratulate the tourist. The show goes on like this with the dolphin in full control and the tourist being asked to do more and more ridiculous and demeaning things. For their mistakes tourists get lots of rude buzzers and as a reward a chocolate dispensed by the dolphin's tapping a lever to release it.

If the tourist completes the instructions from the dolphin, the dolphin gets a fish and the tourist a diploma for their wall saying they have managed to get through one set of instructions from their dolphin trainer, that they show promise and may just turn out to be as bright as a dolphin—but that only time will tell when they return in future for further testing.

The question of who is in charge will be lost on no one, and the more alert visitors will realize that the dolphin only goes through this routine when *it* wants to. Imagine the impact of being selected as a test subject by the dolphin. While people are waiting around for the dolphin to make up its mind to perform, they are also standing, for longer periods than usual, at the underwater viewing windows—and their children are getting a longer chance to become part of that image of the child in the window transfixed.

If the questions that the dolphin could ask were questions it had answered itself in earlier tests, the penny might someday drop and the dolphin realize that by manipulating keys it could learn about people (in order to help the dolphin make this connection, the keys might bear icons—like international signs—representative of the information that the answers divulge and similar to the icons that were on the keys when the dolphin was answering the same questions itself). By putting the dolphin in control of all interviews, it is hard to see just where the limits would lie to the kinds of communication that might ultimately be achieved between dolphins and people. Also, once the dolphin had made the connection, there is no reason it should ask the same questions in the same order each time. One might also use food rewards to encourage the dolphin to select new questions from a large collection, thus providing interesting insights into what subjects interest dolphins most.

I have been speculating about what could be done to improve aquariums without elevating them above their present lowest common denominator of entertainment value. Keeping whales in captivity offers several possibilities for further educating the public about cetaceans. I am referring to the kinds of training experiments that test the language ability of cetaceans. My speculations on the experiments one might perform are offered with the full understanding that the truth, whenever and however it eventuates, will be far more interesting than what I'm proposing.

With whales and primates we are dealing with animals possessing large brains capable of at least some degree of language. Whether their language capability is equivalent to ours has been the subject of some of the most bitter (and at times most mean-spirited) controversy I have seen in science. At the present state of play it appears that human language ability is indeed unique. Even so, a considerable ability with simple sentences has been demonstrated in both primates and dolphins, and even if, as now seems to be the case, these abilities fall short of the human capacity for language, there is much one might do with what language ability these animals do possess without worrying about what its limits may or may not be, or even whether their language ability is comparable to ours.

Let us suppose, for example, that you taught a dolphin a series of words for common emotions like anger, fear, affection, hatred, jealousy, etc. (I am not talking about the dolphin speaking these words, but just depressing keys or manipulating symbols to indicate them.) Once the dolphin can label the proper emotions in the proper context, you put her in with a group of other dolphins of her own species and watch them interact. When you see something whose motivation you don't understand, you ask your dolphin, "Why did you do that?"

And she replies, "Fear," or "Jealousy," etc. A protocol like this could give interesting insights into dolphin behavior. If this system worked on your dolphin, you could go on to ask her while she was observing other dolphins (or movies of other dolphins)—"Why is Santini doing that?" etc.—and expect an answer such as "Fear," or "Jealousy," etc.

If this worked, you might try asking dolphins direct questions. For example: "Are you afraid of boats? Are all dolphins bothered by boats? How many kinds of sharks are there? Are you afraid of sharks? Which of the following sharks scares you most? Is your mother afraid of sharks? Is your brother? Who is most afraid of sharks, you or your brother?" You next interview the subject's brother and ask him the same final question. In fact, to gain insight into how dolphins perceive each other, you could ask the same questions of all the individuals you referred to in the previous questions and get their answers.

Or you might ask your dolphin, "Are you afraid of the dark? Do you like people? Next you could name several people the dolphin knows and ask, "Which of these people do you like most?" Or you could put it in the context of the dolphin's own family. For example: "Who does your mother like most—you? Your brother? Your sister? Your father?" Or "Another male?" Depending on the answer, it might be interesting to ask the other male the same question; and when you have the answer to tell your dolphin's mother what the other male said about her. Over the years, gossips have demonstrated that surprising responses often come from imparting socially important information. Is it entirely unreasonable to suppose that the same may be true with dolphins?

By this means you might find out if dolphins lie to each other regularly the way humans do (I would be surprised if they did not). Or indeed whether their whole social systems are maintained by a tissue of lies, the way most of our social systems are. From which you might be able to conclude that lying may not be part only of the human condition but also of the mammalian condition, or perhaps even of the vertebrate condition, or even of the animalian condition.

The line of reasoning I have been presenting is not altogether fantasy. It should be possible to ask a dolphin questions of the sort referred to above. The majority of the questions I have suggested can be framed as a preference between two or more alternatives, something to which dolphins readily respond. I have in this way chosen questions that should be easy to set up— there are simple ways to get reasonably definitive answers to all of them. Such questions have been asked of and answered by rats and pigeons where preferences for food rather than for other rats or pigeons were the topic. These animals do very well with them. Animals don't need brains that weigh pounds to take part in this rudimentary kind of communication.

There is another experiment that could be performed with whales in captivity that they might find entertaining and that might give us great insights into their minds. It should to some extent be possible to "psychoanalyze" a whale.

There was for many years a male killer whale in the Vancouver Aquarium named Hyak who showed a fascinating response to pictures of dolphins and other killer whales. Biologist John Ford has a window in his office that gives him an underwater view into what was Hyak's tank. Whenever John held up a picture of a killer whale or a dolphin, Hyak would come over and investigate it, looking long and hard at it, first with one eye, then with the other. Seeing that he was looking intently at something, the much smaller female orca, Bjossa, who shared Hyak's tank (and who dominated him entirely), would come over, push him aside and have a look. But after a few moments she would leave, showing no further interest. Hyak would then return and keep looking.

One afternoon, biologist David Bain and I tried holding up pictures of killer whales and dolphins to two other orcas in an aquarium at which David is studying orcas. But other than coming over and looking for a couple of seconds the whales displayed no obvious interest or response. It seemed to me that these killer whales looked for as long at pages without pictures as at pages with them. With Hyak, however, this was clearly not the case; he focused with great interest on the photographs that were shown to him.

Hyak has since died, but if some other whale like him ever appears it might prove interesting to set up a device that would give such an animal access to a TV screen showing short sequences of whales and dolphins, the video recorder being triggered to play in response to the whale pressing a lever. Eventually the task would be modified so that in order to make the film visible, the whale would have to push the lever continuously. It might then prove possible to see what kinds of movies (and what kinds of subjects) the whale worked hardest to see and at what moments in the action it stopped pushing the lever even when the action continued. In this way we might learn a great deal about what interests orcas. (Orcas of the opposite sex? Fish? Orcas of the same pod? Of different pods? Orcas giving birth? Orcas mating? Orcas seen from above water in a view nominally afforded only during a spy-hop or a breach?) Do analysts know their patients any better than you might know a dolphin by this means? (Do analysts know their patients as well?)

There is another experiment I'd love to see someone try that concerns dolphins and art. At the Dolphin Research Center there are two dolphins who have learned to take a paintbrush in their teeth and, while sculling madly with their tails so as to hold their bodies vertically out of the water, to paint on a canvas held by an attendant. Having made a few strokes, the dolphin subsides in the water, returns the brush to the attendant, and is given a different brush with a different color on it and allowed to paint more. Such paintings now sell for several hundred dollars apiece—a bit of capitalism of which I heartily approve. I suspect a lot of people would find these paintings to be no better and no worse than many paintings which sell for much more. It seems to me that there is no telling how well a dolphin might paint if it had a few lessons and if it was not required to do its paintings in this unnatural position (akin to how well you might paint if you were holding a brush in your teeth and balancing on a unicycle). Why not teach the dolphin to use an underwater touch pad attached to a computer that would allow it to select colors and apply them as it liked to a composition of its own choice? If it were given a few lessons in drawing a fish in the simplest kinds of representation, it might then be encouraged to make paintings. Having completed a painting to its satisfaction, it could hit a button that would hang the painting on the walls of its tank (i.e., transfer it to a monitor mounted on the wall) where that painting might stay until the dolphin chose to replace it. How about one-dolphin shows? And galleries of dolphin art? Coffee table books of dolphin paintings? How might that scramble our concept of how unique we are? And what might it do for our appreciation of the wild world? Given that language seems not to be forthcoming from dolphins, is there any other ability that could equal the effect they might have on our thinking comparable to teaching them art? It appeals to me greatly because I have devoted much of my life to trying to blur the distinctions between human beings and the rest of life on earth.

CHAPTER 7

Whaling and Other Delights

The killing of whales by humans dates back to the prehistory of many of the cultures in which it originated. The arctic Inuit peoples are known to have hunted whales for three to four thousand years, possibly even up to eight thousand years. The Japanese have been hunting right whales since time immemorial—though the earliest records date from 1606. The Norwegians have eaten whale meat for four thousand years though whether hunted or scavenged is not known. The first Europeans definitely known to have hunted whales were the early Basques, who hunted right whales along the coast of the Bay of Biscay starting in the tenth and eleventh centuries.

The whaling technique with which most people are familiar is an old one—still in use in some places (the Azores and the Caribbean island of Bequia are examples). It involves a small boat that is sailed and rowed stealthily to within a few feet of a whale, at which point a harpooner stands up in the bow and heaves a harpoon into the back of the whale. The whale, presumably maddened with pain, races through the water or dives deeply while rope by the tubful smokes out through the chocks in the bow of the boat. On its way to the bow the rope passes from the center of the boat to a post in the stern around which a turn or two is taken as a means of adjusting tension on the rope. During the mad ride (North American whalers called it a "Nantucket sleigh ride") the helmsman and the harpooner change places by walking the full length of the wildly careening boat so that when the whale has exhausted itself, the helmsman can be the one to kill it.

Many people think that the harpoon kills the whale, but in fact its only purpose is to attach the boat to it, so that the whale eventually becomes so exhausted by towing against the drag of the boat that the crew can come alongside it without its making an attempt to flee. (Sometimes a drogue is tied to a harpoon and tossed overboard for the whale to drag. Early drogues were constructed of inflated seal skins or barrels.) Only when the whale is exhausted does the killing begin.

The actual killing is done with a long lance or spear that is thrust repeatedly and for many feet of its length into the whale's body in an effort to pierce the lungs or the heart—both areas that bleed so profusely the whale finally expires from loss of blood. However, when the whale feels itself mortally wounded by the spear, it somehow finds a further reserve of strength, rouses itself for a final time, and goes into a "death flurry" (often violent). It was at such moments that the whales' tormentors sometimes died, though mostly not from being bitten by the whale (though sperm whales occasionally did so) or struck by the whale's tail (all species sometimes did this) but by falling out of the boat and drowning when the whale upset it (whalers traditionally never bothered to learn to swim). However, the deaths of such men were blamed on the whale anyway and were used to fuel the myth of whales as savage and dangerous monsters.

When I first heard about all this, it did not strike me that jostling men out of a boat when you are semiconscious and in a death flurry (owing to those same men piercing your lungs with a ten-foot spear) constituted very good evidence that the animal involved was of a naturally savage nature. I felt that if someone could somehow resist the temptation to harpoon and lance whales, it might turn out that they were relatively peaceful animals. It was for this reason that I first drew alongside whales in a small boat and later swam with them, even though in those days the possible consequences of such an activity were unknown and the first few times I did it my heart was in my mouth.

I want to return to that strange custom in which the harpooner and the helmsman change ends of the boat in the midst of the Nantucket sleigh ride. They make this change even though it leaves the boat unsteered for a moment, thus casting the entire operation into the direst jeopardy. Why does the helmsman and not the harpooner do the killing? Is it because the whalers considered the helmsman to be the most skilled person in the boat and thus the one best fit for such a difficult job? Hardly likely. The old whalers made it crystal clear that a skilled harpooner was the most valued man in the boat.

The key to answering this question lies in the fact that the helmsman outranks the harpooner (he's one of the mates on the mother ship). The fact that the helmsman took on the job of killing the whale shows that it must have been considered to be a job with "image." If it was undesirable the helmsman would have had the harpooner do it, just as he had the harpooner do all the rowing during the approach to the whale while he sat on his duff and steered. This swapping of ends in the boat in midcareer indicates clearly that to the whalers killing a whale must have carried a great deal of kudos, I suppose because of the chance it offered to look like a hero (did I hear someone say machismo?) Whaling just brings out a man's best qualities.

One outcome of Captain Cook's voyages of exploration was his report of the numbers of whales he had encountered in the Antarctic Ocean. He had been in some places where he was unable to look toward the horizon without seeing dozens of spouts at once. The whales he saw were inaccessible to the European whalers of his day—they swam too fast, sank when they were killed, and had baleen that was coarse and therefore relatively worthless. Of the great whales that have been the subjects of a major hunt, the right, bowhead, gray, and sperm whales normally float when dead, as do some humpback whales. However, blue, fin, sei, Bryde's, and minke whales sink when dead.

While these sinking whales were a problem to European whalers, at least two tribes of Native Americans living in the Aleutian Islands overcame this. They used poisoned projectiles to kill whales. Once they had hit a whale, they returned to land knowing that it would eventually die and sink, but that a day or two later the corpse would float to the surface, buoyed by the gasses of decomposition. They either retrieved it when it floated ashore or looked out from high cliffs, and when they spotted the corpse (such corpses float very high in the water and are visible a long way off), paddled out and retrieved it. Some of the meat would have spoiled, but there must often have been many tons of it that were still edible.

It was nearly a hundred years after Captain Cook's discovery in 1773 of the antarctic whale herds that a series of inventions were made enabling whalers to catch and kill the species that Cook had found so abundant on the antarctic feeding grounds.

It was the Norwegian Svend Foyn who made in 1864 "a most wonderful invention"—a cannon mounted on the bow of a high-speed, steam-powered "catcher boat" that could fire a harpoon into a whale. But of equal importance was the invention of a long tube with a sharpened tip that could be plunged into the body cavity of the dead whale so that compressed air could be forced into the corpse, preventing its sinking and making those species that sank suddenly available to the whaling industry.

Another important step was the invention of the exploding harpoon— basically a grenade mounted on the tip of a harpoon that exploded a few seconds after impact to blow steel shrapnel through the whale's body, hopefully killing it swiftly. The advantage of exploding harpoons was that the harpoon not only attached the whale to the boat but also killed it. Of course it didn't always work so smoothly. The very long harpoon lines tell you that. The only reason long lines were necessary was that the harpoon might fail to kill the whale and the whale continue to put up a great fight, thus requiring the whalers to "play" it with their winches and with the whole weight and drag of the ship, the way an angler plays a fish by using a reel and moving along a stream. Just how badly things could go awry is indicated by records such as the one describing how it took four hours and nine harpoons to kill a whale. (Incidentally, each of those harpoons would have weighed about two hundred pounds.)

When whaling first began, whales were towed to shore for butchering (called "flensing"). One ancient technique was to make a single spiral cut around the body of the whale. A hook tied to a strong rope was attached to one end of the helical strip of blubber. At high tide the rope was pulled to maximum tension and tied to a rock or a tree on land. As the body floated out on the falling tide the corpse spun slowly and the blubber was stripped off in a single piece—the whale corpse thus skinning itself. But this technique required calm weather, a high tidal amplitude, and sometimes a long wait for a tide when it was high at some inconvenient time. Skinning off the blubber was later accomplished by a winch. At first the winch was a hand-powered windlass; later it was steam powered. A winch is a straightforward and inelegant device. I have watched a winch tear the blubber off a whale's body by brute force, producing as it did so a peculiar, muffled, ripping sound, strangely muted and leaden, as the thousands of pounds of tensile strength generated by the quiet steam-driven winch stretched and then overcame the millions of strands of connective tissue anchoring the blubber to the underlying muscle of the whale. This sound was somehow deeply evocative of the profound impact which the industrial revolution has had on the wild world.

The rest of the butchering is done with the same hockey-stick-shaped "flensing knives" with which the first cuts were made. In modern whaling, steam-powered reciprocating saws and giant band saws are also used. At shore stations small tractors handle the big pieces of meat, but on boats, where the decks are heaving, the same work has to be done by men using flensing hooks—short steel rods bent into a handle at one end with a sharpened hook at the other. The meat is put into pans for flash-freezing and the bones and fat dragged to the immense cookers, whose open tops are natural hazards on the decks. (More than one man has been killed by losing his footing on the heaving deck and slipping into the cooker.) In the cooker the inedible parts of the whale are boiled down for their oil. When all the oil has been "tried out" (extracted) and removed, bonemeal left in the cookers is put into drying ovens. When dry, it is bagged as fertilizer. Everything in the whale is used. As writer Peter Matthieson put it, "Nothing is wasted but the whale itself."

At first whales were towed into shore stations in harbors of subantarctic islands in the Scotia Arc—harbors like Grytviken on South Georgia—where they were cut up and processed. Later, factory ships were developed for processing. These ships were moored in the harbors of the Scotia Arc islands for the season while the catcher boats brought carcasses to them for processing. The carcasses were dragged up a slipway built into the stern of the vessel and processed on deck. These first factory ships remained in the island harbors for the entire whaling season. As their catcher boats killed off all the whales within towing distance, the factory ships could no longer take refuge in these harbors and had to operate in the open Antarctic Ocean through the whaling season. When major storms struck, they sought protection by moving into the lee of large ice flows. Thus truly pelagic modern whaling in the Antarctic was born.

Modern factory ships do not kill whales, as many people think. The pursuit and capture of whales is done by up to twenty-five high-speed catcher boats that accompany each factory ship and that deliver whale carcasses to it for butchering and freezing. (Catcher boats are basically speedboats weighing between 100 and 200 tons that run down whales and kill them with exploding harpoons fired from a cannon in the bow—as noted above, a harpoon that really does kill whales.) The frozen meat is then returned to market aboard freezer ships—a more recent innovation. Freezing of meat only started after blue and humpback whales had been granted protection by the member nations of the International Whaling Commission. Prior to that, the meat was rendered for its fat and all the protein turned into fertilizer.

Because they were systematically destroying the whale herds, whalers began to have to hunt over greater and greater distances. A series of innovations in locating whales was necessary to keep them in business. One was the introduction of helicopters and other spotting aircraft to guide the catcher boats to the whales. Another was the use of radio beacons on the "waif poles" with which floating whale carcasses are marked for pickup, the catcher boats in the meantime having gone on to run down and kill other whales. The radio beacon made it possible for the catcher boat to retrieve dead whales even in fog, thus enabling whalers to extend their catching into much worse conditions and to continue to hunt whales in bad weather.

Another innovation by the whalers was the use of sonar to track whales they were pursuing underwater. But there was a problem; as the boat gained on the whale, the whale started exhaling while still submerged. This produced a cloud of bubbles in the water that reflected sound better than the whale did and made a false target (akin to what a pilot does when releasing metal chaff to create a false radar echo). I suspect that this behavior by whales was simply fortuitous since exhaling while still submerged is simply a means by which a whale can reduce the time it has to remain at the surface, where surface drag will slow it down.

Whalers quickly discovered that a frequency of three thousand hertz seemed to panic the whales, causing them to surface much more often for air. This was a "better" use for sonar because it afforded the whalers more chances to shoot the whales. So they equipped their catcher boats with sonar at that frequency. Of course the sonar also allows the whalers to follow the whale underwater, but that is its secondary use. Its primary use is for scaring whales so that they start "panting" at the surface.

I have been describing some of the most common whaling techniques, but there have been several others over the years. When small whales are the quarry, exploding harpoons are avoided because they spoil too much of the meat—an important consideration once freezer ships began hauling whale meat back to the major market in Japan, where the meat has become much more valuable than either the oil or the baleen. Human ingenuity being what it is, a variety of innovative techniques to kill whales have appeared. There was the amazingly brutal "cold harpoon"—basically a length of steel pipe with no rope on it and with an ordinary end cap screwed onto it that the whalers fired at the whale from the harpoon cannon. If you happened to hit the whale in the right place, these "cold harpoons" killed it by the force of their impact. Of course, with the whale moving and the boat heaving around and the fact that pieces of steel pipe with end caps don't fly very straight, it was hard to hit the right place on the whale. And given that the period of reloading was relatively long and the time necessary to aim and fire long as well, and that sometimes many pieces of pipe were necessary to kill a whale, this was an unspeakably barbaric technique.

Cold harpoons were much used in Norway, particularly when hunting minke whales, since the normal exploding harpoons often blew these small whales to pieces, and anyway exploding harpoons were much more expensive than lengths of steel pipe with end caps screwed onto them.

In response to complaints from more humane people than the Norwegian whalers—in particular pressure from the Humane Killing Subcommittee of the International Whaling Commission—Norway finally began work on—and after several years produced—a smaller exploding harpoon with which to replace the cold harpoon. But those poor Norwegian engineers just had the very old devil of a time trying to perfect such a challenging invention as a smaller grenade-tipped harpoon—they still haven't quite got it right. As the years dragged by, and all of us who attended the International Whaling Commission's meetings read Norway's reports about their slow as cold-molasses progress in perfecting the small exploding harpoon, we knew that the Norwegian whalers were still out there blazing away with the cold harpoon with which they were so reluctant to part—a situation that continued until the use of the cold harpoon was finally outlawed.

The Norwegians also used another technique: a bullet from an elephant gun fired through the brain of a harpooned minke whale to dispatch it. Well, that was where they were aiming anyway. I suppose that a direct hit in a minke whale's brain would kill it relatively quickly, but compared to the entire whale, the brain is a very small target indeed and under the circumstances I have mentioned of trying to hit a moving target from the heaving deck of a small ship in an open seaway, I suspect that many shots were either total misses or might better have been described as remote ablation experiments.

Regardless of your viewpoint about the acceptability of whaling, small arms are not a good way to kill a whale. It usually requires a great many hits before the whale finally dies—of something, who knows what—shock, I suppose. Whales have often been found with several slugs in them and with the bullet holes healed over—the whale having died from another cause years later. The effort to kill a whale with small arms is not likely to succeed. However, those inclined to such practices, including fishermen who don't like whales, don't seem to realize this, and so even today one keeps hearing stories about fishermen blasting away at whales. For example, while studying humpback whales from a sailboat off Greenland in the eighties, whale biologist Hal Whitehead reported seeing a flotilla of Greenlanders, mostly in skiffs powered by outboard motors, roaring along in a kind of festival atmosphere, pursuing a humpback whale and firing repeatedly at it (there were clearly many hits)—the sounds of the shooting still carrying back over the water long after the entire circus had swirled past Hal's boat and was lost to sight in the distance.

Back when blue and fin whales were still fairly plentiful in the Antarctic, there was an effort to invent a means of electrocuting whales in order to speed their death after harpooning. A British engineer got the job of developing the electric harpoon. He wrote to me describing the technique, saying that once the electric harpoon was embedded in the whale, a massive current was turned on. He had discovered that blubber is too good an electrical insulator to be involved very much in the current path, and that the circuit was completed through the mucosal lining (of the mouth, anus, reproductive orifice, nostrils, and eyes as well, of course, as the harpoon wound itself). To get an idea of what kind of death this is, imagine killing a death-row inmate by applying electrodes to the mouth, anus, genitals, eyes, and nostrils, as well as to the back wound you have just made.

The main problem the electric harpoon had to overcome was the tendency of the wires to break when the forerunner—the first few yards of rope attached to the harpoon—became stretched as the rope accelerated from a standing start to the harpoon's muzzle velocity almost instantaneously. The engineer solved the problem by twining the wires into the lay of the rope in such a way that there was room for the stretch to occur without breaking them—he described it as a kind of "Chinese finger trap weave."

Later in his life, this man retired to the island of Montserrat in the Caribbean, where he worked as an X-ray technician in a local hospital. In 1970 I went to visit him there and to interview him about the electric harpoon. When I asked him whether it had proved successful, he told me that the Norwegian who had invented the exploding harpoon tip received a commission of several shillings for every tip sold. The man realized he would lose his commission if the electric harpoon proved successful and so he or someone else set out to scupper the tests.

My friend guessed it was the Norwegian who had the connections and clout to make sure that the boat assigned by the Norwegian whaling fleet to test the electric harpoon was the one that held the previous season's worst record for killing whales by conventional means. Predictably, the results of the test were a failure since the test boat took fewer whales with the electric harpoon than any other Norwegian boat equipped with exploding harpoons (just as it had taken fewer whales the previous season when equipped with those same conventional harpoons). As a result of this "poor performance," the electric harpoon was judged to be a failure and was abandoned.

But not all the methods of killing whales are quite so high-tech. For several hundred years the Japanese caught right whales by maneuvering them into nets and then driving wooden plugs into their nostrils to suffocate them. This form of whaling required many people, and there was competition among the young men to be the first to drive plugs into a whale's nostrils (a perhaps unequaled opportunity for displays of machismo—something that seems to be a recurrent theme in whaling).

There are also the present-day Faeroese who when they have driven a herd of pilot whales into a shallow bay use what amount to kitchen knives to kill them. This particular method of killing is assisted by the "gaff," a sharpened hook made from a piece of heavy steel about eighteen inches long and attached to a small rope. The Faeroese drive the gaff into the whale's body (the preferred target is the melon, i.e., the whale's forehead—one of the areas most richly endowed with sensory nerve endings). With a gaff stuck in its head, a whale can easily be drawn within reach. Sometimes it takes several blows to get a gaff positioned just right. With the whale in reach, the whaler starts sawing away at its neck with his knife, slicing back and forth like someone cutting through a loaf of bread, until eventually the cut he is making has descended through enough inches of muscle to reach close to the whale's backbone, or until he has killed it (or believes he has killed it). What the whaler is trying to do is to slip his knife in between the foramen magnum of the skull and the first cervical vertebra (the atlas) so as to cut the spinal cord along with some major arteries that run inside the spinal column beneath the protection of the neural arches of each vertebra (in humans these same arteries lie outside the protection of the spinal column). Cutting these arteries causes the whale to bleed to death, and it appears to fall unconscious in about half a minute. However, the point into which one can slip a knife is a small target, which the whalers often miss. When a whaler is unsuccessful all he cuts is a pair of veins that run on the outside of the neck. Under these circumstances the whale takes at least five minutes to die, since the brain is protected by a rete (a network of capillaries) that guarantee it to be the last organ deprived of oxygen (an adaptation for deep diving). Because the loss of blood through veins is much slower than through arteries, it takes the whale a much longer time to bleed to death when only the neck veins have been cut.

Sometimes, as the knife nears the backbone, the whale violently arches its back. The Faeroese claim that without the constraint of the neck musculature, this violent flexure breaks the neck, killing the whale. However, a medical doctor who has studied the hunt doubts this is the case.

All efforts to separate Faeroese men from their gaffs and knives have so far failed. The records of the whales killed by this means are among the oldest continuous records of any fishery on earth. They indicate that since 1709 over a quarter of a million pilot whales have died in this particularly ghastly manner at the hands of the Faeroese, with other records going back before that.

Then there are the Iki Islanders of Japan who drive porpoises into bays on their island to kill them because those pesky porpoises have been eating up all their local fish stocks until the poor fishermen have hardly enough to make a living—a problem that has, miraculously, coincided with runaway overfishing of the very same stocks of fish by those selfsame fishermen and their local colleagues (colleagues who *do* in fact compete with them). There is some chance that by killing the porpoises they are actually exacerbating the collapse of their fish stocks, since the porpoises they are killing are known to prey on some of the predators of the young of the most commercially desirable fish species on which the Iki Islanders depend.

It seems miraculous to me that after so many years of this kind of treatment whales approach us at all, let alone with such lack of fear and with such gentleness. Perhaps the sense of fear is not well developed in whales. If so, and if fear is ever selected for in the hearts of whales, it will be men who put it there. For some reason it is these great sea beings that seem to release in us the ultimate in the kind of casual cruelty of which our species is capable. Except for our killing of each other what other mammal have we killed with greater savagery? It puts even bull fights to shame. Yet great fortunes of great families in New England were made by killing whales in this way, and rollicking sea tales written, and museums created to enshrine this kind of brutality in our culture.

Suppose farmers had killed cows on the American prairies by harpooning them from wagons and allowing them to drag the wagon until exhausted enough for the farmer to pull alongside and spear them repeatedly so as to puncture the heart or lungs and make the cow bleed to death? In order to make complete this analogy with whaling it would be important for us think of cowpooners as "iron men in wooden wagons," and never to really take on board the fact that what they were actually doing was killing (brutally) gentle, sweet-breathed, daisy-smelling cows that wanted nothing more violent than a chance to chew their cuds, bear their young, and bury their muzzles in the endless sea of prairie grass.

I have been talking about what whalers do to the whales, but what about what whaling does to the whalers? This is a topic seldom addressed. Whaling is represented as a time-honored tradition by its advocates, but just what is it that they are honoring?

During the eighteenth and nineteenth centuries, when whaling was high adventure, the techniques used to kill whales did not represent an isolated way of perceiving the natural world—they were in harmony with other world perceptions. At the time, our culture was undergoing a peak of religious fervor and self-righteousness and we believed ourselves to be the pinnacle of life on earth. We were outraged by a self-styled naturalist named Darwin who claimed that we and apes had ancestors in common, and farther back than that, we and worms—something repugnant to our sensibilities. At this same period we invented such terms as Manifest Destiny, and while spreading westward under its banner destroyed entire cultures of our own species.

As they opened up the world, the whalers brought to extinction one species after another—most of them animals that they encountered before any other Europeans did. This was particularly the case in the higher latitudes, many of which the whalers were the first to reach. One of the things for which the early whalers are most infamous is having brought about the extinction of Steller's Sea Cow, which was discovered in 1742 and extinct just twenty-seven years later. From what few records exist, Steller's Sea Cow appears to have been an absolutely peaceful species, like the dugong or the manatee, only far bigger—up to twenty-three feet long and weighing nearly nine thousand pounds. Steller's Sea Cow only existed in the vicinity of one North Pacific island group—the Kormandorskies. The only people besides the native Aleuts who ever saw them were the whalers. But the whalers liked the way Steller's Sea Cow tasted—they just got a little carried away, that's all.

They also frequently introduced domestic animals like rabbits, or goats, or cattle, or pigs to the uninhabited islands they passed. They did this so that these species could go forth and multiply, allowing the whalers to stop and kill them for the table when passing the same island on later voyages. By such haphazard introductions they destroyed the indigenous flora and fauna of hundreds if not thousands of islands. This sometimes took some odd turns. I encountered such an example of this on New Island in the Falklands/Malvinas group, where much more modern whalers had released pigs. It hadn't worked out all that well because the pigs took a liking to the eggs and chicks of petrels that they rooted out of their burrows by the thousands. Unfortunately, petrels contain an oil that has a pungent and, to most people, a very unpleasant smell. The oil of the petrels affected the meat unfavorably, and so no one wanted to eat them anymore. And when the whalers abandoned New Island they just left the pigs there. It was hard for the present owners of the island to eradicate the pigs so that the island could return to its present status as a nature reserve. Decades after the whalers had left, my family and I walked past huge, rooted-up areas that the pigs had devastated in their pursuit of burrowing petrels.

When whales couldn't be found, whalers often killed elephant seals, rendering their bodies down for their oil. When the elephant seals became scarce, the whalers sometimes switched to penguins. They drove them into corrals with crude walls made out of stone. In this way the penguins were confined and funneled into a single gate that opened directly into a vat of boiling oil—the tryworks vat borrowed from the whaling ship. Thus they didn't even have to bother to kill the penguins—the boiling oil did that for them and started right in on the rendering process.

Sometimes whaling captains became sealers. One, a Quaker from New England, a very God-fearing man, found a new seal colony on a subantarctic island and put two men ashore to kill and skin the seals, coming back every few weeks to take off the skins they had prepared and to bring them food and provisions. The captain was a great diarist, and in his diary he explains that at the end of the season he was forced to leave the men on the island for the winter—which he regretted because he knew they probably wouldn't survive an antarctic winter. He pointed out that the reason he had to do this was because he knew that there was no way to prevent their telling his competitors about the seal colony—and as he explains reverently, he simply couldn't afford to do that. When he returned the following year he discovered that, unsurprisingly, the men had died.

A whale biologist named Nishiwaki[1] reported seeing from a plane that he was using to locate whales for whale catcher boats a group of sperm whales formed into a circle with their heads at the center and their tails lashing the water into a froth—an obvious protective strategy. In his report he seems bemused at the formation, comparing it to a marguerite flower. He notes that this curious behavior of self-defense on the part of the sperm whales made it easy for the whalers to maneuver their catcher boat around the formation and harpoon them one by one, until in the end they secured the entire herd.

When in the late eighties Japan was unable to persuade the world that whaling in her coastal waters should be reclassified as aboriginal subsistence whaling and thus exempt from the moratorium, she nearly tripled her take on the North Pacific Dall's porpoise. Many conservationists felt this was done as much as anything else as a revenge on conservationists for blocking the whalers' efforts to resume whaling. (Japan was trying to depict her coastal whalers as running what amounted to mom and pop operations owned by poor fishermen who would suffer deeply with no other source of income besides whaling. But conservationist Campbell Plowden had discovered that at least one of the boats involved belonged to the Taiyo Fisheries Company—the largest fishing conglomerate on earth—and his information was important in swinging several key votes.) The Dall's porpoises were killed either by harpooning them with small cold harpoons fired in clusters—the porpoises being drawn by the harpoon into the boat while still very much alive, where they were killed by means too gross to describe—or they were gaffed directly as they swam alongside the boat and hooked up and into the boat by hand (of course a few must have escaped to die later of their wounds).

There are many stories about American whaling crews running rampant on South Seas islands, stealing food and raping young women; apparently this was common practice. In one instance, when the islanders put up resistance, the crew withdrew to their boats, but not without taking revenge. They decided they'd teach these "savages" a thing or two about their "paradise." There were no mosquitoes on this particular island. The captain had a barrel of polluted drinking water on board which had become infested with mosquito larvae at an earlier stop. He had it taken ashore and dumped into a freshwater pond. The island has been plagued by mosquitoes ever since.

The luxury seafood market in America created a major crab fishery in the protected straits and passages of southern Chile. When Chilean crab fishermen needed bait, they began to kill dolphins and cut them up for their crab traps. At the time the killing began, the most abundant species in the area was Commerson's dolphin—a small and particularly lovely animal that is sometimes given the nickname "panda of the sea" because of its striking black and white markings. It appears to mate for life as it is almost invariably encountered in pairs. When the crab fishermen ran out of Commerson's dolphin (which are now close to extinction in the area) they went after other dolphins, and when these ran out, they switched to sea lions. With the sea lions gone, or too shy to catch easily, they started pulling their skiffs up onto the deserted beaches of remote estancias and killing cattle for bait. Here, of course, they finally encountered resistance in the form of the residents of the estancias, who came out shooting.

Whaling is a kind of evanescent enterprise that flickers in and out of business according to the market, the weather, local politics, and so on. In the late fifties, with the utter destruction of the blue whale in the Antarctic all but complete and every indicator available showing that whales would soon be gone, the Soviet Union seized the moment to launch the two largest factory fishing ships in history: the *Sovetskaya Ukrania* (launched in 1959) and the *Sovetskaya Rossiya* (launched in 1961). The *Ukrania* was 32,000 gross tons and the *Rossiya* 33,000 gross tons—roughly the same size class as World War II aircraft carriers. They were not just the largest whaling factory ships ever built, they were the largest fishing boats ever built. One consequence of this incredibly ill-advised decision was that for the next twenty-five years every-one (including me) who attended the International Whaling Commission meetings had to sit and listen to the delegation from the Soviet Union use every trick, every scam, every absurd argument possible to keep their whal-ing industry alive long enough so that the cost of these two fuel-guzzling white elephants could be amortized. Finally, in the eighties, with glasnost and perestroika in full flower, the Soviets changed their tune and announced that their factory ships would not be used for another season in the antarctic whale fishery (one of them had spent the past couple of years engaged in "scientific whaling"). They presumably took this step, which they called a "temporary halt" to whaling, because the ships were finally and mercifully too dilapidated to continue operating in such a remote area as the Antarctic without a major refit.

I used to wonder what had become of the two *Sovetskayas*. A recent article in an Australian newspaper reports that they are to be spruced up for use as floating slaughterhouses for sheep in transit between Australia and the port of Vladivostok (the *Sovetskayas'* old home port). According to the article, ten million sheep per year will get a final cruise aboard these ships, interrupted only by their own deaths. It's a bit tough on the sheep but at least keeps these vessels off the whales' backs for the nonce.

Our savage treatment of whales and dolphins is not limited to our meth-ods of killing them. We have recently started the practice of "impressing" dolphins and pilot whales into the navy—not unlike press gangs that once roamed the bars in seaside towns, kidnapping sailors and forcing them to serve as crew on naval ships during long voyages. In the modern American navy dolphins and pilot whales are impressed for tasks that are classified but which are obviously ways of dealing with people we don't like (well, anyway, whom some of us don't like—or, to be more accurate, whom some of us don't like at the time we are making decisions as to whether to deploy marine mammals to deal with them, but whom we often *do* like later on). The navy has stonewalled the American people and the press about much of what they are doing with these marine mammals but the press did report that the navy has admitted taking dolphins to Vietnam and the Middle East when U.S. troops were engaged there. Even though the navy has never acknowledged the full extent of its activities involving dolphins and pilot whales, according to the fraternity of marine mammal trainers—all of whom know each other and each other's best stories—marine mammals have been trained in the past in particularly savage attack techniques that capitalize on—and pervert—innate behaviors.

Quite apart from the moral issue of involving marine mammals in human disputes, there is the fact that porpoises have traditionally befriended humans, occasionally even saving someone who is drowning by nudging them toward shallower water. It looks as if we may be rewarding this behavior with an ill-advised program using taxpayers' money allegedly to train marine mammals to act aggressively toward people.

And what is the fate of the animals in the navy's programs? With a few exceptions they either die in captivity or escape by going AWOL while on maneuvers at sea. The navy is quick to point out that it takes proper care of its dolphins and whales and that very few of them die in captivity. If this is indeed the case, it means that they must be losing the majority of their animals in the open ocean (presumably during practice runs). Under such circumstances an escapee is never debriefed—that is, taught not to do whatever it was taught to do. (When dogs were used by the military for combat duty during World War II they were detrained before being returned to their owners.)

On a recent television program a remarkable sequence was shown of a woman swimming with a "wild" pilot whale near Hawaii. The whale allowed her to stroke it for awhile after which it took her leg in its jaws and pulled her underwater, holding her down so long she thought she was going to drown. In my experience, pilot whales are not as inclined as some other whale species to allow people to come near them, and I have never seen a wild pilot whale allowing someone to stroke it. When I first saw the film of this woman struggling in the pilot whale's jaws, I wondered whether the bizarre behavior of this animal meant that it might not have been an escapee from one of the navy programs now in progress in the Hawaiian area. The navy's permit request for capturing marine mammals is published in the Federal Register and it is clear that they are using pilot whales. Who knows what techniques the navy is now teaching their pilot whales and dolphins for dealing with people and boats? It would be possible for the navy to reassure us on this point by letting a group of biologists examine for identifying nicks and scratches all photographs of the pilot whales which have escaped from the navy in Hawaiian waters—so as to compare them with the nicks and scratches on the whale in the film. If a match was found it would perhaps be time to ask Congress to ask the navy further questions about its dolphin training programs.

The woman who was pulled under by the pilot whale was on her first trip to see these animals and had no previous experience with them, so it is not clear whether her fears that she might drown were truly justified. However, it seems reasonable to assume that anyone who panicked while in her circumstances might very easily drown. It can be of no benefit to either side in times of peace or war to have escaped pilot whales swimming about pulling people under water.

As species with a long period of dependency between mother and calf, young pilot whales and dolphins are believed to acquire much of their behavior by learning from adults. If there is a long period of dependency during which the calf learns from its mother, what reason do we have to expect that an escapee *won't* teach to its baby what it learned in the navy? What authority in the navy can say that such behavior won't be taught to the young? The naval scientists involved with this work have no more idea than the rest of us in the marine mammal scientific community as to what extent mother dolphins train their young in the behaviors they learn from humans.

At least one chimp who had been taught sign language is credited with teaching it to her baby (people who know Ameslan can, after a fashion, watch mother and young signing to each other—to eavesdrop on them, so to speak). Dolphin trainers tell stories about dolphins learning each other's routines (even when they are not taught to them by trainers) and performing them in place of their companion when he or she refuses to perform. We don't yet know whether wild whales and dolphins learn from observing each other though I suspect it would be hard to find a biologist prepared to argue strongly that they do not learn in this way. To even consider teaching animals who are highly likely to escape into the wild how to hurt people is, at best, fuzzy thinking and, at worst, criminal.

Given the myriad of other ways we have of killing each other, why not leave dolphins and whales out of this part of the human equation? From earliest recorded history they have befriended us; to allow a major governmental body to invest in a program instructing them to attack people would be madness. The idea of involving marine mammals in our wars offends me more deeply than any of the other atrocities I have been describing. In its ways of dealing with the rest of nature, natural human arrogance is already despicable enough to discredit our species entirely without deliberately deciding to stretch the almost invisible wire of our credibility still further by enlisting dolphins and whales to participate in our wars. To use these animals to fight for a cause that concerns one segment (usually a minority) of our species in complete opposition to the views of another is, in my opinion, utterly immoral. When the whalers were destroying the stocks of blue whales at least it was in order to use them as food. Even though it was clearly greed that drove the whalers, the need for nourishment is something that cannot be reasoned around, but the need for fighting wars in utterly immoral ways *is*.

This seems to me an appropriate moment to recall that according to several religious sects, God created man in His own image. If we accept that, then it is we who are the chosen few. What I am talking about here is the behavior of quite a few of the chosen few—a behavior approved of and ordered by those in command—thus rendering it acceptable at the federal level—and as such something of which millions of the rest of us approve—either tacitly or explicitly. If nothing else about the ways that humans have dealt with whales in the past has moved us to act, here is a situation that ought to do so.

And what is it that whalers have achieved with all their years of activity? No one knows for sure how many whales there were of each species before whaling started, and there are no accurate estimates for the worldwide populations of sperm whales, either before or after the moratorium. The estimates that seem to be most widely accepted for the separate species are shown in Table 1.

Table 1: ESTIMATES COMPARING POPULATION NUMBERS OF WHALES BEFORE HUNTING STARTED AND AT THE TIME OF THE WHALING MORATORIUM (1986). [2]

Species	Estimated Original Number	Estimated Number at Moratorium	Percent Left
Blue	250,000	10,000	4
Fin	600,000	50,000	8
Bowhead	13,000	7,000	54
Right	80,000	4,000	5
Sperm	?	?	?
Humpback	150,000	25,000	16
Sei	200,000	60,000	30
Gray	?	20,000	?
Bryde's	60,000	40,000	66
Minke	1,000,000	900,000	90

It is obvious from Table 1 that when the moratorium went into effect blue and right whales had been reduced to less than 5 percent of their original numbers and fin whales to less than 10 percent. The table does not break down the reductions in populations by areas but the greatest such reduction probably occurred in the Antarctic, where, for example, blue whales fell from an original population of perhaps 200,000 animals to a present-day population estimated at about 450—only two tenths of a percent of the original population. It is now apparent that the number is very low because, as has recently been divulged, Soviet whalers continued to kill blue whales long after they were declared a protected species. As for the other species, all but the minke and Bryde's (the two smallest species of baleen whales) are below a population size at which sustained hunting is permitted by the IWC under the New Management Procedure (adopted in 1975 and not to be confused with the more recent Revised Management Procedure). The principle subscribed to by the countries that accepted this procedure was that whale populations should be held at levels that will give a maximum sustainable yield. However, the regulations affected each population separately, which meant that a species could be exploited in some areas even if it was very depleted in terms of world totals.

Estimates of the populations of sperm whales are not given in Table 1, because there is not enough known about this species. It is widely believed, however, that females are abundant in many places but that male sperm whales are so depleted in number that they should be protected throughout their range. Only blue, right, humpback, and bowhead whales were fully protected from commercial whaling under the New Management Procedure. (Aboriginal catches of humpbacks and bowheads were allowed, but this was separate from the New Management Procedure.) Under this procedure, non-zero quotas were set not only for minke whales but also for fin, sei, Bryde's, gray, and sperm whales.

As far as we know, the whaling industry has never brought to extinction any whale species, but it has extirpated some from major portions of their original range. Examples are the right whale, which is now nearly absent in the eastern North Atlantic and eastern North Pacific, and the gray whale, which appears to be missing in the western North Pacific and is extinct in the North Atlantic. It was aboriginal whalers or the early European whalers or the combined efforts of both that brought gray whales to extinction here—something that occurred in historic times.

This otherwise dreary list contains one bright spot—the bowhead whale. In recent years bowheads were thought to be close to extinction. However, it is now apparent that this species is in much more robust health than was feared. In Table 1 I have arrayed the species in order of body bulk, the basis on which they are valued by whalers (in chapter 1, they are shown in order of body length). With the happy exception of the bowhead it can be seen that whalers have brought the largest species closest to extinction and left the smallest species in the best shape. This is simply because a bigger whale is worth more money than a smaller one. The danger has always been that the smaller species of whales would subsidize the costs of bringing the larger species to extinction, simply because whaling on small species would pay the costs of keeping the catcher boats going long enough for them to find and catch the last of the large whale species. Of course, the many years of cheating by the Soviets that I have already mentioned is undoubtedly the reason why the blue whale has not found it possible to recover in the Antarctic since coming under full protection in the 1960s.

Norway has resumed minke whaling. The hope is that the Revised Management Procedure, recently developed by the International Whaling Commission, will allow minke whales to avoid the terrible fate of overfishing that has been visited on other species. However, my money is on the whalers. I'm betting that they will simply kill whales illegally as the Soviets did, or find enough ways to frustrate the system—for example, by whaling under flags of convenience the way the Japanese did, or by dropping out of the commission, the way Iceland has done, or by defying its quotas and stock designations, the way Norway has done, or by claiming that their commercial whaling operations are really science, the way Japan, Norway, and Iceland have done (a scam, however, pioneered by the United States on gray whales back in the 1960s), or by never joining the commission in the first place, the way Portugal has done. Unless there is a very basic change of heart among these whaling nations, I'm betting that minke whales will simply go the way of all their relatives.

What is it that was so desperately needed and that whales alone could supply?

For the first whalers, the Inuit, whales did indeed provide a unique resource. The Inuit lived where no wood was available, and a whale provided not only meat but massive quantities of bone from which to make sleds, spears, the frames for skin-covered summer houses, and many other of the very most basic implements. Given how urgently they needed such things, it is not surprising to me that the first whalers were the Inuit. Indeed, I wonder if the Inuit lifestyle could have evolved in the treeless tundra had whales been unavailable.

When Europeans got into the whaling business, the most valuable products of the industry were oil and baleen—the hundreds of strips of hornlike material that protrude from the gums of the upper jaw of all baleen whales. Baleen is naturally springy, but when placed in boiling water it becomes limp and pliant and can be bent into any desired shape. When it cools and dries out, it retains that shape and its springiness returns. The use of baleen in corsets came into vogue in the early 1600s before spring steel was mass produced. Baleen was used in hundreds of applications, including buggy whips, umbrellas, and occasionally even clocks.

Oil from whales comes in two forms: "sperm oil" and "whale oil." Sperm oil, from sperm whales, is inedible because it is actually a liquid wax rather than a true oil. It is used as a lubricant for fine machinery and was, for a while, stockpiled by the U.S. military for "strategic purposes." Since there are many alternative oils, both natural and synthetic, that can be used for the traditional applications of sperm oil, several of us decided to find out just who it was in the Pentagon responsible for the wise decision of basing the defense of "These United States" on the oil of an endangered species (the Soviets were the baddies at the time so there was plenty of paranoia to highlight the absurdity of such a decision). The result of our investigation was an immediate reversal of policy, the U.S. government putting its entire stock of sperm oil on the market—something that depressed the price and helped put several small sperm whaling operations out of business. At the same time my mother discovered that the New Crops Research Division of the U.S. Department of Agriculture had been developing ways to grow jojoba, a desert plant that produces nuts rich in the same liquid wax that comprises sperm whale oil. It also became apparent that a plot of land between twenty and a hundred miles on a side (and not otherwise usable for agriculture, since jojoba plants like desert conditions) could grow enough jojoba oil to supply the world's annual demand for sperm oil. There were, however, a few unresolved problems in growing and harvesting jojoba oil. But California's then governor, Jerry Brown, came to the rescue by declaring "A Day for Whales" in California. With the whole state attuned to the need to save whales, he introduced a bill which, even though it was winged and crippled by the state legislature, eventually unleashed over $700,000 in funds to complete the work of turning jojoba into a successful cash crop (something that also gave Californians a jump on growing and marketing this now valuable crop). It was one of the brighter moments in showing that politics can actually contribute to the solution rather than to the problem, and in getting the world to recognize that there is nothing we get from whales that can't be gotten elsewhere.

Whale oil comes from baleen whales, and being a true oil, is edible. It is used in prepared foods wherever an edible oil is required. Because both sperm and whale oil can be used for thousands of purposes, it is not reasonable to try to list all their uses any more than it would be reasonable to list all the uses of iron—another raw material.

Sperm oil is valued for its use in the lubrication of fine machinery, because of its chemical stability under high pressures and temperatures. (It is, for example, the oil used in the automatic transmissions of many expensive cars.)

Whale oil can be used in place of any other edible or inedible vegetable or fish oil, in thousands of different applications—from salad dressing to soap. At the height of the destruction of blue and fin whales, it was used most in the manufacture of margarine.

The meat of baleen whales is edible, but the meat of sperm whales is eaten in very few societies. The same cannot be said about other toothed whales, the consumption of which is exploding in popularity. This unfortunate and very recent development results from dolphins and porpoises being caught accidentally in fishing nets, brought into the markets of developing nations, and sold so cheaply that people not otherwise able to afford meat can buy it. Markets for porpoise meat are now developing rapidly in places where they did not formerly exist. In Sri Lanka, the first country in Asia to pass laws against killing dolphins, the dolphin by-catch has stimulated a vigorous dolphin fishery that is believed to kill thousands of porpoises, illegally, each year.

The main international market for whale meat of all kinds is Japan. It is "belly bacon" which the Japanese consider the most valuable delicacy. Belly bacon is actually the pleated muscular tissue in the enormously expandable ventral pouches of lunge-feeding whales (the blues, fins, seis, Bryde's, minkes, and humpbacks). Even though it extends nearly to the whale's navel, this ventral pouch is usually referred to as the whale's throat.

A wide variety of food extracts come from whales, plus the teeth (used for carving) and baleen (used for making brushes or for making artifacts for tourists[3]). These products are of lesser economic value in part because there is so much less of them than there is meat, oil, and bonemeal. The important point, however, is that in spite of the thousands of products which whales provide, there is absolutely nothing that we get from them that is unique— nothing for which there are not far more plentiful naturally occurring or synthetic alternatives.

The most telling evidence of how utterly our perceptions fall short when dealing with whales concerns the uses to which we put them. To look at such an animal as a source of meat is a little like thinking of hummingbirds as hors d'oeuvres. I have no doubt one could come up with several quite tasty ways to prepare hummingbird hors d'oeuvres, and if we put our best battery of farmers on the task, we could probably raise as many tons of hummingbird meat as the tons we can get from whales, but is that the most valuable kind of interaction humans can have with hummingbirds?

It is because whales are such grand and glowing creatures that their destruction for commerce degrades us so. It will confound our descendants. We were the generation that searched Mars for the most tenuous evidence of life but couldn't rouse enough moral outrage to stop the destruction of the grandest manifestations of life here on earth. We will be like the Romans whose works of art, architecture, and engineering we find awesome but whose gladiators and traffic in slaves are mystifying and loathsome to us.

In country after country, as whaling has ceased, those involved in its practice have complained bitterly that they faced ruin—that starvation and social upheaval on a mammoth scale would soon ensue—a surprising complaint when one realizes that in every place where it has occurred, the closing of a whaling industry has been brought about solely through the greed of the whalers. Certainly the world market for whale products is large enough and steady enough to have been sustained indefinitely had the management of whaling been more enlightened. I find whalers reminiscent of the man who killed his parents and threw himself on the mercy of the court on the grounds that he was an orphan.

I have sympathy for anyone who loses a job, but the social upheavals and mass suffering resulting from the loss of jobs in whaling has not even approached the scenarios predicted. Whalers have always been a small fraction of the societies of which they were a part—societies that could absorb them into different sectors of the job market. The whaling communities in America, Britain, the Netherlands, Germany, France, Australia, and Canada have all closed down for what will probably be forever. Yet they have not experienced anything like the apocalypses depicted in whalers' complaints at the time of their closing. Of course there has been suffering—what job loss has ever been attended with anything but suffering? Some psychologists claim that other than the death of a loved one, the two greatest traumas a human being can experience are divorce and the loss of a job. But the vast majority of people lose several jobs in their lives, and in the West divorce now ends more than half of modern marriages. Such losses are now a fact of life, part of the human condition, and not the singling out of a particular group for punishment. One of the most important human attributes is resilience. It is an unrepealable law of nature that no natural population of animals can sustain itself in the face of the full onslaught of a modern industry designed to profit from it. However, history shows us that the lives of humans dispossessed by the collapse of such industries do indeed go on.

And what body is responsible for regulating whaling—what body is supposed to have controlled the industry in such a way that the whale stocks would remain healthy and the whalers would never go out of business? It is the International Whaling Commission (IWC), a consortium of fluctuating membership (but in recent years representing about forty nations) that exists to implement the International Convention for the Regulation of Whaling, ratified by the major whaling nations in 1946.

The IWC grew out of the Convention for the Regulation of Whaling drawn up by the League of Nations in 1931, which did not come into force until 1935—and then protection was only partial. One of the topics it addressed was the need to offer protection to the then most endangered species of great whales, the Northern Hemisphere gray and bowhead whales and the ubiquitous right whale. But not all whaling countries adhered to this convention, though it did establish the principle of the international regulation of whaling. Full protection for gray, right and bowhead whales was finally achieved with ratification in 1937 even though hunts by aboriginal peoples on gray and bowhead whales were still permitted. At this point the Second World War intervened, with profound consequences for whales. Whaling in the Antarctic ceased, and many whaling vessels were torpedoed.[4] While humans were occupied with killing each other, most whales got a rest. In 1946, with whaling resuming, a full International Convention for the Regulation of Whaling was ratified and the first International Whaling Commission meeting convened to implement its agreements. One of the things it stipulated was that the control of whaling would extend into the waters claimed by nations as their own—a most surprising feature when one realizes that signatories to it gave up their right to control whaling in their own coastal waters. However, it was no real threat to whaling since the IWC began more as a whaler's club than as an international body to regulate the orderly development of an industry, and it wasn't until the 1970s that it finally started to become more representative of the interests of humanity at large rather than just of the whalers'.

The IWC was not the only whaling commission. Chile and Peru formed their own—the South Pacific Whaling Commission—whose quotas and restrictions were, if imaginable, even more unrealistic than those of the IWC. The result was that they continued killing blue whales in the 1960s—even after the incredibly unresponsive IWC had finally given them protection. Peru and Chile hunted them not in the Antarctic during summer, but off their own coasts during winter as the last of the antarctic blue whales passed by. In the 1960s these two nations were not members of the IWC and it looked as though the world was going to lose blue whales. But at the eleventh hour Chile and Peru did join the IWC and in so doing made the protection of the last of the blue whales a reality.

It was through the personal efforts of aviator Charles Lindbergh, who made a special trip to Chile and Peru for the purpose of asking them to stop killing the blue whales, that they were persuaded to do so. In many ways it is to Lindbergh that the world owes the continued presence of blue whales. He used to come to IWC meetings as a member of the U.S. delegation. After one particularly frustrating day of meetings I suggested to him that maybe it was time to stop talking and start acting, and I asked him whether he wouldn't be delighted to pick up tomorrow's paper and read that someone had sunk a factory ship. "Ah well," said Lindbergh, "you mustn't forget, Roger; he who lives by the sword, dies by the sword." It was an important lesson of my youth—"one-trial learning" I think it's called. I learned an important lesson from that gentle man. It is clear that on at least one occasion in his very public life, Lindbergh made anti-Semitic remarks that no one can or should condone. He may have been a racist but at least he was not a speciesist. In the late sixties his presence at IWC meetings was like a ray of light, and his untimely death from cancer real cause for whales to mourn— after flying, preserving whales seems to have been Lindbergh's great passion.

In the 1970s, as more and more member nations dropped out of whaling, the IWC became more active in preventing the destruction of whale stocks. Although the IWC has not always included all whaling nations, recently it has included the vast majority of them, and its forty or so member nations have represented the interests of over three billion people—over 60 percent of the world's population.

The legal document that sets forth the agreements that signatories to the Convention for the Regulation of Whaling have signed is called the "Articles of the Convention." These articles are seldom changed and contain several crippling ambiguities—for example, the word "whale" is not clearly defined. This has allowed for a major difference of opinion between signatories to the convention—those nations who believe that what they signed up to protect were *all* cetaceans, and those nations who say they never intended to include the toothed whales (except the sperm whale) in this protection. At the root of this problem lies the fact that the majority of the populations of the small-toothed whales are coastal. Nations like Japan that wish to eat dolphins and porpoises are unwilling to have other nations tell them what they can and cannot do in their own coastal waters—hence their reluctance to have the IWC include the smaller toothed whales under its purview.

The "Schedule of the Convention" is a list of the rules in effect at any given moment, e.g., the quotas for each species. To change a quota one must therefore amend the schedule, and this requires a three-quarters majority. This sword cuts two ways. For example, it means that just as it was hard to get a three-quarters majority to pass the moratorium (what was voted on was not really a moratorium but a zero quota), it is just as difficult for the whaling nations to get it unpassed since that too requires a three-quarters majority.

The IWC meets for a month each year: two weeks of Scientific Committee meetings, a week of Technical Subcommittee meetings, which include the Infractions Subcommittee, the Aboriginal Subsistence Whaling Subcommittee, the Finance Committee, etc., and finally a week of full commission meetings. During this final week of meetings the scientific delegates go home (except for me and a few others benighted individuals) and the full delegations of diplomats, representatives of governmental agencies, lawyers, politicians, and lobbyists come out. It is at this time that international conservation organizations send observers to the meetings (most are not invited onto most national delegations). This week-long meeting of the IWC is what the world at large thinks of as the IWC's annual meeting, even though it comprises but a quarter of the total meetings (and often less than a quarter; e.g., in most recent years there have been extra Scientific Committee meetings as well as scientific workshops on special topics during the year).

The delegates from the whaling countries often complain that the IWC is conservationist in its outlook. However, as a conservationist who attended my first IWC meeting in 1968 (and whose experience with the meetings therefore spans more years than most other delegates), I can say that I truly feel it would be hard to assemble a group of people from around the world who were more pro-whaling. As a result of my years spent on the Scientific Committee of the IWC—a committee including Japanese, Norwegian, and Icelandic scientists all pushing as hard as they can for the largest possible quotas—I have concluded that one of the major advantages to the whalers of convening a scientific body of such a size is that there is perhaps no other way of giving credence to such a small minority opinion (that of scientists from pro-whaling nations) on an issue for which there is such a clear scientific consensus for the opposite viewpoint.

My trips each year to the IWC constitute the most dispiriting, irritating, and outrageously frustrating activity of my life. Every year I watch the whalers' representatives twisting and turning and writhing as they are dragged, kicking and complaining, into the modern age. Annually the IWC provides for my personal Book of Records a fresh entry pertaining to the maximum frustration the human spirit can endure. People attending an IWC meeting for the first time find they need a guide or translator to help them figure out what is going on—not to translate from the many languages to English (for that is quite competently done) but from English to English—from words that are selected by their speakers to be as obfuscating as possible into what the speaker is actually talking about.

The example I offer refers to a period of seven years during which Norway was supposed to give data to the Scientific Committee on their fishing operations so the committee could estimate whale populations, assess the state of the stocks, and work out quotas. Norway had her own agenda, however, and wouldn't comply, even though it is not an option but a requirement of membership that member nations provide data on their whaling operations to the Scientific Committee each year. The conversation I am reporting here takes place during a Technical Committee meeting, which is a kind of practice run for the full plenary session meetings, usually composed of an identical membership but headed by a different chairperson.

The words in my example, however, are not direct quotes, since one of the rules of the commission is that when the meetings are in session you may not quote verbatim from the proceedings. Anyway, in some ways it seems more honest to use fictitious language since so much of what is said is fictitious anyhow. It somehow gives a more honest and accurate picture of what IWC meetings are *really* like.

Commissioner from Norway:

Mr. Chairman, our delegation regrets to inform the Technical Committee that at this year's Scientific Committee meeting we were not able to provide the scientific data for which that committee has been asking. However, I am assured by the head of our scientific delegation that he and his colleagues are working on the matter diligently. They have promised this body a report on their progress at next year's meeting, and we hope we will soon see them reach a conclusion to this important work which our delegation so much endorses and for which we have invested great effort and time.

Translation:

We have no intention whatever of giving the commission our data until we are damn well ready to do so. We didn't offer it this year and have no intention of doing so next.

Chairman:

Thank you, Norway, the Technical Committee report will reflect that fact and we will look forward to receiving your report next year or, if possible, during the interim meeting of the Scientific Committee in January, as I am sure you recognize the urgency which the Scientific Committee chairman attaches to this matter, particularly as the completion of the work of your scientists is long overdue.

Translation:

You're fooling no one. It is perfectly clear you are withholding the report from us. I'll make that clear in my report.

Once the draft report of the committee comes out, we find some rather harsh words in it apparently composed by the chairman but if necessary blameable on the Technical Committee's rapporteur. It reads:

Draft Technical Committee Report: Item 1.13.6

Norway regretted that for the 5th year in a row it was unable to provide the Scientific Committee with its data and has promised to present this to the committee in the coming year.

(Draft reports have to be approved by the entire Technical Committee, so it should prove no problem to the Norwegian commissioner to get the language of the report changed so it won't cause him any problem when he has to report to his government on his return to Norway.)

Chairman:

Are there any comments on the draft report as regards Item 1.13.6? [pause] Norway.

Norwegian commissioner:

Mr. Chairman, I would like to suggest that we strike the words "for the 5th year in a row" as well as the words "and promised it would present it to the committee in the coming year." The item would then read, "Norway regretted that it was unable to provide the Scientific Committee with its data." If I recall correctly, during our discussion of this point there was no mention made to the effect that this might be the fifth, or indeed any other year, that the Scientific Committee has asked for Norway's data, and I know you agree with me that this committee's report should accurately reflect the committee's discussion on the matter. I also regret that I am unable to promise that our scientists will have a report for the Scientific Committee by next year—though I can assure you that they will being expending all of their energies to do so. Perhaps I did not make myself sufficiently clear on that point. Thank you, Mr. Chairman.

Translation:

Gotcha!

And so he does. For when the report comes out it reads:

Final Report of the Technical Committee:

Norway regretted that it was unable to provide the Scientific Committee with its data.

Norway has gotten off scot-free, and the Scientific Committee is no closer to having the data to work with than they were before. Nothing has changed. It is business as usual.

But there were good times too. In fact, I have had some of my most riotous laughs at luncheons and dinners during the meetings—it's the only way to relieve the tension. My all-time favorite was a remark by a whaler's scientist who had failed to see whales during a sightings survey he had carried out (suggesting that the stock of whales he was censusing had collapsed). In explaining his paper on the matter, the scientist concluded: "The sightings were biased owing to a lack of whales."

One famous year we were cooped up in a second-rate hotel in Brighton, England, with threadbare rugs and unsprung furniture. In the hotel lobby there was a little jewelry case exhibiting cuff links, tie clips, rings, and the like, all made of nine-carat gold. None of us Americans had ever heard of nine-carat gold. It just seemed gloriously tatty, and we christened the place "Nine-Carat Brighton." It stuck and became the joke of the meeting.

During the penultimate night of that year's meeting, when the delegates were at each other's throats over a deeply rancorous issue, and tensions were running high—there had even been a shoving match at the bar the previous night with a delegate from a country that hadn't sent one to the meetings for years—everyone was on edge and ready to crack. That same night the hotel was also hosting a convention of Elvis Presley fans, and quite by chance, at the height of the Sturm und Drang between the IWC delegates, the Elvis fans were running an Elvis Presley look-alike contest. There were Elvis Presleys everywhere you looked—in the bar, coming out of the men's room, sitting in every soft chair in the lounge, chatting in little groups. It was surreal. The humor of the situation broke the tension, everyone relaxed a bit, and the meeting was able to proceed.

My great moment came during the 1986 meeting when one of the lawyers on the Japanese delegation (who was, I suppose, assigned to check the credentials of every delegate opposed to Japan's position in hopes of some kind of bonanza) examined my credentials and found a technical flaw. My commissioner had faxed a letter to the IWC secretariat naming me as the scientific advisor to his delegation—all very proper. But there is a law in the IWC that although a fax may be used to transmit credentials to the IWC's secretariat (as a matter of convenience) the original must be sent within a few days. For several days my friends on the inside were warning me that the Japanese delegation was getting ready to strike but that they were waiting until the last moment—presumably to be sure that I would have no time to get the original letter sent up from my ambassador's office in London—a move on my part which would then cause the Japanese to lose face—something that carries stigma in the Japanese culture. Needless to say, everyone—most particularly the Japanese delegation—knew perfectly well that I was there legally, it was just that they had this completely irresistible technical detail with which to try to embarrass me. In matters of this sort the Japanese culture is different from the cultures of most other countries on the commission, and no one on their delegation seemed to realize that what they were offering me was a chance to be seen as the underdog, the victim of a coldhearted bureaucracy—a hero, in other words. At the time I was acting as science advisor to Antigua/Barbuda—a post that ended a few years after the incident herein described when the Japanese moved into the Caribbean and started giving major grants in aid. (Strange to say there was an abrupt, 180-degree shift in the stance of several Caribbean nations, some of whom became rubber stamps to Japanese whaling interests—a great shame considering that before that change they were leaders in the wise management of whale stocks.)

Over the years I had noticed with amusement the success that Greenpeace had in relying on the French to attack them anytime they needed to raise funds. It was clear that all Greenpeace had to do was present themselves to the French somewhere—anywhere: in those South Pacific atolls where France tests her nuclear weapons, or at a base in the Antarctic where the French were cheerfully paving over a penguin colony to build an airstrip. Apparently to the French, Greenpeace is like a red flag waved in front of a bull. Predictably, the French would attack them in some outrageous and wonderfully filmable way and Greenpeace would have their material for the next fund-raiser. This practice culminated several years ago in the famous incident when two French frogpersons (I am not being deliberately provocative, or even just using the politically correct form—one of them was indeed a woman) sank the *Rainbow Warrior* in Auckland harbor, in one stroke giving an unprecedented boost to Greenpeace membership. I can imagine the meeting in which the decision to sink the *Rainbow Warrior* was made:

Mitterrand:

Gentlemen, I want to do something to help those Greenpeace people. They seem overworked. We don't have a lot of money or time to devote to it and I can't see what budget we could charge it to without causing grave problems in some quarters of our government. But I want to do *something* to help them, however small it may turn out to be.

Voice:

Mr. President, if we give them money they will spend it in a few months and have nothing to fall back on when it's gone. But if we give them the basis for another campaign we can help them immeasurably, just as we have in the past. I say let's sink their boat. The sympathy of the world will be with them, their membership will increase, and they can buy and deploy another boat with the money they make from it while continuing to profit in the ensuing years from the support of the members that join during the storm of sympathy.

Mitterrand:

Done. Formidable! Brilliant! But whatever you do, don't tell the press; if they know about it beforehand it wouldn't be newsworthy and the best headline Greenpeace would get out of the whole affair would be FRENCH GOVERNMENT TO ASSIST CONSERVATION GROUP. In the long run that would weaken them, not strengthen them. Everyone would think Greenpeace was getting money from a government and they'd stop contributing. No, if we really want to help these people, we've got to sink their boat.

But no such conversation did take place. The French showed their usual lack of understanding about this kind of politics and decided "to teach Greenpeace a lesson." But even after a rumored eight million dollars paid to Greenpeace, and an admission of guilt, the French still hadn't learned their lesson and it seems more and more likely they never will.

I want to stop long enough to be perfectly clear about two things: my true feelings toward the sinking of the *Rainbow Warrior* and my true feelings toward Japan. When the first explosion aboard the *Rainbow Warrior* went off, the crew was just heading into town and no one was on board. A photographer ran back to save his cameras and was killed by the second explosion. The placement of the explosives on the hull seemed intended to kill. There is nothing in the least bit funny about that.

As regards my feelings for Japan, I have visited Japan several times and have enjoyed everything about those visits. I was wonderfully treated and returned home with the strong feeling that the youth of Japan may well be the best hope the world has for conservation in the future. I like everything about the Japanese culture except its whalers. And to be scrupulously truthful, I even like one of them.

To return to my story: I decided to play the waiting game along with the Japanese delegation. The days slowly dragged by, and with only eight hours of meetings left to go (when it was safely too late for my commissioner to get a letter delivered from London to Sweden, where we were meeting that year), the Japanese delegation struck. Late in the penultimate day the head of the Japanese delegation asked for the floor to point out that he couldn't help noticing that there was someone at the meeting whose credentials were not in proper order. Iain Stewart from New Zealand was in the chair, and having presumably been primed long before as to what was up he turned to me at once and asked me to stand down.

But I was ready too and so I refused, pointing out that I was responsible to the country on whose delegation I was an advisor and that as they had instructed me to attend the meeting I would not stand down without an order from them to do so. Much buzzing in the Japanese delegation. Not quite part of their plan. I wanted to prolong the spectacle of Japan picking on a much smaller country of the IWC for as long as I could, so I sat firm.

There were several exchanges followed by Stewart adjourning the meeting, explaining as he did so that there was no other course open to him. It was obvious to all the delegates that in its absurdly petty vendetta with me the Japanese delegation had managed to precipitate the closing of the meeting and the wasting of everyone's time. While the meeting was closed Stewart approached me and asked me as a personal favor to stand down. He is a good man—someone with whom I had worked for several years and whom I admire. We discussed it, and he returned to the chair and reconvened the meeting. But as I had not agreed to stand down, I refused to do so when he asked me to stand down for a second time. Much apparent consternation in the Japanese delegation. Presumably this was getting dicier than they had intended (though I believe to this day that they had no idea that what was going on was reflecting far worse on them than it was on me). Robert Del Pech, commissioner from the Seychelles, raised his card to say that this seemed like a poor way to be treating a person who had been well-known in the commission for many years and whose presence there could not be doubted (at the time Del Pech was the longest-standing ambassador to the Court of St James from any country and a person whose voting record at the IWC on behalf of whales was impeccable). For a second time Stewart closed the meeting and came down to my table to talk. There were large glass doors at the end of our meeting room offering a full view into the room, and a BBC reporter was standing outside them with a cameraman. It dawned on me that if I got carried out of the meeting, the picture on the nightly news would say more about these meetings than I could say in a lifetime. But it was also clear that Stewart was far too intelligent a man to let that happen.

Meanwhile the tension continued to mount. All my friends were scurrying around, clustering about me in little gusts of consternation asking did I really think I was doing the right thing, and for heaven's sake what was I going to do next, and so on. And then I caught sight of a smallish figure walking slowly toward me down the center of the room. It was the late Sir Peter Scott, one of the founders of the World Wildlife Fund and of the British Wildfowl Trust, a great fighter for whales and one of my favorite human beings on the planet. He was walking along slowly and deliberately, obviously mulling this drama over in his mind—looking at it from every angle as such a wise man is wont to do. He walked up to me and said very plainly, "Roger, I've thought about it and I think that you are doing the right thing. I just wanted you to know that."

I could have hugged him. Of all the people who were flapping around me at that moment Peter was the only one who retained his dignity and managed to think calmly while under the pressure in that cooker. He saw clearly what the underlying values were, and I loved him for it. As I felt I had gotten all the available mileage from this situation, and that it was clear no one was prepared to carry me out, and because I knew that if I kept it up for too long it would soon be me rather than the Japanese delegation that was guilty of holding up the proceedings, I was prepared to stand down and leave the room when Stewart reconvened the meeting. However, before I could volunteer to do so the secretary of the commission spoke up, suggesting to Stewart and to the Japanese delegation that perhaps I could be allowed to stay as an observer representing Werkgroup Zeehund, an organization from the Netherlands whose delegate was absent. Observers are not allowed to speak in the meetings—they do their work by lobbying the delegates at teatime or after hours. But that was fine with me since I hadn't spoken in the plenary meetings that year anyway, except when the chairman addressed me directly to stand down. (It is a matter of etiquette that science advisors do not speak in plenary unless their commissioners are present, and mine had been absent all through the meeting.) I accepted the suggestion to attend as Werkgroup Zeehund's delegate and moved my seat about three feet back from the table. There I sat, smiling at the Japanese delegation until none of them would return my gaze—an entire delegation staring at the table. The Japanese commissioner then raised his card to say something to the effect that inasmuch as it had been established that my credentials were not in order, it seemed that my presence at the many previous committee and subcommittee meetings had not been proper either, and that perhaps we should therefore consider whether to accept the reports of those committees. I supposed that he was trying to get one of the reports that was particularly unfavorable to Japan thrown out of the working documents of the meeting. But it was clearly such an absurd suggestion and such a halfhearted try that Stewart simply looked pained, saying something to the effect that "Well, there is really nothing that we can do about it, I suppose, and there is much work left to complete," and so the Japanese commissioner did not press the matter further. A grand and glorious tempest in a teapot just to move a person three feet.

About an hour after this incident, one of my friends managed to reach my commissioner and that night he sent the commission a strong letter protesting the way a member of his delegation had been treated. (It was only then that I discovered the reason my commissioner had failed to send me the original of my credentials letter—he had been in hospital throughout the month of the meetings.) The following morning the commissioners met in special closed session to discuss the letter from my commissioner and ruled that the original law would be upheld—that credentials had to be confirmed through the mail—faxing them was not enough. If I have been at some pains to describe all this petty nonsense, it is because it is so very typical of what awaits one at the IWC—an example, I suppose, of how whaling brings out the very best in everyone.

Even so, there are people whose presence at the IWC meetings is a blessing and whose contributions are given with dignity. I will focus on three examples: Sidney Holt, Justin Cooke, and Bill de la Mare. All are biometricians—specialists in the study of animal populations—and do much of their work in the context of the Scientific Committee. If you are a lover of whales I suggest you get down on your hands and knees some night and thank God for the efforts of these three men. It is they whose solid and continuous scientific work has brought what semblance there now is of rationality to the whaling issue. None of the three can be beaten in a scientific argument concerning population modeling, stocks, and quotas. They are, quite simply, the best in the business. Justin Cooke is a man of incredibly few words who can without rancor correct another person's flawed scientific argument in fewer sentences than anyone I have ever heard. Bill de la Mare has an equal grasp of the points at issue and a marvelous, dry sense of humor. He is a master at strategy and at drafting resolutions. Sidney Holt has these talents plus thirty years of experience with the IWC, both in their political meetings and on the Scientific Committee. He seems to remember everything that has ever been said in every meeting—what is in every report of every committee and subcommittee, as well as the entire Schedule of the Convention, who proposed what, and every item on every agenda for the past thirty years. It all lies in his mind—straight. There is no one else in the world with this knowledge. One particularly irritating head of a whaling country's delegation spent several years trying to match wits with Sidney in this regard. It was never any contest. I have not seen anyone beat Sidney in a scientific argument, and my sample is very large. I have been in meetings with him in at least twenty different venues, for eight hours or more a day—for what probably totals more than eight continuous months of time. I have no idea how often my heart has sunk as I have thought that all was lost on some point—often a procedural point, the perennial refuge of the lawyers on the whaling delegations—when the card for the Seychelles delegation has slowly been raised (for many years Sidney's seat was on this delegation) and Sidney, having been called upon, has said in his dry and patient voice something like the following:

> Mr. Chairman, I find it difficult to see why it is that the delegate from Iceland is taking this position now, for I recall that back in 1979, at a time when the Scientific Subcommittee was discussing a similar issue, that his delegation said, "[such and such and so and so]," which, as you can see, seems to be the opposite to what he is saying now. Do you suppose he might be given the chance to explain to all of us why it is his delegation took that position then and why he is taking this position now?

Deathly silence. Of course the delegate from Iceland has no idea what his delegation said in 1979 (let alone what the full significance is of what he has just said himself). If he is new to the game he may guess that Sidney Holt is bluffing and decide to call his bluff. But God help him if he does so. For the Seychelles' delegation desk is piled high with the telephone-book-sized "Reports of the International Whaling Commission," and by now Sidney has found the point to which he was referring and has his finger on it. If the other delegate tries to bluff or wriggle his way out of it, Sidney proceeds like a hydraulic press crushing a car chassis.

> Mr. Chairman, I believe that what my distinguished colleague has said is not quite correct. Here is the passage to which I was referring: [he reads it]. What the Icelandic delegate said just now was: [he quotes it verbatim—something its author could not have done—but Sidney has an extraordinary memory]. As you can see we seem to have a problem in squaring these two statements. Perhaps the distinguished delegate from Iceland can help us.

A lot of bluster and hot air from the delegate—to which no one pays the least attention. Having seen by now that the Icelander's point has been defeated utterly, the attention of the other delegates has gone off somewhere else, and they are all talking among themselves. And so the whole threat vanishes, and once again I look over at this white-haired man and think, "Thank you, Sidney Holt, and may the whales thank you as well."

I have seen that kind of thing happen not just once or twice but more than a hundred times. When Sidney retires, heaven help whales. In the meantime, by the excellence of their science and by the fact that they have had to answer every spurious scientific argument and to defeat every possible mischievous interpretation of the data of others, Holt, Cooke and de la Mare have set into place a body of work at the IWC that will act as a model for other international organizations that are trying to preserve the Remains of the Commons. Their work will have had a greater impact on life in the seas than the work of any other three people I could name. There are many of us who might wish to believe that we had a lot to do with saving whales or setting the stage for the moratorium, but it is these three men—Sidney Holt, Justin Cooke, and Bill de la Mare—who through the medium of solid scientific work and an ability to demystify the arguments by what I call "the whalers' tame scientists" showed the flaws in those arguments and in doing so contributed more toward getting a moratorium than any of the rest of us. As it seemed to me, the natural leader of this effort was Sidney. If anyone ever deserved the Getty Prize for conservation—which conservationists consider the Nobel Prize for Conservation—it is Sidney Holt.

But there have been other critically important players—for example, David McTaggart of Greenpeace—a brilliant strategist and master of the surprise move. He has been one of the most important contributors from the environmental movement to bringing whaling under rational control. There is also a man who many see as a somewhat shadowy figure, an extraordinary person who has also played a great role in these affairs but who makes his contributions behind the scenes—Frenchman Jean Paul Fortim-Gouin. When the author of *The Whale Wars* (a book about the Save the Whales movement) inscribed a copy he was giving to Jean Paul he wrote, "To the best friend the whales ever had." When I saw it I thought, "Yes, that's right. It really is Jean Paul who is the best friend the whales had." That's because he has given more of himself than any of the rest of us have. He has put everything he has—all his money, his time, his credibility, and several times his life—on the line for whales.

Jean Paul is a successful businessman who lives in what amounts to a shack on a beach. For years he spent everything he could get his hands on helping to get a moratorium through. To do this he scrimped and saved in ways most other rich men never do. By doing so, he contributed more in the end to the cause. If those of us who also work for the cause gave as freely as

Jean Paul has given the world would be a different place. He travels a lot and wherever he goes he stays in hotels so primitive many of his rooms don't even have a door; some have just a beaded curtain—are in fact the bottle-storage area behind some cafe, with just a cot bearing the remains of a mattress and a torn and threadbare blanket. Many people who know him think of him as a turbulent and hidden character, yet I suppose he is the nearest thing to a saint that the whale movement has yet produced.

I have been discussing how the IWC works but have not said what it accomplishes or might accomplish. The organization has such a deeply flawed history it's amazing to me that it works at all. There is a wonderful series of loopholes the whalers can use to avoid abiding by the will of the majority. In my opinion, the most infamous of these is the ninety-day period for filing objections to any decision that has been taken by a majority of IWC nations but which some country does not wish to obey. In such a case, all that country has to do is send a letter to the IWC secretariat within ninety days saying that it will not be abiding by the law, and it is automatically exempt from it. Thus, as I write this, Norway has resumed commercial whaling even though the moratorium on commercial whaling is still in place—the bad science behind all the attempts by the whalers to lift it having being exposed as bad science and their attempts to justify more killing of a protected stock having failed. But Norway's resumption of commercial whaling is entirely legal. Why? Because back when the moratorium was passed, Norway filed an objection to it within the required ninety days. And so it is perfectly legal for Norway to continue with commercial whaling. Also, back when it was declared that the North Atlantic stock of the minke whales hunted by Norway had been so overexploited as to require protection, Norway also filed an objection to that conclusion within the required ninety days, and so it is entirely legal for her to kill whales of this otherwise protected stock. By this means Norway has her own private North Atlantic whaling ground without the competition from other whaling countries who used to hunt there.

For a while Norway used a wonderful ruse to maintain the pretense that she was abiding by the moratorium. This knavery, which was pioneered by Iceland, is called "scientific whaling." It is quite the thing really. Back in the 1940s, when the Convention for the Regulation of Whaling was being written, one of the scientists present suddenly realized that if he wanted to collect specimens he would have first to apply for permission to do so through the International Whaling Commission, and since it might take several years for such an application to be processed it could interfere deeply with his work. As a result he proposed that each country be allowed to issue permits to their own scientists without general approval from the commission—a suggestion that was accepted and that became part of the Whaling Convention agreements. So when the moratorium was passed we all at once had the spectacle of Norway, Iceland, and Japan suddenly burning with scientific curiosity and expressing with great zeal the desire to do huge amounts of deeply relevant research on whales. Needless to say, the research they did had the unfortunate side effect of producing whale carcasses, and when you have all that meat and oil cluttering up your "research ships," well, I suppose you might as well do something with it—no sense just chucking it overboard and having it go to waste, so I guess. . . well, I guess you just sell it—I mean what else can you do?

When the moratorium came in and Japan, Norway, and Iceland decided to go for science, the difference between scientific whaling and commercial whaling was a little difficult to see. Scientific whaling was done by the same people in the same boats hunting the same whales in the same areas and selling the same products to the same markets. Only now it was called scientific whaling instead of commercial whaling. The big whaling companies had always had a scientist or two on board, and so commercial whaling had produced pretty much the same kind of data now being collected under the new scam. It was as close to business as usual as you can come—or can even imagine that you can come. It is as egregious a misuse of science—the field I love—as I have ever seen. When scientific whaling appeared, it occurred to me that if these people subverted science in this way there was no limit to what they might do—and no end to the kind of destruction that such a precedent might wreak. If scientific whaling is acceptable, what about scientific logging?

The moratorium was passed so that there could be a Comprehensive Assessment of Whale Stocks—a fresh analysis of whale populations during the pause in whaling (the old population estimates and models having been shown to have major flaws). The whalers seized on the Comprehensive Assessment as an excuse for their sudden interest in science, and because it is a requirement that member nations submit proposals of their national research plans to the Scientific Committee (they don't have to abide by its recommendations, but they do have to submit) they wasted the committee's time reviewing their "research plans" when we were supposed to be getting on with the Comprehensive Assessment.

I am sure someone could design a program of scientific logging which had better science in it than many of the proposals we considered. For example, one might propose to clear-cut an area of virgin forest, so as to be able to study the succession of sapling and forest trees which come in—in order to see, for example, which commercially valuable species out-competed which others. But when you had done the clear-cutting you would have all those pesky logs lying about on your experimental lot. And I suppose that you might as well do something with them, not just let them rot.

During my many years of exposure to the IWC I forged friendships with several scientists from whaling nations. At times we would be having a beer together in some bar after a day of meetings in which the Scientific Committee had been considering some "research plan," the principle of which was to enable whaling to continue. And I would look one of these scientists in eye and say, "I know the position you're in and can understand your position, but tell me confidentially, you guys aren't really serious about all this, are you? You don't really mean that we're supposed to be taking this proposal seriously?" And his eyes would lower and in a very soft voice he would say, "Well, we are." In this way, scientific whaling destroyed my respect for several colleagues. It wasn't just those of us on the Scientific Committee who were incredulous about the value of the science associated with scientific whaling; one of the whaling nations even put out a press release clearly aimed at convincing their own population that scientific whaling was important science. Strange that it should have been necessary to point such a thing out to one's countrymen. One usually doesn't see press releases designed to justify the fact that a country's scientists are interested in doing real science.

At the time all of this was going on (it is still going on in Japan), whale science in nonwhaling countries was moving ahead by leaps and bounds through the use of a series of benign field techniques (many of which we pioneered at the Whale Conservation Institute) that made it possible to collect the same kinds of information being obtained by the scientist/whalers, but with this difference: we had demonstrated that if you studied the same questions using benign techniques, you got more representative data, and you got it faster and more cheaply. But the problem is that if you are engaging in scientific inquiry for the sole purpose of justifying a continued whale hunt, you aren't in a position to adopt these benign research techniques because that would defeat the need for scientific whaling. Whaling nation scientists also faced the problem that because these benign techniques really were better, the fact that they weren't able to adopt them put their science way behind the rest of the world. For example, even though the Whales Research Institute of Japan is probably the largest and best-funded such institute on earth, it has not been the leader that such funding and facilities would suggest. Some excellent work has been done there, but with the exception of a couple of remarkable individuals who have adopted the new techniques, the hands of the others are tied. It is a little like what might have happened if for political reasons Sony had not been able to employ microchip technology and had had to keep building all their electronics with vacuum tubes—they would have lost their lead and you would have had to use a wheelbarrow to push around your Sony Walkman.

The Japanese wanted to kill sperm whales in the Antarctic where only males are present. Although there are a great many sperm whales in the world, the vast majority of them are females. (The females live on and near the equator and never show up in the Antarctic.) Because of this it might have been more appropriate for the IWC to calculate quotas for males and females as if they were separate species—the males are probably an endangered species and the females therefore may not be living up to their calf-producing potential simply because of a lack of males to fertilize their eggs.

It is the largest males, the harem bulls, that gain access to females. As a result, everyone is most concerned about saving these rare large males because apparently they are the only ones fertilizing the females. But there's a problem: it is the biggest males that are the most valuable to the whaling industry (which is precisely why they are so rare), and so the Japanese wanted to kill a hundred of the biggest males for "science"—a suggestion which was so clearly a scam that it outraged most of the Scientific Committee. The Japanese proposal stated that what they wanted to kill the bulls for was to study the food habits of large males and to figure out their place in the ecology of the Antarctic. To do this they would have to kill a hundred large males and examine their stomach contents to see what they had been eating. During discussion of this plan, I pointed out that there was data on the stomach contents of thousands of sperm whales from the Antarctic that the Soviets had collected years ago but that had not been analyzed, and that it not only came from a great many more large male sperm whales than Japan was proposing to take, but that the sample came from a much larger area than they were planning to cover. I suggested that perhaps they could gain the same information they were seeking by asking the Soviets to release their data to them, or by getting the Soviets to analyze it themselves.

But the Japanese had done their homework. They knew about that data and were perfectly prepared with an answer to my objection. The Japanese scientist fielding questions on the proposal pointed out that he and his colleagues were interested not just in the stomach contents of the sperm whales, but in what *those stomach contents* (probably mostly squid in the Antarctic) were eating. They were interested in the stomach contents of the stomach contents. There was no data about that in the Soviet sample and the sperm whale stomach contents had not been preserved and could not be used. So in order to come up with an excuse to kill large male sperm whales in the Antarctic, the Japanese delegation had suddenly developed a deep interest in squid biology! They knew that there is no way to catch the squid that sperm whales eat so they were safe in putting forth their proposal to do it by examining the stomach contents of squid the whales caught for them.

From the perspective of a long career in biology I can confidently say that this was probably the most breathtaking piece of nonsense with which I have ever been confronted. It put in deep shade the drama about my credentials. For sheer obliqueness and deceit it simply upended my chessboard, and for once I was speechless. I had grossly miscalculated the depths of deviousness to which my Japanese counterpart was willing to go. I am a scientist. Science is about truth, not about deception. Scientific whaling was bad enough, but I was not prepared for this assault on the very roots of the scientific enterprise. The man who answered me was a colleague on the Scientific Committee, yet he was apparently willing to go to whatever depths of self-deception were necessary in order to please the industry that paid his salary. I was left gasping for air.

Much of the science that the Japanese, Norwegian, and Icelandic scientists were doing during this period was not, in my opinion, science that will make their descendants very proud. It is a matter of record that the Scientific Committee of the IWC didn't see what its relevance to the Comprehensive Assessment was either.

In response to these proposals the Scientific Committee kept pointing out, ever so politely, that the scientific work being proposed was not necessary for the Comprehensive Assessment. Having done so, the Scientific Committee would pass its findings to the commission, which for several years issued resolutions to the member governments politely but firmly criticizing them for the failure of the proposed science to contribute to the Comprehensive Assessment. And every year, the governments of the whaling countries would ignore the recommendations of the Scientific Committee and the resolutions of the International Whaling Commission and proceed in exactly the manner we had always known they would. It was a kind of slow-motion quadrille, a Gothic dance, a posturing in frozen images. The whaling machine ignored everything: reason, public opinion, and the rights of the majority concerning the commons. It simply ground inexorably forward.

One of the most effective strategies of the whalers concerned how their research plans got reviewed by the Scientific Committee. When we reviewed their proposals, the scientists who had written them were present. When the opinion of the Scientific Committee was passed along to the commission, those same authors insisted that it include *their* opinions along with the opinions of the rest of us—no different than if actors insisted on adding their comments to a critic's review. Since most of the scientists whose salaries depended on whaling found the science in each other's proposals deeply relevant to the Comprehensive Assessment, they found a way to hide the clear rejection that the scientists without that vested interest had given to their research plans. They achieved this by insisting on having their own opinions recorded as a separate recommendation. The wording used in these reports was always in the same form: "Some scientists believed that [some viewpoint]. Other scientists believed that [the opposite viewpoint]." This "some" and "others" wording was insidious, because it made it seem to the nonscientist political delegates to the IWC that there was a real debate going on in the Scientific Committee, whereas the strongest support for the proposals came from those who had written them. For a long time the whaling nation scientists even got away with excluding from the Scientific Committee's recommendations the identity of those supporting and those opposing each proposal, because it would have exposed the fact that those supporting most proposals were the proposers themselves.

But the best was yet to come. In 1987 the most senior of the Japanese scientists on the Scientific Committee requested that we exclude in our recommendations to the commission any comment as to whether scientific whaling was or was not relevant to the Comprehensive Assessment of whale stocks. Given that the basis of the moratorium was to have a pause in whaling long enough to enable the Scientific Committee to complete a comprehensive assessment of whale stocks (the very thing that gave Japan the excuse to go whaling in the name of science), we would have been justified in believing that Japan was eager to show us how the whales they were going to kill for "science" would be advancing the Comprehensive Assessment. Yet here was Japan's most senior scientist asking that we not even comment to the main commission meeting on the relevance of their proposal. It was evident that he understood his nation's proposal had little if any relevance to the Comprehensive Assessment and that if we did address the question of relevance directly, the fact that we had done so and found it irrelevant would be stated formally by the Scientific Committee. It was clear that the Japanese strategists had realized they would have a better chance with the full commission if the Scientific Committee said nothing about relevance.

It is for such reasons that I find my days and weeks in IWC meetings such a frustrating experience. One works and works for a year and establishes beyond a doubt that the way forward is X—establishes that fact so clearly that even the most querulous and timid of one's scientific colleagues can find no possible excuse to sit on the fence through the vote—establishing what will become the Scientific Committee's advice. And after they have hesitatingly voted on what is a blazingly obvious point (though watered down into an almost unrecognizably bland version of what everyone knows to be true), the resulting recommendation of the Scientific Committee is forwarded to the Technical Committee, where it gets further watered down before reaching the plenary and where after the full commission has discussed it at length it is finally passed by a majority of the commissioners (in a form which is diluted until it is all but unrecognizable)—even then many diplomats abstain from voting because of political circumstance. But even though the vote is a clear majority, within the next ninety days some whaling country announces that it will not abide by the majority on this point. (The press release bearing this announcement usually states that the nation taking the objection has always abided by the recommendations of scientists in making her decisions—she means her *own* scientists.) It is frustrating—it is maddeningly, dementedly, derangedly frustrating.

For many years Iceland was a member of the commission but has now dropped out. While still a member, Iceland used to treat the rest of the delegates to the commission to periodic scoldings about some decision the commission had taken that Iceland didn't like. As the commissioner for Iceland ranged about over the territory of his speech, I would find myself daydreaming about the fact that with its total population of 240,000[5] people Iceland was one of the smallest nations on the commission. (The four other nations with smaller populations are Caribbean islands, whose combined land area is one-sixtieth of Iceland's but whose combined populations are nearly twice Iceland's.)[6] I wondered how the delegates from China and India who come to the meetings each year might be feeling about Iceland's attitude, given that together these two men represent more people than do the commissioners of all forty or so other IWC nations combined—half again as many, to be precise. I found it curious to look over at those distinguished men as they patiently endured the speeches of a delegation whose entire country's population did not equal the population of many of the cities in their two countries. In China and India there are more than 136 cities with populations larger than all of Iceland (some in this group have populations more than fifteen times as large as Iceland's). Even though many of these have existed for several thousand years longer than Iceland, most of us have heard of only a handful of them. I used to sit and wonder how the Icelandic delegation might feel if it had to sit through the kinds of speeches they gave us from the mayors of those 136 cities—the mayors of Agra, Ahmadabad, Ajmer, Allahabad, Amritsar, Anshan, Bangalore, Baoding, Baotou, Bareilly, Bengbu,

Benxi, Bhatpara, Bhopal, Bhubaneswar, Bikaner, Boshan, Calicut, Canton, Changchun, Changsha, Chengdu, Chongjin, Chongqing, Cochin, Coimbatore, Cuttack, Datong, Faizabad, Fatehgarh, Firozabad, Foshan, Fushin, Fuxin, Fuzhou, Gorakhpur, Guilin, Guiyang, Guntur, Gwalior, Handan, Harbin, Hongzhou, Hefei, Hengyang, Hohhot, Howrah, Huainan, Hubli, Hyderabad, Indore, Jabalpur, Jamshedpur, Jhansi, Jiamusi, Jilin, Jinan, Jinzhou, Jixi, Jodhpur, Jullundur, Kaifeng, Kolhapur, Kanpur, Kowloon, Kunming, Lanzhou, Lianyungang, Liaoyüan, Liuzhou, Ludhiana, Luzhou, Macao, Madurai, Meerut, Moradabad, Munanjiang, Mysore, Nanchang, Nanchong, Nagpur, Nanfong, Nanjing, Nanning, Neijiang, Ningbo, Patna, Pune, Qiqihar, Qinhuangdao, Rajkot, Rampur, Rhotak, Saharanpur, Salem, Shahjahanpur, Shan-t'ou, Shaoguan, Shijiazhuang, Sholapur, Siping, Surat, Suzhou, Taiyüan, Tangshan, Tiruchirapalli, Triivandrum, Tsingtao, Ujjain, Urumchi, Vadodara, Varanasi, Vijayavada, Vishakhaptnam, Wenzhou, Wuhan, Wuhu, Wutunghliao, Wuxi, Xiamen, Xi'an, Xiangtan, Xianyang, Xining, Xinxiang, Xuchang, Xuzhou, Yang-kou, Yangzhou, Yuci, Zhangjiakou, Zhanjiang, Zhengzhou, Zhenjiang, Zigong, Zunyi. You will notice that the above list does not include the really large cities in China and India—for example, Beijing, Bombay, Calcutta, Delhi, Madras, Shanghai, Shenyang, and Tianjin, whose combined population is the equivalent of two hundred Icelands.

Let me be clear about one thing: it is only with the whalers of Iceland that I have my quarrel, not with the rest of the country's population. I have been to Iceland four times, and I admire its strong people and rugged countryside (just as I suspect I would admire the people in the towns I have named above and their countryside if I had been there). But as I see it, because of its distinguished history, Iceland has an outsized responsibility to the world. First, it is a country that did not have an indigenous population of humans whom the Europeans displaced when they arrived. Iceland is also the parent of the concept of parliament (the first European nation to get out from under the rule of kings). So if Iceland's whaling delegation represents one of the smallest minorities on earth—which it does—and if those Icelanders who support Icelandic whaling are to pay anything more than lip service to the concept of democracy, then all Icelanders must encourage their representatives to be less discrepant than they have been in recent years. Iceland's most recent act was to walk out of the commission in order to form another whaling commission—the North Atlantic Whaling Commission—an ill-advised step with an uncertain future that could create great mischief for whales in the North Atlantic, and by its example, elsewhere as well.

Iceland does not own the whales of the North Atlantic. If we accept the concept of human ownership of the world's whales for a moment (an absurd notion, but let it pass for now), then they "belong" to all nations of the world—a world so large that for every Icelander there are twenty-one thousand non-Icelanders—or to put it another way, for every Icelandic family of four, there is an entire city of non-Icelanders the size of Reykjavík.

Having expressed all this frustration about the International Whaling Commission meetings, I feel compelled to express my feelings about what the commission has accomplished. It is my belief that in spite of how terribly flawed its record has been and the fact that it has presided over the destruction of most whale stocks, were it not for the IWC there would probably be no right, bowhead, gray, or blue whales left in the world, and humpbacks (and perhaps fins and seis as well) would probably be extinct in the Southern Hemisphere. For saving those species from final destruction in my lifetime, I profoundly express my gratitude to the IWC.

But I also believe that international organizations like the International Whaling Commission constitute the only way forward . . . are, in fact, the only kind of institutions that ever have made, or ever can make, lasting progress. When the opinions of people are at such deep odds as they are between whalers and conservationists, the lessons of history teach us that the only choice is between this kind of agonizingly slow and tedious negotiation around a table, or the taking up of arms—the latter being a step that has never resolved an issue for more than the time it takes the vanquished to recover enough to raise the same issue again. Of course, it sometimes takes the vanquished many years or even decades to recover, but when recovered, the hostilities resume, often with greater hatred and ferocity.

Every year when I attend the IWC meetings, I am filled with hope that this year will result in some large measure being accomplished, a great stride of progress being made. And every year at the end of my time there I see that we have progressed only a millimeter. But I have been going now for twenty-five years, and that is twenty-five millimeters of progress, and twenty-five millimeters is an inch—a good and solid inch, an inch that I feel is not likely to be entirely reversed over time. I have realized only recently that human progress occurs at something like the rate at which geological processes move continents (it is no faster than the widening of the midatlantic ridge, which opens at a rate of only a centimeter a year), but if it goes on for millions of years, it eventually results in an ocean, stretching out of sight in all directions. I, like many people, keep hoping for more rapid change, but so far we as a species have only been successful in effecting social change at a glacial pace. But if our species can last long enough maybe some future society will finally float in peace on a great ocean of resolved social issues.

What is needed, I believe, is that we face the fact that social change comes incredibly slowly. That is a reason not for despair but to keep negotiating—through this generation, and the next, and the next. For it looks like the only way we will ever be able to make progress out of our own ignorance as a species is to do so through endless negotiation—until we have evolved a common way of being. Until this happens we must never lose faith in the importance of settling our differences by patient agreement—by slow consensus. The process of negotiation is the *only* thing I have ever seen that works toward a true and lasting peace.

Which is to say that I deeply admire my colleagues in the IWC—particularly my political colleagues, the ones about whom I have had the most fun expressing the greatest disdain—men and women who can somehow stand a life of meetings, who can go to them and who through their patience can learn to do what I cannot do—to enable those meetings to create progress. People who have the endurance year after year to drag their bodies through this kind of agony for the tiny grain-of-sand of progress that can be laid in place at the end of each year's meeting—people who see the measure of success in their entire lifetimes as having progressed three inches and yet are mature enough to realize what an extraordinarily solid thing they have wrought. It is these people, not warriors, we should hail as our heroes.

The kinds of twisting and distortion of which some of the delegates to the IWC are guilty of are, in my view, a kind of white-collar crime when you compare them to what goes on on the high seas, the place where the real cheating takes place—the knock-down, hurly-burly world of the open oceans. I have been vilifying the whalers for quite a while, and as we shall see shortly it turns out that there are other dangers besides whalers that pose grave threats to whales. However, it is remarkable that even given what they do in the context of the IWC, many whalers are also simply cheating outright. For instance there was the famous *Sierra*, a catcher boat that behaved more like a miniature factory ship in that it could not just kill a whale but could also bring it aboard to cut it up. It was built in Holland, registered in Somalia, sold to the Run Fishing Company (a company registered in the Bahamas), and backed by Norwegians. It killed almost everything it could harpoon, without regard to age, sex, seasons, or quotas, and is said to have sold its meat to the Portuguese troops fighting SWAPO in Angola. A member of its crew is reported to have said that it once killed a right whale but when they found it was too fat to fit up the stern slipway the whale was abandoned. The *Sierra* was finally rammed intentionally by the *Sea Shepherd* and at about the same time its owners were taken to court for their illegal activities. With so much trouble coming its way, the *Sierra* was finally abandoned.

And then there was the time right after humpback whales had been placed under protection in the Antarctic that the Soviets killed somewhere around seven thousand of them illegally. It was discovered that they were doing so because the Soviet reports included finding a number of Discovery Tags in fin whales that had (according to earlier Soviet reports made when killing humpbacks was still legal) been fired into humpbacks. (Discovery Tags are used to mark a whale so it can be identified later when the tags are discovered in a blubber cooker.) It is probable that whoever was asked to report the tag numbers to the IWC was unaware that the reports from which they were working had been falsified, and that as a result the Soviets reported finding humpback whale tag numbers in fin whales. This resulted in the famous question on the floor of the IWC meeting from the Norwegian delegate Åge Jonsgard to the Soviet delegate Lofitsky. Jonsgard asked: "Lofitsky, can you please tell us how it is you can shoot a tag into a humpback and find it in a finback?" At which everyone laughed, and to which Lofitsky replied simply by smiling and shrugging his shoulders. And that was that— the end of the discussion; all that was ever said about the matter. That was all the justice that those seven thousand illegally killed humpback whales ever saw from the member nations of the International Whaling Commission.

Note Added in Proof

For years most biologists, myself included, assumed that the prohibitions against whaling, though undoubtedly subject to occasional cheating, were probably effective enough to assure that protected species would not go extinct. How naive we all were! With the clarity of hindsight, it seems incredible that we should have been so foolish as to trust the whalers in any way. It is now evident that the only thing that truly saved whales was when the moratorium went into effect in 1986.

Recent revelations by high-ranking officials of the Russian Federation (Alexey V. Yablokov, a science advisor to President Yeltsin, and Ernst Cherny, chairman of the Union of Independent Fishery Workers) indicate that throughout the modern whaling era the Soviets had systematically cheated, and on a massive scale. Yablokov and Cherny were able to unearth the correct data for only a few trips of a few ships—instances in which a scientist who had been on board had kept secret records. The announcement by Yablokov and Cherny was greeted with consternation by those still faithful to the Soviet system and Cherny assumes that much of the secret data from other ships has by now been destroyed. Therefore the numbers they revealed are far from complete and the true degree of the deception will probably never come to light. Even so, the violations they did report are far beyond the wildest speculations of any biologist, myself included.

For example, in 1961 near the coast of southern Argentina the *Sovetskaya Ukrania* killed 1,200 of the rare and completely "protected" right whale. In 1965 two Soviet expeditions (those of the *Vladivostok* and the *Dalnii Vostok*) killed three hundred right whales near Bristol Bay in the Gulf of Alaska, and in the same season a thousand right whales in the Okhotsk Sea. Needless to say, none of these whales was reported to the IWC.

But even when they did report kills, the Soviets under-reported outrageously. For example, in the 1961–62 season (single seasons in the Southern Hemisphere are referred to by the two years spanned by a Southern Hemisphere summer) the *Sovetskaya Rossiya* killed 1,568 humpback whales, although in that year only 270 were reported for all four Soviet fleets combined! Two years later this same ship killed 530 blue whales, though the official reports from the USSR Ministry of Fisheries told of only 74 blue whales being killed that year *by all four fleets*. The total of all these revelations about cheating during the period between World War II and 1972 (with most of the correct data coming from the 1960s) is 48,477 humpbacks of which the Soviets reported only 2,700, and 3,212 right whales of which they reported only one.

Cherny detailed how right from the start the Soviet policy was to cheat. For example, both *Sovetskayas* were designed and built from the ground up with steam pipes installed in their decks so that the decks could be flooded with steam whenever foreign aircraft flew over, thus hiding from view the carcasses of protected species. The KGB orchestrated the entire thing, getting whalers to sign oaths that they would not divulge what was going on. There were always members of the KGB on board, and before entering a foreign port the crews were briefed as to the false numbers they were to give in response to any questions. The KGB also issued codes (changed every few days) so that the whaling fleets could communicate among themselves in secret. As Cherny reports: "The cipher tables contained, for example, such concepts as 'Foreign aircraft have appeared,' 'Foreign fleet is in sight' and, most significantly, 'Sink the prohibited whales'!" (The latter refers to the carcasses of whales being brought back to the factory ship by a catcher boat, or carcasses tied off the factory ship's stern awaiting their turn to be drawn on board for flensing.) Cherny also reported scandals at the highest levels of government involving the smuggling of whale meat to the market in Japan.

Nor are the Japanese whalers without blame. In the 1994 IWC meeting the Russian Federation provided data showing that the Japanese inspector on board a Soviet vessel for which true numbers were found had turned a blind eye to the most flagrant violations. It took years of maneuvering to get even the present pathetically inadequate International Observer Scheme adopted by the IWC. It is now clear that as regards this scheme, the worst fears expressed by conservationists are justified—having Soviets acting as inspectors on Japanese ships and Japanese acting as inspectors on Soviet ships is no guarantee that whales will be protected. It is simply the old routine of the fox tending the chickens.

At the same meeting there was a vote on a sanctuary in the Antarctic first proposed by France. The Japanese had instituted what they called their "Vote Consolidation Operation," a scheme in which they gave aid (usually in the form of the building of some fishery-related project) to a series of tiny island nations in the Caribbean and elsewhere. Such aid, of course, put huge economic pressure on these nations to support the position of Japan in the IWC—a supposition confirmed by the consistent rubber-stamping by these nations of votes important to Japan's interests—in the case of Saint Lucia and Saint Vincent a complete about-face from their record prior to the appearance of Japanese aid.

At the same meeting the sightings data that the Norwegians had been withholding from the commission were finally, though reluctantly, made available. Using this data, Justin Cooke discovered that the Norwegians had made a "mistake" in their data which calculated a population of minke whales twice as large as is actually available. When Cooke recalculated a quota from the corrected population size he discovered it was less than one whale (0.99 of a minke whale to be exact—rather less than the quota of 296 minke whales calculated by Norway for this stock). So even though, technically speaking, the stock of minke whales on which Norway hunts is able to support a quota, it seems a bit tricky for the Norwegians to take 0.99 whales. One might argue that they could wait a couple of years and then kill one minke whale, but the quota is supposed to be spread out over four sub-areas, meaning that they would have to wait five years before being able to take a whale from each area. Faced with this revelation, the IWC decided to ask the Scientific Committee to reconsider the entire situation for Norway. In the process of reaching this decision the Norwegians tried hard to get the IWC to accept the "principle" that their quota would be in effect during the year it took the Scientific Committee to review it. This was a fall-back position from their original attempt to have the quota accepted regardless of what any new calculations might show. Both efforts were failures.

The conclusion to be drawn from of all these revelations is brutally obvious: whalers cannot be trusted. And because there is no way to police the oceans adequately, the only practical way of keeping the whalers from destroying the stocks of whales or even bringing species to extinction is either to stop whaling completely or to set aside a large section of the ocean as off-bounds to whaling. As mentioned above, in 1993 France proposed that the Antarctic Ocean become a sanctuary for whales. At the 1994 meeting of the International Whaling Commission, even though Japan tried to block its formation, a sanctuary encompassing some eleven million square miles of the Antarctic Ocean was adopted by a vote of twenty-three to one—the largest majority in the history of the IWC. (Japan's rubber stamp contingent abstained, and Norway withdrew altogether from the voting.) The sanctuary does not come up for review for fifty years.

On August 12, 1994, Japan announced that she would file an objection to the inclusion of the minke whale as a species protected from hunting in the Antarctic sanctuary. But even if she does try to open her commercial whaling operation there, there is no IWC-approved quota in the Antarctic under which Japan can hunt. But what if she uses her economic leverage to try to get the IWC to pass one? Several nations have already expressed an interest in passing a resolution that will ensure there are no quotas given in sanctuaries. If passed, there will be no Antarctic quota and Japan will not be able to hunt legally in the Antarctic. Unless, of course, she continues her scientific whaling there, perhaps becoming even more interested in the "science" of dead whales by giving her scientists thousands of minke whales to study, rather than the roughly three hundred she has been content to practice science on in recent years. Of course, Japan might persuade nations that are not members of the IWC to hunt whales for her market, or she might hunt whales herself using her own crew and ships but flying the flag of such a nation. This is not unlikely as she has done both before.

Another course open to Japan is to drop out of the IWC as Iceland has done, but that seems an unlikely scenario since Japan presumably has more important economic and social interests on her international agenda than whales. At the 1994 IWC meeting, the BBC's correspondent reported on an interview with the Japanese commissioner, Shima, following the sanctuary vote, in which Shima hinted darkly at Japanese whaling moving into other areas. As I see it, the most likely scenario for Japan is that she will move her whaling operations elsewhere. The humpback whales of Madagascar seem a likely target (and a particularly vulnerable one given Madagascar's economic needs). I fear that what we will soon see is Japan pushing to kill humpback whales there.

The sight of the singer-composer-poets of the sea being served up as strips of raw meat in some high-priced sushi bar would outrage the world and cause more damage to Japan's international image than any nation can afford to sustain. It is time for the Japanese whaling lobby to retire. They have brought destruction to the whales, and disgrace to their country. Both the whales and the Japanese people deserve better.

CHAPTER 8

Killing Whales Accidentally

If I had been born as a whale in the year of my birth (1935), the chances that my parents would have died by harpoon would have been overwhelmingly greater than their chances of dying through other causes. For a whale born in the present day, the chance of dying by harpoon is relatively small—in fact one of the less probable causes. When the Save the Whales movement started, whalers were killing about thirty-three thousand whales a year. When the moratorium was voted in, this had dropped to about one thousand whales a year. The movement managed to stop about 97 percent of whaling. But as it turned out, while we were fighting the whalers two other causes of death for cetaceans had started to rear their heads, which left the problems caused by whaling in the shade. In recent years we had, in effect, our eyes on the wrong ball.

At the same time the careful work in the IWC of scientists Holt, Cooke, and de la Mare was building the foundation for what will undoubtedly become a new way of managing a much wider array of marine species than just whales, the rest of us in the conservation movement were failing to recognize the fact that two new threats to whales, dolphins, and porpoises were growing apace.

One of these was (and still is) the accidental deaths of cetaceans in fishing gear. The best-known killers of cetaceans are the enormous purse seines set around schools of dolphins in order to catch the shoals of large tuna often swimming beneath them. Because the tuna don't necessarily show themselves above the surface, a ship might miss them completely, but dolphins must surface every few minutes for air. Also, the position of the porpoise school is often given away by flocks of birds that fly above the dolphins, tracking them. The reason tuna follow dolphins isn't really known, but the most popular theory is that nothing, not even a dolphin, can outswim a tuna,

302

so the dolphins can't get away from them. And because the dolphins have wonderfully developed sonar and seem to cooperate when hunting for and corralling fish (perhaps coordinating their movements with sound signals), they are able to find and corral prey species that the tuna cannot, or that take tuna much longer to find. So the theory goes that the tuna simply tag along below the dolphin school waiting for it to find prey and then move in and help themselves. The birds that follow the dolphin school from above may well do so for the same reason—that they too are freeloading on what the dolphins catch. Tuna fishermen also exploit the dolphins, not to compete with them for their prey but to catch the tuna that are competing with them, the tuna fishermen thus making up the third species that take advantage of the dolphins' abilities.

When a dolphin shoal is sighted, speedboats are launched from a mother ship. Their job is to round up the dolphins and delay them long enough so that the mother ship (sometimes called a tuna clipper) can drop a "net skiff" off its stern. The net skiff is attached to a mile-long net, and as the clipper encircles the school of dolphins, the resistance of the net skiff and seine net pulls more of the seine off the clipper. The net hangs down about four hundred fathoms and has a cable strung through large rings that are attached every few feet along the bottom. When the clipper has finished surrounding the dolphins and circled back to the net skiff, the skiff passes the other end of the seine to the clipper, and the pursing cable is drawn tight—the rings sliding together along the purse cable until the entire net is bunched up ("pursed") at the bottom. The dolphins and the tuna below them are now confined in an enormous bowl-shaped net that is steadily made smaller by gathering in the net along one side of the perimeter until in the end the fish are confined to a small enough region that they can be removed from the net.

But what about the dolphins, you ask? What happens to them? Indeed, what about the dolphins? That's the problem. If they were sea lions the dolphins would simply jump over the edge of the net known as "the cork line" (the top of the net being buoyed by corks) with ease and grace and leave the scene. But for some reason best known to the dolphins they don't ever do that. Instead they mill around inside the net, and if things go badly they get in under some ballooning bit of net and drown as they try to surface for air. In really bad sets (so-called problem sets), hundreds of dolphins may drown, but a skillful captain can go for an entire season with only a few dolphin deaths. The captain achieves this by a process called backing down in which the pursed seine is dragged sideways through the water and the dolphins allowed to escape across the far edge where the drag submerges the cork line.

When this form of fishing was first invented, hundreds of thousands of dolphins were killed every year in the eastern tropical Pacific. In recent years, thanks to thousands of hours of effort by conservationists, along with several national and international agencies, tuna fishermen finally managed to reduce their kill to around fifty thousand dolphins a year, a kill that is legal and that goes unpunished by that same department of the federal government that (as we saw in chapter 6) fined a man and a woman twelve thousand dollars for filming and patting a pilot whale which dragged the woman under for a few seconds.

There was no real progress in this appalling problem until recently, when several major tuna distributors agreed not to sell tuna fish that were caught by purse seines—a step that seems finally to have had an impact on this problem. That initiative was led by Anthony J. O'Reilly, C.E.O. of Heinz Foods, when he declared that Starkist canned tuna would no longer come from tuna caught under dolphins—something for which dolphin lovers the world over can feel grateful. O'Reilly's move stopped a lot of the setting of purse seines on dolphins but the seines are still used on tuna. A lot of the fishing pressure was transferred to setting on logs or other flotsam under which tuna congregate. (The largest single haul of tuna in history was made by setting a purse seine around an orange crate.) The tuna are smaller than the ones that travel under dolphins, which means we are killing many of them before they have had a chance to reproduce, but at least setting on logs doesn't kill dolphins.

As bad as the problem of dolphins drowning in purse seines still is, it involves fewer dolphins than the number believed to have drowned in drift nets. Drift nets are nearly invisible, very flexible nets made of nylon that entangle any animal larger than the holes in their mesh that touches them. They hang from a long line of floats and catch fish at night, when they are all but indetectable by animals. They were finally banned on the high seas by a UN resolution, except for the Mediterranean, where they are still used by the French, Italians and Irish. Before they were banned, the drift net fishery was the largest fishery on earth. The nets were from six-tenths of a mile to sixty miles, with many between thirty and fifty miles in length. The way drift nets work is as follows: they are set each night and collected each morning along with all the animals that have become entangled and died in them overnight. Every twenty-four hours between thirty and fifty thousand miles of drift nets were set and retrieved in the North Pacific alone. The drift net fleet was principally from Japan, Korea, and Taiwan, when it was the largest fishing fleet on earth.

Drift nets don't limit their catch to fish. It is estimated that each year, in addition to a vast array of nontarget fish (which are simply thrown away), drift nets accidentally killed hundreds of thousands of marine mammals (e.g., whales, dolphins, porpoises, sea lions, and seals) along with millions of seabirds and untold numbers of sea turtles. Entangled in the nets, these animals drowned.

It is likely that in the years drift nets were widely used more whales and dolphins died accidentally this way than from all other causes combined. Though many countries (notably Japan) banned the use of this devastating fishing technique in their own waters, it took the UN resolution to ban their indiscriminate use on the high seas, where only the most rudimentary laws, or none at all, exist to control their use.

Although it is not possible to say just how many porpoises and whales died each year in drift nets, we can get some idea of how bad the true numbers may be by looking at the damage done to porpoises by a very much smaller drift net fishery confined to the shores of the island nation of Sri Lanka (formerly Ceylon). This fishery is minute in comparison to the North Pacific Ocean drift net fishery and is only one of many that exist along the thousands of miles of Southeast Asian coastline, to say nothing of similar fisheries around Africa, Madagascar, and elsewhere. The difference is that the accidental mortality of dolphins in the Sri Lankan fishery was studied and therefore something is known of the size of the dolphin by-catch. The study shows that in the early 1980s somewhere between eighteen and forty-four thousand dolphins were killed accidentally each year in Sri Lankan waters. The nets set by the Sri Lankan fishermen are between three quarters and two miles long. As I have mentioned, nets set in the North Pacific were from thirty to fifty miles long and that entire fishery was the biggest on earth.

Because whales have survived into an age of high technology, they now face threats that make death by harpoons or accidental capture in fishing gear seem pale by comparison: I am referring to the slow but inexorable accumulation of toxic substances in their bodies.

Many toxic compounds are highly soluble in fats but almost insoluble in seawater. For such compounds, the ocean acts not as a means of dissolving them down to harmless levels but as a giant distribution system—a conveyor belt, so to speak—carrying them outward from the continents and depositing them in that ocean of fat collectively comprising the totality of fat droplets and fat deposits in all living oceanic plants and animals. In comparison to the ocean of water, the ocean of fat is minuscule. It is therefore incapable of diluting down to harmless levels the fat-soluble toxic substances that humans have already manufactured and will soon have dumped into the environment.

The most important compounds with these characteristics are called "organohalogens." Many of these are highly toxic organic molecules that also contain one or more halogen atoms (fluorine, chlorine, bromine or iodine). They are widely used as pesticides, fungicides, herbicides, and insecticides—they are, in fact, biocides that are found in hundreds of products. We know them by names like DDT, DDE, Mirex, Aldrin, Endrin, Dieldrin, dioxins (of 75 forms), furans (of 135 forms), PCBs (polychlorinated biphenyls of 209 forms, of varying toxicity), PBBs (polybrominated biphenyls), hexa-chlorobenzene (HCB), benzo[a]pyrene (b[a]p), one of a large family of poly-aromatic hydrocarbons (PAHs), etc. Most organohalogens are no longer produced intentionally, but many arise as accidental by-products of im-proper burning or in manufacturing processes using chlorine. Some are also contaminants found in chlorinated pesticides. As a practical matter, organohalogens are unintentionally produced in such things as combustion of fossil fuels as well as wood (including forest trees during forest fires), in the production of paper (while it is pulp), and in waste incineration, includ-ing the burning of tires. Organohalogens have thousands of uses and are uni-versal in their occurrence.

I will focus on just one of these groups—the PCBs. They are particularly damaging to vertebrates that live at or near the top of food chains where bioaccumulation causes an increase in concentration of any substance that cannot be excreted by animals. I am referring to a process that concerns food pyramids (also known as "food chains" or "food webs").

Diatoms are the smallest plants in the ocean. They are also the most numerous and constitute as well the greatest total biomass of any plants on earth. All life in the oceans, from the tiniest planktonic animals to the largest whales, is absolutely dependent on diatoms to trap energy from the sun. Diatoms are single cells encased in silica shells. Silica is basically sand and these outer shells are really constructed of what we think of as stone. Diatoms would sink like stones and end up in the dark depths of the ocean out of the light they need to nourish them if they didn't have something to prevent this from happening and to keep them up near the sunlight where they can trap its energy. The thing they use for flotation is a tiny droplet of oil. (All plants, even single-celled oceanic plants, contain fats and oils.)

Let us consider the consequences of that tiny drop of oil. When sub-stances like PCBs enter seawater, they are so nearly insoluble that their con-centrations can only be measured in parts per trillion, that is, parts per thou-sand thousand million. But when any molecule of, say, a PCB touches the droplet of oil in a diatom, it will immediately go into solution in that oil—that is, in the diatom. Because the diatom has no way to break down the PCB molecule, it just stores it. Diatoms have fierce microscopic predators, and as a general rule these predators must consume at least ten diatoms before they can divide their cells to reproduce themselves. But the predators can't digest PCBs either, and the result is that each predator ends up with about ten times as many PCBs as there were in each diatom it preyed upon.

The same process repeats itself with each level of the food pyramid; slightly larger predators each feed on prey smaller than itself, and with each new level of predator there is a further multiplication of the concentration of PCBs by about ten times. Whales feed on prey that live between the second and seventh levels of the food chain. This means that the concentration of PCBs they take into their bodies with each meal is between 10^2 and 10^7. The highest concentrations (10^7) represent a concentration of toxic substances ten million times higher than those in the ocean through which the whale is swimming. In fact, scientists have measured levels of PCBs in fish more than twenty-five million times higher than the levels of PCBs in the sea around them. When you take something that is measured in a single part per trillion and concentrate it ten million times, its concentration becomes ten parts per million. With substances as toxic as some PCBs, ten parts per million turns out to be a dangerous level.

For example, in the United States the federal government forbids the sale of any food containing more than two parts per million of PCBs.[1] The law also states that anything containing fifty parts per million of PCBs has to be disposed of in sealed, marked containers at special facilities in which they can be incinerated at high temperatures into harmless components.

Recent analyses of the tissues of killer whales caught in midocean (i.e., far from any local sources of industrial wastes where they might be getting above-normal concentrations of PCBs) have revealed PCBs in concentrations of four hundred parts per million, while there are also records of beluga whales from the gulf of St. Lawrence with concentrations as high as thirty-two hundred parts per million.

But let us now go to Cape Cod, that part of the United States coastal waters so much like Península Valdés. Recently there was a bottle-nosed dolphin from that area whose tissues were analyzed and shown to contain sixty-eight hundred parts per million of PCBs, a concentration 3,400 times what the federal government considers safe to sell, and 136 times higher than the level that would designate it as toxic waste. This animal was, by definition, a swimming toxic waste dump. (By the way, the same species of dolphin also occurs in the waters of Golfos San José and Nuevo.)

Because humans also live at the top of the food pyramids in the sea, people and whales are the animals most at risk from PCBs.

In spite of the high levels of PCBs that have already been found in whales and porpoises, there is no direct evidence about what constitutes a lethal dose of PCBs for any marine mammal. However, there is excellent evidence that one of the general effects of PCBs on mammals and birds is to diminish the ability of their immune systems to fight infection.

In the western North Atlantic about half of the population of bottle-nosed dolphins and 10 percent of the feeding population of humpback whales died in 1987 from what was declared to be an organism similar to red tide. Although they have not yet made their suspicions public, two of the scientists involved in the autopsies of these animals told me that they believed the porpoises probably died from having their immune systems suppressed by pollutants. Since these cetacean species have coexisted for a very long time with the same pathogens that killed them, one wonders why so many suddenly succumbed to these pathogens.

There was recently a die-off of seals in Northern Europe that is also suspicious in this regard. Although it was clearly established that the die-off was caused by well-known viruses (related to canine distemper and human measles), seals too have presumably undergone their entire evolution in coexistence with these diseases. There is growing concern now that these outbreaks could have been the result of damage to the immune systems of these marine mammals, possibly from the accumulation of such toxic substances as PCBs, PBBs, etc. If the current indications are borne out by further research—that these and other toxic substances indeed have a deleterious effect on cetacean immune systems (as they are known to have for other vertebrates)—then one can conclude that marine mammals are being affected by a condition strikingly similar to AIDS as regards its effects on its victims' immune systems.

The AIDS virus is, of course, harmless in itself. No one has ever died of the HIV virus, which causes AIDS. What kills HIV patients is some other pathogen that they are unable to survive owing to the fact that their immune systems have been compromised by the HIV virus. If toxic substances are indeed damaging vertebrate immune systems, then they are affecting life in the oceans in the same way that AIDS affects its human victims, and it is not unreasonable to conclude that the oceans themselves have the functional equivalent of AIDS.

What we have been discussing is the effect of increased concentrations of PCBs achieved, for the most part, by bioamplification as we move up the food chain. There is, however, another mechanism of bioamplification that has not been generally recognized. It only occurs in mammals, and it depends on the fact that when a mother mammal nurses her first young, she also passes to her baby, dissolved in her milk, her lifetime accumulation[2] of those toxic substances that are soluble in fat but relatively insoluble in water. The result of this is that her baby does not start out with a clean slate but with roughly its mother's concentration of PCBs. If the baby is a female, she will, when she matures and has a baby of her own, pass on in her milk an even higher concentration of toxic substances. This toxic load will consist of the substances that the baby who is now a mother collected in the meals that she obtained for herself plus whatever she received from her mother in her mother's milk. The result of this is that as long as we are dealing with substances that persist in an animal's body longer than the intergeneration time, there will be an accumulation of toxic substances from one generation to the next. As far as is presently known, PCBs seem to fit this pattern. If future evidence continues to support this conclusion, then whales, dolphins, porpoises, seals, sea lions, sea otters, and polar bears may all be doomed to extinction. Of course, human beings would face a similar threat were it not for the fact that we can easily sidestep this danger of passing fat-soluble pollutants to our offspring simply by feeding our babies formula instead of breast milk.

Regardless of whether a solid correlation is made between PCBs and damage to vertebrate immune systems, there is one prediction that *can* be made regarding the damage that these substances may cause for humanity if they continue to increase in concentration in the seas.

Of the roughly 1.2 million tons of PCBs that were manufactured before their production was halted, about 15 percent were sold to developing nations, mostly as coolants contained in the capacitors and transformers of power company substations. The proper disposal of these coolants, once the components burn out in the normal course of daily use, involves an expense that most developing nations cannot be expected to sustain, given their other priorities. However, if these PCBs are not disposed of properly, many of them will eventually reach the oceans, and it has been predicted that when they do so, the concentration of PCBs in commercially valuable oceanic fish will rise to levels at which they will no longer be saleable (i.e., above two parts per million). There are no additional steps we must take in order to have this dire prediction fulfill itself. All we have to do to achieve this disaster is to do nothing, to take no steps to collect the PCBs in these components and dispose of them properly.

If we fail to act, the only way out of this predicament in the future may well be to decide that two parts per million of PCBs is too low a measure of toxicity and that in fact it is okay to consume fish with a higher concentration than that. Lest we think that this kind of scenario is unreasonable, we need only realize that it is made with the assumption that all the remaining PCBs scattered around the developed world will be disposed of properly so that just the 15 percent originally sold to developing nations is at issue—a most unrealistic assumption. It is also well to point out that in Lake Ontario, one of the Great Lakes of the United States, the largest freshwater lakes in the world, there is no longer any significant commercial fishery for trout— once its most important fish. The reason commercial lake trout fishing has ceased here is because the concentrations of toxic substances in commercially valuable trout are too high to allow them to be sold.

I have been talking about the effects of organohalogens on the immune system, but there is another effect they have on living systems that is at least as serious and probably more so. That is the ability of many organohalogens to mimic female hormones. In effect we are bathing all of life on earth in female hormones. Examination of this issue also helps to illuminate one of the questions about these compounds that most people ask: why they are so dangerous in such minute concentrations. It is because they mimic hormones.

Hormones are substances produced by one tissue in an animal's body and conveyed by the bloodstream to another, where they affect such physiological activities as development, growth or metabolism. In other words, hormones are chemical messengers which deliver a message important to development, growth or metabolism of an organism. The endocrine system is a set of organs responsible for producing the hormones. Its major organs include the sex organs, the liver, the brain, the pituitary gland, the pancreas and the adrenal gland. Not only does the endocrine system regulate metabolism and respond to stress, it also synchronizes processes such as reproduction and sexual development. Examples of hormones are adrenaline, estrogen and testosterone. The endocrine system is complex and involves interactions (most of them feedback mechanisms) between the hormone-producing organs, the central nervous system, and the immune system. The feedback mechanisms control the levels of hormones circulating in the blood. Thus, the hormones circulating in the blood are chemical signals to some specific part of the body where some specific action of some specific group of cells is required. The way hormones induce this action is to bind to receptors in cells at the receptor site. Once either a natural hormone or a chemical mimic is bound, the activity of the cell is altered in such a way that some specific gene or genes are activated. Thus hormones help a cell to modify itself to become what it must become in order to contribute to the body of which it is a part. Every body cell has within it the exact same collection of directions, i.e., the same genes. It is the specific genes that are encouraged to become active along with the timing and the order in which they do so that determines what a cell becomes (whether nerve cell or a kidney cell, for example, and this in turn determines how the organism develops, grows and metabolizes).

Binding also can increase enzyme activity directly (enzymes are biological catalysts which change the speed of chemical reactions in cells). If the change involves the activation of genes, the genes may produce enzymes that build new cells or modify the metabolism of the cells or change the secretory activity of the cell (which will create a secondary reaction in some target cell that is affected by the secretion, thus unleashing whatever effects those cells are responsible for).

Many hormones are highly complex molecules in which only some relatively small part of the molecule is responsible for producing the significant reaction. The problems with some chemical pollutants is that they have the same kinds of active sites on their molecules that the hormones do, and so those sites bind to the receptor sites of the cells targeted normally by the hormone. Or they block those binding sites so the true hormones can't bind to them when the time comes, say during some critical stage of development. Or some pollutants cause the cell to make extra receptor sites, which amplifies the impact of the hormones on the cell's activity. Other pollutants interact with the true hormones and change the nature of the message they are delivering to a specific cell. And finally, some contaminants simply destroy or stimulate overproduction of hormones so that the natural balance is thrown out.

The human body is designed to respond to hormone messages in the range of parts per quadrillion! But that is the same kind of dose that we get every day from pollutants in what we normally eat. We are now living in a man-made sea of estrogenic chemicals and other toxic compounds. Let us consider just one of these hormones, estrogen. It is one of the most potent hormones controlling human life. When prescribed by a doctor it is given in carefully controlled doses, yet because hormone mimics of estrogens are everywhere, we might as well be using estrogen as a spice with which to lace our food in unpredictable amounts, sprinkling it on our children's meals and adding it to everything they eat, even such healthy foods as vegetables and fish (in fact it is particularly likely to be present in vegetables and fish, which is why these substances are such a threat to whales that eat fish). Fortunately, many hormone mimics are held in places like the liver for long periods before the time comes when they can do their mischief. But when a woman becomes pregnant they are lying in wait within her, ready to deliver masses of copies of the wrong message at just the time when such information has the most devastating effects on her growing fetus. The same copies of the same spurious messages might not affect her husband even though he may be carrying far more of the offending substance than she is—but that's only because he is incapable of becoming pregnant.

I wish to explore a somewhat elaborate analogy. A major skyscraper is a complex environment containing a variety of mechanisms for controlling such basic functions as its temperature, the flow of water within it as well as its consumption of power and air, and the removal of such wastes within it as waste water and air. Let us suppose that our skyscraper weighs 110,000 tons, which is about a trillion grams. Somewhere in that building there is an instruction card with the directions on it for operating the building's heating system. For the sake of argument, let us say that the ink on the instruction manual weighs just one gram (it is thus one part per trillion of the weight of the building). By sheer chance the directions for operating the heating system occupy just 1,000 letters on the card. Among the instructions on the card is the sentence: "Set the thermostat to 70° Fahrenheit." During the summer when the heating system is shut down for the season, some person who isn't employed at the building prints ten instruction cards which differ by only one of the letters on the true card and they scatter those ten cards around the building where the people who run it are likely to pick them up and use them to set the controls. The mimic card says "Set the thermostat to 700° Fahrenheit." In relation to the normal, properly functioning building this single extra zero weighs only a thousandth of a gram, a milligram, and is therefore only one part per thousand trillion, i.e., one part per quadrillion of the whole weight of the building. But when winter comes and it's time for someone to pick up the instruction card and activate the heating system, lo and behold they get the wrong card (there are ten times more of them so the chances they will get the wrong card are ten times as great). The wrong message is delivered to the heating system, the temperature soars toward 700° Fahrenheit and the entire building burns down. A pretty serious consequence of one part in a quadrillion of the weight of the skyscraper.

The example we have been considering is the control system of a skyscraper. But a skyscraper is infinitely less complex than even the very simplest cell, and when you have vast arrays of cells as is the case in higher animals like whales and people, the chances that wrong messages will significantly upset the system are great. That is why even in parts per quadrillion or parts per trillion, hormone mimics can have such devastating effects on living organisms at particular moments in their life cycle. It's because these molecules are really messages responsible for controlling the most basic operations of the living systems that rely on them.

And what sort of effects have they had on human beings? It is all but impossible to make hard and fast connections between industrial pollutants like hormone mimics and human health. Besides, any effort to do so is made far more difficult owing to the efforts of corporations who fear the consequences of such connections and who do everything in their power to discredit the science of anyone who thinks they have demonstrated such a connection. However, there is a burgeoning weight of evidence supporting the theory that several recent conditions have been caused by, or exacerbated by, hormone mimics. The average man today may be producing only half as much sperm as did his grandfather and is at far greater risk of contracting such cancers as testicular and prostate cancer; the incidence of undescended testicles in baby boys has at least doubled in the past thirty to forty years, to say nothing of such genital abnormalities as very short penises, which are found in boys whose mothers were exposed to relatively high concentrations of PCBs prior to becoming pregnant. Not only men are affected. The average woman today is twice as likely to contract breast cancer as was her grandmother. The disease is now an epidemic with one woman in nine due to get it in her lifetime. Endometriosis, an extraordinarily painful uterine disease, has increased dramatically so that among women of reproductive age one in ten will be afflicted by this condition. As for children, those who are exposed to high levels of these pollutants show increased aggression as well as poor performance in school. Both conditions have been tentatively linked with environmental pollutants such as PCB, dioxin, and other organonalogens.

And where do we get these pollutants that are possibly causing such havoc? They are in everything we eat or touch. They are such things as the widely used herbicide atrazine (used on such crops as corn) of which in the U.S. about 100 million pounds are spread annually. Or endosulfan, a highly toxic insecticide used to control insects and mites on vegetables. (Twenty million pounds per year are in use worldwide.) Or hexachlorobenzene—which is simply a by-product of producing pesticides or of burning compounds that contain chlorine. Or alkylphenols, substances used in food and beverage packaging as well as in detergents, and which are also used in the production of polyvinyl chloride and polystyrene plastics (from which they later leach out). Or Bisphenol-A, another estrogen mimic that is ubiquitous in consumer goods such as plastic bottles containing "pure" water and plastic dishes in which prepared baby foods are heated. It leaches out of these plastic containers into the liquids contained within them and gets into the user's body when the contents are drunk or eaten.

These substances also affect wildlife, and because they have fewer friends in court it is possible to do experiments on wild animals and thus to draw tighter conclusions as to what's ailing them. Hormone mimics are now known to be responsible for such things as short penises in alligators; female bears, fish, and snails growing penises; feminized male gulls; and fish-eating birds like bald eagles and cormorants having twisted beaks from eating fish contaminated with organohalogens.

And how did we get into this terrible mess? It's the old story: we looked only at the short term and acted too quickly, looking for deleterious effects over too short a term. The havoc was caused by what were hailed at first as miracle chemicals like DDT or PCBs. For decades we used them indiscriminately, welcoming them into our lives as pesticides, herbicides, fungicides, plastics, and cleaners. Then, finally, in the late sixties and seventies, we began to measure their true long-term costs, but by then our lifestyle was thoroughly addicted to their benefits, and so the costs they exact from us have just kept on rolling up.

We can take control of this situation, as dreadful as it seems, and change our fate, or we can sit back and do nothing about cleaning up the legacy of these highly toxic chemicals and let them keep escaping to the sea until they remove our access to oceanic fish, and kill off all marine mammals but the manatees (which are vegetarians and thus not so susceptible to the substances as animals living higher on the food chains).

It has traditionally been the case that the things that scare us most are those that will kill us suddenly and violently—things like nuclear war. I believe that humanity will not have a swift death but a slow and lingering one. It appears to be not only probable but certain that unless you and I dramatically change our ways, the cumulative effect of the slow, inexorable changes we wreak on the environment will, in fact, destroy all of us as well as many of the most complex life forms.

This can be seen nowhere more clearly than the changes that the ocean is undergoing. And I am not just referring here to large animals like whales and dolphins that are so obvious to us, but also to the vast subarray of organisms on which they depend. One could ask for no better example than the copepod, the food on which the entire host of right whales is absolutely dependent, a species so little known to us that we don't even have a common name for it. Suppose that something we introduced into the sea began to kill off the copepods. And suppose that someone was trying to interest the world in stopping the destruction of them. It would be next to impossible to do so because we would have so little idea of what it was we were trying to stop the destruction of. But copepods have a life; they have an existence.

For example, to a copepod a whale must represent the very concept of fear, a terror so vast there is nothing in human experience or human history with which it could possibly be compared. In order to get some idea of the scale of a copepod's life, let us try for a moment to become a copepod (only one of normal human size) in a crowd of a million other copepods (which would, by the way, be a modest meal for a right whale). Crowds of a million fellow humans are rare but they do happen. Imagine how incomprehensibly horrifying it would be to be standing in such a crowd when suddenly you became aware of something moving across the sky—something so vast that you couldn't quite comprehend its form—something so immense that most of its body was lost within and beyond the clouds—something so expansive that it blocked out the sun, casting a chill over the earth. And imagine a mouth opening slowly into an unplumbable cavern the size of the blackest thunderhead. Then picture incalculably huge, black, rubbery lips sliding noiselessly along the ground on each side of the crowd near the limits of your peripheral vision (moving far faster than anyone could run to escape them), smoothly engulfing all one million of the screaming throng (even including a grove of trees crowded with small boys who were by now dropping onto the ground in their frantic efforts to escape—the trees and the boys just a garnish for this horrible meal). And imagine that having engulfed the crowd, the huge formlessness wheeled slowly in the sky and eased itself unhurriedly above the clouds, leaving stark staring empty and utterly silent the field that only a few seconds before had been seething with a million screaming and frantic people. And suppose that by some miracle, perhaps by being on one edge of the crowd, you, along with a few others, escaped those immense rubbery lips so that now you were standing, motionless and dazed—gazing blankly at the spot toward which this incomprehensibly destructive thing had vanished.

How would you describe what you had experienced? Would anyone believe you? Would you believe it yourself? Would you ever pass a peaceful night again? Or would the horror of that terrible vision invest all your waking hours as well as all your sleepless nights—the possibility of its return slowly but inexorably driving you mad with fear? Isn't it perhaps a positive advantage not to have a brain like ours if such a brain can so easily become a slave to terror—become frozen with images of such insurmountable horror that it can perform no normal function? Would it not just be mindless cruelty to give a reasoning brain to some tiny creature that, because of its size, was completely incapable of doing anything at all to alter its fate? If you were very small, wouldn't it perhaps be a mercy to have a simple brain—one that forgets easily or never comprehends at all—one that simply does not notice or perceive the inescapable jaws yawning above it, no matter how obvious they might be to a reasoning brain? Is it better to have a mind that is numb to risk and whistles a merry tune as the world burns around it than it is to have a mind willing to perceive the threat of a great danger and try to do something to avoid it?

The answer to this is of more than theoretical interest, for there *is* a monster loose out there, one which broods over the world with hot breath, threatening every living thing on earth . . . whose rubbery lips are at this very moment closing over you and me, blocking out the light, ending humanity's brief day, truncating all our futures. The monster is pollution—the accumulation of toxic stuff; the slow poisoning of the earth; industrial wastes for everyone; the diminution of everything we love, believe in, and hold dear; the erosion of earth's ability to sustain us; the graying of all life. We can whistle a merry tune and pretend it doesn't exist even as it swallows us whole. Or we can galvanize as never before and attempt to escape its jaws . . . or drive it back . . . or dismantle it . . . or break our addiction to the lifestyle that breeds it. Maybe it will still swallow us whole in the end but that doesn't matter—for we know it will *surely* get us if we don't act. Even if the attempt fails in the end, the only thing to do is try.

We might like to think it otherwise, but the madmen who made this monster are you and me. Although we try to put the blame on mad scientists or selfish industrialists, it is we, the mad consumers, the selfish shoppers, who are its ultimate architects—because it is we who funded its creation and then went on from excess to excess, wildly multiplying the insane consequences through our insatiable addiction to the heedless lifestyle that is its genesis. We are still addicted. Even as we speak we are still addicted; in fact speaking is about as far as we have gotten.

The incredible thing is that we refuse to acknowledge our creation or deal with the problems it is causing—even irreversible devastation, like extinctions.

There has never before in history been such a dangerous situation, such an iniquitously ubiquitous monster, such an all-pervasive monster, such an attendant participator of a monster. Unlike "the monster who ate the million copepods," this one never flies back up into the clouds. It just hangs around . . . participating . . . joining you. If you sit down you find you have sat upon one of its webbed toes (it wiggles it a bit, smiles, and waves at you). If you take a drink you feel it stirring in the glass. When you rejoice at a fresh salad, it's there rejoicing too. At night it sleeps on your skin and in your hair; and on the clean glasses sitting in the dishwasher awaiting the breakfast juice; and in the orange juice itself nestled in the freezer awaiting the dawn when it will be put in those glasses; and in the tap water that will wash the glasses when you are finished; and on the towels that will dry them; and on the shelves on which they will be set. It is so eager to be a part of you, this monster, so eager to rejoin the rest of its parts which you have already swallowed, that it has splintered itself into a hundred billion pieces of a hundred thousand forms and spread itself like a powder over every surface: on the soil, on the grass, on the trees, on the flowers, in the water, and on everything that you touch and eat and that touches and eats you.

Never before has there been so little response to a grave situation. But this is probably just a consequence of the fact that we have never before had the chance to test just how indolent we were capable of being.

When it's people who have offended us—because they happen to have different political beliefs, or different religious beliefs (or oil we want)—we're quick to spend seventy cents of every tax dollar on a military that will kill them for us by the hundreds of thousands—you know, that will "deal" with the problem. But when the problem is something like runaway pollution that will inexorably make the lives of our children and grandchildren utterly intolerable, killing them not by the hundreds of thousands but eventually by the hundreds of millions (and will disgrace you and me and everyone else in our generation utterly), we don't seem to be willing to do anything at all—even raise taxes by a few dollars a year. We would rather not hear of its existence—rather not even glance in its direction, even though it has fixed us with its burning eyes and is rolling down on us like a towering black cloud in a Kansas dust storm.

Our behavior is that of copepods. We have disconnected from our rational brain and are denying what our senses are shrieking at us. If ever there was a time to act, it is now. There has never before in history been a time when acting fast was nearly so important to the fates of everyone on earth—never a time when it was literally true that every day counts.

Most politicians just seem to wish that the problem of pollution would go away, because openly discussing its dangers won't keep them in power, or get them reelected as readily as outrageously irresponsible statements appealing directly (and very effectively, by the way) to human selfishness—statements like "Read my lips, no new taxes," or refusing to sign endangered species accords because it might cost every American fifty dollars more.

There will come a time, one not very far in the future, when we would fall to our knees with gratitude if only someone could come up with a way to solve the problems of the environment for fifty dollars more per American.

Or five hundred dollars more.

Or five thousand more.

Or fifty thousand more.

Here is a scary question about scary monsters: Should you die in the maw of an omniprevalent monster just because there is no law saying that you have to acknowledge its existence? The future of thousands of species, including ours, is tied up with how we answer that question—not just with words but with deeds.

In 1957 scientists began to monitor carbon dioxide in the earth's atmosphere from the top of Mauna Kea mountain in Hawaii. The reason they chose to work from the Hawaiian Islands is that they are not only the most isolated islands in the world, but also lack heavy industry. They are therefore as unaffected by industrial gasses like carbon dioxide as any place on earth can be, and because they are isolated islands with a market that is too small to support heavy industry, they are likely to stay that way. The reason they chose Mauna Kea is that it is the first point on Hawaii to be hit by the prevailing wind—a wind that has been blowing over thousands of miles of ocean and is therefore thoroughly mixed—and thus constitutes a representative sample of the earth's average concentration of CO_2. The resulting data show the world's average concentration of carbon dioxide. It also reveals that carbon dioxide is increasing rapidly at a rate unprecedented in history and that this rate of increase is accelerating.

These simple data, showing carbon dioxide concentrations over time, have had a profound effect on world affairs. They have triggered a series of national and international conferences and meetings, have played a role in a presidential campaign, have engendered several congressional bills, and have sparked the "Montreal Protocol," an international accord by the world's major powers controlling the future production of "greenhouse gasses." What has happened because of these data has been a wonderful example of the fact that the establishment *does* sometimes respond to very grim news. If the data on carbon dioxide is someday perceived as having alerted humanity in time to save itself, what dollar value might we fairly place on it? A billion dollars? A trillion? More?

Unlike carbon dioxide, the levels of organohalogens in the seas and in marine life have never been measured. However, if they were known, I believe the information might have the same kind of effect that information on carbon dioxide has had. The Whale Conservation Institute has supported the studies of Dr. James Ludwig on the far-ranging Laysan albatross, a species that collects its food from all over the North Pacific. Analysis of what these birds catch in the open ocean helps us determine baseline levels of pollutants in the open seas, away from local effects that may exist downcurrent of some industrial area. Ludwig's work gives us the first inkling of the concentrations of organohalogens that are out there. But other studies will be needed to know how much damage individual organohalogens are doing by themselves, let alone what they may do in combination with each other (a point about which nothing whatever is known).

As this book goes to print, the results of Ludwig's work are not yet in. However, during the course of his research, Ludwig has made a shocking and surprising find. People with whom he is working on Midway Island in the North Pacific started collecting the contents of the crops of dead Laysan albatross chicks whenever they found them. In just eight chicks they found a heap of trash—enough to fill about half a shopping bag. In the crops of these eight dead albatross chicks, there were forty-two bottle caps, eighteen cigarette lighters, a plastic motorcycle, and a double handful of other flotsam, most of it bits of plastic. By carelessly discarding a bottle cap, you can kill an albatross. Albatrosses aren't fools for mistaking cigarette lighters for food; it is we who should know better than to discard them carelessly.

Ludwig went looking for chemicals that kill and found in passing that albatrosses are murdering their own chicks by feeding them bottle caps and cigarette lighters. Ironically, because it's laced with invisible pollutants, the real food of these birds may be just as deadly to them anyway. As his research continues, he's bound to make discoveries that are no less bizarre.

One often hears that because humanity's impact has become so great, the rest of life on this planet now depends on us for its succession and that we are going to have to get used to managing natural systems in the future—the idea being that since we now threaten everything on earth we must take responsibility for holding the fate of everything in our hands. This bespeaks a form of unreality that takes my breath away. Taking responsibility for all of the problems we have created involves not only the necessity that we become intimate with our trash but also that we recognize the consequences of all of humanity's individual and collective actions (e.g., not just the effects of each and every one of the hundreds of thousands of chemical compounds we throw away but the synergistic effects of all these in every possible combination as well as every effect of their combined interactions in every combination—not just with whales but with all eleven million species of living things, or however many there are). We will also have to learn about the effects of these things on the larval forms of these species, and superimposed on this the changing geographical distributions of every species as they respond to the climatic changes occasioned by the increase of greenhouse gasses, etc., etc.

The fact of the matter is that there is no way we can possibly even begin to have enough insight into the system to run it properly—I have seen that in spades when I was dealing with something as relatively simple as a group of about a hundred scientists in the Scientific Committee of the IWC trying to provide the data for management of the populations of whales. The problem is so complicated I know of only three people who even understand it and they have no power with which to put their knowledge into effect. The cost of just finding out enough about the environment to become proper stewards of it—to say nothing of the costs of acting in such a way as to ameliorate serious problems we already understand, as well as problems about which we haven't a clue—is utterly prohibitive. And the fact that monitoring must proceed indefinitely means that on economic grounds alone the only possible way to proceed is to face the fact that by far the cheapest means of continuing life on earth as we know it is to curb ourselves instead of trying to take on the proper management of the ecosystems we have so entirely disrupted.

We can only possibly stop this foolishness if each and every one of us pitches in to change our ways utterly. Nothing less will do. The people whose actions are most critical are those of us who have good educations and live in the developed world. Indeed, it is a symbol of having a good education that we are able to recognize the importance of taking action now. Those who live in the less-developed world should not be expected to respond happily to requests from us (who have squandered our own biological heritage in an orgy of greed) that they now avoid using *their* biological heritage to make their lives better as well. The only way to prevent them from taking that step is by sharing with them the wealth we have stolen from humanity's inheritance.

We do great damage by allowing deadly, nonbiodegradable pollutants to wash downstream and get into the sea, where the sea can methodically distribute them across the planet. And in spite of this fact, we then reach out and tell developing nations how important it is for them to clean up the world we are using as our cesspool. No wonder they tell us to get lost; if it is we who did the lion's share of messing up the world, it is we who should pay the lion's share of cleaning it up. If we want to preserve more natural habitats, maybe we should pay a rental premium to those nations that have not yet done to theirs what we have done to ours.

It is true that many of the people from developing countries would not be acting in their own interests if they failed to do whatever they could to assist in the process of cleaning up, but our request for their assistance might well be preceded with an apology for the part that our nation has played in creating the problem in the first place, as well as an explanation of what steps we are taking to change things now, and of how much money we are spending on it now compared to the amount of money that will be lost by other countries if they are good enough to pay their contribution toward cleaning things up. And if we find that theirs is a greater percentage contribution than our own, we should not be surprised if they reduce their contribution to our level. We should not think of them as ungenerous, but only no more selfish than ourselves.

Organohalogens are among the most dangerous compounds that have ever been released into the environment on a large scale. So why did we produce them? As I have already said, for an enormous variety of things—everything from insecticides, to herbicides, to making plastics shine, or tires more flexible, or cooling large components in power stations. We have stopped producing PCBs now but plastics still shine and power transformers aren't burning out any more often than they ever did, and you have about the same ratio of grass to weeds in your lawn that you always did and the insects have not taken over agriculture the way the lobbyists from the pesticide companies would have had us believe, and the companies that made DDT have not gone out of business—they have just switched to making pesticides that are less appalling. If you think you have suffered because of these changes, ask yourself what year these items became unavailable on the market. You can't remember? Has your life been a nightmare since? My point entirely.

We get along just fine with safe alternatives. For example, to avoid PCBs we should be glad enough to try to get used to eating fruit that is not quite so perfect—it might turn out that we even preferred such fruit if as buyers we were made more fully aware that by eating perfect fruit we were risking appalling developmental problems for our children, involving not just whether they develop normally in the womb, but their ability to concentrate on their schoolwork through childhood and whether or not they are normal sexually when they reach puberty, and if they are boys, whether they can produce enough sperm to sire children. Is serving beautiful fruit on our tables worth those trade-offs? Would it be all that hard to give up our addiction to perfect fruit if we knew what we were actually getting? Once we know the dangers, if we should fail to act it would be safe to conclude that we have a well-developed death wish, or perhaps that the human brain is just a misadaptation—you might say the greatest misadaptation that has yet appeared on earth, threatening its owners with extinction in fewer years than any other adaptation of which there is evidence.

The problem of pollution that I am discussing is one that has been around for a long time without our really addressing it. We started dumping drums of nuclear wastes into the ocean at least fifty years ago, and we still do. It is a problem that we have not begun to solve and which offers consequences we cannot even list. We still have no plan on which we can agree as to where to begin or what to do. There's a lot of that in our history. The castles of Ireland, or indeed of any part of Europe, testify to the fact that if one can successfully avoid the negotiations necessary to settle them, bad problems will last for centuries. The way to maintain intolerably unacceptable situations is to withdraw behind armor.

As weapons became more devastating and we reached the nuclear age we as human beings became so vulnerable to the completely unacceptable risks of a nuclear confrontation that we were finally able to see how critical it had become to solve our problems with each other rather than just continuing to hide from them behind increasingly devastating weaponry. It was at this point that we learned that the stuff of which great heroes are made are not the skills of a warrior but the skills of the statesman and diplomat.

When the Allies defeated Germany and Japan in the Second World War, they prevented both countries from building up armies that could threaten the rest of the world. In doing so both nations were launched into the future in a way they could probably never have accomplished for themselves (it seems clear that the Allies did this without even realizing what they were doing for their former enemies). By requiring Germany and Japan to seek their ends without resorting to force, we prevented them from squandering their resources on arms. In this way we gave Germany and Japan a fifty-year jump on the rest of humanity and a wonderful chance to enjoy the kinds of benefits that the peaceful ways of resolving conflicts have to offer. It seems an unfair reward to two countries whose earlier greed had had such horrible consequences for the rest of us. We now find ourselves up against another threat stemming from our "success"—the destruction of nature and the total pollution of the continents and seas. Although it is a slower death than nuclear holocaust, it may prove just as lethal—maybe more so by killing more of us in the end and destroying more of our resource base. Worldwide pollution offers a good parallel to nuclear war. It wields a power so great that once unleashed it will kill everyone without regard to whose side they are on. We can take a leaf from the book on saving the world from nuclear winter and use it to start the process of saving ourselves from the slow graying and final destruction of humanity through pollution.

We have progressed beyond whaling—well, most of us have progressed beyond it—and have begun, thankfully, to realize that the single greatest problem facing humanity is overpopulation and its single greatest consequence the stress that ever more people put on the environment. The inexorable accumulation of toxic stuff is as dangerous in its own way as an all-out nuclear confrontation. There is little difference in the final result. Although both would drastically affect our world, we seem for some reason more afraid of nuclear war. My guess is that we will be wise enough to avoid a nuclear confrontation but that unless we undertake a massive restructuring of our society to achieve ecological balance, we will not be able to avoid fatally polluting the world, and with it, ourselves. It seems as though massive destruction of the environment is more likely to come about as a result of pollution than of nuclear war—and that unless we act soon, we as masters of the land, and whales as masters of the seas, will meet our end together, and it will come not with a bang but a whimper.

CHAPTER 9

Saved by the Whales

In my view, *Moby-Dick* is the greatest novel, the most inordinate book ever written. That a whale scientist should fancy a book in which a whale is one of the central characters may seem unsurprising, but I find the whale himself the least interesting character in the book. When he was researching *Moby-Dick*, Herman Melville tells us that he had the assistance of "a late consumptive usher to a grammar school" and of "a sub-sub-librarian." In spite of that help, a lot of what Melville wrote about whales we now know to be wrong. It was with Melville as it was with Shakespeare—each viewed the world in the light of the truth of their times and mastered whatever science existed then. Nor were they fooled by shadows (or afraid of the dark). We might suppose that *Moby-Dick* would suit our times better if Melville had based it on better information about whales. But not even Melville could have written a story like *Moby-Dick* now—its view of whales would be too unpopular. In some ways accuracy has constrained as much as it has expanded the literary possibilities of whales. However, there is an essence in *Moby-Dick* far greater than the facts. Alongside the profundity of his observations the fact that so many of Melville's perceptions about whales were wrong is entirely irrelevant—something that would be disturbing only to "a late consumptive usher to a grammar school" or to "a sub-sub-librarian."

On several occasions Melville put aside his perceptions of the "panther heart" of the sea and of the "dangers and affrights" of whaling and wrote lyrical passages about whales that show what he could do when he turned his back on the nineteenth century's fashionable misconceptions about the ferocity of Leviathan and addressed his readers more along lines with which we have only recently grown comfortable ourselves. He was decades ahead of his time.

When creating these passages Melville wasn't just writing an adventure story. His soul was speaking. I have always suspected that he fully understood the role whales might serve in human consciousness if they could ever be properly installed there. It is clear that he knew how to position them best to penetrate the defenses of the human imagination. I have wondered whether the underlying genius of Melville's book isn't that he knew just how and by what steps whales would enter our minds, and how once inside they would metastasize and diffuse throughout the whole engine of human ingenuity, mastering and predisposing it to their purpose. And I think he knew that having penetrated the last defenses of the system, that whales would reconstitute themselves, reintegrate at the point of origin of all the meridians of the imagination, its very pole, and there tie themselves forever into human consciousness by a kind of zenith knot.

Might not Melville have perceived that when this process had completed itself the whale as symbol would have become the whale as puppeteer— would start orchestrating, manipulating, and directing the connections that people perceive between themselves and the beating heart of nature?

We are climbing a mountain, struggling to reach its summit. Several routes seem plausible, but none has yet been proven (since no one has yet made it to the top—though several have died trying). The one who has come closest (the Mallory and Irving among us) is Melville—last seen within an ace of success before a cloud moved across to block his progress from view. But we do know the path along which he was climbing. That is the one on which I am now staking my life. That path is a path into the human mind along which whales swim more easily than we do and with which this chapter is concerned—the same path that Melville started to ascend and that brought him closer than anyone has ever come to demonstrating that whales can help humanity save itself—help us to make the transition from Save the Whales to Saved by the Whales.

In *Moby-Dick*, Captain Ahab meets his nemesis in a whale—I feel it more appropriate that whales are our apotheosis rather than our nemesis. Even with his nineteenth-century view of whales, Melville might find it easy to agree with this view—all he would need to say is: "Go to the heart of the danger and there you will find safety."

The Save the Whales movement was an important first step, but now I think we need to mature by turning that around and making it into a Saved by the Whales movement. Sir Peter Scott remarked that "If we can't save whales we can't save anything." I have come to believe that if whales can't save *us*, nothing can.

This chapter is about whales saving people—what whales can tell us about ourselves and about our predicament. It tries to answer such questions as:

What's wrong with killing whales? Why should we save whales? What do whales really offer humans? What can whales and their songs teach us that could possibly be worth more to the average person than the meat and oil we get from them? Well, for one thing, look at how whale songs have changed our perceptions of whales and how that change has started to affect our views on the rest of life on earth.

Let me offer an analogy: What lessons did the Jews teach the Nazis? One must surely be that the Nazis' beliefs about the inherent supremacy of one group of people over all others were utterly wrong. The Jews put the appalling consequences of that view on public display in an overwhelmingly unforgettable way and thus refuted it forever. Whales offer to human beings very nearly the same lesson—they demonstrate to us that our ancient and ignorant belief in the inherent supremacy of our species over all others is utterly wrong. They put the appalling consequences of that view on public display in an overwhelmingly unforgettable way—and thus refute it forever. What whales offer us is a lesson about tolerance. If we take it on board, it could be the most important lesson we learn during this century.

In 1884 Chief Seattle made an extraordinary statement regarding the way that he and his people felt about the natural world. It has recently been disclosed that the best-known version of this statement was written by a modern writer. Although this has damaged many people's feelings about the speech, Chief Seattle did in fact say some of the things included in the popular version. One statement attributed to him is the following:

> What happens to beasts will happen to man. All things are connected. If the great beasts are gone, men would surely die of a great loneliness of spirit.

However accurate the rendering of Seattle's words, this remarkable statement expresses exactly what I sense will be the most painful loss when "the great beasts are gone" and when we are condemned to live alone for all eternity in the unspeakably boring and monochromatically human world of our own creation. When the whales are in our bay in Argentina, and our days are spent watching them spouting, swimming, courting, sailing, breaching, pushing, and shoving—all at their majestic, glacial pace—or when I see them suspended and floating in the shallows—great, gentle, cloudlike beings drifting with currents too slow to perceive—my spirits soar and I am moved in ways that nothing which is smaller ever moves me.

And then comes a day—usually in mid-December—when I awaken, look out across the bay, and see nothing. They are gone—have departed in the night—leaving me behind. The bay returns to silence, loses its mystery and allure. It is no longer unique, but just like any other body of water. My mind, which only hours before was free and gliding with the whales, is reoccupied with annoying details. I feel peevish and irritable—symptoms, I suppose, of loneliness of spirit.

The emptiness of the bay without whales is a little like the emptiness of a life without the sea. (I could not live in the heartland of a continent.) One of the things that makes the study of whales so alluring is that it puts one into boats and onto the sea. The silence of sailing boats makes them the best choice for studying whales—something I perceive as a kind of miracle of serendipity since I enjoy all that sailing offers; some of the happiest days of my life having been spent aboard sailboats. It is the fact that whales do not come to where you live, that you must go to where they live, that offers the best rewards. I even like the obstinacy of the sea—the way it makes the simplest thing, like trying to take a sighting on a star, a trial of frustration. You wedge yourself between the shrouds that guy the mast and try to make all your alignments of the horizon and some star come out right as the boat reels and at each most crucial moment chooses to all but pitch you and your sextant overboard.

It would be difficult to dissect out from my love of the ocean my love of whales. Perhaps I could explain it more convincingly if somehow I could include a whiff of the sea in this book or the feeling of an ocean swell slipping beneath the beds in which readers are lying, to lift and lower them a few times and give that stately feel which only the ocean evokes. I recall a very rough day off Bermuda in the North Atlantic. It was April 13, 1970, and I was recording humpback whales and had to take a reading on a star that was very close to the Bermuda lighthouse called Gibb's Hill—the highest point on the island. We were so far from land that all Bermuda lay beneath the horizon, with only Gibb's Hill light barely visible. I kept confusing the star I was trying to shoot with the lighthouse, as both were flickering off and on, owing to distant and proximate swells interposing themselves between boat and horizon. It took a long time, but by the time I had finally gotten a star fix, I felt I had somehow placed myself better in the universe than I had ever done before. It is this kind of grounding that living among whales gives to a life.

The brains of whales suggest by their size and complexity a potential for function and/or thought equal to or surpassing our own. Yet we cannot really imagine what it would be like to experience the world through a whale's senses—to staff its control center, so to speak. I once saw another species try to do so. It was a mouse.

Some years ago a sei whale—said to be the fastest swimming of all whales—appeared in our bay. For several days our hydrophones picked up its low calls in the distance, surely one of the most mysterious and eerie sounds on this planet. And then the calls stopped. A few days later we had word that the whale had died and was ashore many miles from our camp. We mounted an excursion to save the skeleton, and we trucked the bones back to camp and stored them along the back of the beach, beyond the reach of spring tides and storm waves. But the truck carrying the skull was too large to negotiate the steep road that descends the cliffs to the bay, and so we off-loaded the skull on the plateau above, where it now lies, alone in the desert, out of sight of the sea, surrounded by bushes. A few years later I paid the skull a visit to see how it was faring. As I surveyed the "decay of that colossal wreck" I thought I saw something move. It appeared momentarily at a round hole in the base of the skull—the so-called foramen magnum, that passage-way through which the spinal cord enters the brain. A few moments later I saw it again: it was the face of a mouse. I investigated at closer range and found that she had built her nest in the brain case of the whale.

This seemed to me a grand transaction between a mouse and a whale. In exchange for the shelter that had once housed the whale's vaunted and enig-matic mind the lady mouse had filled that now-vacant chamber with a whole tumult of smaller, more compact intelligences—and then stuffed in a hatful of twigs and grass to make up for any shortfalls that might otherwise have been perceived.

Could the mind of the mouse possibly comprehend what an extraordi-nary sanctuary she had selected for her nest? While nursing her young inside that allegory-filled cave of the whale's skull, could she imagine the whale's sunless world beneath the sea, into which only the keels of the deepest ice-bergs penetrate; or whole galaxies of phosphorescent creatures, wheeling slowly along; or giant, goggle-eyed sea turtles flying weightlessly past? No matter, it was good, solid housing. It is curious to what uses we and other mammals put whales. It is as if we suffered from some lapse of spirit causing us, in the end, only to seek utility from that which in itself is incomprehensi-ble to us.

We do the same when we hunt animals for sport. To me such hunting shows a lack of imagination. I suspect that the sport hunter is fascinated by animals; loves them, but except by hunting them, sees no other way of bring-ing them into the circle of his or her life. Our greatest hunters—the ones who have spent their entire lives venerating, and killing, big animals—seem to me always to have fallen short of finding an enduring way to interact with what they love. I suspect that in the hunter's heart is a yearning which those who have never hunted can never understand and which, of course, the hunting itself can never fulfill.

I know a man in Japan who has killed more than two thousand whales but who has now abandoned whaling and makes his living taking tourists out to see them. He says he is no longer attracted by whaling and claims to much prefer his present way of interacting with whales. When I met him on my first trip to Japan, I did not know his history, but my attention was drawn to him because his questions about whales were the most penetrating and intelligent of any directed at me during my stay there. When someone told me of his background, it seemed immediately obvious why he had become a whaler. He was fascinated by whales just as I am. He, however, was born into a poor family in a poor fishing village, whereas I was born into a middle-class family in New York City and had every benefit of an excellent education. In his case the only way he could get out on the ocean and see whales was to become a whaler. It seemed clear enough that what fueled his ambition was not his love of hunting but a fascination with whales. If my opportunities had been no better than his I suppose I might have done the same as he.

When I was a child my father thought it important that boys know how to shoot, and I was, briefly, a hunter. However, I soon realized that what hunting offered me was a chance to learn about animals, but that by killing them I killed my chances of knowing even more. So I gave up hunting and started watching animals—a move toward which my hunting buddies were unsympathetic. At first it bothered me to come home empty-handed, but I soon gained confidence that the grace of what was being revealed to me through watching animals was more rewarding than what my hunting friends got from their experiences.

I also saw that they seemed arrested in their development as they became hooked by the pursuit of game bags and trophies—of "larger and larger," and "bigger and bigger."

According to the newspapers, Prince Philip, president of the World Wide Fund for Nature, set as his personal goal the killing of ten thousand pheasants during the 1993 hunting season—a goal that he achieved and for which, having done so, he expressed personal satisfaction. Although I suspect that the papers have it wrong and ten thousand must represent the number of pheasants shot on the Sandringham Estate by Prince Philip and his guests (I have tried, without success, to confirm this), it seems to me that this kind of slaughter represents an extraordinary anachronism in the modern world. Imagine the loading and firing of ten thousand shotgun shells (well, of more than ten thousand shells, since I suppose the shooters must have missed from time to time). Imagine inflicting that much suffering on domestic animals (pheasants in these hunts are really domestic animals since they are raised in pens for the hunt—raised with people feeding them so they must grow to believe people are harmless). And imagine the retrieval of that many dead and dying birds, of the need to wring the necks of the still alive (or whatever technique was used to kill them). And imagine the ones that got away, with only a pellet in them, to crawl deep within some hedgerow to die some days later—perhaps during the hunting party's final celebration as everyone is raising a glass to toast their personal satisfaction for a job well done. And imagine one host and his guests doing all of this—a man who is comfortably maintained by his society to be an example to us all of the best and most-enduring values. And imagine to boot that he has been entrusted by people like you and me to be the head of one of the world's best-known international conservation organizations—I feel that killing ten thousand pheasants in a single season makes the prince of conservationists seem hypocritical.

Trophy hunting is another shortfall in imagination. I began studying whales at the New York Zoological Society, now the Wildlife Conservation Society, whose "Heads and Horns Building" then contained one of the greatest collections of world-record heads and horns on earth—many being gifts from the society's nineteenth-century trustees—at that time the cream of animal-loving (and killing) society. When I was in residence there, these, their most famous trophies, were from an even earlier era and were dusty and slightly munched around the edges by dermestid beetle larvae.

Because the Wildlife Conservation Society is one of the main players in preserving animals and ecosystems around the world, this collection was clearly an anachronism, an all-too-vivid reminder of how unenlightened many of our broadly accepted outlooks have been in the all-too-recent past. The whole collection was indeed an embarrassment and had about it a kind of grandiose moth-eaten irrelevance—not unlike the aristocracy (in fact very like the aristocracy). I thought of past ceremonies in which new trophy heads must have been installed on the wall of the main Heads and Horns room to replace smaller ones, while the tipsy huntsmen swirled the ice in their glasses and laughed loudly at jibes and japes and jests that no one else would have found funny (undoubtedly causing the waiters who served them to withdraw ever deeper into their own inner sanctums—much as the smaller relatives of the animals now hanging on the walls must have withdrawn into their most inner sanctuaries when these selfsame hunters were smashing about their dominions, preparing, as it were, for this party, shooting at them for their heads, hastening the demise of the last of the Pleistocene fauna, and generally desecrating everything—not least their own human natures—or, to put a different slant on it, most clearly demonstrating their human natures).

When in pursuit of a trophy animal, even on the very longest and best stalks, hunters catch only distant glimpses of their quarry during at most half a day. When they get close to an animal's true magnificence it is only for a few seconds. This they call "being in range" and respond to the animal's resplendence by killing it. If bears could shoot, it would be no different than a bear reacting to the most beautiful human in the world by killing him or her so it could stuff her head and mount it on the wall of its den. If the bear could speak and we asked it why it felt it had the right to do such a thing, it might respond that it is a God-given right of the stronger creatures to do what they like to the weaker ones. However, if bears were trying to impress us with how advanced they were, that reply probably wouldn't cut much ice.

From Prince Philip and from trophy hunting I learned two things: 1) the further removed from reality the man, the more offensive he is to those whose lives aren't as far removed, and 2) there is a relationship between the size (and/or the number) of the game killed and the degree to which the moral question is engaged—the rule being: the bigger the bag and the bigger the trophy, the bigger the crime.

Hunters are no strangers to the fact that there is more to be obtained from animals than food. One of the rewards men seek from hunting (though it usually appears that it is sought unconsciously) is an affirmation of their manhood. This machismo (I prefer to think of it as testosterone poisoning) seems to be particularly prevalent in some societies. The effects of this affliction on endangered species are devastating. One discovers again and again that the reason many plants and animals are destroyed is for their supposed properties as aphrodisiacs—even though there is no evidence that there is anything but a possible placebo effect to be had from any such substances. It is in this context that rhinoceros are destroyed for their horns, Amazon dolphins for the lenses in their eyes, monkeys for their testicles, tigers for their penises, snakes of many species for a variety of organs, Houbara bustards for their bodies, and so on. Of all the actions that disgrace men, surely this is one of the worst. How will the endless generations of our descendants deal with the fact that for the most venal and absurdly pathetic reasons there are no more rhinoceros, Amazon dolphins, monkeys, tigers, snakes or Houbara bustards? Is there any deeper disgrace awaiting us down the long road to the future? I don't believe there is.

In 1970 I spoke with Athneal Oliviere, leader of the whalers who still kill humpback whales from open rowboats near the island of Bequia in the Caribbean. At that time they usually killed fewer than three whales a year. In some years they killed none. But every time there was a kill, people came from all over the island to feast on the whale, and the occasion turned into a grand fiesta. I was particularly interested in why they were still killing humpbacks and asked Oliviere if they needed the meat. "Oh no," he said, "we catch plenty of fish here."

"So why do you need to kill whales?" I asked.

"It's not so much that we need to," he replied, "but you simply can't imagine how it feels when you're towing a whale home, and the whole island is lined up along the shore, and with every stroke of your oars everyone is cheering you on." He paused and seemed to think about it for a while, smiling to himself, and then, speaking softly, added, "It's a wonderful feeling."

Whaling off Bequia has become a sport hunt. If you're a member of the whaling crew and have just killed a whale, you're a local hero. You have no trouble getting a date that night. Since a man who needs an aphrodisiac also needs a date, how much different is killing a whale for a date from killing an Amazon dolphin for the lenses in its eyes because you think they're an aphrodisiac? In a world that provides little or no opportunity for men to be heroic, the need to be so (not pettily but truly so) is a serious problem. After all, all that testosterone is there for a reason—ask any biologist. In an earlier time one of its main effects was to encourage its victims to leap into action to save the occupants of the cave (the next generation of its own genes) from danger. But cave bears and saber-toothed cats didn't have .38 Specials; you had a good chance of bluffing them or fighting them off. There were lots of chances, real chances, to be a hero. In spite of its side effects, testosterone was both relevant and welcome. But having accepted the easy life, we find many of the effects of testosterone not only irrelevant but disruptive and downright harmful, not just to us but to other species. Our greatest problem seems to be that many of the adaptations that worked so well to bring us into the dawn of our own history are now clearly maladaptive.

The relationship that hunting has to men's hang-ups about their sexuality is usually more obvious to the onlooker than to the afflicted. For people who don't have to hunt and kill animals in order to feel fulfilled (most women, for example), the complex way in which the primal urges of hunting and sexuality intertwine are at the deepest root of what makes sport hunting offensive to so many people.

When describing their love of hunting, big-game hunters speak of the excitement of the stalk, of having to overcome their fear, and finally of the grandeur of their quarry, and their respect for it. I accept what they say and believe they are speaking the truth. But I also feel that the problem with trophy hunters is that although they are brave enough to face and kill their prizes, they are not imaginative enough to risk a sustained relationship with them, except when they are dead and all possible danger in such relationships is laid to rest. From which it follows that they are not brave enough to admit first to themselves, and then to their friends, and then to the world at large, that they love animals so much that they will, so to speak, embrace them rather than kill them. The challenge is in learning how to live with your quarry—learning how to extract the same thrill, without in the end straddling its dead body—without dominating it utterly and claiming ownership of it.

It is in our human desire to dominate that we have laid waste to even the grandest manifestations of life on this planet—the whales—and we are going from one excess to another as we lay waste to the world itself. Healing this kind of madness must be akin to healing a womanizer who in the end marries and settles down, when he finally learns the deeper pleasure of living with what he loves rather than just continuing to dominate more and primer examples of it. As Eric Hoffer says, "You can never get enough of what you don't really want." How strange it is to discover that what you want most is not what you think you want most (the person you see whom you know you could achieve, the victory within your reach), but to live according to your beliefs—to nurture your soul and watch that take effect on the person you love by interacting truthfully with yourself and with that person—to have nothing to hide from yourself or from them or from others—to live consistently rather than mired in inconsistencies—to enjoy the ease of sitting back and letting truth freewheel through your household—to be what you are by living your word.

How similar this all is to what we must do in order to repair our relationship with the natural world. The challenge before us is to confederate with nature in new ways, without straddling its dead body, or claiming ownership of it, or using it for nothing but short-lived self-gratification. In this way, I believe, we will also heal ourselves.

The hunter shares an outlook with many wealthy men. Each seems to have invested in the belief that happiness arises out of dominating situations, out of controlling and owning things; whereas happiness has nothing whatever to do with these things, any more than it has to do with not owning things, or not being in control. Owning and controlling are simply irrelevant to happiness, have no connection with it. They don't summon happiness any more than owning Melville's writing desk would summon his wit to your page.

Absolute power not only corrupts absolutely, it is absolutely not the path to happiness. Happiness originates in the domestic details of one's life, not in what one commands. I feel that happiness is most likely to be released by the kinds of simple things that are common to all human societies—things like the love of a child, sharing a meal with friends and family, or sharing work, and hard times. I suppose that the sensation of being happy, like many other human feelings, must must have been selected for and shaped through thousands of generations. I guess it to be older than our species—to have its origins in species that antedate ours. That means it would have been triggered for thousands of generations by very simple things—things that were common to the lives of our ancestors and to our ancestral species—things like good health, enough food (too much is irrelevant), or a sense of well-being that comes from being surrounded by troop mates who don't dominate you and who you know well and get along with and on whom you can rely for support when danger threatens. Or having so few predators you feel secure as you watch your family growing or at play around you.

(I think that even avaricious people understand at some level that they can't buy happiness. They *can* buy comfort, and that isn't so bad. But as I see it, most people find the real stuff of the world inaccessible. I presume they don't really disbelieve in its existence—just that they don't know how to get it. Thus they set out to control and command as much as they possibly can—to bring back the biggest trophy.)

Because whales are the biggest animals, whaling is, I feel, the biggest crime. Most whalers seem to have an extreme case of machismo—the iron-men-in-wooden-ships myth. I have often thought that whalers are remarkably similar to the conquistadors. I consider that the conquistadors fixed for all time a price on ignorance. The Vikings were nearly as bad but at least they didn't conquer in God's name. The eyewitness accounts of Viking raids are less detailed than the conquistadors' simply because most of the Vikings left no written record of their activities. Most of them couldn't write. The conquistadors, on the other hand, usually had someone along, some priest-chronicler, who could.

These chroniclers described the unique civilizations that the conquistadors discovered. They described the marketplace in Mexico City, giving a detailed description of the articles of clothing sold there—including head-dresses and capes woven of gold and feathers, made by artisans employing a technique never found elsewhere and never achieved since. The Aztecs created architectural wonders that put us in awe but which the conquistadors simply tore down. This fact suggests that when the conquistadors were impressed by the garments they saw in the markets of Mexico City those garments must have been astonishingly beautiful.

On one occasion Cortés heard that a rival group of would-be conquistadors had landed on the coast and were headed for Mexico City. He marched half his force back to the coast, killed the rival leader, incorporated that man's followers into his own forces, marched them back to Mexico City, and added them to his army. While accomplishing all of this, Cortés left one of his generals, Pedro de Alvarado, in command in Mexico City. Unbeknownst to the Spaniards, a great Aztec religious festival—a kind of harvest celebration—was scheduled during Cortés's absence, in which the citizens of Mexico City appeared in the main temple at night to dance the Macehualixtli. They danced naked under torchlight. Their bodies were oiled and covered with pearls and jewels and precious stones with "plumes of brilliant feathers nodding from their heads." Cortés's general, Alvarado, sealed the doors to the temple, slaughtered almost every one of the thousand people inside, and stole all their jewels. Here is the way the Indian chroniclers described this event:

> They ran among the dancers, forcing their way to the place where the drums were being played. They attacked the man who was drumming and cut off his arms. Then they cut off his head, and it rolled across the floor. They attacked all the celebrants, stabbing them, spearing them, striking them with their swords. They attacked some of them from behind, and these fell instantly to the ground with their entrails hanging out. Others they beheaded; they cut off their heads, or split their heads to pieces. They struck others in their shoulders, and their arms were torn from their bodies. They wounded some in the thigh and some in the calf. They slashed others in the abdomen, and their entrails all spilled to the ground. Some attempted to run away but their intestines dragged as they ran; they seemed to tangle their feet in their own entrails. No matter how they tried to save themselves, they could find no escape.

One of the things which Cortés's priest-chronicler stresses is the way in which the practices of the Mexicans deeply offended the god-fearing Christian Spaniards. The conquistadors explained away their behavior by pointing out that they were christianizing idolatrous pagans and saving souls for God.

When, in response to this and other atrocities, the people of Mexico City started to resist more forcefully, Cortés formed an alliance with a jealous neighboring tribe (from which his mistress came), attacked the city, and destroyed it utterly. The city was organized in a string of island blocks raised above the level of the lake and connected by causeways. The technique Cortés used was to fight each day for another block. Having conquered it his men would burn it to the ground, reducing everything that remained to masonry debris, "until there were no two stones on top of each other." The following day they would conquer the next block and repeat the process. Thus they continued, in the most methodical way, until they had rendered the entire city into rubble.

Cortés and his men were the only Europeans who ever saw Mexico City or the culture of the Aztecs intact. Having discovered this remarkable civilization, they destroyed it utterly, before anyone else even got a glimpse. Of course, they turned even the art of the Aztecs into rubble—melting down countless uninventoried treasures into relatively worthless lumps of gold (which they sent back to Spain aboard galleons, many of which were lost at sea in storms).

I see in the history of the conquistadors something very similar to the history of the whalers. These men reduced the civilizations of whales that only they ever saw intact to rubble by rendering them into casks of fat (later into freezersful of meat). Having discovered in the Antarctic the greatest herds of whales on earth, they destroyed them utterly, before anyone else even got a glimpse.

What we do with whales (or with other large mammals with the potential to inspire us) takes the measure of our souls. When we turn them into meat and oil, we demonstrate that we have no souls (or only little, wizened souls). We reveal that we aren't up to the challenge of whales—that our ignorance of what they offer humanity and our prejudice against nonhuman life are too profound. When we kill off populations of any large mammal it is the same; it makes no real difference whether we are destroying giraffes, or rhinoceros, or elephants, or whales. It is the same crime. It requires exactly the same shortfall of imagination to mount a rhinoceros on a wall as it does to turn a whale into cat food.

Large animals are intimately entwined with our history. We have come far together: they have been with us all the way. But along the way we have killed off so many species that walked the earth when we first appeared. We have killed off the relatives of modern elephants, rhinos, deer, horses, ostriches, tigers, etc. The versions of those species that are still with us are just a remnant, all that remains of the once-great Pleistocene fauna. It is only in historic times that we have been able to threaten whales. Before that we didn't have vessels that were seaworthy enough. The Pleistocene fauna found a refuge in the seas—a stay of execution. As a result, a much greater percentage of the Pleistocene fauna remains in the oceans than has survived on land.

Whalers are turning the largest animal that has ever lived (and as far as we know that has ever lived anywhere in the universe) into meat and oil. We excuse this by saying that we have the right to put other species to human uses. And our leaders often justify their arguments against conserving species whose benefit to us is not visible to most of us by asking why we should save an animal that has no direct benefit to humans. The demand that species should be in service to humanity, coupled with our failure to see the benefit we could find in most individual species (to say nothing of the totality of species—the global ecosystem), is probably the most expensive and irreversible piece of ignorance our species has ever exhibited. The problem stems from being unable to appreciate the value of another species unless that value is measured as a commodity.

As a species we should have now progressed far enough to put aside forever the presumptuous and primitive view that to justify its continuance the wild world should be of some use to us. It's at best a nineteenth-century point of view—and, by the way, the clearest possible indicator of an inadequate level of education in any country professing that view. Whales have so much more of value to offer people than what we have taken from them. From a lifetime of living among whales I have grown to see that one of the lessons they can teach us best is the folly of thinking of life solely in economic terms. Their present status shows clearly the results of that approach.

When we started killing whales we were harvesting them for economic gain. But now we have gone beyond that and have begun to realize that though we can put their direct killing under quasi-rational control, the killing won't stop. In fact it is accelerating. What is killing whales now is the destruction of the seas. The only way we can stop this is to change the basis of our ways, to change utterly the value we accord nature. This seems to many a daunting task, since the only way we can change ourselves enough is to develop a universal respect and love for nature.

If we are to turn ourselves around by the millions, we need to look at our options. The Church used the power of love. Ecologists might profit from what the Church has found to be a successful strategy. If the power of love can change people on a grand scale, then perhaps it could be used to try to save what's left of the wild world.

But how can people fall in love with nature when all but a small percentage of them never see anything but the inside of a city? One way to do this is to start with an animal, any animal capable of capturing the imagination. My candidate for an animal commensurate with everyone's capacity for wonder is, unsurprisingly, a whale. I think that television carries the key to getting city dwellers interested in whales, and that it is not unreasonable to assume that once sparked, their interest will lead to a wider interest in nature. City dwellers are not automatically opposed to nature, they are simply uneducated about it. For the first eighteen years of my life I was raised in the heart of New York City and therefore know what it's like to have that start and nevertheless end up falling in love with the natural world.

Why are whales a good choice through which to get people to act to save the world? Why not some other animal, or even no animal? Why can't people alone inspire other people to act? I think it's because people don't really trust each other enough. They look at someone who is trying to help solve a problem as someone trying to sell them something.

But we do trust children, and we trust animals. We trust the reality of animals—and we trust big animals more than small animals, which is to say that we trust the reality of big animals more. We are all more easily captivated by something big. The bigger it is, the more captivated we seem to be by it. It is not just a coincidence that as of this writing the most successful film ever made (as measured by its success at the box office) is about dinosaurs—not about some sports figure, or war hero, or president, not some love story, but a story about dinosaurs. People are fascinated by big animals. They should be even more fascinated by a whale, since next to a whale, *Tyrannosaurus rex* is just a cute li'l tyke.

This should make whales the champion captivators of all. People simply don't forget the first time in their lives that they saw a whale. They never say to you, "Well, I just can't remember whether I've ever seen a whale or not." (Or if they do, then you know they haven't seen one.) Unless someone had first cultivated some kind of interest in art, they might forget whether they'd seen an original Rembrandt, but they wouldn't forget whether they'd seen a whale. The French writer La Rochefoucauld once remarked, "I doubt that anyone would fall in love who had not first read of it." I believe, however, that when seen up close a whale is such an awesome presence that one need not have heard about it first to be deeply impressed. Whales are intrinsically impressive and are therefore uniquely suited to introduce people to a feeling of awe about the wild world.

Besides being impressed, we are all much more likely to be interested in an animal if we know something about it—if there is a body of information that tells us fascinating things about it. Suppose for a moment that fleas were endangered. If you were trying to save them, I think that your only hope would be to learn a lot about them. You would have to know enough to fascinate people into action to save them. You would have to learn about what kinds of lives they led, how they dealt with getting from cat to cat, how they handled a crisis when the single hair they were holding onto broke off, how they avoided the cat's tongue, how they survived when the temperature dropped to twenty degrees below zero, how they made it when the sun was fully on the cat, why they wouldn't dry out then, how they selected the best place on the cat to lay eggs, whether they caught on to the trick of taking up residence on some spot on the cat out of reach of its tongue or its hind legs (or are fleas what make cats so supple?), how they avoided jumping right off the cat in surprise (and thus losing their free ride—and perhaps their life), and so on and so forth. Answers to all these questions might just prove sufficiently fascinating to lead others to act on behalf of fleas and from that first step to widen their interest in the environment.

What I am saying in this example is that conservation is simply a state of mind. That all we have to do to save the world is to change how we view the importance of the wild world. Saving the world is not a job that requires some highly developed technology, or some arcane new science, or some hitherto undeveloped social system. It requires that simplest of things— changing our minds. One could argue that the most difficult thing anyone ever does is to adapt to a new view, but that would not change the most salient fact about what's needed: the fact that what one believes to be important is under one's total control. The fact that only we ourselves have control over our own minds puts the job of saving the world squarely in the lap of each of us. It is not some other person's responsibility, but ours. We are not waiting for something to happen before the time is right. We are simply waiting for each one of us to make up our own mind about how we treat the wild world. Not someone else's mind (we cannot change that), but our own mind. This is the challenge of the future—what we must accomplish if we are to save ourselves and some significant fragment of life on earth.

I feel that most conservationists are looking for less-sweeping reforms— approaches that are only Band-Aids when what is needed is major surgery. Band-Aids like establishing watchdog committees, or passing new laws, won't work. The way through to the future is by rethinking our priorities and by starting reforms—as sweeping as the moral shift that ended slavery.

If what I'm saying contains a grain of truth, how do we go about achieving such a moral shift? Again, I feel it can be started by getting people to fall in love with the wild world. We defend freedom with our lives; we don't defend it because it has a favorable cost-benefit ratio. We preserve it, fight for it, even die for it, because we love it so passionately that we will not live without it. I feel the same way about the wild world, and I sense that I am not alone.

I love freedom as much as anyone, but I place the value of the wild world above the value of freedom—at least above a freedom that can only be defended by spending a trillion dollars on military hardware while ignoring the stress we are putting on the environment.

I doubt that you can get people to fall in love with whales in general; I think it's more effective to start with a particular individual whale. It is knowing an individual that causes us finally and inexorably to be bonded to a species (to fall in love with it). And it is this kind of bonding that finally sets our feet on a path to action. There are many whale-adoption programs that give people information on a particular individual whale. Once a person sees (several years from now) that their animal is fighting a curiously persistent infection and hears that several of its compatriots have died of what seems to be the same infection the person gets mad—mad enough perhaps to do something about it.

People who live near the sea may get to know a particular whale, but people with access to whales comprise a tiny percentage of us. So how do we get this process started for people who live nowhere near whales? I think the process can start by adopting a whale and following its progress, or by injecting whales into all of human culture. This means getting whales and images of whales and sounds of whales into films, schools, offices, art, poetry, sculpture, dance, theater, ballet, opera, literature, music, churches, public spaces, etc. I have spent much of my life trying to get creative people to build into their films, curricula, logos, paintings, poems, sculptures, dances, plays, ballets, operas, books, songs, sermons, murals, etc., the beauty of whales and of the natural world. I did so because I feared that unless we negotiate a peace with the rest of life on earth, we will spend the rest of our existence in a world made entirely by humans, where nature is gone, a world whose bible—in which the virtuosity of the creator is extolled on every page—is the mail-order catalog.

By becoming a focus for human creative energies, whales have taken hold of our collective imagination to the point where many people now value them not just as animals but as part of our heritage—classifying them as World Heritage Sites along with Druid stone rings, ancient Indian burial grounds, or the Dreaming Places of the Australian Aborigines. Because they fire our imaginations so effectively, we can often marshal the political clout needed to set aside areas of the earth to protect whales—the recently established sanctuary for whales in the Antarctic (the largest sanctuary in the history of the world) is an example. Such sanctuaries also become havens for lesser-known species of animals and plants that are so necessary for life but that because they have not inspired us have no friends and therefore die alone. The principle seems to be this: if you wish to save an area, save its most inspiring inhabitant. The rest will be maintained along with it.

Because whales now have so many advocates and have taken on an international luster, it is not surprising that they have also attracted opponents among the ranks of those from whom one might expect support. One sometimes hears the complaint that too much time is being spent on such glamorous beasts while the bootless cries of a myriad of lesser-known species go unanswered. That is, of course, partly true—*but* there is a vastly practical reason for focusing one's efforts on saving major species. This relates to the fact that whales are the apex of the pyramids of life in the sea. Many cetaceans are top predators and feed on animals that are themselves the second through the seventh steps in food chains that start with the single-celled microscopic plants called diatoms. If you wish to save the apex of a pyramid, you must save the entire pyramid. If we are trying to ensure a viable population of whales—the monarchs of the sea—we will have to set aside enough of the oceans to ensure an abundance of everything on which whales feed and through which they swim.

The irreducible minimum ecosystem is a food pyramid with a single pair of predators on top. But it is a doomed ecosystem unless enough such pyramids are preserved to ensure the perpetuity of the predator species. In this sense a whale does not exist apart from its pyramid . . . it is one with its pyramid . . . it *is* the pyramid. It is much the same with kings and queens. The word "king" or "queen" defines an office, not an individual. Monarchs who have lost their subjects and been dethroned have no meaningful existence. They are like anybody else—lost in the crowd and soon forgotten. It was once good strategy in conservation to identify animal and plant monarchs and work to guarantee their kingdoms. This seemed to be enough, but now we are aware that the ways in which we have an impact on the world, particularly through pollution, have cumulative and synergistic effects that destroy the substrate on which all life depends. We now see that if we are to save ourselves and at least some of the rest of life with us, we must change our actions and our premises in the most fundamental ways. We must be concerned with the totality of all the intersecting, interlocking, interacting pyramids—the whole of life on earth.

It has been accepted for many years that integrated animal societies that are made up of individual organisms (for example, ant colonies or beehives) are in fact a single entity—a "superorganism." Some years ago the concept was advanced that the whole of life on earth is a super-superorganism called Gaia, and that it is responsible for regulating and maintaining the conditions on which its own life depends. The elements of this super-superorganism, though individually mortal, are collectively immortal, and the laws that govern them are natural laws.

Would it therefore be outrageous to call these mortal elements which are collectively immortal and which define life on earth God? And to call the immutable laws that explain them God's laws? When I take this step, several things fall immediately into place: for example, I can understand why I feel rage when a species is destroyed—the destruction of any element in the totality is a blow struck directly at the God I worship—my God being life on earth—Gaia. It also points out that there need not be a dichotomy between religion and science, since we can use science to learn about God. In fact we can, through science, beat a direct path to God, always staying on course and never being diverted, no matter how slow our progress.

Science is not antithetical to religion. A scientist is more like a surveyor than the preacher of another religion. Scientists run sight lines and formalize boundaries around religion, occasionally taking over some of the ground that religion was claiming as its own (the creation myths of several religions have yielded ground to science).

The study of whales is not just a collection of curious facts about big, blubbery animals that cavort in the seas; it is for many people (though I am not one of them) the study of a mystical presence with which we share the planet. In the present state of affairs, whales are perceived by these people more as prophets than as monsters or barrels of oil. It is an interesting switch from how we viewed them a century ago.

There are two ways for religion to accept this state of affairs: one is to fight it, the other to adopt it. Rather than being threatened by science, religion could make science its strongest ally—could recognize that as a means of understanding the works of God, science may be what religion has been praying for. It seems to me that although they are produced by mortal human intellects, the distinct discoveries of science are fragments of an all-encompassing immortal intelligence called natural laws. They are unit ideas contained within an incomprehensibly larger idea. In this sense they are rather like those mice nesting within the braincase of the whale. I sense that if the human mind could be made visible we would find a tiny mouse mind nesting in the overarching mind of the cosmos.

I have long felt that the love of all life on earth (a concept that is interchangeable with the word "conservation") needs to be written into religions—is, in fact, overdue to become a religion in its own right. Should religions accept this and it come to pass that there was a religion with science at its root, I would not feel that science was an inadequate base upon which to build a belief system like a religion. On the contrary, I think science can uplift the soul, give the spirit wings, and teach it how to soar. Science can lead us to revelations that faith cannot. As I see it, it can provide insights as deep or deeper than those faith provides. Some scientific truths transcend religious beliefs and illuminate Gaia. In this way they are more like artistic creations which "do not imitate actuality but transcend it and illuminate reality."[1]

In my own experience I have found that at their best the revelations of science are as inspiring as art. I am a cellist and at several periods of my life have spent more time playing chamber music than I have doing science. Although there is nothing I have enjoyed more than music, I can testify that even the intense delight of playing a Beethoven quartet does not exceed what I felt when I learned about black holes, or drifting continents, or replicating molecules, or how life might evolve spontaneously, or even, dare I say it, that the complex utterances of whales were actually songs. In fact I find these are spiritual delights and compare favorably with those derived from religion and music. They make interesting companions and do not clash, as my formal education tried to persuade me they did.

I feel that science has a role to play not just in conservation (in my view the most important current human activity) but also in the more spiritual parts of our lives. We have long recognized the essential value of science for resolving conflicts over how a species could be managed (for instance, how quotas could be set or hunting seasons fixed). But that is just its journeyman's duty. Unless we can inspire our own species with a sense of the magnitude and sweep of what will be lost by our failure to act, we cannot ever hope to inspire any major changes in how we view other species and hence in how we treat them. I feel that just as the only way to save the wild world is by developing a deep love for it, so must we rely on science for the evidence needed to convince us of how serious our mistakes are and how crucial the need to act is.

In the process of making such a major change at least two steps are needed: 1) what a friend of mine calls "getting the listening," followed by 2) presentation of the most compelling arguments. Science can provide the compelling arguments, but it has been shown over and over again that it cannot "get the listening." Art and literature and myth are the things by which we "get the listening."

Even if we don't survive ourselves, we won't kill life off completely. But we will do it great damage. Though deeply disfigured, life on earth will continue nevertheless. The sun is not due to balloon out and burn away the earth's atmosphere for another six billion years. That is long enough to evolve life on earth again from scratch to its present state, with one and a half billion years to spare. It is twelve times longer than the period since the pre-cambrian—the time it has taken to evolve animals that look like what we think of when we think of animals. (Before that everything had a soft body and a largely unfamiliar form.) So even if we do self-destruct, or if some successor species with our foibles arises to make the same mistakes we have made, the earth will probably have time to re-create the prehuman paradise at least twelve times over. There have been many mass extinction events, the most famous of which ended the dinosaurs a mere sixty-five million years ago. Mammals, birds, reptiles, amphibians, and fish all survived that mass extinction, while fish have survived four others, amphibians and reptiles three others, and mammals one other such event. So if what we ever do to life on earth is no worse than what ended the dinosaurs, there could be ninety-two re-creations of the prehuman paradise before the sun ends life on earth for good.

I suspect, however, that what will happen will be a little less violent, though inconceivably tragic. I think that again and again we will be thrown back to a very primitive form of ourselves in which we will eke out life in a primitive state, recovering slowly as the life on which we depend re-speciates and eventually recovers. Every time we gain enough control to live comfortably once more, I suspect we will blow it all once more by overproducing ourselves and, like Sisyphus, will fall back to a primitive state and have to start all over again, straining to roll our boulder up the hill.

The only way I can imagine that we will kill ourselves off entirely is to poison the atmosphere and the oceans so badly that we cannot survive in them—or that our food cannot survive in them (though we would, I am certain, be shocked to see the kinds of things on which a truly desperate human can subsist). If we do that, however, I suspect that only the very hardiest life-forms will make it, which means there will be a throwback to a far more primitive earth—perhaps one similar to that which existed before plants and animals—one with the kind of atmosphere that we could not breathe. But perhaps we will so damage the atmosphere that only single-celled living organisms like bacteria will survive—or, unthinkably worse, that we will create a runaway greenhouse effect and incinerate the earth with temperatures on the surface hot enough to melt lead, as has happened (from unknown causes) on the surface of the planet Venus. If that should happen, life on earth will never recover, and our greatest monument will be that it was we, who so prided ourselves on our wit and intelligence, who destroyed Gaia single-handedly—destroyed her with our own seamless greed and ignorance. I can imagine the mind of Gaia dreading the advent of the human mind—praying with each passing aeon to postpone it for yet a little longer.

If through our own greed and addiction to our present easy lifestyle we should take ourselves out, or do so through some all-out confrontation over some incalculably minor differences between a couple of groups of us, I could somehow understand that. I will get it. For I realize that this is one of those terrible flaws in the human way of being. I am prepared for that possibility, but the thing I cannot stand is the thought that we might take the rest of life with us. This fills me with a greater rage than any I have ever felt. It heaps me, it overmasters and overflows me like some kind of mental volcanic lava. There are failures and there are failures, but such a one would be beyond grief—beyond all pales, all possible forgiveness. I don't wish to be a member of a species that could do such an insane thing. I don't care what name it does it in. I don't care how seriously it takes its mission, it would simply be too lunatic to countenance. When I think how near the Soviets and we Americans came to confronting each other fatally with our full nuclear arsenals (the threat, of course, still very much exists) over differences we never really fully understood and which now are a little hard even to recall, and when I think what has happened recently in the Soviet Union, and how hard we in the United States are trying now to help the very people we were prepared to confront with a force so violent it would have sacrificed our entire civilization and perhaps life itself, I am thunderstruck by how out of touch with reality we can be. That kind of quixotic behavior—that willingness to trample all life in the dust and mire of some overblown confrontation of concern only to some small group of humans—is symptomatic of a mind that simply isn't worth it—that cannot be forgiven for this ultimate madness—not even in the light of its greatest past accomplishments. The work of no Shakespeare, no Beethoven, no van Gogh could ever atone for the consequences of such a huge measure of insanity. If we were to destroy life on earth, whatever else our accomplishments, we could only be considered a mind that never should have happened—a failure too vast to be countenanced even by the very brain in which it was housed.

I want to ask now, in greater detail, just what is it that we can learn from the brains of whales. The great problem we face is that we don't really understand what it is that whales do with their brains. So I will have to approach what their brains might mean to us through a rather indirect route.

In chapter 4 I discussed songs of humpback whales and tried to guess at what they mean. But because they are still so deeply enshrouded in mystery, I want to look at the songs in a different way: I want to consider the possible value of humpback whale songs as a message about the seas and about life on earth that whales can convey to people.

Whales and humans seem to have an interesting kind of bond—call it a bond of mutual curiosity—which appears to form automatically and surprisingly often when whales and people find themselves face to face. This bond also seems to occur when people hear the songs of whales for the first time. It is as though our two mammalian brains have more in common than we are aware and that we really may have significant things to say to each other—despite our isolation for the last sixty-five million years—if only we could find a communication channel. Meanwhile we are signaling to each other with every gesture, every sound, every hint of what may someday qualify as meaningful communication but for which meanings are not yet known.

It is fascinating that it should be in the sea that we find a brain as fancy and complex as our own (perhaps even more so). It invites us to make comparisons between our brains and those of whales. The most obvious difference seems to be that we have a lethal component in the way we use our brains that is missing in whales. They haven't threatened their own survival in the past few hundred years—not even in the past thirty million years, as we shall see.

In the past twenty years there has been repeated speculation about whether we or whales possess the greater intelligence. I have stayed out of this discussion because it is obvious that we have no clear idea as to the nature of the intelligence abiding in the brains of whales (or our own, really). It all depends on what we mean by intelligence. If we mean an enduring intelligence, then whales are the winners hands down, simply because they have been around for tens of millions of years longer than we have. Besides, they do not use their extraordinary brains to do things that can destroy the world; judging from the rate at which we are increasing the threats to our own existence it is hard to feel much confidence that the human line can match the whales' term on earth by persisting for fifty-eight million more years. Whales show that it is possible to own a complex brain without threatening one's existence and the rest of life on earth with it. Whales have had their most advanced brains for almost thirty million years. Our species has existed for about one-thousandth of that time. We have a lot to learn from whales. They know how to avoid destroying the world. We don't. We could learn how to use our brains in such a way as not to destroy the world with them. (What would a lesson like that be worth? A trillion dollars? More? All the money that was ever minted and printed?)

Whenever anyone tries to measure the difference between humans and other closely related animals (e.g., our closest relative, the pygmy chimpanzee), the only significant difference seems to be that we invented language. It is language, of course, that enabled us to go on to invent cosmologies, philosophies, mathematics, vocal music, art, poetry, and nuclear weapons.

Language is such a complex and intricately colored art that once an animal has a brain that can handle language, the same brain appears to be able to handle Hegelian philosophy, Boolean algebra, or string physics as well. If that is the kind of mental activity that we call intelligent, then it is all but certain that *we* are the greatest intelligence on earth. However, one of the unwelcome fruits of a language-capable, thinking mechanism like our own is that we now have the power to threaten our own existence, and with it that of millions of other species. What moral can we draw from this? That the human brain is a wonderfully exciting thing to own but when there are billions of copies of it around all working away at once with different and in some cases directly conflicting agendas it can take on an uncontrollably destructive potential that can cause us to question seriously whether it can coexist much longer with the rest of life on earth. (Just how much of a compliment is it to a dolphin to claim that it has the same mental capacities that we have?)

The function that humanity can serve in the scheme of things is to be the omnigalactic brain of it all, the final miracle of the creation—matter able to meditate upon itself and by this process to elucidate the miracle of life. If we detach entirely from our roots, rip them out and burn them, we find that we become self-creations in a self-created world, and we abrogate our responsibility entirely and no longer serve the one kind of function that such an otherwise destructive creature can serve.

This is just what we appear to be doing now. We are destroying the complexity and variety of life rather than illuminating the miracle of the creation and displaying the magic for all to marvel at. Once we have completed our destruction, we will, from that time on, be condemned to study only our own trivial concepts.

By failing to take any action to prevent further extinctions we are killing the big mysteries, and our understanding of the complexities of life on earth will be forever frozen at whatever level of comprehension we will have reached when we destroy the last whale and the last flower and allow them to take to their graves their last secrets.

All of this must surely also have consequences for our own mental health. I believe that as surely as it is destroying biological diversity by bringing species to extinction, our destruction of the wild world is affecting our sanity—we need whales not only for possibly valuable pharmaceuticals, but for songs, for inspiration, adventure, wonder and excitement—in other words, to help make life worth living. If we are only comfortable thinking of whales as a resource, let us think of them as a resource for sanity.

I recently returned from New Zealand, where I slept on board a boat in

Milford Sound, a spectacular fjord on the South Island, inhaled the purest, sweetest air, and saw the stars so bright they seemed like members of our party. In the morning a sunlight so clear fell on the land that it restored my life and my sanity from the eroded condition it had been in when I arrived there jaded from Los Angeles and London.

I believe there is something akin to a substance that flows into one's being from the wild that cannot be seen or measured, and which is not tangible in terms we recognize as scientific, or economic, or in any way yet demonstrable, but which is nevertheless very real and very important to mental well-being.

It is a sort of celestial phlogiston, which comes from flowers and vast beaches and deserts and oceans populated by species other than our own. This substance restores souls, and sets minds straight, and rebuilds moralities, and cleans up the wreck and wrack and rust that we generate by endlessly rubbing against our fellow humans. It is the substance that is drained entirely out of city dwellers until they are a hollow husk of the full ripe ear of their pastoral ancestors. In this husklike state, urban humanity falls prey to such things as heart attacks, hypertension, stroke, and addictions to violence, drugs, and God knows what—a syndrome I'll call urbanicide. It is a kind of self-destruction by reason of nervousness, an aggressive state that is somehow hastened by disconnection from the fountain of nature.

Millions of dollars are spent each year in efforts to cure this plague of humankind. The cure is already at hand. What is needed is long draughts of the natural world. Not beaches or small national parks shared with tens of thousands of other humans but areas that owe their existence to nature and not to humanity. Silence is an incredibly important part of the cure, as are restful views with no human-made things in view, not even sky glow at night—nothing but stars, sand, and sea. That will do us well. The only hope for making such cures available when their value is finally appreciated is to let the land that can produce them be.

The admonition in the Beatles song "Let It Be" is, in fact, consummate medical advice for an ailing world suffering from an overdose of its own civilization. It is dead obvious to anyone who has ever taken a vacation that involved hiking or camping that the farther they got from the rest of humanity the more refreshed they felt when they returned. There seems to have been no serious investigation of the restorative medicinal value of the wild world. As I see it, one of the most terrible deprivations that inner-city children endure is their lack of contact with the natural world—rather like a plant growing in a pot that is too small so that it becomes root bound. I expect that for such a person the discovery of nature is no less of a shock than that which a homeless child feels when it first lives in a house that has a bed, a bathroom, a kitchen, a roof over it all—and a door the child can shut. This is what I love so deeply about the wild world. It is a door I can shut on the city—a room of one's own—on that frantic, empty, hollow, glitzy, violent, myopic, aggressive, dead-blind lifestyle which is called urban.

I feel that we should recognize that our progress lies behind, not ahead, of us. That to make progress is to undo the knots we have tied and the snarls we have created. Anyone who has watched an army march into a cul-de-sac would tell its commanding officers, "Your future lies in going back."

In that respect what is happening to some whales offers a parable for our time. When I first started to study the right whales at Península Valdés in Argentina, there were only a few of them. In the twenty-five years since, they have increased strongly. They have gone from being a tiny band to a boisterous rabble. Because I watched this river of living whales from the start of its flow, I have seen it change from a freshet to a torrent. When I see the bay now it is starting to feel a bit more faceless, crowded, strangely the way you feel when you witness a quiet rural place become populated, then suburbanized, and finally incorporated as a town. At Valdés the right whales now seem to exist everywhere. The bay is riotous with their presence. It is truly a miracle in this otherwise waning world to watch a species wax, and start reaching back in time to its former abundance. The sea lions and elephant seals in the area are also doing this and now their harems stretch for miles and miles. They practically encircle the entire hundred-mile outer coastline of Península Valdés.

How deeply exciting to be able to re-create the Pleistocene simply by leaving things alone—the fact is that there is a creator waiting to create the perfection we destroy. This creation can start simply by our leaving nature alone.

The progress that we are making with right whales is not that they are being exploited but that they are being unexploited. In so doing they are being returned to their original untouched numbers where they achieve more good for humankind than they ever could possibly have achieved as blubber, or margarine, or meat for cats and dogs. We have saved them in time for them to become our salvation. In my view we are more in need of what the example of their peaceful lives (led in remote but beautiful places) has to offer than we are in need of anything else that ever came from the sea. The sea has never offered us a better lesson than that of the whales that recovered and brought back something of our sanity before it left us entirely.

So what will we lose if we fail to slow down our mad rush forward before we destroy thousands of other species? What would we lose if we were to continue polluting the seas long enough to lose the humpback whales and with them their songs?

We have witnessed a similar event on land with the red wolf in Texas. Coyotes and red wolves are closely related and have such similar chromosomal structure that they began to interbreed after 1940, when the numbers of red wolves had fallen and coyotes were moving in from the west to fill the predatory niche that the wolves were vacating. Through genetic swamping the remnant red wolf populations gradually faded away until by about 1970 the last pure group of the Texas subspecies which had once lived south of Houston along the Gulf Coast was gone. A similar fate overtook the central subspecies though it survived for a few more years in southern Louisiana and in extreme southeastern Texas. However, it no longer exists in its pure form. Back in the late 1960s a friend from my youth described an experience he had one Texas night with a graduate student, far from towns, howling for wolves. They were red wolves, now the rarest form of that increasingly lonely species. He and the graduate student were unsuccessful, though they tried repeatedly to raise an answer. Once my friend imagined he heard a reply, a wavering sylvan cry from the infinite stars and grass surrounding him, and then it was gone. He wonders if he really did hear a call. From my discussions with him I suspect he did. If my friend Tom is right, the last contact anyone ever had with red wolves in Texas was when some unnamed graduate student called to them and was answered by a lilting, fading cry that only *may* have been there. Since then there has been nothing but arid, utter, numb silence.

The passing of some species has been measured by the year, day, or even hour when the last surviving captive has been found dead on the spotless floor of its cage in some zoo. Thus the last passenger pigeon, a female, died in the Cincinnati Zoo on September 1, 1914, eighteen years after the last of her kind was seen in the wild. The last Carolina parakeet died alone and far from its haunts, in 1918.

With most species it is otherwise. Only by examining recent history is it slowly realized that So-and-So, a farmer, returning late one evening on his tractor from his fields, was the last to see, flashing through his lights, such and such a species. These are the last visual records of the last of a species. But the visual presence of some animal is not all that will be missed when it is gone. I care more for the howl of the wolf than for its merely doglike look, and when the last howl of the last wolf has filled the night, echoed and died out, something of us all will pass with it into a kind of mute invisibility.

And so it is with whales. There may come a time when, in some remote, moonlit ocean glade, deserted of humanity, the last call of a humpback whale will start, and spread out, and then vanish, until those who heard it last will only wonder if they heard it at all. And in this way each whale species will make its final exit until the blind continents, banked in their beds of silent ooze and moving like slow clouds across the molten face of the earth, will no longer have whales to cheer and guide them but will take their way in silence and alone.

Wolves, redwoods, eagles, whooping cranes, peregrine falcons, and whales have in common that they are large examples of their kind whose numbers have been drastically reduced in recent times by the activities of humans. Remote and imperturbable, the lives of whales are somehow enough to match any fantasy humanity can create. They are what we have lost, what we yearn for. They are in some ways the last wild voice calling to the consciousness of terminally civilized humanity, our last contact before we submerge forever in our own manufacture and irretrievably lose the last fragments of our wild selves.

I have wondered whether, as we lie on our deathbed, drifting ever closer to oblivion, surrounded by increasingly elegant televisions and computers, plugging more and more directly into ever more electro-optical links, more videographic, stereo-electronic nonrealities (all the while looking forward to the onslaught of 3-D, holographic, high-definition, virtual reality), slipping, submerging, subsiding into mental oblivion—into terminal civilization—I have wondered, I say, whether the whales are trying to call us back from the edge, back from our lost and mesmerized state, or whether they, along with the rest of life on earth, are just relieved to see us self-destruct?

The major obstacle to solving the environmental crisis is clearly apathy— the feeling that it is already too late and that nothing we can realistically expect to achieve will be able to reverse the kinds of problems we face. I see this as being at the root of the self-destructive behavior of many young people who have obviously lost all faith in society and now believe there is no future and so have simply dropped out. They, along with many, many others, appear to be completely daunted.

In contrast to this view it is my feeling that the problems we face provide us with the most singular opportunity for greatness ever offered to any generation in any civilization. Although I share everyone's frustration at how slowly environmental awareness is spreading, I have not the slightest doubt that in a very short time, environmental problems will be the major focus of everyone's concern. People will all be fighting for their lives and will finally have identified the enemy. I am just old enough to remember the attention that people gave during World War II to international news. Local problems took the back burner, and had anyone suggested that it would be nice to start, say, a natural history museum in their town in the middle of World War II they would have been greeted with incredulity and reminded emphatically, "There's a war on!" I have no doubts that this will be the kind of greeting nonenvironmental concerns will receive in the not-too-distant future.

The whole trick, obviously, is to get the attention of the world as early in the process as possible while solutions are still feasible. That is why I believe that mass education is the most urgent step we must take and why it will be the most important field on which the battle to save the world will be fought.

I have discussed earlier the fact that humans have a lethal aspect to their brains that whales lack. I wish to go further in asking the question of how our brains differ, but to do that I need first to determine just how far our brains have gotten us in figuring out our rightful place on this earth. One way to approach this problem is to examine the kind of environments human brains have made possible about which we can feel unqualifiedly proud. I want to know what our proudest boast is.

The usual answer to this question is that we have put a person on the moon and a robot on Mars that could search for life there, and most recently we have completed a grand tour of the solar system past Jupiter, Saturn, Uranus, and Neptune with the unprecedentedly successful *Voyager* space-craft, both of which are still in good health and are now moving so fast that they will leave the gravitational influence of our own star and spend the rest of their expected 1.2 billion years of life (making them, by the way, the longest-lasting of all human creations) drifting through the rest of our galaxy.

I can relate to that answer. When *Voyager II* passed Neptune I was out in Pasadena at the Jet Propulsion Laboratory, where I had the privilege of watching the images it sent as they formed on the JPL monitors. And I learned all kinds of new things—for example that there are scientists pas-sionately concerned with such arcane things as how the solar wind—that blast of particles constantly radiating outward from the sun—interacts with the magnetic fields of the planets.

On one of the days I was there, *Voyager II* passed through the interactive zone where the solar wind is deformed by the planet's magnetic field—the so-called bow shock wave—of Neptune. All that night we could hear the engineers celebrating over how well *Voyager*'s aging instruments had re-corded that rite of passage.

But when I refer to assessing the progress of our species and identifying what our proudest boast should be, I am not talking about technological whizbangery or more comfortable living through science, I'm talking about something else: how we as a species would be perceived before, say, the court of intergalactic opinion. I think that today a visiting alien from some other space-faring civilization of equal or superior engineering competence to our own would give us an encouraging pat for our recent increase of toleration to other members of our own species but would judge us harshly on how unclearly we perceive our place on this planet and how unrealistic our view is of our own importance in relation to the rest of that larger miracle called life.

Let me spare us further embarrassing judgments at the hands of the galaxy's more advanced civilizations or before the court of intergalactic opinion, and instead take a deep, honest look at ourselves. Let's look more closely at *Voyagers I* and *II*, and their grand tour of the solar system. Having flown by all of the planets beyond the earth except Pluto, they will carry on out of the solar system, spending the rest of their lives wandering elsewhere in the galaxy. On the incredibly small chance that in that time some other space-faring civilization should encounter one of these spacecraft, messages were put on board them—pictures, sounds, human voices sending greetings in sixty-one human languages, music including African chants, works of Bach, and even something by Bill Haley and the Comets. But also on board was a recording of a few minutes of a humpback whale singing. Suppose some other being does find this "bottle cast into the cosmic ocean," as Carl Sagan put it so well. Think of what will be communicated. After all, it is not just the words, music, and pictures in a spacecraft that would carry the message. The whole concept of sending a spacecraft carrying words, music, and whale sounds conveys a message about what we are like and what we believe in, conveys it in a way that perhaps few things could have done more forcefully. For it tells another civilization that by the time we sent this message, we had begun to recognize some other species besides our own enough to give it at least a little bit of room on board. If we had sent a recording with the songs of tens of other species and only one sound of human voices sending greetings it would have been an even prouder boast as to where it is we see ourselves in the scheme of things.

So just where do we stand? Just how far have we advanced in the direction of wisdom? I feel that true wisdom amounts to one thing: it is tolerance—plain and simple. From which it follows that more tolerance is more wisdom, and that the growth of wisdom is the growth of tolerance, and that it is tolerance of others, not domination of them, that is the mark of a wise civilization.

Speciesism is like racism—neither is any less ignorant than the other. Let me consider racism first. People are unaware of how closely related we are as a species and fail to note that whether we are black, white, brown, yellow, red, or fluorescent, we are one family, one people, deeply and intimately and inextricably related through millions of complex connections and interweavings. For example, the races of humans have 99.9 percent of their genes in common. That includes all of us—Aborigine (Australian), Amerindian, Aztec, Chinese, Indian, Inuit, Ju/hua (Bushman), Korean, Maori, Masai, Mediterranean, Melanesian, North European, Polynesian, Pygmy, Tibetan, and Yanomamo. The reasons our similarities seem so obscure to many people is that it is the mostly insignificant genetic differences between us that tend to find their expression in the way we look, while the more important, underlying genes controlling the things about us that aren't visible (the way we are, our biochemistry, probably even most, or all, of the way we think) are almost identical.

The 99.9 percent similarity of the key human genes means that 999 out of every thousand key genes in us are the same. How pathetic to be thrown so horribly by differences that amount to less than one thousandth part of our beings. Would anyone in their right mind die over one thousandth of their share in some contract? Would a thousandth of any deal be so important that you should walk away from it unless you got the last one thousandth part? Yet that is what we do when we are ruled by racial prejudice. Are there any grounds for not feeling ridiculous about this?

There's another argument that applies here: the race of *Homo sapiens* that had the longest period of relative isolation from other races, is probably the Australian Aborigines. However, even if we assume that a generation (the time between the birth of parents and the birth of their offspring) was only about fifteen years in our relatively short-lived ancestors, the isolation of the Australian Aborigines from even the most opalescently white of the Nordic races has probably not been longer than twenty-seven hundred generations (40 percent of the sixty-seven-hundred-generation history of our species) and much less than 1.6 percent of the total generations of our genus, *Homo*, which, surely, amount at the very least to 167,000.

If we could trace our ancestors earlier than one hundred thousand years ago, we would find that every human now on earth had precisely the same ancestry. Of course, those 40,000 years constitute less than one one-hundred thousandth of the 4.5-billion-year history of life on earth. Regardless of your race and mine, given that 99.99999 percent of our ancestors were exactly the same, is it not ridiculous to consider that the last hundred thousandth of our history is so profoundly important that we should subjugate, enslave, even kill each other over it? It seems to me that many of our worst human problems stem from the way in which our incredibly short lifetimes distort our view of the relationships between ourselves and others, and between ourselves and the rest of life on earth. Our tendency to kill other people because of the most minute distinctions between us (e.g., different political beliefs) is madness when you realize that one thousand years from now people will have no idea what we were quarrelling over. (For example they will probably not even know what or where the Soviet Union or the United States was—how many of us could discuss the chief issues at stake in the Battle of Salamis in 480 BC? Yet thousands of men died fighting over them.) This kind of struggle presumably comes from the fact that from the standpoint of reproductive success, people are programmed to fight over everything. You may be only 0.001 percent different from me genetically, but I am still in competition with you over resources (e.g., who pays for a meal, who gets to date the best-looking person in our school, etc.). Because the payoff is reproductive success—representation of one's genes in future generations—modern sociobiology predicts conflict between unrelated individuals. We try to counter this ancient force with philosophic and moral argument—a form of mental activity we call rationality and in which we take great pride (it has been pointed out, however, that if the world was rational men, not women, would ride sidesaddle). Presumably if we pay more than lip service to the desirability of acting rational, then we should be beyond letting minute differences between ourselves destroy our lives and those of others, and we should get on with preserving the world together so as to insure that our ancestors have at least some chance of survival.

The most recent human who is common to the ancestry of all modern humans has been named "Eve"—I'm not referring to the Bible but to the "Eve hypothesis," which states that we are all the descendants of a single female of the genus *Homo* (and almost certainly of the species *sapiens*) who lived in Africa between 140 and 290 thousand years ago. Although it is now agreed that we will have to learn more than scientists know at present before we can figure out where, and how long ago, "Eve" lived, there *is* general agreement that all humans are, in fact, the descendants of a single female. (Her father was, of course, our common male ancestor.)

As regards classism, racism, and speciesism, what can be said about how far we as a human species have progressed? Well, let's start at the basics: we have learned that murder is just not acceptable. We have also learned, although it certainly took us far too long to do so, that slavery is a no-no. And we are slowly learning that other religions and other races have rights that are equal to our own. We are learning as well to tolerate a wide variety of sexual preferences in others and we are learning that women must be given equal opportunities. And, surprise of surprises, we have discovered that even children have rights, as do the homeless and those with incurable illnesses like alcoholism, as well as the mentally ill. In short, we are, more and more, at least professing that we understand the importance of being tolerant, even though we may fall far short in our practice of it. What does all this amount to? It says to me that we have learned to tolerate (at least in principle) a lot of variability in our own species and in that sense have begun to put our own species' house in order—but that's about it. This we have done to the extent that we have learned to recognize the value of most forms of ourselves.

What about our recognition of the rights of anything beyond ourselves? That needs work.

Where do we stand as speciesists? I think that at the moment we are stuck on the bottom step of a long and daunting stairway that any primitive species must climb in order to make its long, slow way upward out of ignorance and prejudice and toward the light of tolerance.

We understand in a theoretical way the importance of maintaining peace within just one species—our own. Although you and I may like them, African farmers don't like elephants, or rhinos, or hippos, or lions. And sheep farmers don't like wolves. And Eskimos don't like polar bears. And Iki Islanders don't like porpoises. And Newfoundland fishermen don't like humpback whales.

Thousands of species may be irritating to you and me—things like weeds, rodents, coyotes, snakes, crocodiles, sharks, insects, ticks, spiders, centipedes, sand fleas, worms, jellyfish, parasites, mildews, molds, yeasts, bacteria, viruses, retroviruses, and so on. Presumably each of these nonhuman organisms is also irritated by a host of other organisms. They probably do their best to overcome the things that compete with and annoy them, but no matter how hard they try, none of them is able to threaten the whole system that supports them.

But we can. And we do.

We now have the power to devastate pretty much anything we don't like, as well as a lot of things we do. In fact we are now finding that the things we don't intend to destroy are the things we are destroying most (we achieve this through overpopulation, erosion, habitat loss, reduction of biodiversity, pollution, accidental entanglement, etc.). We have become an incalculably powerful force for unintentional annihilation. We wield more power than we can even comprehend. It is our latest stage of development—our newest talent—that recently acquired characteristic of which we have yet to become aware.

Because of the position in which we find ourselves, we need to make respect for the rest of life our highest priority—not just respect for our own species and those species we like, but for the thousands of life-forms that are "of no benefit to us" or are irritants to us. (It is unlikely that any species is "of no benefit to us," and very likely that we fail to recognize the benefits it offers.) The reason it is so important that we learn to tolerate the rest of life is that it is only through diversity and complexity that the stability of the ecosystem on which we are entirely dependent is maintained. Thus when we destroy other species unintentionally, we destroy diversity—a step that always moves us in the direction of destabilization of the world.

The most simplistic solution to this problem is to learn to put the rights of all other species on a par with the rights we claim for ourselves. This doesn't mean we have to stop eating other species, but it does mean that we have to harvest sustainably what we use and learn to stop sacrificing the rest of life just to satisfy our whims. When we have learned to accord the rest of life on earth equal rights, we can finally take our place in the court of inter-galactic opinion and while holding our heads high claim: "Yes, there is intel-ligent life on earth. And it is our species which demonstrates that the blind force of evolution is capable not just of self-destruction but of self-enlight-enment."

I feel that the message we have sent to the rest of our galaxy by putting whale songs aboard the *Voyager* spacecraft is evidence that we are just begin-ning to have a new awareness. (The message is not some hokey nonsense about how superintelligent and humanoid whales are—we have no idea whether such is the case and anyway it wouldn't be much of a compliment to them if they were.) I believe that we are just now entering a new age, one in which we will perhaps find it possible to set aside the arrogance of human-ism and in its place realize that life on earth transcends human civilization. We will achieve a new enlightenment when, to paraphrase a famous docu-ment, we declare that we hold these truths to be self-evident, that all species are created equal, that they are endowed by their creator with certain inalienable rights, that among these rights are life, liberty, and the pursuit of happiness.

As I see it, the message we put aboard *Voyager* is evidence that we are near-ing that point. When I first began studying whales, few people seemed to care much about animals, even whales. Whales were being killed wholesale, and the powerful message contained in their song was going unheard. I recall that night of April 13, 1970, off Bermuda that I mentioned earlier, for it is the recordings we made that night that were put on board *Voyagers I* and *II*. The songs of whales so long confined within the oceans have welled up and out of that prison, overflowed the rim of the sea, conquered the hearts of their age-old enemies, us, and are now aboard a spacecraft bound on a 1.2-billion-year voyage that will spread their message throughout the galaxy.

I think of that star so close to the Gibb's Hill light and wonder whether it was not perhaps the very star toward which those sounds are bound.

If our species is to survive throughout even a tiny part of the journey of *Voyagers I* and *II*, the most important thing we must learn as a species is how incalculably evanescent, how inconceivably fleeting the human species and its ephemeral human lifetime is. Ours is the briefest of candles. We need to appreciate how short our species' life has so far been, how untried we are, how balanced on a knife edge and how perilously close to the yawning precipice of failure. It seems all but certain that never in the history of life on earth has any species threatened its own existence in so few years, or so few generations. Though I suppose that the reason there is no evidence of other species doing worse than we could be because when you last for as brief a period as we are in danger of lasting, you probably don't leave a large enough fossil record to stand much of a chance of being detected.

No other species of which there is any evidence can hold a candle to us for acting so contrary to its own interests or for unleashing so much widespread destruction. Even at the height of their ascendancy the most rapacious herd of *Tyrannosaurus rex* would have been a walk in the park alongside *Homo sapiens*.

If we could recognize our limitations, learn to staunch our arrogance, and realize that we are not the master of ceremonies, not the master of nature (but her servant), not the thing for which God made the earth, not a species created in God's image but just one species among millions of other beguiling species—just another pretty face (and a rank newcomer at that)—then I think we could make it. If we could just accept the fact that we are not the star of the show but just a very small player in a very large play, and that even though the role our species plays might be considered important, ours is nevertheless just a bit part—a little like the messenger who runs in and shouts, "The city's on fire"—important for moving along the plot but certainly not the lead. If we can learn to stop upstaging the main act (which is nature) and start to use human ingenuity to keep the earth alive rather than just to make our lives easier—then the show can go on, the earth can recover, the great beasts can endure, and we will not have to face the prospect of dying of a great loneliness of spirit.

APPENDIX: A PRIMER OF
OCEAN ACOUSTICS

In the course of this appendix, I will calculate the distance at which a fin whale sound can be heard, and comment on the ways in which whales can take advantage of a variety of sound propagation paths in the sea. I will also consider some of the acoustic tricks that whales might be playing and that I did not mention in chapter 5.

I have included this appendix because the study of ocean acoustics is full of surprises—at every point counterintuitive—and will in the course of the next few years become, I feel sure, the source of many of our greatest revelations about whales. In ocean acoustics the expected almost never occurs, and the fantastic is commonplace. It has been claimed that the reason God created economics was to give credibility to astrology. I have wondered whether God created the laws of ocean acoustics to give credibility to science fiction.

If we look at the way sounds propagate in the sea we can see what bizarre but important consequences the acoustic properties of seawater have for the lives of whales. It is worth the effort to learn a bit about ocean acoustics because the most interesting feature of the loud, low-frequency songs of fin and blue whales is the incredible distance they can travel in deep ocean and the odd consequences that the unexpected paths taken by these sounds may have. Even though it is true that blue whale sounds may travel farther than fin whale sounds, I will take fin whales as my example, because theirs are much simpler sounds and therefore lend themselves more readily to calculations of range of transmission. However, any conclusions we draw for fin whales will be an underestimate of how far the sounds of blue whales can be heard.

In order to figure out how far a particular sound can travel in the ocean before it has fallen to the same loudness as the background noise, we need information about several things. We must know about:

1. the characteristics of the sound itself—its frequency, duration, loudness, bandwidth, and directionality;
2. the characteristics of the receiver—its sensitivity and directionality, and how well it can pick the signal out of noise;
3. the nature of the background noise against which the sound will be heard—which is to say the noise going on in the vicinity of the receiver;
4. the path the sound will follow in the sea, including the things from which it will reflect along the way; and
5. the rate at which sound is converted to heat as it travels—called acoustic attenuation.

We need to look at each of these characteristics, but before we can do so we need to know something about ocean acoustics.

DEFINING UNDERWATER SOUND

Airborne sounds are rapid successions of compressions and rarefactions of the air molecules through which these sounds pass. Underwater sounds are rapid successions of compressions and rarefactions of the water molecules through which waterborne sounds pass. With all sounds, the molecules are compressed and expanded many times per second. The numbers of times per second determines the pitch (also called tone, or frequency). The lowest tone audible to people of normal hearing is about twenty such compressions and rarefications per second—twenty cycles per second. Or, more properly, twenty hertz (Hz). The highest tone we can hear is about twenty thousand compressions and rarefications per second, or twenty thousand hertz (well, twenty hertz and twenty thousand hertz were the lowest and highest tones we used to be able to hear when we were all younger).

MEASURING ACOUSTIC IMPEDANCE

Suppose you were so tiny you could take a seat on an oxygen molecule and observe a sound wave as it passed through the air around you. And suppose that you compared that experience to sitting on a molecule of water in the sea and watching as a sound wave passed through the seawater around you. Suppose also that you had a pressure gauge sensitive to the very minute pressures associated with sounds, and that you had a ruler with which you could measure the distance between the molecule on which you were seated and other molecules of air or water closest to you. And lastly, let's say that the sounds you observe, both those through water and those through air, were of equal loudness.

As the sound waves pass and the molecules around you are alternately pushed close together (compressed) and then moved farther apart (rarefied) you can use your ruler to measure how much of an excursion these molecules make in closing together and pulling apart. As this is going on, you can use your pressure gauge to measure the pressure of the sound that is causing the compressions and rarefactions. By comparing your readings of molecular motion and pressure in the air with the ones you got in water you would find a difference in the relationship between pressure and motion in the two media. You would find that for any given loudness of sound the pressure in air is always lower than it is in water, but that the back-and-forth motions of the molecules in the air are always greater than they are for sounds of the same loudness in water.

We are ready to measure the "acoustic impedance" of air and of water. It is simply the ratio of the things we have been measuring—the pressure and the particle velocity. It has been found that the ratio depends on the density of the medium and the speed of sound rather than on the actual pressure level (except for very high pressure signals). What have you been measuring? When you measure the distance that known sound pressures displace the molecules of a medium through which a sound is being conducted, you are measuring the "acoustic impedance" of that medium.

MATCHING ACOUSTIC IMPEDANCES

Because of the differences in acoustic impedance of air and water, in order to make a sound go from air to water, we must somehow increase the pressure and reduce the amount of movement between the water molecules. (If we want a sound to go from water to air we must do the reverse—make an increase in the amount of molecular movement at the expense of a reduction of sound pressure.) This process is called "impedance matching," and if we lack a device to help us do it, then only a little of the sound passing from one medium to another will actually get there. A good impedance matching device that allows an efficient transfer of sound from air into water swaps large movements at low pressures for small movements at high pressures. The energy needed to create the high pressures is stolen from the energy needed to move the molecules for longer distances, and in the end it all balances out.

We go through an impedance matching process when we use a simple mechanical device like a lever to move a rock that weighs, say, a thousand pounds. We cannot lift a thousand pounds directly with our muscles, so we place one tip of a steel bar under the rock, rest the bar on some fulcrum (say another stone close to the rock), and then push down on the long end of the bar. In that way we *can* lift the rock with our muscles, only we lift it a shorter distance than the arc through which we pushed the long end of the lever. We trade the relatively small muscular force we can exert throughout a long downward motion of the lever for the much larger force that the tip of the bar exerts over a lesser distance. We are not applying any energy to the system from any source but our own muscles; we are simply arranging things so the energy we *can* apply will do the job we wish to have done. The lever is simply an impedance matching device. In the world of physics, a job is work, and work is defined as a force moving something through a distance. The impedance matching device simply takes the force we are able to exert and matches it to the job at hand so the rock moves. Without the impedance matching device, the rock wouldn't move and no work would get done.

When you have such an impedance mismatch as that between sound traveling in air and sound traveling in water, if you have no way to match those impedances, then energy is lost and only a small amount of the sound will transfer between the two media. As a result, a robust sound like a shout in air will sound feeble to you as you lie on the bottom of a swimming pool holding your breath and listening. The same case holds true for loud sounds made underwater: humpback whales sing so loudly they could deafen an ear as sensitive as a human's were it designed to hear underwater. As it is, if you were in a boat directly over a singing humpback and trying to hear its song, you would find it sounded very faint in the air.

Most impedance matching devices for listening to underwater sounds are electrical circuits interposed between an underwater microphone and a loudspeaker. (Or if you're trying to get in-air sounds into the water—between a microphone and an underwater loudspeaker.) What might a simple mechanical impedance matching device that could change underwater sound into airborne sound look like? The physician's stethoscope in which things are arranged so as to maximize the transfer of sound from the patient's body to the tube full of air leading to the doctor's ear is an impedance matching device from which an early version of an underwater, directional listening device was derived. The device had a stethoscope-like chamber outside the ship that delivered sound to a circular set of tubes that a listener could rotate from inside the ship so as to change the length of the sound path from each underwater stethoscope until the phase of the sound matched in both ears. By noting the degrees of rotation of the tubes the listener could estimate the direction to the sound source.

However, long before the invention of this apparatus Aristotle made an impedance matching device for listening underwater. He found he could hear dolphin whistles by putting the capped end of a hollow wooden tube in the water and listening at the open, in-air end. It wasn't perfect, but it was a great improvement over listening with his unaided ear. The sounds coming through the water pressing against the walls of the wooden tube caused them to vibrate, and the transfer of sound energy was fairly efficient—well, a bit better than it would have been had sound just passed into the air over the water between Aristotle and the porpoise. Because the acoustic impedance of the tube's wooden walls was about midway between that of water and that of air, the walls transferred sounds to the air in the tube rather better than the water could have done alone. Also, because the air in the tube was confined at one end by Aristotle's ear and at the other by the cap on the underwater end of the tube, the sound energy in the air inside the tube was conducted directly into his ear with no disturbance from outside sounds. It is curious that this discovery of Aristotle's is not widely remembered. In my view, it was one of the things Aristotle did that actually advanced science rather than holding it back.

Sea sounds that pass through the hulls of wooden boats are partially impedance-matched to air. As mentioned in chapter 4, the humpback whales' songs may be the origin for the myth about the Sirens' song in the *Odyssey*.

MEASURING HOW LOUD A SOUND IS

The unit in which loudness of sounds is measured is the decibel (abbreviated as db). Decibels are not based on an arithmetic sequence of values; they are exponential. Zero sound energy therefore cannot be expressed in decibels, because zero cannot be expressed on any exponential scale (except as ten to the minus infinity). What one does is to decide arbitrarily what constitutes so little sound energy that lesser sound energies are of no real interest. That loudness is then called zero decibels. Most biologists use zero decibels to mean the human threshold of hearing (0.0002 dynes per square centimeter—the faintest sound we can hear under ideally quiet conditions when listening to the frequencies we hear best). A navy acoustician is likely to select a much louder sound to represent zero decibels simply because the sea is such a noisy place that one never has a chance to hear a sound as faint as a human ear can hear under ideally quiet conditions. For purposes of this discussion, I will refer to zero decibels as the softest sound a human being can hear.

If you are sitting in a quiet room under controlled conditions, listening carefully and concentrating fully, you can just barely detect a difference of one decibel (1db) between two otherwise identical sounds. Under the circumstances of normal living, two sounds usually have to differ in loudness by at least three decibels before you notice the difference. Radio and television advertisements are broadcast about three decibels louder than regular programming. You're usually not conscious of the ads being louder; they just seem a bit clearer (or a bit more irritating).

THE SENSITIVITY OF WHALE EARS

We don't know how sensitive the ears of large whales are, but there are lines of evidence we can use to estimate this. The human ear is at the theoretical limit of sensitivity. It can detect a sound so faint it displaces the eardrum no more than the diameter of a hydrogen molecule. If the human ear were any more sensitive it would hear as a background roar the collisions of the molecules that make up the ear.

People often speak of the ears of animals such as dogs being more sensitive than ours, but if the frequencies they hear best were the same as those we hear best their ears could not be any more sensitive than ours. There are, however, some ways a species can appear to be more sensitive: it can collect more sound (e.g., the large external ears, or pinnae, of horses) or emphasize a different acoustic spectrum (either higher, as in bats and porpoises, or lower, as in elephants and whales). However, none of these strategies will result in an ear that is any more sensitive than the human ear is at those particular frequencies we hear best.

The deep ocean is very noisy, as we shall see, and there is no such thing as a perfectly quiet place that a whale would need to be in if we wished to test whether it could hear the very softest sounds humans can hear. The vast majority of studies with animals of many kinds show that in spite of many independent evolutions of many different hearing organs, the selective pressures for more sensitive hearing are apparently so great that every kind of ear soon evolves to the point at which its hearing is pushed to the theoretical limit of sensitivity. This means that when we come to try to guess how well a whale hears (so we can calculate how far away from another whale it can be and still hear it) it is almost certainly safe to assume that its ears are sensitive enough to hear sounds as faint as the quietest background noise in the deep sea. It is also true that in the vast majority of species in which hearing has been tested, the frequencies each species makes loudest are also the frequencies it hears best, suggesting that even though fin and blue whales make sounds at the bottom end of human hearing they are likely to be the frequencies they hear best.

One of the most remarkable things about the low notes made by fin whales is the purity of their frequency. Most of the sound energy falls within the single frequency of twenty hertz. An instrument such as a flute produces a comparably pure tone—just the fundamental frequency and a few overtones. But a noise like a stick of dynamite exploding produces all frequencies, from the very highest to the very lowest, which is to say that the probability of any given frequency being present at any given moment is the same as the probability of any other given frequency being present at the same moment (this is also the definition of pure noise). In such a blast, in order to study a given frequency, you simply filter out the ones that don't interest you and listen for the ones that do. This is why a stick of dynamite is a useful noise source when you are trying to see how far different sound frequencies travel in the sea—it produces any frequency you might want.

Most natural "noises" don't contain all frequencies at equal intensity. Instead, they emphasize certain frequencies. Even though such sounds are called noises, they aren't the ideal noises of theory. This makes it impossible to express the loudness of such noises with a single decibel value. Instead loudness is measured according to its "spectrum level." This simply means that the loudness of each frequency present in a sound is given its own value. When I described the twenty hertz noises of fin whales (chapter 5) as having a loudness of 155 decibels I meant spectrum level. This means that the principal frequency of twenty hertz has a loudness of 155 decibels. The decibel scale is logarithmic which is convenient for expressing sound intensities over a very large range of values. It also permits sound intensities to be multiplied by the simpler procedure of adding their decibel equivalents. In recent years the Newton has started to replace the dyne as a unit of force. I have used the older "dyne" because more people are familiar with it. The loudness is also measured at a standard distance, usually one meter. This doesn't mean our measuring device has to be set up one meter from a stick of dynamite. We measure the loudness remotely, but when we quote the loudness later we refer it back to how loud it would have been at one meter. By sheer coincidence, it turns out that when a standard stick of dynamite is exploded in the sound channel, the spectrum level of the twenty hertz component of the total blast is also about 155 decibels—the intensity of an average fin whale blip. Thus, if you are interested in seeing how far away fin whale sounds can be heard, a stick of dynamite makes a useful model.

In order to make sure that the example is fair we must, of course, be listening only for that portion of the energy from the stick of dynamite which is at twenty hertz. We must discard all the rest of the frequencies by filtering them out. For although it is true that a fin whale can produce twenty hertz sounds as loud as sticks of dynamite produce twenty hertz sounds, it is not true that a fin whale can make a sound as loud as a stick of dynamite—since the whale cannot begin to produce all those other frequencies at the great loudness at which the dynamite produces them.

BANDWIDTH OF SOUND

In the example above we narrowed our filters and listened to a very narrow band signal down the line. If we had widened our filters and listened to, say, all frequencies between ten hertz and a thousand hertz we would have let in a lot more sound energy from the stick of dynamite. The proper way to describe such a change is to say that we are listening in a wider bandwidth. It should be clear from all this that if we are trying to figure out how far a sound can travel underwater, we must know its bandwidth.

I have pointed out that the purity of the twenty hertz sounds made by fin whales is surprisingly great. However, that doesn't express it precisely enough; we need to know more. We need to know just how much energy the different frequencies on each side of twenty hertz contain. When we know that we will be ready to state the signal's bandwidth. If the signal we are listening for has a very narrow bandwidth we can slide our filters in from either side until they admit only a very narrow band of frequencies, and yet we will still be able to find our signal. If the sound we are listening for has a broader bandwidth we will have to widen our filters if we wish to hear all of the signal. Widening the filters lets in more energy but it also lets in more noise. However, it is possible to gain an advantage in the end because the broader the signal band, the more information it contains, and with more information we can increase the certainty that the signal we have found is the one we were looking for.

BACKGROUND NOISE IN THE SEA

Back in the 1950s Jacques Cousteau produced a film called *The Silent World*. Like millions of others, I was fascinated when I saw it. It had a magnetic allure for attracting people to the sea. The title, however, is a misnomer, for one of the sea's most inexorable characteristics is that it is an exceptionally noisy place. In the low frequencies at which most whales speak, the noise comes from a great variety of sources. Wind is the chief noise source and, after that (at least in the modern world), ship traffic. Even in the most remote areas of deep ocean it is not possible to lower a hydrophone into the sea without hearing the roar of ship traffic.

Other sources of background noise are: the scouring of tides as they rattle pebbles and rocks along the bottom; the sound of surf beating on the shore; storms; rain; hail; the grinding of ice; whales and porpoises; several species of fish and shrimp; the pops, crackles, and creaks due to heating of the earth by the sun or to the cooling of its night side, or the sounds of microseisms—minute earthquakes which thump and bump away twenty-four hours a day as the earth groans and strains under the deformation imparted to it by the fact that its attraction to the sun and moon causes whatever part of the earth's surface that is facing those bodies to bulge slightly toward them. We mustn't underestimate the pummeling that the earth takes by dint of its attraction to the sun and the moon.

When the satellite of any planet is in an exceptionally eccentric orbit around it, it is kneaded gravitationally as it comes closer to and moves farther from the planet. This action can keep its core molten long after it might otherwise have cooled. Triton, a satellite of Neptune, is an example. We think of tides as only affecting water, but the moon also causes deformation in the earth's crust, creating tides in the rock of the crust that are nearly twice the amplitude of the average tides in the ocean. Even when a satellite's orbit is not eccentric the stress from tides alone can keep the core molten. Io, a satellite of Jupiter, is such a case. The sulfur dioxide that erupts from Io's volcanoes appears to be kept liquid by the tidal stress exerted on Io by Jupiter—the most massive of the planets. But even when there is not enough kneading and pummeling to melt the core (as in the case of earth), a planet will nevertheless make a lot of noise as the tides in its rocks deform the crust, bulging outward whatever surface is facing the star around which the planet is revolving. No wonder the earth's microseisms make a lot of noise.

Because water is so much better a conductor of sound than air, many oceanic noise sources propagate for miles through the sea. The summed racket from them and from many other causes makes a din that is ever present in all oceans. When a whale wishes to hear one of its comrades it must search for its sound among all that noise. (When we are determining the noise background against which a whale has to hear another whale, the only noise which matters to the listening whale is noise in its vicinity—not noise in the vicinity of the source of the sound, or noise in regions through which the sound passes on its way to the listener, but only in the vicinity of the listener.)

Figure 1 shows a typical distribution of ocean noise across the sound

FIGURE 1

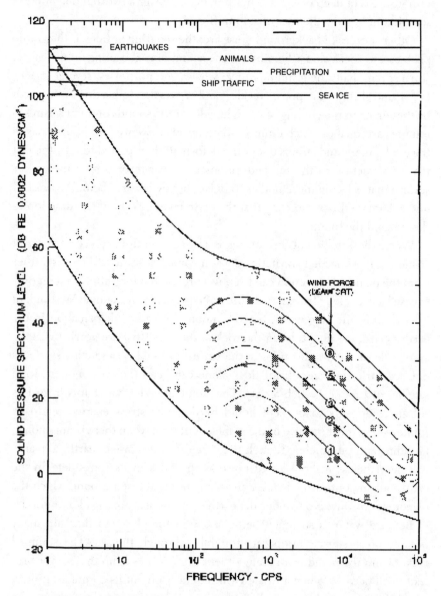

spectrum. It is immediately apparent that the loudest background noises are low frequencies and that at very high frequencies there is very little noise. But it is also apparent that the ocean noise around twenty hertz, where fin whales speak, can be very intense. The main contribution is from ship traffic and from storms, and, of course, the finbacks themselves, as well as other low-voiced whales.[1]

Storms in the vicinity of the listener are intermittent, but noise from ship

FIGURE 2

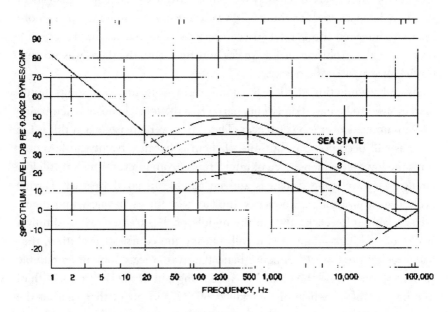

traffic is of fairly constant loudness, except when nearby ships increase it temporarily. The noise goes on twenty-four hours a day, 365 days a year. However, ship noise is a relatively recent phenomenon. Ships' propellers cause most of it. The noise from ships' motors is a much less important contributing cause. Sailing ships don't make any significant noise. Before propeller-driven ships, although all other sources of sound would have still been present, there was absolutely no ship traffic noise at all, and as a result the ocean was a quieter place at those frequencies except when strong winds were blowing. Back before ship traffic noise twenty hertz would have been a very good frequency for whales to speak at, because if you remove the noise from ships and extrapolate the noise spectrum generated by wind and waves you find that there appears to be a slight dip in the background noise at twenty hertz (see figure 2).

A modern test conducted in an area of ocean very remote from shipping lanes has shown that storms do indeed generate frequencies as low as twenty hertz (normally you cannot hear them because they are masked by the louder ship traffic). Even so, in an ocean devoid of propeller-driven ships, twenty hertz would have been (under average wind conditions) the lowest frequency that was relatively devoid of wind noise before the low frequencies generated by microseisms started to dominate the noise spectrum.

Whales that looked enough like a modern fin whale that you or I probably wouldn't notice the difference with a casual glance have probably been around for twenty-six million years. Ships driven by propellers instead of sails have been around for about 150 years. Twenty-six million years is more than one hundred thousand 150-year periods. This means that for 99.999 percent of the evolution of fin whales and their sounds, there was no ship traffic noise at all in the oceans.

As we have mentioned, there are good reasons why fin whale songs should have evolved to be based on twenty hertz. It is the logical choice when trying to communicate over long distances. There are several reasons that this is the case, as will become clear, but one of them is because twenty hertz represents the lowest frequency free of interference from microseisms yet still low enough to travel long distances and be audible in good weather. Having evolved to utilize such a frequency, the fact that fin whales now find themselves listening for each other in the middle of ship traffic noise is simply a stroke of bad luck—fate, if you will. During the course of evolution, they had selected the lowest frequency band that was at least sometimes audible (in fair weather), and then humans came along and in the last thousandth of one percent of fin whale history killed off 92 percent of them and at the same time started jamming their songs with traffic noise. The question is whether fin whales can survive the racket. Can "he" still find "she" at useful distances over the din? I suspect that for a number of reasons, the answer is yes, as we shall see.

I suggest that the reason fin whale sounds are so loud has to do with hearing each other across oceans and not with overcoming traffic noise—a speculation supported by the fact that the voices of fin whales who live permanently in the rather small and nearly landlocked Sea of Cortéz are much softer than those of fin whales living in the major ocean basins like the Pacific and Atlantic, even though there is now a lot of propeller noise in the Sea of Cortéz.

Because the ocean is so noisy there should be a very strong selective advantage favoring any adaptation that extends the range at which one whale can hear another.

There are several ways of extending range. In chapter 5, I referred to the advantages of shouting louder and to the advantages and disadvantages of directional and nondirectional sounds. But there is yet another very powerful way to increase range, and that is by employing any adaptation, any strategy, that can improve a listener's ability to find a signal in noise. In efforts to keep track of each other's submarines the United States and the USSR (back when there was both a USSR and a reason to keep track) invested billions of dollars and rubles in improving their techniques for finding signals in noise.

They became very good at it, but they were up against a limit defined by information theory.

Signal-to-Noise Ratios

According to information theory, it is theoretically possible to detect a signal if the background noise isn't more than sixty decibels louder than the signal you are trying to hear. When it gets louder than that you can no longer detect your signal. A more formal way to say this is that according to information theory a signal is detectable if its signal-to-noise ratio—its S/N—is greater than minus sixty decibels. (Sound ratios less than one are written as a negative number of decibels—e.g., a sound ten decibels less loud than the noise around it is expressed as having a signal-to-noise ratio [S/N] of $\frac{1}{10}$ = minus ten decibels.) In practice the detection of signals buried deep in noise requires relatively long analysis periods, which is one reason why sounds of short duration are harder to detect than sounds lasting for longer periods.

Sound Duration

When you are listening for a sound, the duration of it is a bit like its bandwidth. Up to a point; the more sound energy you have—even if it takes you more time to accumulate that energy—the better your chances are of detecting a signal in noise. Other things being equal, if you are trying to hear a sound that is buried in noise, the longer it lasts, the better your chances will be of detecting it. For humans, the signal-to-noise ratio necessary for detection decreases by about fifteen decibels as a signal is lengthened from a few milliseconds to one second. Beyond one second there is no improvement, the signal-to-noise ratio having reached an asymptotic value (an interesting coincidence considering the one-second duration of a fin whale's twenty hertz blips). Even though the mechanism of analysis in the human brain is locked onto samples of about a second's duration there is nothing to say that a fin whale should be limited in its integration time to one second. It might profit greatly from longer integration times because a brain that could analyze longer samples might be able to track a signal still deeper into noise.

It's not just duration; repetition can be useful. With a repetitive sound like a ship's propeller, the redundancy of the repeated pattern is very useful for detecting the sound against background noise—particularly if you are familiar with the sound you are trying to hear.

Unless special structures surround them, sound sources make sounds that are omnidirectional, the sound spreading evenly outward from the source in all directions, like an expanding sphere. Basically, the way animals make directional sounds is to collect the energy from the source that would otherwise be spreading in inappropriate directions and direct that energy in the direction they wish it to go. Other things being equal, the sound will be louder when it reaches the ears of the intended listener. This is how megaphones work. It is also why you cup your hands around your mouth, face someone, and shout when you wish to be heard far away.

When you are listening, the advantage of cupping your hands behind your ears in order to hear a distant sound is twofold: 1) it widens the area over which sound is collected, and 2) it somewhat excludes noises coming from directions other than the one in which you are trying to listen. The value of collecting more sound from a wider area is obvious, but the value of excluding noise from unwanted directions is a bit subtler—it has to do with finding signals in noise. When you are trying to hear a signal in noise what you are really trying to do is improve the ratio of that signal to the noise in which it is embedded. A good trick used by brains for improving this ratio is to pay attention to the direction of all noises. That way the brain can subtract out noises coming from directions other than the one in which you wish to listen, and this will improve your signal-to-noise ratio. If you have a directional receiver (one that hears sounds better if they come from one direction than from others), it is possible to get rid of much of the noise that is coming from directions in which you don't expect your signal to be present.

When an animal has some special feature of its anatomy that makes its sounds directional, it usually aims its sounds straight ahead. The large swelling on the front of the skull of many porpoises and toothed whales appears to be an acoustic lens with which they can form and direct beams of sound. This swelling is called the "melon." Melons are those features of their heads that give whales like the beluga, pilot, and sperm whale their characteristic appearances. The melon is filled with fat or a liquid wax that conducts sound more slowly than does water. Sound is bent when the speed of conduction changes in the medium through which it is passing. This is true whether it propagates between different areas of the same substance or from one medium to another (for example, from water to air). When the speed of conduction changes, a ray of sound bends.

All forms of energy propagating in waves behave the same way, whether ocean waves, or light waves, or sound waves, or heat waves, etc.—when energy traveling in any waveform enters a region that conducts it at a different speed, it bends. This is why a light beam bends when it enters the glass of a lens—glass conducts light more slowly than does air. The difference in the speed of conduction of sound in the fat of a whale's melon (its acoustic lens) coupled with the whale's ability to change the melon's shape (thus changing the convexity of the acoustic lens) gives the melon the ability to focus sound rays into a beam that is directed forward. Even species like the common dolphin have what appear to be well-formed acoustic lenses—only the lens is more streamlined, presumably to enable the dolphin to swim at higher speeds.

If baleen whales have acoustic lenses they are not obvious. They are the only whales that appear definitely to lack them. When an animal has a low voice, it needs much bigger structures to focus or direct that voice. It may simply be that because the voices of baleen whales are so much lower than the voices of other well-studied whale species, a lens able to focus such low tones would have to be too large even for an animal the size of a baleen whale to carry around. However, some pretty big acoustic lenses do get carried around by whales. The biggest melon of all resides in the head of the male sperm whale.

As I have already mentioned, this truly extraordinary structure may enable a sperm whale to focus a loud sound generated in its head so narrowly that it creates a ray intense enough to confuse or perhaps even stun its prey. This could enable the sperm whale to rush up and swallow its prey whole before it could regain its wits.

It is easy to see the advantages of producing directional sounds or listening directionally, but it is also all too easy to lose sight of the very real disadvantages of directional systems. For keeping herding animals together, directional systems are virtually worthless. The main problem is that when you are listening intently for sounds from a particular direction, you won't hear your sound if it is coming from a different direction. The same holds true for generating directional sounds; if you are shouting in one direction, you may be directing the energy of your sound just to one side of the whale you wish to contact. And suppose the whale you are trying to contact has directional hearing and has directed its most sensitive hearing in another direction from you just at the moment when you finally get your directional system pointed accurately and are hitting that whale properly. Your signal would be undetected by the directional listening system of your intended recipient.

It is clear that a much better strategy would be to make a sound so loud, and to possess an acoustic analysis system so good, that you could be heard by your chums no matter where they were. Then you could speak omnidirectionally and listen omnidirectionally, and always contact them when you wanted to. And, of course, they could also always contact you.

If herds are kept together by sound, it is self-evident that at any moment when you need to contact your herd and don't know where they are, you will not know which way to listen for them.

For animals that use echolocation the exact opposite holds true. In this case the animal has full control over making the sound and can point it in any direction it likes. Thus it also knows exactly the direction from which the echoes will be returning and will therefore always be pointing its directional receiver in the right direction. It is obvious that the kind of information an animal seeks to get from a sound will determine whether it will benefit from the ability to produce and sense directional sound. This is not to say that omnidirectional clicks are useless to echolocating animals. For example, using such clicks to make an initial detection of small targets before locking onto them is a valuable strategy when searching for food in the great three-dimensional space of the sea.

SPEED OF SOUND

Let's return to that swimming pool you were lying in before and listen again while your friend shouts to you. Even though you might not be aware of it, your friend's voice traveled to you much faster through the water than through the air. That's because sound travels almost five times faster in water than it does in air (about 1,100 feet per second in air and about a mile per second in water). If the distance between you and your friend is short, the difference in arrival time between the sounds in the two media will be small and you won't notice it. But if the distance between you and your friend is large, the difference starts to become very noticeable.

On a calm day when you are standing on a beach and a whale breaches nearby, the sound of the impact alerts you to look up in time to catch the tail end of the splash where the breacher has just landed. In that way you are ready to see the next breach when the same whale breaches a few moments later. But when the whale is several miles away, the main splash has usually died down before the sound reaches your ears through the air. So that when you hear a breach and look about, trying to see where it was, there's no sign left of the disturbance to the water and you can't see where the breach took place. When the whale breaches again, you're usually again looking in the wrong direction, and because the whale is so far away you don't notice it (unless by luck your line of sight happens to be aimed just right). Even if the whale breaches every now and then over the next twenty minutes (as often happens), you'll probably keep missing it because the sound of the splash always alerts you much too late—very frustrating. However, if you listen through a hydrophone instead of through the air, the sounds of distant breaches will reach your ears five times faster—which means there will usually still be enough wavelets left over from the splash to enable you to spot the distant patch of disturbed water and thus know where you should look to see the next breach. It's a trick we used to use in Argentina to see breaches during years when we had hydrophones permanently installed off our field station.

WAVELENGTH

Different frequencies have different wavelengths. Wavelength refers to the distance a sound has traveled between the onset of one compression and the next. If the compressions and rarefactions are coming in quick succession, as they will for a high-frequency sound like twenty thousand hertz, the sound doesn't get very far between compressions. Recalling that in water sound travels about a mile each second, a sound of twenty thousand hertz will have traveled about $\frac{1}{20,000}$ of a mile (about three inches) between compressions (we say that twenty thousand hertz has a wavelength of three inches). But if we consider a twenty hertz fin whale sound, it will have gone a twentieth of a mile (one thousand times farther) between compressions, which means the wavelength is very long—$\frac{1}{20}$ of a mile (about 250 feet).

There is another curious fact about the wavelength of a sound, which is that unless an object has dimensions at least as great as (or greater than) the wavelength of the sound wave that hits it, the object won't reflect that sound significantly. This same rule applies to any waveform, including not just sound but ocean waves, light, heat, etc. It is why light microscopes can't see extremely small objects—they are smaller than the wavelength of the light itself and so they are simply too small to reflect that light. In order to see them you have to illuminate them with an electron beam (electron beams have significantly shorter wavelengths).

This simple law of reflection is intuitively obvious. For example, it is obvious that if you erected a long, nearly submerged breakwater of rock in the path of an ocean swell, and near it a steel post, the post wouldn't reflect the swell at all but the breakwater would. The reason the swell goes right past the post is because the width of the post is not nearly as great as the wavelength of the ocean swell and so it cannot reflect the swell. (I am not talking here about the height of the crests but the distance between crests.) However, when the same swell encounters the breakwater of rock, the breakwater is much longer than the crest-to-crest distance of the swell (the wavelength of the swell) and so the wave *does* reflect off it (you can see the effect as the

swell crashes against the breakwater, expending all its energy by madly stirring up white water, foam, and wavelets—the elements that characterize
crashing waves). All that mad stirring up of the water takes energy, which is
what becomes of the energy that had propagated across the ocean as the
swell, lifting and lowering tons and tons of water as it went. Of course if
larger swells come along with longer distances between crests, until the
wavelengths are greater than the length of the breakwater you have made, the
swell will then propagate right past the breakwater and through to the lagoon
on the other side, the reason being that the wavelength of the swell has
become too long to reflect off the breakwater.

This same need for objects to have dimensions as large as the wavelengths that they reflect explains why the sound you get in a car when you
are passing a line of closely spaced fence posts next to the road is a series of
high-pitched rapid-fire hisses—*tss tss tss tss tss tss tss tss tss tss tss tss*—versus
the sound you get when the same car, traveling at the same speed, goes past
a tall cement retaining wall flanking the highway—a lower sound like
rraaaaahhhhhhhhhshh. When cars are going down a road without fence posts
or retaining walls next to them there is often nothing to reflect significant
portions of the sound of the car back toward it, so normally the sound simply propagates outward over the countryside and is only heard by the locals.
But when there are potential sound reflectors like fence posts or retaining
walls or trees, the sound of the car reflects back and passengers inside the
car can hear it clearly. Cars makes noise, and as we have said, noises are
characterized by the fact that they contain all frequencies. Fence posts are
too small to reflect anything but relatively short wavelengths (which is to say
relatively high frequencies), so of all the frequencies that the car is producing the only ones the fence posts reflect back are the high frequencies.
And so the sound is a rather hissy: *tss tss tss tss tss*. A tall cement retaining
wall is big enough to reflect not just short but also much longer wavelengths
which are, of course, the lower frequencies, so that the sound reflected
back contains some much lower frequencies, and therefore sounds lower:
rraaaaahhhhhhhhhshh.

I have examined all this in detail because this concept has several important consequences for whales. It means, for example, that a frequency as low
as the twenty hertz sounds of fin whales cannot be useful for echolocating a
fish—the fish would be too small to reflect the sound. It might, however, be
useful for echolocating a school of fish or an island and therefore for navigation (the overall dimensions of the school of fish or of an island are large
enough to reflect the sound back to the whale).

Wavelength implies a very interesting thing about the directionality of the
sounds as well. If we are dealing with a sound as low as twenty hertz with a

250-foot wavelength, it is hard to imagine that sound could be very directional as it leaves the whale, simply because there is no structure in a big whale (even in a 100-foot whale) big enough to reflect, and thus to shape, a 250-foot wavelength sound into a directional beam of sound.

There is another rule of thumb that is useful in this regard: if you wish to focus a sound, for example by reflecting it off some curved surface, say, a parabolic reflector, the reflector should be several wavelengths across (at least six is the usual number needed for respectable focusing). Parabolas which are smaller in relation to the wavelengths they are trying to focus are not very directional. A parabola more than one but smaller than six wavelengths *will* act as a somewhat directional device to the extent that it will partially block any sounds of the frequency in question coming from the direction opposite to that in which the parabola is pointing—as long as the wavelengths of those sounds aren't significantly longer than the diameter of the parabola. All of which tells us that when a fin whale makes its twenty hertz sounds, because they have a wavelength of 250 feet, there is nothing the whale could cup around its ear (not even its whole body would be long enough) to make the sound directional. From all of this I conclude that the twenty hertz sounds of fin whales are omnidirectional. There is confirmation of this fact from several recordings of fin whales made concurrently on several widely spaced hydrophones. By noting the delays in arrival times between the various hydrophones, the fin whale's position could be determined and the animal thus tracked. The results show clearly that even though the fin whale making the noise was slowly swimming about along a very tortuous course, twisting and turning back as it went, the sounds at each hydrophone remained at practically the same loudness throughout. Since the fin whale's head must have been pointing in all directions during this process, the only reasonable explanation for why the sounds remained at the same loudness is that the sound was omnidirectional.

The same line of argument must hold true for whales that are listening for a twenty hertz sound. It seems most unlikely that the listener could cup any part of its body behind its ears in order to make them directional. There is a way, however, in which the whale could gain useful directional information from the sound. This is a consequence of the fact that whales have two ears. By attending to the time of arrival of the sound as it strikes first one ear and then the other, the whale could determine the direction from which the sound was coming. This strategy works best when the sound has an abrupt transition (for example, an abrupt beginning or ending). The twenty hertz sounds of fin whales lack such features, meaning that the whale must resort to a second strategy for gaining directional information—by attending to the phase of the sound in each ear.

PHASE

Because sounds consist of fluctuating pressure waves (alternating compressions and rarefactions) the sound pressure alternates between positive and negative pressures several times each second (the number of times being the frequency of the sound). If a sound source is coming at a whale from directly ahead, the compressions and rarefactions will occur at the same moment in each ear (such sounds are said to be in phase). However, if the source is to one side, the sound pressure will increase and decrease at different moments in each ear (such sounds are said to be "out of phase" in each ear). By paying attention to the phase of the sound wave in each ear (i.e., to the state of the wave, whether sound pressure is rising or falling), an animal can make quite accurate determinations of the direction to a low-frequency sound source. By attending to phase differences in sounds arriving in both ears, it is possible to ignore even quite loud sounds that arrive from directions other than the one in which the whale is trying to listen. By this means it can hear a faint sound better, and determine its direction.

Though it is not widely recognized, low frequencies are especially useful for determining the direction to a sound source. In human beings, where it has been studied in detail, the most accurate determination of the direction to a sound results from facing the sound and moving the head from side to side by small amounts until the subject gains the impression that the sound is coming from straight ahead. This ability has been studied by testing a subject's "minimum audible angle" (the largest angle through which a sound can be moved without a subject who is facing the source knowing that it has been moved). Surprisingly enough the best directional hearing (i.e., the smallest minimum audible angle) occurs not with high but with low frequencies. In humans, 125 hertz is the lowest frequency for which the minimum audible angle has been tested. It is also the frequency which gave the best result.[2] It is clear from other considerations that need not concern us here that the way this is achieved is through phase comparisons between both ears. The ability to determine direction to a sound source by paying attention to its phase is one of the ways in which we keep locked onto the relatively weak signal of a person with whom we are conversing in the loud background noise of a cocktail party. As long as the person stands still and keeps a steady orientation to us their voice will have a constant phase delay. Our brains can then discard sounds with different phase delays—a process which improves the ratio of the person's signal to the background noise. It is my belief that whales could use a similar mechanism to increase the signal-to-noise ratio of sounds that interest them.

The technique of comparing phases in two ears depends on the two ears being separated by enough distance to provide a respectable time delay between sounds which are presented from one side as they reach first the near and then the far ear. The minimum time it takes for a sound wave to get from one side of the human head to the other is about 650 millionths of a second (650 μsecs). Another way to put this is that the length of the acoustic path in humans is 650 μsecs. The smallest time difference a person can detect between the arrival of pressure maxima in sound waves hitting two ears is about 10 μsecs. Because sound travels about five times as fast in water as it does in air, the acoustic path for a human head underwater would be about 130 μsecs (650 ÷ 5 = 130). For a whale to be capable of meaningful phase comparisons it would presumably need an acoustic path comparable in length to a human's in-air acoustic path. It is not clear what the length of the acoustic path is for a whale, since the path taken by a sound wave in traveling from the whale's body surface to the cochlea (the inner ear, where sound waves are transduced into nerve action potentials) is the subject of almost as many theories as there are investigators studying it. Although the interaural acoustic path length therefore cannot be measured, we can measure what must be the minimum path by measuring the distance between the entrances to a whale's left and right inner ears. For an average adult fin whale, this distance is about 600 μsecs in water. Thus an aquatic animal gains another advantage for hearing low sounds simply by being large. The animal's size makes useful acoustic separations possible in spite of the high speed of sound conduction in water. If fin whales can detect phase differences as well as but no better than people, they would, I suspect, do very well at determining the direction of sounds as low as twenty hertz.

I conclude from all this that though it rules out the realistic possibility of structures that would add significant directionality either to outgoing or incoming sounds, the 250-foot wavelength of twenty hertz sounds is probably no obstacle to a whale if it can employ phase comparisons to determine the direction of a sound.

WHY SOUNDS LOSE ENERGY

When sounds are traveling (propagating) through the ocean, there are three main reasons they become fainter with distance: 1) they are slowly converted to heat as they pass through seawater—called oceanic attenuation; 2) they are reflected from the surface and bottom; and 3) they spread out as they travel.

It is worth looking at each of these sound reduction mechanisms in more detail.

Losses Due to Oceanic Attenuation

Earlier in this appendix I described the noise background in the sea and pointed out that less background noise occurs with higher frequencies. So why don't fin whales speak at high frequencies if they wish to be heard a long way off? It would mean that the conditions in which other fin whales listened for them would be far quieter. The answer concerns the rate at which high- and low-frequency sounds are converted to heat as they pass through the sea.

When sounds compress and rarefy water (or any other medium, for that matter), the compacting and expanding of the molecules in the medium stirs them up a bit and imparts to them a certain amount of random motion (= heat). Thus when sound compresses and rarefies the medium through which it is propagating, some of the sound energy is converted to heat, which robs the original sound of this energy. The result is that the sound gets softer.

Since sounds of high and low frequency travel at practically the same rate, it is obvious that high-frequency sounds will die out in far fewer seconds (or miles) than low-frequency sounds, simply because high frequencies generate more compressions and rarefactions per second (and therefore per mile traveled) than do low-frequency sounds. Small wonder that the more compressions and rarefactions it undergoes per second, the shorter the distance the sound gets before its loudness is significantly diminished by having slightly heated the water through which it is propagating.

When the conversion of sound energy to heat energy is complete, there is no longer any sound left to hear. The very highest sounds—such as the ultrahigh frequencies made by porpoises (180 thousand hertz higher than anything you and I can hear)—propagate for only a few hundred feet before all their energy is converted to heat. Very low frequencies like those made in fin and blue whale songs have to travel for far longer before they are noticeably reduced by conversion to heat. Thus oceanic attenuation losses are said to be frequency dependent.

Reflections from Surface and Bottom

Reflections from surface and bottom cost sounds significant energy. Several things determine to what extent this occurs. The type of bottom is important: a soft, muddy bottom absorbs more sound energy than a hard, rocky bottom. The amount of absorption is dependent both on the sound frequency and on the "grazing angle"—the angle at which the sound strikes the bottom. When a sound hits the bottom, the nearer it hits to a right angle, the more of it is absorbed. Ocean bottoms that are rough or porous are more absorptive than smooth bottoms, but how effective the pores (the roughnesses) are in absorbing sound depends on the frequency of the sound. This has to do with the wavelength of the sound.

Relatively enormous bottom relief is required to capture a sound with a wavelength of 250 feet—meaning that twenty hertz sounds lose hardly any energy from reflections off most ocean bottoms. Very low sounds have another unexpected attribute—the amount of energy they lose when they contact the bottom is practically independent of the angle at which they strike it. Only a few decibels more of their energy is captured when they strike the bottom at right angles than when they merely graze it.

To summarize: when we are dealing with very low frequency sounds like those in the songs of blue and fin whales, oceanic attenuation losses, reflection losses, and grazing angle losses are relatively minor (because low frequencies are only slightly affected by them).

However, one factor that robs all sounds of energy, regardless of their frequency, is the way they spread out as they travel through the sea. These are the so-called spreading losses.

LOSSES DUE TO SPREADING

This is an area where ocean acoustics start to get weird and surprising. Some of the paths sounds take through the ocean are quite complex, others entirely unexpected. For animals trying to hear distant sounds, the consequences of these paths are profound. I will consider four cases: how sound propagates at short distances; the ducting of sounds between surface and bottom; how sound propagates for long distances (sofar channeling); and how sound propagates in water covered with broken ice (underice propagation).

Case 1: Propagation over Short Distances: Spherical Spreading Losses

As wave energy of any kind—sound, light, heat, etc.—spreads out from a single source, it spreads evenly over the ever-increasing surface of an ever-expanding sphere until such time as it reflects from or is bent by (i.e., refracted by) something. The surface area of an expanding sphere is proportional to the length of the radius of that sphere squared (multiplied by itself). If we "freeze frame" the expanding sphere and examine it, the reasons for this become more obvious. At any given moment, the radius of an expanding sphere is, of course, the distance of the surface of the sphere from the sound source. If a sensor (B) is twice as far from a source of sound (or light, or heat, etc.) as some other sensor (A), the more distant sensor at B will hear the sound one-quarter as loud (or see one-quarter the light, or sense one-quarter the heat) simply because the original energy is now spread over four times the surface area it was spread over at sensor A. Because the surface of a sphere varies as the square of its radius, by doubling the radius we square the area of a sphere's surface: $2^2 = 4$. If B is four times as far away from the source of sound as A, its sphere will be sixteen times the area of the sphere at A ($4^2 = 16$). Because your ears (or eyes, heat receptors, etc.) don't change size, the amount of energy they can collect of the original sound (or light, or heat, etc.) at the source becomes less, the greater the distance to the source, simply because the area of the sound receptor (or light receptor, or heat receptor, etc.) is a smaller and smaller percentage of the surface area of the expanding sphere over which the energy emanating from the original source is distributed. (This is formally expressed by the statement that the intensity of the energy available at a distance from a source is inversely proportional to the square of the distance to that source.)

So these are the properties of spherical spreading losses—the amount of sound energy lost is proportional to the square of the distance between listener and source. When we are dealing with sounds in the sea the only trouble with a concept like spherical spreading is that sounds cannot expand like spheres for very long before the surface of the sphere encounters the ocean surface (and/or its bottom). This is because the depth of the ocean is very much less than its length and width (the ocean is, of course, the thinnest of liquid films stretched across the globe). Once the surface of our idealized expanding sphere has reached either the surface or bottom of the sea, the sound begins a second phase of conduction in which it is channeled or ducted between the surface and the bottom. This means that in the sea, spherical spreading only applies to propagation of sounds for a relatively short distance from the source and then it becomes ducting between surface and bottom.

Case 2: Ducting of Sounds Between Surface and Bottom
Now comes a problem. Because the sea's surface is often fairly rough, the rough undersurface of the waves is often at a scale about equal in size to the sounds that are audible to you and me—and presumably to large whales (sounds with wavelengths between three inches and 250 feet). Some of the energy in such sounds gets trapped by the undulating underside of the ocean's surface. But we also know that some of the sound goes through

FIGURE 3

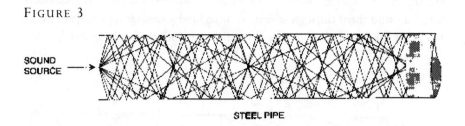

SOUND
SOURCE ——>

STEEL PIPE

the surface and passes into the air above it. It is apparent that each time an underwater sound strikes the underside of the sea's surface it loses some energy through the surface and, if it is a rough day, to being trapped in the roughness of the underside of the waves. It also loses some energy every time the sound hits the bottom (though this loss is very little for very low frequency sounds).

The whole process is lossy, meaning that sounds lose energy all along the way and are not ducted for great distances between surface and bottom the way they would be were they traveling inside an idealized steel pipe such as the one shown in figure 3.

But let us suppose for a moment that by some means as yet to be explained we were able to arrange things in our duct so that the sound waves did not strike the walls but bent away from them before they hit. We would then have reflection-free propagation of the sounds, and this would allow the sounds to reach great ranges. There is just such a duct in deep ocean. It is called the deep sound channel, or sofar channel.

Case 3: Propagation over Long Distances in Deep Ocean: Sofar Channeling
The deep sound channel is not really a channel in the way we usually think of channels—narrow ducts. It is, in fact, all the water in the ocean from very near the surface to very near the bottom—almost the entire depth regime, a layer of water as broad and as wide as the deep oceans themselves. It is in this "layer" of ocean that some of the energy in a whale's sound can transmit for very long distances. Because "deep ocean" includes roughly 60 percent of the area of the seas, this sound channel is of great potential value to any whale that lives in deep ocean and might find some benefit in being able to be heard a long way off.

To see how this ducting layer works, we need a source of loud sound. A stick of dynamite will do. We drop it into the deep sea, and when it has sunk to a depth of 4,200 feet—about halfway between surface and bottom—we detonate it. (I shall explain why I have chosen this depth shortly.) We do this experiment off the Hawaiian islands because they rise out of deep water and are the most isolated island chain in the world—so there's lots of open ocean around them through which our imagined sounds can propagate without being interrupted by striking a continent or other islands or shoals.

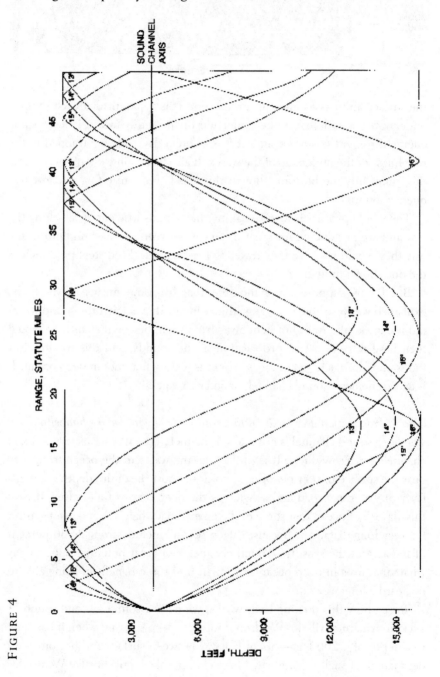

FIGURE 4

Once the explosion has occurred, the radius of the spreading sphere of sound will reach the bottom at about the same time it reaches the surface and at that moment the sound will have run out of the third dimension of ocean into which to expand. Nevertheless it will continue expanding laterally. The way it expands laterally is not obvious, and is one of the most interesting and unexpected facets of ocean acoustics.

To examine this phenomenon let us follow the fate of several rays of sound (although sound rays don't really exist, they are a useful fiction). We will draw one ray for each degree of angle so that all around the sound source there will be a circle composed of 360 rays. Each ray will represent the sound energy confined within an angle of one degree as it spreads out from the sound source. Actually, of course, because sound spreads outward not as a circle but as a sphere, the number of rays of a solid one-degree angle leaving any sound source will be 360 times 360 rays, or 129,600 rays. Figure 4 shows a sound source in midwater with several selected rays drawn in.

The rays that go straight up or even steeply up hit the surface, ricochet off it, hit the bottom, echo back up to hit the surface again, and so on. With each reflection they are diminished as the sound leaks through the surface into the air or gets absorbed by bottom material or is trapped in the under-surfaces of waves created by rough weather. These rays continue to bounce back and forth between surface and bottom until their energy is used up and they die out. (Just the same fate is shared by rays that start out headed straight down or even steeply down.)

However, there is at least one sound ray that can travel a long way, since it does not reflect from either surface or bottom. That is the sound ray that leaves its source horizontally. Like any other ray it should propagate indefinitely in a straight line. But like any straight line drawn inside any sphere (e.g., the earth), it should eventually intersect with the sphere's curved surface. (In our case this fact will cause the sound ray to reflect off the underside of the surface of the sea.) However, something bends this ray so that it stays at the same depth and never hits the surface or the bottom no matter how far it may travel.

Just what is it that causes this horizontal sound ray to bend? In the description of how whales use their melons, I mentioned that sound, like any waveform, is bent when it propagates through a medium in which it is conducted at a different speed.

So now it has become important to measure the rate of conduction of sound to see whether there is anything in the structure of deep ocean that might bend sounds. If you were to go offshore near Hawaii to deep water and measure the speed of sound conduction all the way from the surface to the bottom, you would find that sound was conducted faster near the surface and slower as you went deeper until you reached a depth of about 4,200 feet. However, as you went deeper still you would find that the speed of sound conduction would slowly increase again all the way to the bottom, several thousand feet below.

This high-speed, low-speed, high-speed sound conduction profile is due to two things: the change in water temperature with depth, and the fact that as you go deeper, increasing water pressure squeezes water molecules closer together, making the water denser. (In school we were taught that water is incompressible—a "fact" which is simply not true. Great pressures are necessary to compress water measurably, but great pressures occur in the abyss.)

In water the effects on sound transmission of increasing temperature and increasing pressure are the same—both increase the speed at which sound travels through water. An abrupt change in water temperature refracts (i.e., bends) a sound ray abruptly, a gradual change refracts it gradually.

The effects on temperature and pressure of increasing depth are the opposite (temperature decreases and pressure increases with increasing depth). The question is, which effect wins out? Temperature does—and by quite a lot. Ocean water gets colder with depth, and the temperature change involved has a much greater effect on speed of sound conduction than does the increase of density with increasing pressure. Therefore as you go deeper into the ocean, you observe that the speed of sound conduction decreases. The sea's surface waters are warmed by the sun, and because, like light, the heat from the sun cannot penetrate very far, the sea gets colder with depth. But even where the ocean is warm (e.g., around Hawaii), once you have descended to 4,200 feet, the water is almost at freezing temperature. From there on down to the bottom it is isothermal (the same uniform temperature). So if you were descending in a deep-diving submersible off Hawaii, once you reached a depth where the water temperature was near freezing, the temperature would stop changing significantly, and the increase in water density caused by increasing pressure would take over as the major influence affecting the speed of sound conduction (since sound travels faster the denser the medium through which it is propagating). Thus, once you dive below the depth of the sound speed minimum in the ocean, the speed of sound conduction starts to increase again as you go deeper. The depth at which sound speed is at a minimum (about 4,200 feet near Hawaii) is referred to as the "axis" of the deep sound channel.

The axis occurs at different depths at different latitudes. This is because the depth of the sound channel axis is determined by the depth of warm water at the latitude in question—the closer to the equator, the deeper the depth at which water temperature falls to near freezing (i.e., the deeper the axis of the channel). In Hawaii that depth lies at about 4,200 feet, but in cold polar waters there is no overlying layer of warm water and so the axis of the channel is at the surface. This has important consequences for whales and is a point to which I will return below (see "Case 4," p.393).

The part of the deep sound channel that conducts sound slowest—the axis of the channel—is overlaid and underlaid by water in which the speed of sound conduction is faster. This fact gives the ocean the properties of a gigantic lens—one that runs from the surface of the sea to its bottom—a lens that focuses sound horizontally in such a way as to keep horizontal sound rays from hitting the surface or the bottom as they propagate along, mile after mile, maintaining a constant depth. What causes the sound wave to bend just enough to keep it parallel to the surface is the fact that sound (or any other form of energy that travels in waves) always bends toward that part of the conducting medium in which it travels slowest.

Let us return to a consideration of that sound ray in figure 4, which, as it leaves the source, is parallel to the surface—I am talking about the ray that, if it went far enough in a straight line, was obviously destined to intersect with the curvature of the earth, causing the sound ray to reflect off the underside of the sea's surface. What we find is that the thermal structure of the water bends the horizontal sound ray just enough to keep it following the depth of the sound speed minimum—the axis of the sound channel—which because it is at a constant depth is, by definition, curved perfectly to match the curvature of the planet. Thus if it were loud enough, the horizontal ray of low frequency might travel completely across the Pacific, say, to the Philippines (because every time the earth's curvature dropped down into its path and the ray found itself aimed toward the surface, the ray would also find itself entering water that conducts sound faster, which would bend the ray back toward the slower conducting water at the depth of the sound channel axis, thus returning it to the axis of the sound channel).

One horizontal sound ray does not represent very much of the sound energy from the dynamite blast we used as our experimental sound source. If there were some factor that bent many sound rays in some similar way so as to avoid reflections but kept them following along the axis of the sound channel, it would mean we would have more sound rays (= more sound energy) propagating along a path that avoided losses, thus increasing the sound energy that propagated to very long distances—perhaps even letting enough through to have it be audible to distant listening whales.

There is just such a mechanism. Aside from the one horizontal ray that didn't die out, all the rays we saw in figure 4 reflected off the surface and

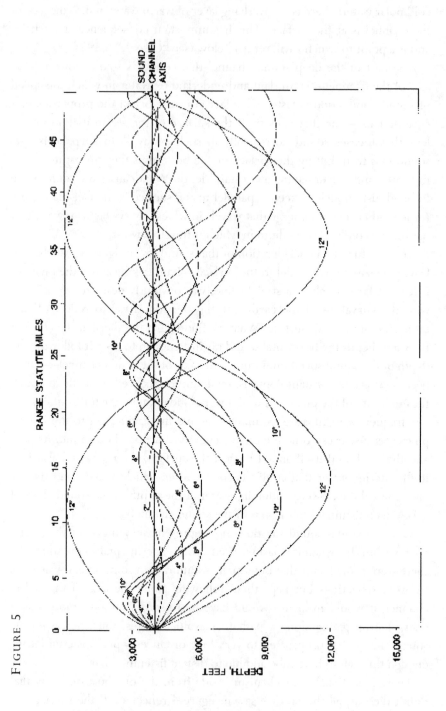

FIGURE 5

bottom and eventually died out. They failed to start ducting within the sofar channel. But figure 4 doesn't show the fate of sound rays a few degrees above and below the horizontal. Let's get another stick of dynamite, lower it to the axis of the sound channel the way we did with the first one, and set it off. This time we'll ignore the rays in figure 4—the rays that die out in a few miles by reflecting off surface and bottom—and look only at a special set of the rays we didn't look at in figure 4. The result is figure 5.

Let's focus on the ray in figure 5 which is at a ten-degree angle above the horizontal. As it leaves the source it is aimed at the ocean's surface and seems destined to hit it and reflect off it. But as it streaks toward the surface it enters water that conducts sound faster. This bends it back toward water that conducts it more slowly—that is, toward the axis of the sound channel. But because this ray is propagating at an angle of ten degrees to the axis of the channel, it will pass back through the axis layer at a ten-degree angle and carry on into deeper water below the axis. But as it goes deeper it will again encounter water that conducts sound faster, which will, of course, bend the sound ray back toward the slowest conducting water—the channel axis— once again. But as it will be coming up from below the axis depth at a ten-degree angle it will carry through the axis depth and up into water above the axis—again water which conducts sound faster. This, of course, will bend the sound ray back toward the slowest conducting water of the axis of the channel once again, and so on. Because this process keeps repeating, it keeps this sound ray that started out headed toward the surface at a ten-degree angle with the horizontal undulating back and forth across the axis depth in such a way that it never reaches either surface or bottom and therefore never experiences a reflection.

Just as the fate of the horizontal ray was to be kept propagating along the channel axis depth, so all the rays up to ten degrees (actually all the rays up to twelve degrees above the horizontal and down to fifteen degrees below it) are bent in such a way as to avoid contact with surface and bottom. Thus they not only retain the energy they would otherwise lose in reflections with the surface and bottom, they also propagate in a way that spreads them out over the surface of an expanding cylinder rather than over the surface of an expanding sphere. This point is not obvious, so I will elaborate.

The way sound waves that are undulating about the axis of the sound channel expand is not like an expanding sphere but like an expanding cylinder—albeit the cylinder in which the sound is spreading has a very small height (the depth of the sea) in relation to its diameter (the entire length and breadth of the surface of deep ocean). It is, nonetheless, a cylinder. This kind of spreading is called cylindrical spreading.

A phonograph record is also a cylinder of very low height in relation to its diameter. Both the record and the pattern of sound propagation in the deep sound channel are cylinders with very skewed dimensions—but they are cylinders nevertheless.

We saw before that the surface area of an expanding sphere increases as the square of the radius. The surface area of an expanding cylinder, however, increases in direct proportion to its radius—not in proportion to its radius squared the way the surface of a sphere does. This means that when sound is propagating as an expanding cylinder, if sensor B is twice as far from a source of sound as sensor A, the more distant sensor at B will hear the sound one-half as loud (not one-quarter as loud as was the case with the sphere). And if B is four times as far away from the source of sound as A, the surface of B's cylinder will be four times the area of the cylinder at A (not sixteen times its area as it would be if the expansion was spherical and its surface area increased with the square of the radius). This means that all else being equal, with cylindrical spreading you retain about an order of magnitude (a power of ten) of the loudness of a sound.

To get to the point where it starts spreading cylindrically, sound must first expand spherically as it leaves its source until it reaches a distance where the refraction of sound keeps bending the earlier diverging rays back toward the axis depth. This distance is called the "transition range." For a sound source near Hawaii this would occur about four miles from the source.

In spite of the factors that can reduce spreading losses of sounds made by whales, we have what could be a serious problem: we have been talking about cylindrical spreading of sound along the axis of a sound channel which is at a depth of about 4,200 feet near Hawaii. There is no direct evidence that either fin or blue whales can dive to such depths or that they can make their sounds once there. The deepest record we have of fin whales making sounds is a single instance in which it was shown that the sounds were made at "at least 1,200 feet." From what is known about other whales, however, I see no reason to suppose fin whales would not be able to create sounds at greater depths—but we simply don't yet know. (I would be less surprised if it turned out that they can and do make their sounds at such depths than I would if it turned out that they can't or don't.)

However, a whale need not be able to dive to the depth of the channel axis in order to inject its sounds into it or to hear sounds carried in it. Some of the sound energy propagating in the deep sound channel refracts along paths that carry it just beneath the ocean's surface. The roar of propellers from surface ships gets into the deep sound channel and once in it propagates across oceans. The sloping bottom of an island or continent or seamount acts to lift sounds propagating in the channel up to the surface (it also can help to inject descending sound rays into it). This means that whales near deep ocean islands or seamounts could, without diving to the depth of the deep sound channel, both hear sounds that had been propagating in it as well as launch their own sounds into it. It is noteworthy in this regard that several of the best-known humpback whale breeding areas are in the vicinity of islands that rise out of deep ocean. Hawaii and Bermuda, as well as Silver, Navidad, and Mouchoir banks in the Caribbean, are examples. The whales that sing along the perimeter of a breeding bank at any given moment must provide a beacon for others migrating toward it—though whether other humpbacks use this beacon has yet to be demonstrated.

But none of these special conditions for getting sounds into and out of the sound channel are absolutely necessary for whales to hear a long way. It is merely that the best sound transmission over the very longest ranges is found at the depth of the channel axis. We must not overlook the fact that sound gets into the channel even from sources at the surface (I have already mentioned that the sound channel is roaring with the sounds made by surface shipping—in fact, even the sounds of supersonic jet aircraft have been heard over hydrophones lying deep in the sound channel). The reason that almost every low-frequency sound travels via the sound channel is that the sound channel is not a finite layer of water but almost the entire mass of the ocean from very near the surface to very near the bottom. The only reason for diving to its axis depth is to get the very best out of it, either as regards projecting sounds to the greatest distance or listening for sounds from far away.

We can see how sounds get into the channel from shallow sources by getting another stick of dynamite and blowing it up at a much shallower depth (but we mustn't forget that even though the stick may now be quite shallow, if our propagation path is to have enough thickness to allow for cylindrical spreading we will still have to perform our experiment in deep ocean). In figure 6 we see the results of exploding a stick of dynamite at a depth of only three hundred feet in deep ocean (three hundred feet really isn't very deep—only about four fin whale lengths). In this figure I have included only those sound rays that never hit either the surface or the bottom. They turn out to be just those few that were aimed a little below the horizontal and that refract in such a way as to miss the bottom. Though there are very few rays involved, they propagate with true cylindrical spreading—the vast majority of the sound rays from the same explosion having been used up because of reflections from surface and bottom. It is clear that the rays we are looking at return to the same three-hundred-foot depth at which the sound was made before they start to bend back down again.

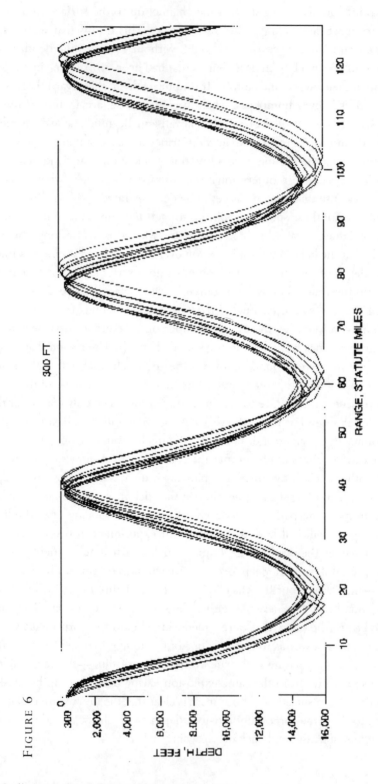

FIGURE 6

300 FT

DEPTH, FEET

RANGE, STATUTE MILES

This case produces something very peculiar: if we assume for a moment that the whale listening to the whale making sounds is also at a depth of three hundred feet, the listener will have to be at a particular distance—some multiple of forty miles from the source—in order to hear it. At intermediate distances the path along which the sound rays are propagating will carry them deep down below the listening whale, where they will be inaudible to a shallow listener. So here we have a very strange circumstance: a kind of sound propagation in which if whales wish to hear each other they must be at some distance that is an even multiple of forty miles (eighty miles, one hundred twenty miles, and so on).

Because all this occurs in three dimensions, the area in which one whale can hear another without having to dive deep is actually a set of concentric bands of seawater centered on the whale making the sounds. These bands are spaced forty miles apart. If a listener is fifty miles from a sound-maker and both are at a depth of three hundred feet, the listener may not hear the soundmaker. However, if either swims *farther* away from the other until there are eighty miles between them, they will suddenly be able to hear each other just fine. Of course the listener could also hear its friend from fifty miles away if when it wished to listen it dived to a depth of ten thousand feet. However, there is no evidence for such deep diving by baleen whales.

One might well question whether a system of communication that only worked when the users were at even multiples of forty miles apart would be of much use to those users. But of course it would be, if the information in the messages to be received wasn't terribly urgent and if the message was repeated over and over again for long periods. A fin whale song is monotonously repeated for hours over a period of days and is composed of only a few notes—it's my candidate for just such a message. Also, if the main use of songs is to enable whales to home on each other when trying to get together, and if these sounds travel for many miles, it will take whales several days or weeks to swim between them anyway. Meanwhile, it won't much matter whether they hear each other all the time. Sextants aren't useless because they only work on cloud-free days.

Case 4: Propagation over Long Distances in Deep Ocean Underice Transmission
There is a special case of sofar transmission that uses some of the properties of the deep sound channel—actually just that half of the deep sound channel lying below the sound velocity minimum. It is particularly relevant to fin and blue whales because it concerns the propagation of sound under a surface covered with floating ice, and both of these whale species do much of their

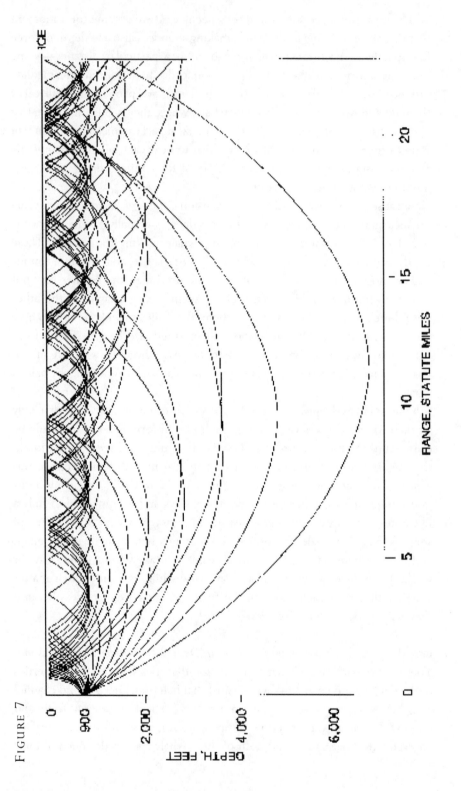

FIGURE 7

ICE

DEPTH, FEET

0

900

2,000

4,000

6,000

5

10

15

20

RANGE, STATUTE MILES

feeding in polar regions where they presumably can profit from being able to contact each other.

As I have already mentioned, in this case only that half of the deep sound channel lying below the depth of the sound velocity minimum is used, the reason being that there isn't any overlying layer of warmer water in polar regions.

Figure 7 shows the paths of rays from a source at six hundred feet in polar seas. If polar waters are deep enough (and they are throughout the Antarctic Ocean and in some parts of the Arctic Ocean), a ray of sound from near the surface which is headed down at any angle between zero degrees and about minus fifteen degrees below the horizontal will be bent throughout its travel so that it misses the bottom and returns to near the surface. When it reaches the surface it will be reflected from it and some energy will indeed be lost. However, the angle of the reflection will be the same as the angle at which the ray first started out from the surface and so it will repeat its fully refracted excursion toward the bottom and back up to the surface again (from which it will reflect again). A ray that propagates this way is called a "surface-reflected-bottom-refracted" ray. It doesn't travel as far as do fully surface-refracted-bottom-refracted rays from sources on the axis of the channel in lower latitudes, but it travels farther than surface-reflected-bot- tom-reflected sounds. A sound that is reflecting from the bottom is not gain- ing the benefits of ducting within the channel. However, bottom reflection is important in shallow water and when a sound that is destined for propaga- tion within the sofar channel is launched into it or received from it in coastal areas. Bottom reflection is also important in deep water for detecting seamounts and ridges.

In the Arctic Ocean the fact that the undersurface of ice is a good sound absorber has interesting consequences for whales. Frequencies higher than about one hundred hertz are of the right wavelengths to be absorbed in rela- tively short distances by the average dimensions of the roughness of the undersurfaces of floating ice. Wavelengths of twenty hertz are too long to be captured by them. Frequencies much lower than twenty hertz have wave- lengths too long to "fit" into the sound channel under floating ice. The result is that the frequency of twenty hertz is just right to travel farthest in the spe- cial conditions of underice sound transmission. I suspect this is no coinci- dence—that a good reason fin and blue whales speak at the frequencies they do is to be heard more effectively in polar latitudes when they are feeding among floating bergs—a situation in which they spend much of their lives.

I have gone through these lengthy considerations of how sounds lose their energy while propagating in the sea in preparation for calculating the dis-

tance to which the sounds of whales propagate. The results of that calculation are surprising.

Let us now calculate the distance that the sounds of a fin whale can travel
before they are lost in the background noise of the sea. For our calculation
we need to know several things. As regards the sound, we must know its frequency, duration, loudness, bandwidth, and directionality. As regards the
receiver, its sensitivity, directionality, and the lowest ratio of signal intensity
to noise intensity at which it can detect the signal. We also need to know the
background noise against which the sound being listened for must be heard.
And we need to know how many decibels per mile the signal will lose
because of how the sound spreads during its trip from source to receiver,
what it reflects off along the way (and how many decibels that costs it), and
how many decibels it loses owing to oceanic attenuation.

In 1969 Douglas Webb (then at the Woods Hole Oceanographic Institution) and I calculated the distance fin whale sounds travel. We based our calculations on the following values:

Characteristics of the Sound

1. *Frequency*: 20 Hz.
2. *Duration*: About 1 second.
3. *Loudness* (more properly known as intensity): About 155 db (spectrum
   level).
4. *Bandwidth* (in this case the bandwidth within which 95 percent of the
   sound's energy lies): 4 Hz.
5. *Directionality of Sound Source*: Omnidirectional.

Characteristics of the Receiver

6. *Sensitivity*: Adequate.
7. *Directionality of Receiver*: Omnidirectional.
8. *Lowest Detectable Signal-to-Noise Ratio*: 0 db. We assume that a whale has
   no ability whatsoever to hear a signal against noise and that for the whale
   to hear it, the signal must be as loud as the noise. Zero db represents the
   signal-to-noise ratio in which signal and noise are equally loud. This is
   because the decibel scale is exponential and any number raised to the 0
   power is 1. As we shall see later the assumption that a whale cannot
   detect its signal at all unless it is at least as loud as the noise which sur-
   rounds it is almost certainly an absurdly conservative assumption.

9. *Background Noise*: Webb and I chose three background noise conditions at 20 Hz:
   (1) Average twenty hertz noise in modern times (ship traffic included) at Sea State 6 (i.e., winds less than 33–38 mph, waves up to 8 feet high): 49 db.
   (2) Average background noise prior to ship traffic (an estimate of what the ocean was like then): 39 db.
   (3) Quiet background noise prior to ship traffic: 29 db.

All of these values are spectrum levels—the energy in a single frequency of twenty hertz. However, to hear 95 percent of the energy of the sound we have to listen over a bandwidth of 4 Hz. When we open the filters on our receiver by 4 Hz we let in four times as much noise, which is 6 db more. This means that the noise backgrounds in our three cases will be 6 db higher than we have indicated above. Therefore, their real values are:

   (1) Average twenty hertz noise in modern times: 55 db.
   (2) Average background noise prior to ship traffic: 45 db.
   (3) Quiet background noise prior to ship traffic: 35 db.

10. *Geometrical Spreading Losses*: Again we assumed two conditions:
    (1) *Spherical spreading losses* (this will give a minimum figure for how far these sounds travel in deep ocean before they fall to the level of background noise).
    (2) *Cylindrical spreading losses* (deep sound channel propagation). The calculation we made assumed that both the singing and listening whales were in midlatitudes and at the depth of the axis of the sound channel. If fin whales don't dive to such depths or if they only listen at them but don't make noises while there, or if they never descend that far, the distances Webb and I calculated will be overestimates. Because our assumptions were so conservative, Webb and I considered these figures to be extreme upper limits of range at which fin whale sounds could be heard, just as spherical spreading is the extreme lower limit of range. However, when we credit whales with even the slightest ability to hear a signal in noise we will see that these calculated ranges are probably underestimates.
    There is one other assumption we had to make when considering cylindrical spreading, and that was the distance at which spherical spreading

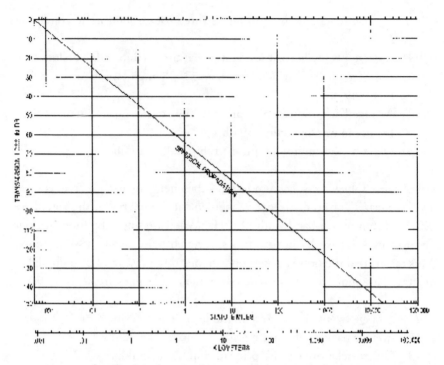

ceases and cylindrical spreading, with its much lower transmission losses, begins—the so-called "transition range." We used the standard transition range of four miles.

11. *Losses Due to Reflections*: We ignored reflection losses in our calculations because reflections are absent in the kind of unimpeded spherical spreading we were considering, as well as in cylindrical spreading via the deep sound channel. (Besides, even if our sounds were ducting for long distances, twenty hertz sounds lose less than 1 db with each reflection, meaning that during ducting of twenty hertz sounds, reflective losses are likely to be much less important than spreading losses.)

12. *Oceanic Attenuation Losses*: At twenty hertz, sounds must travel 2,300 miles to lose just 1 db to oceanic attenuation. This means that out to distances of 2,300 miles we can ignore the effects of attenuation losses on twenty hertz whale sounds. It is also why the transmission loss curve in figure 8b only starts to show the effects of attenuation losses (i.e., only starts to curve downward) after 2,300 miles. A higher frequency would show downward curvature at a shorter range, and the curvature would be more pronounced.

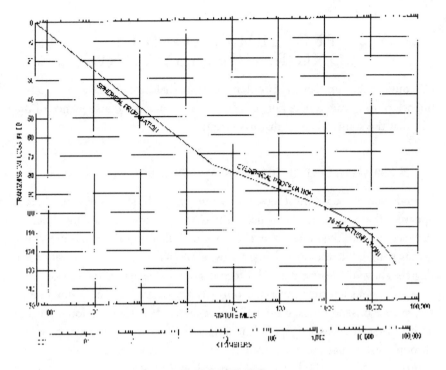

RESULTS

Figures 8a and 8b show a curve of the losses versus distance for two cases: spherical spreading and cylindrical spreading. We assumed three conditions of noise against which the signal has to be heard: fifty-five decibels for moderate shipping noise in the twentieth century; forty-five decibels for average background noise before there were propeller-driven ships; and thirty-five decibels for quiet conditions in the pre-propeller ocean. We see that in the twentieth century fin whale sounds can travel by spherical spreading for about 50 miles and via the deep sound channel about 600 miles before their intensity has faded to the same level as background noise. Before ship traffic noise permeated the oceans, they would have gone about 160 miles by spherical spreading and about 4,000 miles by sofar channeling under average background noise conditions. In quiet conditions in the pre-propeller oceans they would only have fallen to the level of background noise after 500 miles of spherical spreading and 13,000 miles via the deep sound channel!

The spherical spreading cases are undoubtedly underestimates and the sofar channeling ranges probably overestimates (since the sofar ranges given assume both source and receiver to be at the depth of the deep sound channel axis). We assume that the correct answer must lie somewhere between our calculated values.

PROBLEMS RAISED BY LONG-RANGE SIGNALING

Of course there are several problems that a whale would have as a consequence of long-range signaling. One of these comes as a consequence of the way that the sound channel distorts sounds.

SMEARING OUT OF SOUNDS BY THE DEEP SOUND CHANNEL

To understand this we must look again at the ray paths shown in figure 5. It is apparent that sounds traveling along different ray paths are traveling different distances toward the same listener. The ray path that is horizontal is the shortest ray path, while the ones that are most extremely refracted (those at twelve degrees above the horizontal and fifteen degrees below it) are the longest.

Here comes another surprise from ocean acoustics: if we go downrange for, say, a thousand miles, we will find that the ray that took the longest route arrives first (because it spent the greatest part of its journey traveling through water that conducts sounds fastest) whereas the ray that took the shortest route (i.e., the horizontal ray) will arrive last because it spent all its time traveling in water that conducts sounds slowest. But because the slowest ray has had the shortest journey it will be loudest because it has lost the least intensity along the way.

So when we listen to our explosion downrange, expecting to hear a loud bang, what we hear instead is not at all like that. Instead of a single bang, we hear a roar which rises out of background noise, increases steadily in intensity for about ten seconds, and stops abruptly on the loudest note of all (as the last sounds carried in the shortest, and therefore loudest, horizontal sound ray arrive). The sounds carried by the many rays thus arrive over a period of several seconds, which means that their trip via the deep sound channel has smeared out the discrete sound of the explosion, thoroughly distorting it.

The amount of smearing lengthens by about ten seconds for every thousand miles traveled, so that if we listened to a single bang that had traveled the entire seven thousand miles across the Pacific, we would hear a roar that slowly increased in loudness for a minute and ten seconds from its onset before the final loudest rendition of the sound arrived.

It should be apparent from this that you can make a rough estimate of the distance to a sound source if you know the characteristics of the sound you are listening for and can detect the rate at which the sound you expect is increasing in loudness as it rises to its final loudest note.

I would be very surprised if estimating range from smeared-out signals is the only advantage that whales can take from such signals. Modern modems and fax machines are able to transmit information at rates beyond which elementary theory would let you believe it was possible. The way it is achieved is very similar to decoding distant messages through the sofar channel. A pulse produced by the transmitter does not arrive at the receiver as a single pulse but is smeared out into a chain of pulses traveling by different paths. In the fax machine a test pulse is repeatedly sent and the distortion of the signal observed and compensated for. This kind of testing and compensation is done several times a second, which essentially changes an imperfect transmission line into a near perfect transmission line by digital processing. Because they are so constant the blips of fin whales should constitute excellent test signals with which to compensate for observed distortions by the sound channel. This should give fin whales considerable opportunities to examine specific areas of the oceans between them and the whale they are listening for by means of acoustic tomography. In ocean acoustic tomography (the passive imaging of specific areas of the ocean using sound) the imperfections in the transmissions contain the "fingerprints" of everything the sound has touched. Acoustic tomography is a relatively young science and the current job is to learn to read those fingerprints. If we could communicate with them I suspect cetaceans could teach us a lot about interpreting acoustic fingerprints.

HOW WHALES MIGHT HEAR EACH OTHER FROM FARTHER AWAY

If fin whales cannot indeed dive to the depth of the axis of the sound channel and make their sounds once there, there may be several considerations that would offset in part the losses inherent in off-axis deep sound channel signaling.

1. There is good evidence that some blips have signal source levels five or more decibels higher than the values we have assumed.
2. By attending to phase, whales may sometimes use the directional characteristics of their receivers.
3. Lower noise conditions may exist—something that would be unwise to count on in designing a system demanding reliability but that nevertheless ought to be strongly entertained when the task is to calculate maxi-

mum possible range and where reliability may be of relatively little importance.

4. The analysis time of the whale might be able to accommodate samples of sound long enough to have sequences of blips sum at the receiver, thus providing signal energy greater than that from single blips. I am aware of no acoustic research on animals indicating a time base long enough to make such a mechanism very plausible. A signal retrieval system relying on a monotonously repeated signal, such as that from a whale or from a ship's propeller, would require sampling times of several seconds or minutes if it were to detect signals buried deeper than fifteen decibels in noise. Should whales have developed such a mechanism, then a fin whale's sounds would, even today, be audible to another whale that knew its "signature" from anywhere within the same ocean basin—even under quite noisy conditions.

5. Several whales might sometimes shout in synchrony (this need not be intentional) so that their signals would add, making it possible for a distant whale to detect their summed voices at a range greater than it could otherwise hear a single individual.

6. The zero-decibel signal-to-noise ratio we specified for a just-detectable signal may be much too conservative.

Of all of the possibilities listed here, the last seems to be the most likely and is the one with the most profound potential impact on the maximum propagation range of twenty hertz sounds. I have considered it at some length in chapter 5.

NOTES

CHAPTER 1—Whales

1. Listing whales by length can give a very skewed idea of mass. For example, though longer than a right whale, a large sei whale is far more slender and only weighs a fraction as much as a large right whale.

2. Properly speaking, krill is *Euphausia superba*, but sometimes a series of similar crustacean species are referred to collectively as "krill."

3. To be strict, it is probably only very rarely that a whale fasts entirely for a period as long as eight months. Whales, like any other animals, are opportunists and will undoubtedly feed whenever they get a chance. By fasting, I mean the same thing we might experience if we ceased to have substantive meals and ate an occasional cracker or carrot while otherwise starving. The point is that when fasting, whales are not getting anything resembling a diet that would maintain their metabolism.

4. For the mouse, the body volume is roughly 1.57 cubic inches and its surface area 7.07 square inches, for a ratio of body surface area to volume of about 4.5 to one. For the whale, the body volume is roughly 9,772,000 cubic inches, and its surface area 247,700 square inches, for a ratio of body surface area to body volume of 0.025. The mouse's surface-to-volume ratio is more than 175 times as big as the whale's.

5. Lockyer, C. 1976. "Growth and energy budgets of large baleen whales from the Southern Hemisphere." *FAO Fisheries Series No. 5, Volume III* [Mammals in the Seas], pp. 379–487.

6. Kanwisher, J., and G. Sundness. 1966. "Thermal regulation in cetaceans." In *Whales, Dolphins, and Porpoises.* K. S. Norris, ed. Berkeley: Univ. of Calif. Press, pp. 397–409.

7. Tomilin, A. G. 1957. "Mammals of the U.S.S.R. and adjacent countries." Volume IX, *Cetacea.* O. Ronen, tr. Jerusalem: Israel Program for Scientific Translation, 1967.

8. Mayo, C., M. K. Marx, and B. H. Letcher. 1987. "Estimated zooplankton consumption rate and calorie intake of the North Atlantic right whale (*Eubalaena glacialis*)." Abstr. 7th Biennial Conference on the Biol. of Mar. Mamm., p. 46.

9. Zenkovich, B. A. 1937. "Gorbatyi ili dlinnorukii kit (*Megaptera nodosa*, Bonnaterre, 1789)." ("The humpback whale *Megaptera nodosa,* Bonnaterre, 1789.") *Akademiia Nauk*, SSSR. Dal'nevostochnyi Filial 37(27): 37–62 (Russian).

10. Palmer, E., and G. Weddell. 1964. "The relationship between structure, function and innervation in the skin of the bottlenosed dolphin (*Tursiops truncatus*)." *Proc. Zool. Soc. London* 143: 553–568.

11. Barnes, L. G., and S. A. McLeod. 1984. "The fossil record and phyletic relationships of gray whales." In *The Gray Whale*. M. L. Jones, S. Leatherwood, and S. L. Swartz, eds. Orlando, Fla.: Academic Press.

12. Nishiwaki, M. 1972. "Ryukyuan Whaling in 1961." *Sci. Rep. Whales Res. Inst. Tokyo* 16: 19–28.

    Ohsumi, S., and Y. Masaki. 1975. "Japanese whale marking in the North Pacific 1963–72." *Bull. Far Seas Fish. Res. Lab.* (Shimadzu) 19: 171–219.

    Rice, D. 1978. "The humpback whale in the North Pacific: distribution, exploitation and numbers." In K. S. Norris and R. Reeves, eds. *Report on a workshop on problems related to humpback whales* (Megaptera novaeangliae) *in Hawaii.* U.S. Dept. of Commer. NTIS PB-280 794, pp. 29–44.

13. Chittleborough, R. G. 1965. "Dynamics of two populations of the humpback whale, *Megaptera novaeangliae* (Borowski)." *Aust. J. Mar. Freshwat. Res.* 16(1): 33–128.

    Dawbin, W. H. 1960. "Problems of humpback whale migration in the Pacific Ocean." *Rep. Challenger Soc.* 3(12).

14. This work was the product of efforts by Dawbin, Chittleborough, and others and is well reviewed in Dawbin, W. 1966. "The seasonal migratory cycle of humpback whales." In Norris ed., op. cit. pp. 145–170.

15. Lambertson, R. H. 1983. "The internal mechanism of rorqual feeding." *Jour. Mammal.* 64: 76–88.

16. Pivorunas, A. 1979. "The feeding mechanisms of baleen whales." *Amer. Sci.* 67: 432–440.

    Storro-Patterson, R. 1981. "The great gulping blue whales." *Oceans* 14: 16–17.

CHAPTER 2—Living Among Whales in Patagonia

1. *Lagenorhynchus obscurus*, also called Fitzroy's dolphin, a name given to it by Darwin in honor of Captain Fitzroy of the *Beagle*. Darwin described this species from a specimen captured during the time that Darwin and Captain Fitzroy were still getting along well. However, their friendship was eventually destroyed, owing to Fitzroy's resentment of what he saw as heresies in Darwin's theory that humans had not been created specially by God but had evolved from other species.
2. Bernd Wuersig—a graduate student at the time. He and his wife Mel were working and living with us.
3. Hugo Callejas is now the pilot of the governor of Chubut's plane. But for years he flew us over whales. I have flown with pilots from all over the world in efforts to observe or photograph whales from the air. It is a great skill and requires, among other things, that the pilot read a whale's intentions and adjust the size of the plane's circle so as to arrive over the whale when it is breathing. But there are at least four other critical requisites: the pilot must allow properly for the wind, arrive over the whale at the correct altitude (since we search from a higher altitude than we photograph and the pilot has to descend to the right altitude while making all other maneuvers), avoid colliding with the cliffs since the whales are right offshore and in some places the cliffs are higher than picture-taking altitude, and make sure that the plane's closest approach occurs with the sun at the right angle in relation to the whale so it isn't obscured by glare. Most pilots never get this right. Hugo always got it right.
4. A friend and pilot (and Bernd's graduate sponsor at the time) who had just been visiting us.

CHAPTER 3—Behavior of Right Whales

1. Best, P. B., and L. G. Underhill. 1990. "Estimating population size in Southern right whales (*Eubalaena australis*) using naturally marked animals." *Rept. Intl. Whal. Comm.* Special Issue 12: 183–193.
2. 64.9 feet. Leatherwood, S., and R. Reeves. 1983. *The Sierra Club Handbook of Whales and Dolphins.* San Francisco: Sierra Club Books.
3. Leatherwood and Reeves, 1983.
4. I have also seen the spellings "Ingotok" and "Inutuq."
5. See page 269.
6. See page 269.

7. 18.3 meters.
8. Given as 10.7 meters.
9. Given as 6.4 meters. Leatherwood and Reeves.
10. 1991. "Recovery plan for the northern right whale (*Eubalaena glacialis*)." Prepared by the Right Whale Recovery Team for the National Marine Fisheries Service, Silver Spring, Md.
11. Rowntree, V. 1983. "Cyamids, the louse that moored." *Whalewatcher*, 17 (4):14–17.
12. Based on the assumption that aging right whales are probably at least in their sixties and that they join the migration each year, traveling a distance equal to at least the round trip between Península Valdés and South Georgia (2,800 miles).
13. Mayo, C. A., and M. K. Marx. 1990. "Surface foraging behaviour of the North Atlantic right whale, *Eubalaena glacialis*, and associated Zooplankton characteristics." *Can. J. Zool.* 68: 2214–2220.
14. Ford, T., and S. Kraus. 1992. "A rete in the right whale." *Nature* (Lond.) 359: 680.
15. E.g., Mayo and Marx.
16. There was also the possibility that she had moved to a new area.
17. From our data between 1971 and 1986 we have 119 three-year intervals out of a total of 233. We have never seen a female in our population calve in the year following the birth of a calf (though we see this commonly in humpback whales). We have had four females who had calves with them after a two-year interval, sixteen that had them after four years and twenty-four after five calfless years. We have also witnessed intervals of six to thirteen years, but we cannot distinguish such intervals from either 1) a female who was present with a calf in some year when we failed to see her, or 2) a female who miscarried, or whose calf died before we saw it. So we cannot know whether records of calving intervals longer than five years are true or just represent our failure to see calves. It may seem that we are already being too careless by assuming that four- or five-year intervals exist. Maybe the four-year interval is two two-year intervals, and the five-year interval a two- and a three-year interval. (We even have examples of a some whales that had calves after a two-year and a three-year interval.) But since both of these interpretations require pure two-year intervals, which are so much rarer than either four- or five-year intervals, explanations invoking two-year intervals are unlikely. (It is bad practice to explain a common event by invoking a rare one.)
18. Kraus, S. D., M. J. Krone, and A. R. Knowlton. 1988. "The North Atlantic right whale." In W. E. Chandler, ed., *Audubon Wildlife Report 1988/89*. Academic Press, pp. 685–698.

19. We measured a dead female near our camp at 16 meters in length (52.49 feet).

20. Reid, W. V., and K. R. Miller. 1989. "Keeping options alive: the scientific bases for conserving biodiversity." *World Res. Inst.,* Wash., D.C.

21. Bose, N., and J. Lien. 1990. "Energy absorption from ocean waves: a free ride for whales." *Proc. Roy. Soc. Lond.* 240: 591–605.

22. Some biologists have denied that right whales feed on fish, though it has been reported by E. S. Clark (Clark, E. S. Jr. 1958. "Right whale [*Balaena glacialis*] enters Cape Cod Canal, Massachusetts, U.S.A." *Norsk Hvalfangst Tid.* 47(3): 141–143). Some feel that right whales are too slow to catch even small minnows. However, Guillermo Vanegas, who spent his youth as a fisherman on Golfo San José and is a good observer of whales, reported seeing right whales feeding on minnows on two occasions. I have seen right whales in Golfo San José feeding in this way by breaching into what appeared from the disturbances at the surfaces to be shoals of minnows. Following a breach they would circle back through the breach area with their mouths open.

23. The brown-hooded gull is *Larus maculipennis,* and the kelp gull, *Larus dominicanus.*

24. *Larus fuscus.*

25. 14.79 years according to Gaillard, J. M., D. Pontiere, D. Allainé, J. D. Lebreton, J. Trouvilliez, and J. Clobert. 1989. "An analysis of demographic tactics in mammals and birds." *Oikos* 56: 59–76.

26. Kraus, Krone and Knowlton, *op. cit.*

27. Only 42 instances out of 460 opportunities (= 9 percent) in our data taken between 1971 and 1986.

28. This was first done by A. H. Harcourt, P. H. Harvey, S. G. Larson, and R. V. Short. 1981. "*Testes weight, body weight and breeding system in primates.*" *Nature* 293: 55–57.

29. Kraus, Krone and Knowlton, *op. cit.*

CHAPTER 4—The Song of the Humpback Whale

1. Stone, G. S., L. Flores-Gonzalez, and S. Katona. 1990. "Whale migration record." *Nature* (Lond.) 346: 705.

2. Nishiwaki, M., and K. Hayashi. 1950. "Copulation of humpback whales." *Sci. Rep. Whale Res. Inst.* 3: 183–185.

3. Payne, R., and S. McVay. 1971. "Songs of humpback whales." *Science* 173: 585–597.

4. Stone et al. *op. cit.*

5. Jones, M. L., and S. L. Swarz. 1984. "Demography and phenology of gray whales and evaluation of whale watching activities in Laguna San Ignacio, Baja California Sur, Mexico." In Jones et al. *op. cit.*

6. Kraus, S. & Katona, S. (1977) Humpback whales (*Megaptera novaeangliae*) in the Western North Atlantic: A catalogue of identified individuals. College of the Atlantic, Bar Harbour, Maine.

7. This number is based on the fact that just one of the groups studying humpback whales on Stellwagen Bank near Boston (the area in which the most intensive humpback studies are made) has photographically identified some individual humpback whales a hundred times in the same year. However, there are at least three other research groups working in the same area, all of whom are identifying the same individuals, making two hundred sightings a year of these most-seen single individuals a more likely, though undoubtedly conservative, estimate. Given that some of the most-seen individuals have been observed for fifteen consecutive years, one of these animals must have been seen something like three thousand times (let's say two thousand times, to allow for differences in effort in different years). Of course the individuals concerned are still alive, meaning that more data on them will pour in every year so that several individuals will have been seen many thousand times more in their lifetimes before they die.

8. Agilar, A. 1989. "A record of two humpback whales (*Megaptera novaeangliae*) in the Western Mediterranean Sea." *Mar. Mam. Sci.* 5 (1): 211–215.

9. The Carolina wren is *Thryothorus ludovicianus,* and the wood thrush is *Hylocichla mustelina.*

10. "The Music of the Fireball." 1986 lecture by Brian Swimme.

CHAPTER 5—A Heard of Whales

1. Glockner-Ferrari, D., M. J. Ferrari, and S. Atkinson. 1993. "Occurrence and analysis of mucous secretions of humpback whales." Abstr. 9th Biennial Conference on the Biol. of Mar. Mamm., p. 53.

2. See the appendix for a detailed discussion of the differences.

3. The relationship between frequency and how far a sound can carry underwater is explored more extensively in the appendix.

4. See appendix for a description of decibels.

5. Payne, R., and D. Webb. 1971. "Orientation by means of long-range acoustic signaling in baleen whales." *Ann N.Y. Acad. Sci.* 188: 110–142.

6. For a review see Payne and Webb. *op. cit.*
7. See appendix for a discussion of wavelength and how it relates to the size of objects from which a sound will reflect.
8. A decibel is the smallest difference in loudness we can detect between two sounds that are in all other respects identical. Decibels are discussed at length in the appendix.
9. Beklemishev, C. W. 1960. "Southern atmospheric cyclones and the whale feeding grounds in the Antarctic." *Nature* (Lond.) 4736: 530–531.
10. Norris, K. D., and B. Mohl. 1983. "Can odontocetes debilitate prey with sound?" *Amer. Nat.* 122: 85–103.

CHAPTER 6 — Making Friends with Whales

1. This claim is based on the following assumptions: when a 150-pound person runs up a ten-foot stairway in one second they generate about 2.7 horsepower for that second (one horsepower = 552 foot-pounds per second). When a blue whale breaches, it is able to lift its entire body clear of the water in about a second. If such a whale weighs 250,000 pounds and the average distance the body is lifted out of water is twenty-five feet (this may be a serious underestimate), the whale is generating 11,322 horsepower, or 4,194 times as much as the person running upstairs.
2. Based on the following assumptions: that there are between twenty and sixty capelin per kilo (I used forty). The annual capelin catch peaked in 1976 at 370 thousand tons but has averaged about 8 thousand tons in recent years. The catch is thought to represent between 5 and 10 percent of the total capelin population. Therefore the total number of capelin visiting the shores of Newfoundland probably lies between about three billion and three hundred billion animals.
3. The death occurred in a skiff loaded with tourists when a mother gray whale whose calf was getting very close to the boat slapped it with her tail, killing a man. The second incident concerns a woman who worked in my laboratory who was in a small boat photographing a breaching humpback when the whale breached directly on top of her boat, landing across the bow. (It was not a glancing blow but a direct hit.) The impact of the whale hurled her and two other passengers through the air. They landed in the water badly shaken but with no one seriously hurt. They swam back to the boat, which was still floating even though the sides near

the bow had been crushed and it was filled with water (the boat was of sandwich-foam construction and was unsinkable). Because only the bow had been submerged, the outboard had not been inundated, and they were able to start it and clear the boat of water by driving it forward. At this point they noticed that the same whale was still breaching, though it must surely have realized it had hit the boat, as they found large pieces of its skin in the bottom of the boat when the water was removed.

4. Individual gray whales are identifiable from the blotchy markings on their skin, which are constant enough to allow the identification of individuals from year to year.

5. They seem to favor the term "curious" behavior over "friendly" behavior. They also point out that we don't really know yet why gray whales do this.

6. The quotes are from Steve Swartz.

7. Hoyt, Erich. 1992. "Whale watching around the world: A report on its value, extent and prospects." *The Intl. Whale Bulletin.* Whale and Dolphin Conservation Society (Bath, England) 7.

8. "Kujiri watching: Whales and dolphins alive and being watched by the Japanese." *Special Pub. of Whale and Dolphin Conservation Society*, pp. 1–16.

9. Ronnie Fitzgibbon wrote a pamphlet about it that he printed privately and that is sold in Dingle stores: *The Dingle Dolphin.* He gives the date of his first meeting with Fungie as April 14, 1984.

10. Occam's razor is a rule that states that the simplest of competing theories is likely to be preferable to more complex ones and that the best explanation is likely to refer as little as possible to unknown conditions and phenomena.

CHAPTER 7—Whaling and Other Delights

1. Nishiwaki, M. 1962. "Aerial photographs show sperm whales' interesting habits." *Norsk Hvalfangst Tid.* 51: 393–398.

2. Data primarily from Klinowska, M. 1991. "Dolphins, porpoises and whales of the world." *The IUCN Red Data Book.* IUCN, Gland, Switzerland, and Cambridge, U.K.

3. This is particularly true of the baleen of the bowhead whale, which is the finest baleen and is engraved and woven into baskets by the Inuit peoples.

4. Japan had pressed all of her whaling factory ships into service carrying fuel to her island bases because the tanks that had once carried the whale oil back from the Antarctic gave them such a large fuel-carrying capacity. Every one of them was sunk.

5. The population of Iceland is 240,000 and of Reykjavik 87,000. Land area is 39,768 square miles. *World Atlas*. 1990. Earthbooks Inc., Esselte Map Service AB (Sweden).

6. Antigua/Barbuda: population, 64,000, land area, 170 square miles. Grenada, population, 84,000, land area, 131 square miles. St. Lucia: Population, 153,000, land area, 239 square miles. St. Vincent: population, 113,000, land area, 150 square miles. *World Atlas. op. cit.*

CHAPTER 8—Killing Whales Accidentally

1. Fish advisories for human consumption are based on two parts PCBs per million—a concentration based on the amount of fish the average person consumes. I know of no study that has determined what is or is not a safe PCB concentration to have in one's tissues. Such a study has not even been done in animals.

2. If it is a second or later calf, she passes on to it much of what she had left after nursing her previous calf plus what she has accumulated since she dumped much of her toxic load into her previous calf.

CHAPTER 9—Saved by the Whales

1. René Dubos.

APPENDIX A—A Primer of Ocean Accoustics

1. There is a curious increase of noise in the twenty hertz band that occurs at local noon every day at deep water listening stations spaced out across entire oceans. It is called the "noon effect." It couldn't be a ship's traffic noise since that remains relatively constant twenty-four hours a day. I have postulated that it could be whales—perhaps fin whales—increasing their calling at midday. If this is the case the noon effect must now be less pronounced than it was before fin whales were so decimated in the '50s and '60s. It would be interesting to compare the data on the noon effect from early in those years with its value in the present day. If whales are responsible for the noon effect, its loudness should be related to the total population of them in each ocean—it might even prove useful for making rough assessments of the stocks of whales.

There is also a general seasonal increase in twenty hertz sound energy in the ocean background noise. Available data suggest that fin whales may contribute to this seasonal effect, but more data is needed to confirm the theory.

2. Mills, A. W. 1958. On the Minimum Audible Angle. J. Acoust. Soc. Amer. 30: 237-245.

INDEX

aboriginal peoples, whaling exemptions for, 264, 270, 275

acoustic censusing, 181–82, 196

acoustic communication, for collision avoidance, 173–74

acoustic communication, long range, 174–204

  analytic abilities and, 171, 193, 194, 196, 197–200

  background noise and, 194–96, 366–71, 380

  benefits of, 188–92

  as determinant of herd size, 176, 188–89

  directional factors and, 198–200, 372–74, 376–77

  distance estimation and, 198

  earth's mantle as conductor for, 202

  evolutionary selection for, 174, 189, 200–202, 370

  on food sources, 36–37, 186, 187, 188, 189–90, 196–97, 202

  for herd maintenance, 174–75, 176, 186–87, 188–89, 202, 203, 373–74

  human-generated noise as obstruction to, 183–84, 195

  low frequency sounds for, 176, 177, 193, 203, 360, 370, 375–78, 395

  mating behavior and, 184–86, 187, 203

  maximum effective range of, 175, 179–81, 187, 198, 200–202, 396

  for navigational purposes, 188

  sonar systems vs., 192

  species requirements for, 193

  see also ocean acoustics; sound

acoustic images, visual images vs., 171–72, 206–7

acoustic impedances, 360–63

adrenaline, 210

aerial censuses, 88–89, 96

age, determination of, 39

Agriculture Department, U.S., 272

air compressors, 27

Alba (whale), 89

albatrosses, 75–78, 119, 185, 319

Aldrin, 306

Alice's Adventures in Wonderland (Carroll), 77–78

alkylphenols, 313

Allen, John, 233

alligators, 313

Alvarado, Pedro de, 335

Amazon dolphins, 331, 332

Ameslan, 268

amniotic fluid, 56

anal glands, 170

anchoetas, 76, 77

anechoic surfaces, 246–47

animal behaviorists, 218

animals:

  Christian views on, 228

  as objects of moral concern, 239–40

Antarctic Ocean:

  nutritive content of, 33–34

  winter storms in, 197

Antarctic Ocean, whales in:

  factory ships used for, 257

  food sources for, 25, 33, 190–91

  population levels of, 265, 269, 271

  sanctuary established for, 300, 301

  sperm whales among, 291

  tour boat sightings of, 26

  whaling tools for, 27, 255–56

antifouling bottom paint, 43

aphrodisiacs, animal sources for, 331, 332

aquariums:

  acoustic properties of, 246–47

  limited stays for animals in, 242–43

  public education value of, 241–42, 249

  stress reduction improvements for, 245–48

Aristotle, 326–63

arrow grass (flecha), 72

calves:
blubber insulation in, 37
calm waters sought for, 37–39
cyamid infestations on, 135
deaths of, 136
group responsibility for, 55–56
growth rate of, 24, 99
learning process for, 209–10, 268
male protection of, 135–38
mating groups and, 135–36
nursing of, 99, 135
observer boats approached by, 104
play behavior of, 119, 120, 134, 135, 140
in polar seas vs. warm waters, 37
predators of, 38, 39–40, 136, 137
punishment of, 114
shallow waters sought for, 38–39, 103, 105
in utero, 55, 209–11
Campbell Island, right whales near, 37–38
Camus, Albert, 92
cancer rates, toxic pollution and, 313
Canute, King of Britain, 179
Cape Cod:
PCB concentrations near, 307
Península Valdés vs., 57, 59
capelin fishing, 213–14, 409n
captivity:
display facilities in, 246–47
dolphins in, 229–31, 234, 235, 237–38, 242, 243, 244, 246–51, 252
improvement in conditions of, 245–48
intelligence experiments in, 249–52
killer whales in, 237, 238, 242–43, 247, 251–52
limitations on time spent in, 242–43
as moral concern, 239–40, 241
public education and, 241–42
for species preservation, 243–45
stresses of, 244, 245
transport conditions for, 245–46
carbon dioxide, world's average concentration of, 318
Caribbean, humpback whales in, 23
Caribbean nations, Japanese whaling interests and, 281, 300
Carolina parakeets, 350
catcher boats, 27, 255, 256, 257–58, 264, 297, 299
Cauble, Bruce, 219
cavitation, 208, 209
cetacean, 20
change ringing, 155
chemoreceptors, 169–70
Cherny, Ernst, 298, 299
Chile:
crab fishing in, 265
in whaling commissions, 275

chimpanzees:
multiple-male mating system of, 128–29
pygmy, 346
sign language taught to, 268
chlorine compounds, toxic, 306, 313
polychlorinated biphenyls, 306–9, 313, 314, 321
Christianity, 228, 335, 337
circularity, 31–32
city dwellers, natural education for, 240–42, 337–38
Clark, Christopher:
acoustic censusing and, 182, 196
gunshotlike sounds noted by, 136, 208, 209
long-range whale sounds tracked by, 179–81, 184, 187, 198
right whale vocabulary studied by, 204
target strength calculated by, 191
on whale responses to recorded sounds, 164
on whales' acoustic analytic abilities, 199
Coast Guard, U.S., 124
cold harpoons, 258, 259, 264–65
collision avoidance, 173–74
Commerce, U.S. Department of, 221
Commerson's dolphins, 265
communication:
breaching noise as, 120
coastline habitats and, 115
in utero, 208–11
water slapping used for, 120
see also acoustic communication, long-range
Comprehensive Assessment of Whale Stocks, 289, 292–93
conquistadors, Aztec civilization destroyed by, 334–36
conservation, public education in, 337–41
contour plowing, 30
Convention for the Regulation of Whaling (1931), 274–75, 276
convergent evolution, 163–64
Conway, Bill, 57–58, 61
Cook, James, 255
Cooke, Justin, 285, 287, 300, 302
coolants, PCBs in, 309
cooperative efforts:
in feeding techniques, 50, 51, 54
on food finds, 36
in group defense maneuver, 107
among males in mating groups, 126, 129–30
reciprocal altruism and, 38, 98, 104–5
copepods, 100, 314–15
coral reefs, 42
cork lines, 303
cormorants, 314
coronula, 42, 43–45
corset stays, baleen used in, 95, 271
Cortés, Hernando, 335–36

Costello, Lisa, 222
Cousteau, Jacques, 366
coyotes, 350
crab fishermen, animals used as bait by, 265
Crusader, 51
cyamids (whale lice), 98, 100, 118, 135

Daisy (humpback whale), 229
Dall's porpoises, 264–65
Darling, James, 153–54, 220
Darwin, Charles, 262–63, 405*n*
DDE, 306
DDT, 306, 314, 321
death flurry, 254
decibels, 363
deep ocean herd, 189
deep sound channel, 193
deer, Père David's, 243–44
de la Mare, Bill, 285, 287, 302
Del Pech, Robert, 283
De Vincent, Cynthia, 51
diatoms, 306–7, 341
Dieldrin, 306
diet, *see* food consumption
Dingle, Ireland, celebrity dolphin near, 229, 231, 232–36
dinosaurs:
    extinction of, 344
    whale size vs., 21, 24, 338
dioxins, 306, 313
Discovery Tags, 298
dives:
    of humpback whales, 142
    by pregnant females, 55
    pressure differentials and, 28
Doak, Wade, 228
dogs, military use of, 267
dolphin(s):
    acoustic lenses in, 373
    aphrodisiacs from, 331, 332
    begging behavior of, 231–32
    boat race with, 235–36
    as by-catch in fishing nets, 273, 302–5
    in captivity, 229–31, 234, 235, 237–38, 242, 243, 244, 246–51, 252
    classified U.S. naval uses of, 266–67, 268
    as crab bait, 265
    drowning humans saved by, 227, 266–67
    echolocation used by, 171, 206, 209, 211, 303
    feeding practices of, 76, 77
    fishermen aided by, 227
    freshwater, 243, 244
    in Greek history, 227–28
    hearing abilities of, 171
    human contacts with, 227–28, 229–38
    language capabilities of, 205–6, 249–51
    legislative protection of, 273

mating behavior of, 128
as meat source, 273
mother/calf relationships of, 268
1987 North Atlantic die-off of, 308
paintings by, 252
PCB concentrations in, 307
sexual arousal of, 235
show tricks performed by, 248–49, 268
in toothed-whale group, 20
tourist business boosted by, 234–35
tuna found beneath, 302–3
in utero, 211
vocal pitch of, 203
see also porpoise
Dolphin Research Center (DRC), 229–31, 234, 252
domestic animals, pheasants as, 330
domination, domestic pleasures vs., 333–34
domination behavior, among whales, 109
dorsal fins:
    absence of, 93
    of humpback whales, 142
    of males vs. females, 144
doublets, 177
DRC (Dolphin Research Center), 229–31, 234, 252
drift nets, 304–5
drogues, 116, 253–54
dugongs, 55, 263
Dulce (right whale), 228, 229
dusky dolphins, 76, 77, 405*n*
dynamic soaring, 76, 119

eagles, 70–71, 74, 314
ear canal, growth rings in wax of, 39
Earle, Sylvia, 221
ear separation, 193, 379
earth's mantle, whale sounds propagated through, 202
echelon feeding, 54
echolocation (sonar), 194
    basics of, 206–7
    directional sound and, 374
    dolphin use of, 171, 206, 209, 211, 303
    by killer whales, 172
    navigation and, 181, 188
    sound frequencies and, 192, 207
    target strength in, 191
    in utero experience of, 209, 211
    whalers' use of, 257–58
electric harpoons, 259–60
electric sense, 170–71
elephant seals:
    noises made by, 61, 108
    oil rendered from, 263
Ellison, Bill, 181, 191
El Niño, 189

Hayashi, K., 143, 144
HCB (hexachlorobenzene), 306, 313
Head Catalog, 63, 96, 101
heart size, 24
Heinz Foods, 304
helmsmen, harpooners vs., 253, 254–55
herbicides, 306, 313
herd:
    acoustic communication system for, 173–75,
        186–87, 188–89, 202, 203, 373–74
    determination of membership in, 168–69,
        175–76
    sense modality used for maintenance of, 168,
        169–71
herd size:
    communication range as determinant for,
        176, 188–89, 203
    largest, 168, 203
    of toothed whales vs. baleen whales, 168,
        175, 203
Herman, Louis, 205, 206
Hero, 57
hexachlorobenzene (HCB), 306, 313
hibernation, 35
HIV virus, 308
Hoffer, Eric, 333
Holey Fin (bottlenosed dolphin), 232
Holmes, Brian, 232–33
Holt, Sidney, 285–87, 302
Homer, 161, 162
hominids, 166
hooks, flensing, 256
hormones, toxic-pollutant effect on, 310–14
horses:
    chemical sensing by, 169–70
    extinct, 243
Houbara bustards, 331
Hoyt, Erich, 222–23
human births, whale deaths vs., 56
humans:
    acoustic limitations of, 177, 194–95
    mating systems of, 129, 138
    reciprocal altruism linked to intelligence of,
        130–32
    reproduction limited by, 54
    see also whales, human contact with
humpback whale(s), 141–67
    aboriginal hunts permitted for, 270
    acoustic tracking of, 187
    belly bacon from, 273
    breeding grounds varied by, 156, 157
    in Caribbean, 23
    color patterns used in identification of, 46,
        152–53
    cooling mechanism for, 143
    coronula barnacles carried by, 42, 43–45
    diving posture of, 142

dorsal fin of, 142
early illustrations of, 58
east-west migrations of, 46, 47
in equatorial waters, 143, 152
feeding techniques used by, 49–52, 53
fighting among, 44, 153–54
films of, 226, 229
flippers of, 142–43
floating carcasses of, 255
frequent breaching by, 121
gunshotlike sounds made by, 209
near Hawaii, 22–23, 42, 43–44
heartbeat of, 24
human contacts with, 141, 145–46, 229
hunting of, 227, 255, 257, 259, 270,
    297–98, 299, 301, 332
IWC protections for, 257, 270, 297–98
lek system of, 158
mating of, 143, 158–59
in Mediterranean Sea, 162
migratory destinations of, 42, 43–45, 141,
    143, 152–53
mouth size of, 49
name of, 142
Newfoundland fishing nets removed from,
    213–16
1987 die-off of, 308
population levels for, 269, 308, 408n
as rorqual, 49, 142
in Sacramento River, 22
sage grouse vs., 158–59
scent marking by, 170
size of, 20
humpback whale songs, 144–67, 204
    audibility ranges for, 193
    birdsongs vs., 144, 146, 164–65
    boat's hull as sounding board for, 160,
        161–62
    in breeding season, 144
    as change ringing, 155
    for competitive mating displays, 154,
        156–57, 158
    composition process for, 147–51, 157
    cycling of, 31
    as evidence of intelligence, 240
    frequencies vs. complexity of, 193
    group behavior and, 151–52, 156, 157
    head-down posture adopted for, 145
    human music vs., 145–46, 148–50, 155,
        162–67
    human responses to, 141, 145–46, 147,
        160–62, 166
    hydrophone listening device for, 144
    language content of, 154
    length of, 144, 146
    mating and, 154, 156–57, 159
    as migration markers, 152–53

note intervals in, 146
octave range of, 146–47
overall structure of, 147
percussive elements vs. tonal notes in, 147
physical mechanism for, 159–60
practical information conveyed through, 148,
   154, 155
purpose of, 153–57, 159
record albums of, 164–65
repetitive phrases in, 146
rhyme elements in, 147, 151, 240
rhythms of, 144, 146
Siren myth and, 160–62, 363
on *Voyager* spacecraft, 353, 357–58
Humphrey (humpback whale), 22
hunting, sport of, 328–34
Hyak (killer whale), 251
hydrophones, 144, 173
   dipole array of, 199
   directional analysis and, 198, 199
   navy network of, 182–83

Iceland:
   democratic government in, 295
   IWC withdrawal of, 271, 294, 295, 301
   scientific whaling pursued by, 289, 292
   size of, 294–96, 411n
Iki Islanders, porpoises killed by, 261–62
immune systems, 308, 309
impedance matching, 361–63
Incas, 119
Ingutuk, 93
inner ear, 171
insecticides, 306, 313
International Convention for the Regulation of
   Whaling (1946), 93, 274, 275, 288–89
International Observer Scheme, 300
International Whaling Commission (IWC),
   274–301
   accomplishments of, 296–97
   annual meeting of, 238, 276–77
   blue whales protected by, 257, 270, 271,
      275–76
   bowhead whales protected by, 270, 275
   committees of, 276
   conservationist contributions to, 285–88,
      302
   current quota list for, 276
   development of, 274–75
   gray whales protected by, 270, 271, 275
   Humane Killing Subcommittee of, 258
   humpbacks protected by, 257, 270, 297–98
   Icelandic withdrawal from, 271, 294, 295,
      301
   International Observer Scheme used for, 300
   killing techniques scrutinized by, 258, 259
   meat processing and, 257

member nations of, 239, 275, 276, 294
   on minimum population for hunting, 270
   minke whale protections and, 270, 288, 300,
      301
   national research plans presented to, 289–93
   New Management Procedure of, 270
   noncompliance with, 270–71, 277–80,
      288–93, 297–301
   observers vs. national delegations to, 277,
      284
   other whaling commissions vs., 275, 295
   procedural politics in, 278–81, 283–85
   pro-whaling delegates to, 277
   quotas determined by, 93, 270, 276, 291,
      300
   Revised Management Procedure of, 270, 271
   right whales protected by, 270, 275, 299
   Scientific Committee of, 276, 277–80, 285,
      289–93, 294, 300, 319–20
   scientific whaling and, 271, 288–93, 301
   smaller whales and, 238
   Soviet delegation to, 266
   survey data for, 277–80, 289, 292–93, 300
   Technical Committee of, 276, 277–80, 294
Inuit whale hunters, 93, 253, 271
Io, 367

Jacksonville, Fla., right whale protection near,
   124
Jacobsen's organ, 169–70
Japan:
   aboriginal whaling protections claimed by,
      264
   Caribbean aid from, 281, 300
   drift net fishing banned by, 305
   history of whaling in, 253, 411n
   in IWC politics, 280–81, 282–85, 300
   new breeding grounds sought by, 184, 301
   postwar restrictions on, 322
   whale meat marketed in, 258, 273
   whale protections evaded by, 271, 289,
      290–92, 293, 299–300, 301
   whale-watch industry in, 223, 329
   whaling techniques in, 260
Jason (right whale), 101, 102
Jehl, Joe, 100
Jet Propulsion Laboratory, 352
Jews, Nazi persecution of, 326
jojoba oil, sperm whale oil vs., 272
Jones, Mary Lou, 219–20
Jonsgard, Åge, 298
Jupiter, satellites of, 367
Jurasz, Charles, 50, 51

Kanwisher, John, 56
Katona, Steve, 152
kelp gulls, 121–22, 123

shallow water used for avoidance of, 125
sibling relationships and, 133–35
of sperm whales, 291
tailing behavior and, 124, 125
testes size and, 126–27, 128–29
whale songs and, 154, 156–57, 159
as year-round practice, 137–38
Matthieson, Peter, 257
Mauna Kea, carbon dioxide levels monitored at, 318
Mayo, Charles, 41
meat, whale:
    market for, 258, 273
    whalers' processing of, 256, 257
Mediterranean Sea:
    drift net fishing in, 304
    humpback whales in, 162
Megaptera novaeangliae, see humpback whale
melons, 372–73
Melville, Herman, 95, 324–25, 334
Messiaen, Olivier, 164–65
Mexico City, conquistadors' destruction of, 334–36
mice:
    body temperature maintenance for, 34, 35–36
    convergent evolution of, 163
    nest of, 328
midocean waters, nutrient paucity of, 33–34
migration, 32–47
    barnacle growth and, 42, 43–45
    of birds, 32
    birth conditions as motive for, 37, 143
    of bowheads, 45–46, 47
    east-west movement in, 45–47
    fasting and, 34–36, 98, 134
    of fin whales, 187
    food sources linked to, 33–37, 41–42
    fossil evidence on, 45
    of gray whales, 45, 152, 155, 219
    of humpback whales, 42, 43–45, 46, 47, 141, 143, 152–53
    longest, 152
    marking methods used in studies of, 46–47, 152–53
    mating and, 39
    by old whales, 39–41
    by pregnant females, 37–39, 98–99
    of subadults, 39
    whale songs as markers for, 152–53
milk:
    production, 24–25, 98
    toxic substances passed through, 308–9
minerals, ocean water enriched with, 33–34, 196–97
minke whale(s):
    belly bacon from, 273

feeding techniques of, 49
genus of, 142
hunting of, 27, 255, 259, 271, 288, 300, 301
IWC protections for, 270, 288, 300, 301
population estimates for, 269, 270
pygmy right whale vs., 94
as rorqual, 49, 142
size of, 20, 94
Miocene:
    ancestral whales in, 23
    fossil barnacles from, 45
Mirex, 306
Mitterrand, François, 281–82
Moby-Dick (Melville), 324–25
Möhl, Bertil, 207, 208
Monkey Mia, dolphins at, 229, 231
monkeys, hunting of, 331
Monterey Bay, underwater loudspeakers in, 183
Montreal Protocol, 318
Mora eagles, 70–71, 74
mosquitoes, 265
mothers, motherhood:
    calves' play limited by, 134, 135
    group support for, 55–56
    learning process and, 268
    lowest age for, 110
    migration patterns and, 37–39, 98–99
    milk production and, 24–25, 134
    patience of, 135
    play behavior and, 119, 120
    protective behavior and, 104, 105–7
    punishment by, 114
moths, 21–22
mouth:
    in feeding techniques, 47–49
    heat exchange mechanism in, 99
    size of, 48–49
Mozart, Wolfgang Amadeus, 116
mud filtering, 48
multipath propagation, 197
multiple-male mating systems, testes size linked to, 127–29

Nacho (gray whale), 219
Nantucket sleigh ride, 253, 254
National Geographic Society, 64
National Marine Fisheries Service, 221, 223
National Oceanographic and Atmospheric Administration (NOAA), 221
navigation, long-range acoustic communication for, 188
Navy, U.S., marine mammals used for classified purposes by, 266–68
Nazism, 326
Neobalaenidae, 94
Neptune, *Voyager II* observation of, 352

San Ignacio Lagoon, whale watching in, 219–20
Santini (dolphin), 229–30
Save the Whales movement, 287, 302, 325
Scammon, Captain, 218–19, 220
Scammon's Lagoon, 226
scent marking, 170
Schedule of the Convention, 276
Schevill, William, 178
science, religion vs., 342–43
scientific whaling, 271, 288–93, 301
Scotia Arc, whale butchery stations in, 257
Scott, Sir Peter, 284, 325
seabirds:
    drift net fishery and, 305
    in feeding swarms, 76–77
    krill eaten by, 33
    ocean pollution and, 318–19
    see also specific species
sea lions, 61
    breeding grounds for, 185
    as crab bait, 265
    dominance patterns among, 132
    in drift nets, 305
    human contact with, 112
    whales at play with, 111, 139–40
seals:
    breeding sites for, 185
    in drift nets, 305
    elephant, 61, 108, 263
    hunting of, 264
    krill eaten by, 33
    noises made by, 61, 108
    oil rendered from, 263
    viral infections in, 308
Sea Shepherd, 297
Seattle, Chief, 326
sea turtles, 185, 305
seawater, see ocean water
seaweed, whale play with, 139
seismosaurus, 24
sei whale(s):
    acoustic communication and, 177
    belly bacon from, 273
    calls of, 328
    feeding techniques of, 49
    genus of, 142
    hunting of, 27, 255
    IWC quotas set for, 270
    population levels of, 269
    as rorqual, 49, 142
    size of, 20
    swimming speed of, 328
self-awareness, 239–40
setting on logs, 303
sex-role reversals, 111
sexuality, hunting behavior and, 332–33
sexual maturity, 38

Shakers, 31
Shakespeare, William, 324
shallow water:
    for avoidance of mating, 125
    calves brought to, 38–39, 103, 105
    nursing avoidance in, 135
    sleeping in, 108–9
sharks:
    electric sensitivity of, 170
    whale calves attacked by, 38, 40
Shaw, George Bernard, 237
shipping lanes, 124
ships, ocean background noise from, 198,
        368–70
shrew(s):
    food consumption required by, 34, 35
    heartbeat of, 24
shrimp, krill vs., 33
sibling relationships, 133–35
Sierra, 297
signatures, 198
sign language, 268
Silber, Gregory, 208–9
Silent World, The, 366
silica, 306
silver-back gorillas, 129
Sirens, songs of, 160–62, 363
size:
    appetite and, 24–25
    of blue whales, 20, 23–30, 126, 174
    of brain, 193, 200
    comparative models for, 30, 338
    fasting ability linked to, 35–36
    food consumption and, 24–25
    growth rate and, 24
    of largest-known individual whale, 25–26
    of males vs. females, 97, 111, 126
    of penis, 129
    population levels and, 270
    pressure differentials and, 28–29
    sound production and, 165
    of ten great whale species, 20
    of testes, 126–27, 128–29
    tranquility linked to, 20–21
skimming, 48, 99
skin:
    near blowhole, 139
    growth rate for, 43
    sloughing of, 42–43, 121–22
    sunburn and, 121
    tenderness of, 173
skin surface area, body-temperature mainte-
        nance linked to, 35–36
skyscrapers, 312
sleep:
    body positions for, 121
    breathing during, 107–8

sleep (cont.)
    favored times for, 121
    grounding during, 108–9
    after storms, 246
    tail position in, 121
smell, sense of, 169
snakes, aphrodisiac qualities ascribed to, 331
snores, 108
Snow, C. P., 17
snow leopards, 239
social change, slow pace of, 296–97
social organization:
    for care of calves, 55–56
    for cooperation on food finds, 36–37
    evolutionary similarity of, 158
    for multiple-male mating systems, 127–29
    reciprocal altruism in, 130–33
sofar channeling, 381, 383–93
sonar, see echolocation
songbirds, migratory patterns of, 32
songs, see humpback whale songs; whale songs
Songs of the Humpback Whale, 165
Sosus array, 182–83
sound:
    airborne vs. waterborne, 172–73, 360, 361
    bandwidth of, 366
    directionality of, 198–200, 372–74, 376–77
    energy losses and, 379–400
    imagery in, 171–72
    loudness of, 363–66
    pitch of, 176, 177, 193, 198
    speed of, 374–75
    see also acoustic communication, long-range;
        ocean acoustics
sound signals, water-slapping techniques as,
    120
South Africa, right whale population off, 93,
    122, 123, 124
Southern Hemisphere:
    baleen whales concentrated in, 33
    rough seas in, 38
southern right whale (Eubalaena australis), 94
South Georgia Island, Península Valdés whale
    sighted at, 100, 101, 102
South Pacific Whaling Commission, 275
Sovietskaya Rossiya, 265–66, 299
Sovietskaya Ukrania, 265–66, 299
Soviet Union:
    factory fishing ships run by, 265–66
    nuclear weapons of, 345
    sperm whale data collected by, 291
    whale protections ignored by, 117–18, 269,
        270–71, 298–300
space exploration, 352–53
species, separation of, 94
speciesism, 353, 356–57

sperm oil, 271–72
sperm whale(s):
    annual food consumption by, 56
    calves tended by, 55–56
    feeding grounds for, 208
    group protective strategy of, 264
    gunshotlike sounds made by, 208
    hunting of, 95, 254, 255, 291–92
    IWC quotas set for, 270
    male populations vs. female populations of,
        291
    mating of, 291
    meat of, 273
    melon of, 372, 373
    population levels for, 269, 270, 291
    right whales vs., 93
    single blowhole of, 93
    size of, 20
    social organization among, 55–56
    in toothed-whale group, 20
    whalers bitten by, 254
sport hunting, 328–34
spotted dolphin, 171
squid, 19, 291–92
Sri Lanka:
    dolphin killing prohibited in, 273
    drift net fishery near, 305
Starkist canned tuna, 304
starvation, 34–36, 98, 99, 134, 186
steam-powered catcher boats, 27
Steller's Sea Cow, 263
Stewart, Iain, 283–84, 285
Stokes, Sheila, 232–33, 234–35
Stone, Gregory, 152
storms:
    mineral-enriched water left by, 197
    roughness of, 38
    sleep increased after, 246
straight lines, human predilection for, 30–31
Strait of Messina, 162
Struhsaker, Paul, 42, 43–44
subadults:
    human contacts with, 111, 112
    sea lions at play with, 111
    sibling relationships of, 134–35
sunburn, 121
Swartz, Steve, 219–20
Swimme, Brian, 166–67
synthetic aperture, 199

tail(s):
    defensive use of, 105–7
    domination expressed with, 109
    few barnacles on, 43
    in mating behavior, 124, 125
    in play behavior, 119, 140
    repeated thrashing of, 43, 120

whale(s) (*cont.*)
  self-awareness of, 239–40
  sensory abilities of, 169–75
  size of, 20, 23–30, 403n
  slow rhythms of, 21
  as source of enlightenment, 324–29,
    336–41, 342, 345–46, 347, 349, 357–
    358
  swiftest, 328
  two major groupings of, 20
  see also specific species
Whale Camp, 63–64
Whale Conservation Institute, 151, 181, 208,
    290, 318
whale lice (cyamids), 98, 100, 118, 135
whales, human contact with, 212–52
  boat traffic and, 104, 111, 113–14, 224,
    225–26
  bond of mutual curiosity in, 345–46
  in captivity, 237–38, 239–52
  in cooperative hunting efforts, 227
  dolphins, 227–28, 229–38
  expectations of, 22–23
  eye contact in, 214
  for feeding, 230, 231–33, 235
  filming of, 221–22, 226, 229, 267
  in freeing from fishing nets, 213–16
  history of, 165–66
  legal limitations on, 217, 221–22, 223–27
  profound impact of, 238–39
  public education through, 240–41, 337–39
  right whales, 104, 111, 112–14, 228–29
  while swimming, 112, 212–13, 221, 228–30,
    233–34
  tourist economy boosted by, 26, 233–34
  see also whale watching
whales, protections for:
  aboriginal exemptions from, 264, 270, 275
  adoption programs and, 340
  boat traffic and, 122, 124
  census methods and, 181–82
  filmmaking and, 221–22, 225, 226
  from fishing nets, 213–16, 273, 302–5
  from human-generated underwater sound,
    183–84
  inspection protocols and, 300
  international agreements on, 105, 110, 117;
    see also International Whaling Commission
  job losses entailed in, 274
  1986 whaling moratorium and, 269, 298
  noncompliance and, 269, 270–71, 277–80,
    297–301
  overprotection and, 217, 226–27
  politics of, 225–27
  population levels and, 269–71
  scientific cover for evasion of, 271, 288–93,
    301

through songs of whales, 19–20, 141,
    145–46, 147, 160–62, 166, 345–46
  whale products and, 272, 273
  whale watching and, 222, 223–24, 225, 237
Whales Alive, 164–65
whale songs:
  curving paths of, 19
  endless cycling of, 31
  fin whale blips as, 176–77
  human reactions to, 19–20, 141, 145–46,
    147, 160–62, 166, 345–46
  pitch vs. complexity in, 193
  see also acoustic communication, long-range;
    humpback whale songs
whale sounds:
  aggressive behavior accompanied by, 208–9
  for communication within bays, 115
  for coordination of communal breach, 51
  difficulties in observation of, 204–5
  through earth's mantle, 202
  gunshotlike quality in, 207–9
  as long–range communication system,
    174–204
  maximum duration of, 210
  of mothers, 209–10, 211
  physical production of, 28, 154, 159–160,
    204–5, 210, 211
  for predation, 207, 208
  specific meanings of, 204
  in utero experience of, 209–11
  vast assortment of, 204
  see also acoustic communication, long-range;
    blips; humpback whale songs
Whales Research Institute, 290
Whale Wars, The (Fortim-Gouin), 287
whale watching:
  in Baja California, 219–20
  economic success of, 124, 222–23, 233–34
  fears confronted by, 238
  of gray whales, 219–21
  hunting vs., 329
  legal limits proposed for, 222, 223–24, 237
  at Península Valdés, 122–24
  recreational boating vs., 114, 225
  worldwide participation in, 222–23
whaling, whaling industry, 253–66, 269–301
  by aboriginal peoples, 93, 253, 264, 270,
    271, 275
  annual take in, 302
  blubber stripping and, 25–26
  capture methods in, 115–16, 254, 257–58,
    264
  catcher boats in, 27, 255, 256, 257–58, 264,
    297, 299
  census techniques and, 181–82
  consumer products derived from, 271–73
  cultural attitudes toward, 262–63